AF361465

CERVANTES' ARCHITECTURES

Cervantes' Architectures

The Dangers Outside

FREDERICK A. DE ARMAS

UNIVERSITY OF TORONTO PRESS
Toronto Buffalo London

© University of Toronto Press 2022
Toronto Buffalo London
utorontopress.com

ISBN 978-1-4875-4239-9 (cloth)   ISBN 978-1-4875-4240-5 (EPUB)
                                  ISBN 978-1-4875-4241-2 (PDF)

Toronto Iberic

Library and Archives Canada Cataloguing in Publication

Title: Cervantes' architectures : the dangers outside / Frederick A. de Armas.
Names: De Armas, Frederick A., 1945– author.
Series: Toronto Iberic.
Description: Series statement: Toronto Iberic | Includes bibliographical
    references and index.
Identifiers: Canadiana (print) 20210395168 | Canadiana (ebook) 20210395389 |
    ISBN 9781487542399 (cloth) | ISBN 9781487542405 (EPUB) |
    ISBN 9781487542412 (PDF)
Subjects: LCSH: Cervantes Saavedra, Miguel de, 1547–1616 – Criticism and
    interpretation. | LCSH: Architecture in literature.
Classification: LCC PQ6351.D4 2022 | DDC 863/.3–dc23

We wish to acknowledge the land on which the University of Toronto Press
operates. This land is the traditional territory of the Wendat, the Anishnaabeg,
the Haudenosaunee, the Métis, and the Mississaugas of the Credit First Nation.

University of Toronto Press acknowledges the financial support of the
Government of Canada, the Canada Council for the Arts, and the Ontario Arts
Council, an agency of the Government of Ontario, for its publishing activities.

Contents

Illustrations

Preface

More than a decade has passed since I conceived the idea of writing a book on architectures of Miguel de Cervantes. The scaffolding of the book always eluded me, along with the ways in which I would approach very unstable buildings. Although I published essays on the subject as far back as 2004 and 2009, I began to write this book in earnest in 2016 when *Los trabajos de Persiles y Sigismunda* helped me to come up with some new ways of approaching the matter. I spoke on the subject at symposia from Princeton to Tromsø, Norway. Then I expanded my reach to include other works in talks I was asked to give from Calgary to Ohio State University. At one point I abandoned the idea of a coherent book because there were numerous aspects that did not seem to come together. In February of 2020, however, as I looked over some two hundred pages of text that had failed to fully coalesce, the book acquired a new urgency: the University of Chicago started considering teaching online instead of in the classroom because of an unexpected worldwide pandemic. I left Chicago and taught for a while from the relative safety of a small cottage in Fairfield, Iowa. When I returned, I found it difficult to access my office as I kept teaching on Zoom. While many were told to shelter in place, I started to consider again the notion of *place as safety* in Cervantes' novels, further incorporating Yi-Fu Tuan's dichotomy between place (safety) and space (freedom, adventure). I also came to consider *pastoral* as a place cordoned off from danger. Safe spaces, in a different sense, are a topic much talked about at universities, although my institution tends to reject the notion in favour of more vigorous dialogue.[1] Does Cervantes' *La Galatea* echo safe spaces or reject them? In addition, I had already dealt with *touch isolation*, another current notion that touches upon early modern works.[2] Other contemporary terms, such as *cancel culture*, surface but only briefly because they may resonate with today's readers.

As I looked out the window of my Iowa cabin into a kind of bucolic surroundings, albeit eerily silent since few people were venturing out, I redoubled my efforts to understand the role of open spaces, inner places, and even windows in Cervantes' architectures. I began to rewrite or simply shift the angle in some chapters. In some ways, this study is not so distant from my previous work dealing with ekphrasis. After all, an ekphrasis is a description of a work of art, and here I was looking at the description of buildings, at the art of architecture. However, buildings coalesce with the architecture of the text, and in Cervantes' imagination they acquire the metamorphic qualities that Don Quixote utilizes to turn inn into castle.

Cervantes' narratives go much further than the knight's imagination might visualize. I have come to believe that a kind of shapelessness and a kind of haunting aura pervade many of Cervantes' architectures. Although many of Cervantes' structures are shadowed by his Algerian captivity and by his experiences in jail, his edifices are not just a reflection of the trauma and (paradoxically) of the creative power that was triggered in the "wrong" spaces. His architectures arise at times from the superposition of a series of buildings, one upon another; in the transformation of one structure into a different one; or even in the very absence of solid architectures, in phantom-like buildings and in the sudden appearance of an architectural feature, as if materializing from thin air – a corner, a keyhole, some stairs, a window. At the same time, a number of his structures dialogue with the classical architectures encapsulated in Vitruvius' famous text and his Renaissance followers.

It would be impossible to express my heartfelt gratitude to all who have listened to my lectures on the subject and contributed to the shaping of my thoughts. Let me just thank a very few and let this stand for the many. The list is perhaps as unconstructed as Cervantes' own buildings. My deepest gratitude goes to the following colleagues and friends: Randi L. Davenport and Carlos Cabanillas Cárdenas from UiT Norges Arktiske Universitet, who showed me the North and helped me envision the *Persiles* from Tromsø, Norway; Marina Brownlee and Christina Lee, who led me at a Princeton symposium to refine my view of Rome's architectures in the *Persiles*; Elizabeth Davies, Lisa Voigt, and many others at Ohio State University where I first presented some of my ideas on place in the first part of *Don Quixote*; Elizabeth Amann for inviting me to present these initial ideas at the University of Ghent; and María Chouza-Calo for her warm welcome at Central Michigan

University. I owe a debt of gratitude to Mercedes Alcalá-Galán and Steven Hutchinson for influential conversations on the subject; Ryan Giles and Steven Wagschal, whose work always inspires me; Thomas Pavel, a mighty thinker, with whom I taught Cervantes' novel; Armando Maggi, with whom I share a passion for the art of memory; and my many friends and colleagues in Spain, Luciano García-Lorenzo, Julio Vélez-Sainz, and so many more. A special thanks goes to Adrián Saez, to whom I still owe a trip to Venice and a lecture on Cervantes. I would also like to express my gratitude to my former graduate students from Penn State University and the University of Chicago, many now tenured faculty members, from whom I always continue to learn. In particular, I would like to express my appreciation to Carmela Mattza for tracking down many of the images and permissions used in this book. My thanks also go to Juan Pablo Gil-Oslé with whom I had many conversations on climate change and the plague in early modern Iberia. These discussions expanded my way of approaching the topic of architecture. Also I want to single out my research assistants at the University of Chicago over the last decade (all of whom are now assistant or associate professors elsewhere), José Estrada, Felipe Rojas, Medardo Rosario, and Manuel Olmedo Gobante. To Daniela Gutiérrez Flores and Matías Spector I offer my heartfelt thanks for their efforts in putting together this book. And my thanks go to my friends Robert Ducasse, Sam Perrone, and Powell Woods: as we spent time meditating and talking in the confines of my place in Iowa, they ended up listening to some of the ideas for this volume and helped me clarify some of my arguments. Finally, my deepest appreciation goes to the two anonymous readers of the manuscript, who provided invaluable suggestions.

Over the years some of this material, now reworked, has been published in journals and book chapters. Selected sections have been reconfigured and revised to focus on buildings and architectures. They appear scattered throughout this book as sections in several chapters. I would like to thank in particular Bruce Burningham, the editor of *Cervantes: Bulletin of the Cervantes Society of America*, who has allowed me to include portions of an essay from 2004 and a second from 2009 in this volume. I have also used sections of "Hercules and the Statue Garden: Sansón Carrasco's Ekphrastic Contests in *Don Quijote* II.14," in *Signs of Power in Habsburg Spain and the New World*, edited by Ignacio Lopez and Jason McCloskey (Lanham, MD: Bucknell University Press, 2013), 59–76. The last chapter revises and augments "Cervantes' Hermetic Architectures: The Dangers Outside in *Persiles* IV," in *Cervantes' Persiles and the Travails of Romance*, edited by Marina Brownlee (Toronto: University of Toronto

Press, 2019), 17–34. I would like to thank Bucknell University Press and University of Toronto Press for permission to use this material.

A bibliographical note: since all revisions to this work were done during the pandemic and without access to many of my books, or to those at the University of Chicago library, I have had to make some accommodations. I can only provide chapters rather than pages for Pedro de León, and I have used more than one edition of Covarrubias' *Tesoro* and of Pérez de Moya's *Philosofía secreta*. I have cited from the editions of Cervantes' works that I had at hand, but seldom could I consult others. For *La Galatea*, I used the Cátedra edition by Francisco López Estrada and María Teresa López García-Berdoy; for *Don Quixote*, the Castalia edition by Andrés Murillo; for *Novelas ejempares*, the Penguin edition by José Montero Reguera; and for the *Persiles*, the Cátedra edition by Carlos Romero Muñoz. In this context my thanks go to Juan Montero, whose many insights and erudition in his edition of *La Galatea* I wished I could have used to a greater extent, but his text was locked away, in these perilous times. My efforts were as futile as those of Don Quixote's search for his walled-in library. Most translations are mine, except those of *La Galatea*, *Don Quixote*, and *Persiles*. For the first I use the 1892 edition of the translation of Gordon Willoughby and James Gyll; for the second, the Charles Jarvis translation, edited by E.C. Riley in Oxford World Classics (2008); and for the third, the electronic version created by T.L. Darby and B.W. Ife. If I either change or add to these translations, the words or sentences will be in italics.

CERVANTES' ARCHITECTURES

1 Breaking Eurithmia

In death I life desire to see,
Health in disease, in tortures rest;
In chains and prisons liberty,
And truth in a disloyal breast.

Don Quixote, pt. 1, ch. 33

One night I had two books opened before me. *Don Quixote* invited me to reread the passage where late into the night Maritornes, a servant at an inn, stealthily tries to bypass the knight's bed in order to reach the muleteer with whom she had an assignation, only to be caught by our crazed gentleman. The mad and agitated knight, thinking that he was in a castle and that he was being pursued by the daughter of the castellan, takes hold of her to implore her to leave him alone. This double impulse, to take hold of her and to send her away, is folded into a second impulse, where he will paint and construct the scene in his own manner. Through Don Quixote's eyes we see a very different structure, one in which the lady with golden hair, wearing a bracelet of oriental pearls, glides as easily in her lavish dress and palace as Elisena searching for a new lover in the *Amadís de Gaula*. The knight was never asleep, his eyes, like those of a hare, staring into the night. Was he gazing at Venus, the goddess and star that rules the hare? He could have done so, for the roof of his room had ruptured long ago, and the architecture of the sky enveloped him. The comic and the cosmic meet as the ceiling seems to be transformed into one of those zodiacal vaults so typical of Renaissance palaces.

I also took up the *Persiles*, Miguel de Cervantes' posthumous novel, opened it to the scene in which, also in the dark, a woman enters Antonio's room in Policarpo's immense palace. The details are all in the action, as Antonio realizes who has intruded, and acts according to his "barbarous" code of honour:

> Sucedió en este tiempo que, estando Antonio el mozo solo en su aposento, *entró* a deshora una mujer en él [...] *Levantose* Antonio a recebirla cortésmente, porque no era tan bárbaro que no fuese bien criado. *Sentáronse* [...] [Cenotia] *se levantó* para ir a abrazarle. Antonio viendo lo cual, lleno de confusión, [...] *levantándose*, fue a tomar su arco [...] y, poniendo en él una flecha, hasta *veinte pasos* desviado de la Cenotia, le encaró la flecha. [...] a este instante, *entraba por la puerta* de la estancia el maldiciente Clodio.

> (At this time it happened that while the young Antonio was alone in his chamber, there *came in* a woman [...] He courteously rose up to receive her, not being so barbarous as he was well brought up; both of them sat down [... Cenotia] rose up to embrace him. Antonio, full of confusion, rose up and took his bow [...] and putting an arrow in it, shot Cenotia from a distance of about twenty steps [...] at the same instant, the unhappy Clodio entered through the door and came inside the chamber.) (Cervantes 2015a, 229–34)

There are no descriptions here. We may conceive of a bed and a place to sit, but these are not described. There are no wall hangings or other ornaments. Not even clothing is of importance. What attract us to the passage are the verbs. As in the first passage, it is night; again, there is a surprise guest, as a door seems to form out of nothingness in this evanescent palace. Both moments reveal a sense of intimacy as well as danger. The first is written with great *enargeia*, as if we had right before our eyes the very architecture of the rooms and the feelings of those involved, as if the words were acting upon us and expanding our visual imagination.[1] The second moves us along with rapidity, creating its verbal magic through its verbs. For years I have felt the astonishment of discovery when turning to Cervantes' changing and compelling language, one that is disguised in apparent simplicity, one that can astonish through tangible narration or through actions that increase suspense and allow us to construct, albeit very thinly, the surroundings, thus calling for a different type of phantom-like vision. Curiously, the *Persiles* passage ends very differently, suddenly evoking an emblem and returning us to the visual imagination, having us pause in order to ponder the significance of the emblematic moment. For years I have sought to explain Cervantes' ever-changing but always compelling scenes through Renaissance art or through the construction of cosmos.

But that night, I was recalling a brief note by Matteo Pericoli: "Great architects build structures that can make us feel enclosed, liberated or suspended. They lead us through space, make us slow down, speed up or stop to contemplate. Great writers, in devising their literary structures, do exactly the same" (2013). And some of them do even more. Authors like Cervantes, it seems to me, go beyond the literary structure because their works are always about motion. Steven Hutchinson said it well: "Within Hispanic literature, Cervantes is certainly the most prolific and diverse inventor of journeys. As is the case with a great number of the world's narratives, and especially with the European novel from around the fifteenth to the eighteenth century, his three long novels and twelve *novelas* set his characters en route, and most coincide from beginning to end with journeys" (1992, x). During their journeys the characters encounter numerous buildings. Cervantes carefully construct buildings within his fiction to augment the feel created by architects. This is possible because, as Terence Cave said more than forty years ago, "'things' are presumed to inhabit 'words.' Yet that such a habitation may be possible at all is a strange notion [… it] entails the absence of that which it purports to represent" (1976, 5). Another kind of absence is told in a poem in the tale of *El curioso impertinente* (*The Curious Impertinent*). In the midst of it the narrator intrudes to chastise Anselmo, ending his questioning of his self-destructive endeavour with a quotation from a poet he does not name. Among the impossibilities evoked, the verses call for freedom in a prison and an exit from a hermetic space (Cervantes 1978, 1.33.416; 2008, 294).[2] I am arguing not that Cervantes was a student of architecture (although he carefully noticed numerous buildings around him and read some architectural treatises), but that over time he came to realize the importance of architecture in the scaffolding of his literary career and in the structure of his works, and, more importantly, how it affected the tale he was telling, how it magnified or obscured whatever feeling, emotion, or action he wished to display. He may do so, as Terence Cave suggests, through words but also through space. Pericoli, in his course on Laboratory of Literary Architecture, asks students to break down the text: "In writing, once you discard language itself, the actual words, what's left? Thus we also work toward the questions that architects, knowingly or unknowingly, must always address: how does one design and build using emptiness as a construction material? How do we perceive space? And how does it affect us?" (2013). I am convinced that at times Cervantes starts with this empty space and, like an architect, he not only builds a tentative architecture of the chapter or prose text he is writing, but also constructs within them edifices of many types, at times impossible structures that find support, paradoxically, in the literary architecture of the work. He is a new Daedalus that dazzles us with new and unexpected turns in his labyrinth.

In the past I had been looking at objects of art that inhabit works of fiction, but I had neglected inns, castles, palaces, temples, and even smaller architectural pointers such as corners and keyholes, all images of habitation inhabiting these words. In the pages that follow I interrogate places and spaces that are perceived through words or even through their absence, through ellipsis – the intentional omission of words, phrases, direct allusions, and so on. I would like to envision what Cervantes constructs – how some habitations are immensely visual, while others remain unconstructed. I would like to see what habitational shapes coalesce in these narratives and what spaces comfort us, haunt us, or have us forget they even exist.

Although this is not my main focus, a reader can come to realize how Cervantes, over time, came to think more closely and deeply about the buildings he included in his texts and about the spaces in which his characters roam. It may appear that in his early pastoral he is only thinking of natural spaces, but the huts and temples within are built in harmony with nature, almost as if he were thinking of these spaces from the point of view of a modern architect such as Frank Lloyd Wright. Turning to the inn as depicted in the first part of *Don Quixote*, the reader may think of it as a hotel, and its occupied space as following the principles delineated by Robert A. Davidson (2018). Or, if looking at the secret and enclosed spaces of the interpolated tale of *El curioso impertinente*, we could consider the modern demonic spaces as perceived by David Spurr (2012); or even the sense of atmosphere as defined by Finnish architect Juhani Pallasmaa. When Cervantes deals with windows, his views seem to coalesce to some degree with Laura Mulvey's discussions of a Hitchcock film, or perhaps even the studies of windows and paintings within paintings as evoked by Victor Stoichita. Moving on to part 2 of Cervantes' novel, we are astounded by the leap he makes in his critical thinking on architecture. His view of the Pantheon, for example, recalls that of the contemporary Spanish architect Alberto Campo Baeza. His posthumous text, *Persiles y Sigismunda*, goes far beyond, thinking with great intricacy about the question of ellipsis, the missing words in a description, and about the elliptical space with two foci, much like Severo Sarduy has posited regarding the baroque. But almost from the start there is a tension in Cervantes' prose between space and place, between confinement and freedom, between the visible and the invisible. Cervantes' prose also delights in the construction of monstrous buildings that pile one on top of the other, which may well recall the fantastic structures in *Carceri d'invenzione* (Imaginary prisons) by Giovanni Battista Piranesi. My point then is that Cervantes, while at times pointing to the classical past, was often far ahead of his time in imagining structures. Not only is he tilting with baroque (and postmodern) metafictions, as Bruce Burningham would have it, but he is tilting with the many intricate windmills of his texts, edifices that metamorphose before our eyes as we come to view one architecture within another and within another, creating an abyss of space.

Yet, we are also surprised by what is not there in some cases. Don Quixote's mind is filled with memories of the many books of chivalry he has read. Thus, his imagination can erect new structures, replete with welcoming or threatening architectures, their variety and marvel clearly illustrated by Stefano Neri.[3] These structures could be sites of danger and adventure, places of refuge, or spaces of contemplation, in which allegorical images would confound the traveller or yield new insights.[4] Castles or towers could loom over the landscape, protecting some, being a bulwark against enemies, seeking to prevent attacks or intrusions. Or they could be guarded by evil enchanters, giants, or evil dwarves, who would dare knights to attack them. And yet, we often note how the narrative avoids presenting the crazed knight "painting" such portentous buildings upon the landscape. He fails to fabricate them. *Don Quixote* functions differently from chivalric places or spaces that are often more elaborately described for the purposes of wonder;[5] Cervantes also differs from later realistic novels that seek to bring out the materiality of the world. Cervantes' architectures are always partial, pointing to specific aspects while leaving others unconstructed. Since most of the first part of *Don Quixote* takes place in the rusticity of La Mancha, the ever-present inn evokes a real, albeit far from marvellous, structure. One of my purposes then is to come to an understanding of how Cervantes transforms these sites of chivalric books into the less magical world of *Don Quixote*, while at the same time infusing them with the mystery of complex architectures, thus retaining a partial magic that, as I hope to explain, derives at times from the metamorphosis of one building into another and back again. And I am not just speaking of the knight's transformation of an inn into a castle. Instead I will evoke myriad metamorphoses that take place at the level of the narrative itself or are constructed by other characters. This is where Cervantes is most compelling, as buildings become other buildings and then transform yet again, establishing an unstable architecture, conjuring a mirage that suddenly turns into another mirage and then transforms into an unexpected edifice.

Although the prologue to *Don Quixote* takes place in the author's study, the first sentences divert the reader to a prison where the novel was born. Thus, the study is overlaid by a second architecture. Through allusion the passage also evokes a third space, the Vatican Palace. In Cervantes' biography veiled allusions can turn a home described in fiction into a historical referent or even into a monastery; the crystals in a cave can lead us to legendary wonderings, such as Merlin's abode. There is much that can be said as to the mechanics of these changes, but what interests me here is the way in which buildings absorb different architectures, making them less stable and much more difficult to materialize fully as a space or a place.

Cervantes' novels are peopled with characters that are constantly on the move, under the tutelage of Hermes, or Mercury the light footed, always going from here to there, pursuing their unfulfilled desires through amorous, spiritual, picaresque, or chivalric quests.[6] This movement also introduces an autobiographical subtext: Cervantes' own life, journeying through Andalucía to earn a living. Moments of rest also shadow the text with yet other autobiographical elements. Cervantes, who travelled to collect taxes, was accused of appropriating public moneys and was incarcerated at the Royal Jail of Seville, where he spent the last months of 1597. He claims to have imagined and started writing his *Don Quixote* at this time, an almost impossible feat given the noise, filth, and stench that emerged from a site where hundreds of prisoners roamed about, caged.[7] Upon release from jail, he remained in Seville. The dangers inside led him to imagine the dangers outside, those of his knight.

Curiously, Spain was struck by the plague, starting in Santander in the north and reaching Madrid by 1599 and Seville by 1600. Cervantes, who had witnessed the exequies at the death of Philip II and composed a famous sonnet on the subject in 1598, left Seville in 1600 with the advent of the plague, going to Madrid and then on to Valladolid. While he was following the court, he was going in the opposite direction of the spread of the plague. It may be possible that Cervantes conflated his time in jail with his experience during this devastating epidemic. Some have attributed Cervantes' captivity in Algiers as a major impulse in his writings, but María Antonia Garcés goes further, arguing that the trauma he endured in North Africa served as a catalyst for his work. Over time, she sees through his writing "a gradual liberation of the chains of captivity in Cervantes" (2002, 242). In this study we may be able to glimpse some of Cervantes' written architectures as somehow related to his many incarcerations: Algiers, the jail in Seville, and, to a much lesser extent, the constraints of the plague, which included confinement as a means to alleviate contagion and rapid spread.[8] In addition, he had to deal with the uncertainty of climate change. The "Little Ice Age" is said to have begun around 1550 with glacial expansion, which may have been caused partly by lower solar activity and increased volcanic activity (Parker 2013, 668–9). Javier Martín Vide and José Olcina Campos claim that, in Spain, one of this age's four catastrophic periods took place during 1570–1610, with alternatings times of heavy rainstorms and great drought.[9]

In periods of great danger the outside seems to turn against humanity in order to become the opposite of a site for *negotium*, the pursuit of wealth, fame, and power. What may appear as paradisiacal settings or spaces for activity and the discovery of new challenges become menacing environments as people flee to the relative safety of the home. Several decades have passed since Gaston Bachelard assured us that the home represents our "protected intimacy" (1994, 3), that such architectures bring comfort and trigger the benefic imagination as we recall its wardrobes, chests and corners. However, in modern times and perhaps in the cities of early modern urban settings, such places of safety harbour much less of those feelings. Bachelard argues that instead of the cosmic vertical sensation of basement to attic, a new horizontality ruptures both cosmos and intimacy. This disruption that is felt in much of modern architecture was not absent from Spain at the time of the Habsburg empire, where the haphazard placement of architectures in growing towns and cities led to disorientation and anxiety. We need only remember the birds-eye view of Madrid in *El diablo cojuelo* (*The Limping Devil*).[10] As population centres grew, they became overcrowded, filled with abodes that did not seem to belong. The marvellous growth of the court could be contrasted with the concomitant danger of urban spaces, their lack of order, and the absence of a harmonious cosmos.

This disruption is easily reflected in the metamorphosis of constant change and in the ellipsis of the absent, as a description is left out, as an edifice vanishes in favour of another. Thus, the term *ellipsis*, which often refers to the omission of words using three dots, is extended to mean gaps in writing where something is understood; from there it leaps to a more metaphorical use of the term when in Cervantes, something vanishes; at times something else appears in its place (as in the case of descriptions of buildings). In addition, we consider the geometrical form of the ellipse, which during the early modern period acquired immense importance as the circular orbit of planets was transformed into an elliptical one. While the circle has one centre, both the geometrical form of the ellipse and the celestial orbit create a second, obscured centre. Severo Sarduy has applied elliptical orbits to the ellipsis of the baroque: "supresión en general, ocultación teatral de un término en beneficio de otro que recibe la luz abruptamente, caravaggismo" (1973, 24; general suppression, theatrical concealment of a term in favour of another one that is suddenly brought to light in the manner of Caravaggio). We are then presented with a double focus, typical of a geometrical form related to the ellipse, the elliptical. Let us remember that by 1609 Johannes Kepler had come out with his first insights into planetary gravitation. The notion of circular orbits, that is orbits that exemplified the perfection of the circle, were suddenly replaced by the idea that planets revolved around the sun in an elliptical orbit, thus having a double focus. As a structure shines and another is shadowed, which one takes precedence? This sense of insecurity affects how we look at space and place.

In these chapters I will consider whether architectures abide by the basic concept of place and space as delineated by Yi-Fu Tuan. Although in our day, according to Tim Cresswell, "the literature that uses places is endless" (2015, 194), and from the theories of Gaston Bachelard to those of Henri Lefebvre and Paul Zumthor,[11] there is a certain consensus about place as a term. Pointing to how we make a previously inhabited apartment our own place and how "a child's room, an urban garden, a market town and New York city" become places, Cresswell explains that "they are all spaces which people have made meaningful. They are spaces people are attached to in one way or another. This is the most straightforward and common definition of place – a meaningful location" (2015, 12). More important for this volume is Yi-Fu Tuan's original distinction between space and place: "Place is security, space is freedom; we are attached to the one and long for the other" (1977, 3). Thus, a home would generally be equated with security. After all, as archeologist Ian Hodder states, the house is linked to the emergence of human society since it "provided a way of thinking about the control of the wild and thus for the larger oppositions between culture and nature, social and unsocial" (1990, 39). Since the beginnings of time the home has kept humans safe from roaming beasts or other threats. Indeed, for the ancient Greeks and Romans, the domicile was inviolable, and it was sacrilegious to violate it (Fustel de Coulanges 1980, 50). In early modern cultures a similar notion prevailed, when the dictum "an Englishman's home is his castle" was incorporated into English law as early as 1628. In the literature of early modern Spain we can find numerous moments when the violation of the law of hospitality in one's home is condemned.[12] If the home is sacred, the temple or church possesses an even greater sense of inviolability. Swift punishment from the gods was the result of trespassing, as detailed in classical mythology. In early modern Europe it was often used as sanctuary by those pursued by the law.

I would ask, Can architectural places in Cervantes' fiction guard from the danger outside? Or do some of these sites become hermetic enclosures, spaces that wall in certain dangers? Also, can some of these spaces evoke Hermes and conceal hermetic mysteries?[13] Or can they also evoke Janus, god of thresholds as a way to break confinement? The concepts of space and place are rather complex, and Yi-Fu Tuan seeks to explain their many meanings through specific examples. He also shows the paradoxical nature of each. Even though "[s]pace is a common symbol of freedom in the Western world" because "it suggests the future and invites action," it has a negative side: "space and freedom are a threat" (1977, 54). Although following his notions, this book sometimes extrapolates, extends, and seeks to understand contradictory statements. For example, though we understand place as security, we must also keep in mind that as a centre of "value" such a place can "attract or repel in finely shaded degrees" (18). In addition, we will see that the bond of love and friendship as two people join together can bring about a sense of place, no matter where they may be. The human anatomy and surely the shape of the heavens partake of the notion of architecture. Although Yi-Fu Tuan does not actually state this, he does tell anecdotes that point to these conclusions. Early modern readers would have had available Vitruvius' *Ten Books on Architecture*, written at the time of Augustus Caesar, in which the heavens are discussed as a divine architecture, and the proportions of human bodies and temples are discussed side by side.

This book represents a first attempt to understand Cervantes' architectures. As such, it does not pretend to be comprehensive or strive for a panoramic view of all four of the writer's novels or works of lengthy prose fiction: *La Galatea* (1585), *Don Quixote*, part 1 (1605), *Don Quixote*, part 2 (1615), and *Persiles y Sigismunda* (1617). Through a series of discrete sections on specific passages, it serves as an invitation to open up this field for further research, to open the door into palaces and inns, and to scrutinize windows, ceilings, towers and even large noses that turn the human body into a grotesque architecture. These chapters may suggest contexts and may point to moments in which history, architectural history, biography, and the environment are at play. López Estrada argues: "la arquitectura aparece como la manifestación artística de las diversas gentes, tanto en relación con sus vidas como en cuanto a las creencias que las sostienen" (1999, 78; architecture appears as the artistic manifestation of different peoples, in relation both to their lives and to the beliefs that support them). Thus, it is impossible to neglect the notions and beliefs that led to such constructions. From evidence of Roman architecture in the crystal palaces of the Cave of Montesinos to the presence of a Jewish ghetto in Rome, and from suggestions that jail and plague coexist in Cervantes' prologue to a questioning of the non-threatening outside at a time of great environmental changes, this volume seeks to include those contexts that allow for a more expansive understanding of Cervantine architectures.

The complexities of architectural structures extend backwards and forwards in Cervantes' prose and challenge the readers' senses as well as notions of reality. Leo Spitzer in his famous article on linguistic perspectivism in Cervantes, as well as Américo Castro in his evocation of the *engaño a los ojos*, point to the notion that "reality varies in the way it is perceived, that the 'what' of reality is determined by the 'who' perceiving it [...] By the time we come upon the *baciyelmo* in the *Quixote*, we already know that the world is susceptible to different interpretations [...] We know, from the clash of perspectives between Don Quixote and Sancho, that we must guard against taking reality to be one way without pausing to question its alternative identifications or to account for the personal histories which might alter any perception of it" (Cascardi 1986, 14–15).

The composite nature of Cervantes' architectures turns against Vitruvius. His *Ten Books on Architecture* was the only treatise on the subject that survived from classical antiquity, and thus it became central to Renaissance artists, builders, and theorists. He based his theory on the six principles of order, arrangement, eurithmia, symmetry, propriety, and economy (1960, 13) and advanced the three orders of columns as Doric, Ionic and Corinthian, adding the Tuscan (102, 120). Rediscovered in 1419 by Poggio Bracciolini in the Abbey of Saint Gall (Switzerland), the book was first published some seventy years later, in 1486. Although at first it was difficult to understand and evaluate,[14] it had an impact on all major Renaissance artists from Leonardo to Raphael. Although some criticized Vitruvius when measuring actual ruined temples and comparing them with his measures, many still followed his theories.[15]

Leon Battista Alberti popularized the work in his treatise on architecture. In addition to the many Latin editions such as the illustrated and influential text by Fra Giovanni Giocondo (1511), with 136 woodcuts, dedicated to Pope Julius II,[16] Vitruvius' *Ten Books on Architecture* was translated into the vernacular as early as the fifteenth century by Francesco Di Giorgio Martini.[17]

The Venetian Daniele Barbaro prepared a lavish edition together with a commentary in 1556. Indeed, Barbaro's volume contains woodcuts by Andrea Palladio, who was deeply involved with the author in the elaboration of this work. Architecture was considered from the time of Plato to be the highest of the arts, combining a number of other disciplines, including arithmetic, geometry, and art (Cellauro 2004, 301–2). There was then a desire to include it among the liberal arts. Vitruvius is very careful to remedy any misperception of a building on the part of the observer that may derive from the site on which it is constructed. He gives examples of how "the eye does not always give a true impression, but very often leads the mind to form a false judgment. In painted scenery, for example, columns may appear to jut out, *mutules* to project, and statues to be standing in the foreground, although the picture is of course perfectly flat" (1960, 175). Throughout his treatise Vitruvius is concerned with transforming elements to conform to perception. In his commentary Daniele Barbaro points to the science of optics and the art of perspective as key to understanding Vitruvius and ancient architecture: "highly placed parts such as architraves, friezes, cornices […] should be inclined forward one-twelfth of their height to make them appear perpendicular" (Cellauro 2004, 305). Since "things are represented by the eye as other than they are" (Vitruvius 1960, 175), some changes can be made to the building. Symmetry and proportion are essential so that the viewer "may feel no doubt of the eurythmy of its effect" (158). Eurithmia,[18] although based on exact principles, must at times be modified to give the appearance of perfect grace, proportion, and a kind of rhythmic order to a building.

Francesco Di Giorgio Martini, in his own treatise on architecture, explains that eurithmia relates to the beautiful appearance of a building and derives from the harmony of its parts and its composition (Marder 1989, 640)[19] Indeed, Elizabeth Mays Merrill (2013) believes that eurithmia in his treatise is synonymous with proportion. In his commentary Daniele Barbaro relates it to music and harmony and describes it as "*bel numero* [beautiful number], *bellezza* [beauty], *gratiosa maniera* [graceful manner] or *aspetto gratioso* [graceful appearance]" (Cellauro 2004, 320). In the seventeenth century Gioseffe Viola Zanini reasserts these ideas. In chapter 30 of his *On Architecture* (1629), he claims that eurithmia is the grace and shape of the work, out of which symmetry arises (1629, 128–9). Hanno-Walter Kruft has summarized the meaning and connotations of eurithmia for Vitruvius and the Renaissance: "an appearance that is graceful and agreeable in the way in which its individual elements are arranged. It is achieved when these are of a height and proportionally suited to their breadth and of a breadth suited to their length; which, in short, they all correspond symmetrically" (1994, 25).

The popularity of Vitruvius' work returned architecture to its rightful place as a liberal art, something that had been lost during the Middle Ages. This Renaissance ideal was soon echoed in Spain. Hanno-Walter Kruft asserts that "[i]n the sixteenth century Spanish writing on architecture was completely under the spell of the Italians. Vitruvius, Alberti, Serlio and Vignola dominate the scene" (1994, 219). As early as 1526, Diego de Sagredo published a dialogue, *Medidas del romano* (Measurements of the Romans), which became very popular, borrowing from Alberti, Di Giorgio, and Vitruvius and often paraphrasing the latter.[20] With Sagredo, the notion that architecture was based on human proportions was given full attention in Spain. He is actually much more detailed than Vitruvius is and even corrects him: "hombre bien proporcionado se puede llamar aquel que contiene en su alto (según Vitruvio) diez rostros [...] Pero los modernos auténticos quieren que tenga nueve y un tercio" (one can call a well-proportioned man he who measures ten visages in height [...] But the true moderns wish him to be only nine and a third; 1526, 5r). Sagredo also develops the notion of architecture as a liberal art (Bassegoda i Hugas 1985, 121–2). He argues that the architect is the first maker (an analogy to *Deus artifex*) and that his hands do not do work because this is executed by all his assistants.[21] Sagredo also popularizes the orders of architecture (related to the forms of the capitals of different types of columns) and adds original chapiter on balustrades, candelabra, and, particularly, monstrous columns, with a rounded or belly-like bottom part.[22] This could have opened the way for Cervantes to conceive of a whole range of architectures, from the classical to the monstrous to the grotesque.

Not until 1582 was there a full translation of Vitruvius into Spanish, done by Miguel de Urrea, although we must note a couple of manuscripts: the translation of the first book by Hernán Ruiz (the younger, whom we will encounter later in this volume) and a complete translation by Lázaro de Velasco. As the term *architect* is recuperated, particularly at the time Philip II ordered the building of the Escorial, Juan Bautista de Toledo, Juan de Herrera, and Francisco de Mora, adopted this term for their profession. Indeed, Juan Bautista de Toledo is given the title of royal architect as opposed to the earlier *maestro de obras* (master of the works). He is thus an intellectual who designs the plans, learning from theorists such as Vitruvius, Alberti, and Palladio. Someone else, an *aparejador*, would be in charge of the day-to-day construction. Indeed, in the early seventeenth century Juan Gómez de Mora insisted that the architect should not be on site because this was the job of the foreman or technician (Losada Varela 2007, 47).[23]

In a curious text published in 1600, Gaspar Gutiérrez de los Ríos, citing Vitruvius, declares that architecture stands above other "arts" that help it: "… la architectura, que (según Vitruvio) es arte architectónica y señora, que contiene debaxo de sí a otras, sirvientes y menores, como son el cantero, carpintero, cerrajero, albañil; y todas las demás artes estructiorias, cuyos fines sirven de medio al architecto para conseguir su principal fin, que es formar un edificio." ([A]rchitecture (according to Vitruvius) is an architectural art that rules or mistresses over and contains within others that serve it and are minor, such as the stonecutter, carpenter, locksmith, builder – and all other structuring arts which serve as means for the architect to reach his main goal, which is to structure a building; Gutiérrez de los Ríos 2000, 31.) Thus, only five years before Cervantes published the first part of his *Don Quixote*, it was clear that the architect dealt with form, with the invention of the structure as noted by Vitruvius, while others such as builders used their craft and their hands to serve in the materialization of the architect's idea.

The term *architect*, then, became a most fashionable one during Cervantes' lifetime. Knowing its value as an expression that evokes the Graeco-Roman world, Cervantes uses it just once, when a gentleman is explaining to Charles V the subtleties of the Pantheon in Rome. It thus behoves us to understand the way in which the writer conceived of his structures. It is also important to understand Cervantes' view of eurithmia because the most important building of his time followed this precept. The Escorial seeks to unite Vitruvian and biblical ideals, making use of eurithmia, and thus it appears in the late seventeenth-century treatise by the mathematician, astronomer, and philosopher Juan Caramuel y Lobkowitz, *Arquitectura civil recta y oblicua* (Straight and oblique civil architecture).[24]

Although Vitruvius and his Renaissance followers used eurithmia to construct graceful buildings that appeared harmonious and beautiful to the naked eye, even if their proportions were somewhat altered to take into account human perception, Cervantes began *Don Quixote* by absolutely negating this type of architecture, turning instead to a prison where grace, harmony, and proportion were sorely missing. Many Renaissance architects rejected the steadfast rules propounded by Vitruvius, preferring, as in the case of Di Giorgio, that architecture develop "'according to the infinite invention that occurs in the mind of the architect" (Di Giorgio Martini 1967, 372–3). Cervantes, who would have read Vitruvius in either Italian or Spanish and who would have perused with some care Sagredo's book, may have even looked at other texts and illustrations on architecture – but he was certainly not an expert on the topic. He knew enough for his purposes and must have been acquainted with Hernán Ruiz, whose many works in Seville he encountered. He knew enough to invent edifices so far removed from Renaissance harmonious structures that it is as if his invention had gone astray. At times he creates monstrous habitations rather than temples for the gods. As the architectures become unstable, pointing to more than one kind of edifice, the readers begin to mistrust the senses and acquire a sense of caution and uncertainty in reading itself, for the very solidity of objects and architectures that seek to emerge from words are no more than illusions.[25] Eurithmia becomes a kind of "plurithmia" (plural harmonies) and even a "dysrithmia" (ruptured harmonies) as structures are reconstructed through the use of other architectures. Vitruvius sought to make small changes to architectural structures in order to deceive the eye into seeing a perfectly harmonious work, but Cervantes actually enhanced changes and transformations to underline the deceptiveness of the senses, the deceptiveness of words as configuring a solid structure, and the deceptiveness of a world in which appearances can be subjective. Cervantes inserts elements from classical architecture and art, often to deny harmony. After all, for the ancients, each structure reaffirmed the perfect order of the cosmos and the perfection of the human being. Cervantes takes the classical and the senses and provides readers with new and unimagined forms and structures that even defy the imagination. And he further breaks down the dichotomy of space and place, creating sites with a plurality of meanings. The instability of these architectures points to the impossibility of presence, the exasperation that comes when words fail to create;[26] however, they also reveal the illusion of a world beyond words. Just as place and space can be reversed, a safe place can become a constricted and frightening space and vice versa. The constant flux of words and things and the constant changes of experience allow us to see danger and comfort in the same edifice or the same outside. Perhaps only the very inner architecture of the self can be trusted. Somewhere deeper than the intellect and the senses we may seek a changeless and peaceful place, the marvellous silence felt in the home of the Knight of the Greek Cloak. But this infinite moment is paradoxically fleeting in the work of Cervantes, who is constantly showing the world as change, and the spaces and places as unstable as the perception we may have of them.

The proliferation of homes as closed places or spaces brings to mind the importance of windows as a way to look out from the inside and even at times to peer in from the outside. These liminal structures, as Cervantes himself recalls, recreate the body. The eyes as windows of the soul point to the body's interiority. What is inside? What is the human body expressing or concealing? According to Vitruvius, Socrates bemoaned the fact that the human body lacked windows so that we could understand its emotions (Vitruvius 1960, 69). Rather than turning to the human body's performances, these chapters will look instead at the house in terms of such a body, and vice versa. Windows not only conceal and reveal the self but also allow characters to gaze at what lies beyond. Do these windows open to interior patios, to outside landscapes, to the sight of other buildings with their own windows and balconies? In *Don Quixote*, part 1, for example, Luis is able to see Clara even though her father keeps her window as draped as possible. She can peek and perceive his freedom of movement as he stands on his balcony. While some urban spaces call for windows, other spaces, as in the northern land of the *Persiles*, depict vanishing architectures and windowless spaces. While moving through different spaces and places, we may come upon a specific architecture that calls for viewing, be it towers, stairways, or corners. From the home to the villa and the church, from the palace to the tower and the tombstone, from the window to the corner and the library, the architectural sites of Cervantes' novels invite us to learn more about them and to inquire about the transformation of human interaction in different places or spaces.

The book consists of nine chapters. This introduction will be followed by chapter 2, which takes a look at *La Galatea*, written after Cervantes' Italian sojourn and his captivity in Algiers but before the Seville incarceration and the plague. And yet there is much that is untold here; there is much that calls upon ellipsis. The pastoral setting seems to be a safe place, away from disasters, a place that conforms to a Ptolemaic universe at the centre of which the human being sits snuggly. Already here, even before Kepler, we can detect a decentring, an anxiety even within the "circle" of perfection. The pastoral space is contiguous to large towns – perhaps even Seville – that threaten the environment. The absence of Moriscos who often partook of shepherding leads us to other absences. The pestilence of jealousy reminds us that readers sought safety in such books at difficult times. Even while painting the pastoral, Cervantes points to empire, and even while embracing Renaissance contrapposto, the novel shows it as a figure of antithesis. Temples of joy foreground dangers, while tombs for mourning call upon heterodox figures.

If nothing is as it seems in Cervantes' pastoral, what are we to make of his *Quixote*? Chapters 3 and 4 herein focus on *Don Quixote*, part 1 (1605). Chapter 3 is entitled "Unstable Architectures." After all, the first edifice ever mentioned in the novel appears in the prologue, the Royal Jail in Seville where Cervantes was incarcerated. A careful look at this prison shows how a number of its features will be replicated in the novel. The knight, as a figure first imagined, and thus born, in prison, echoes the desires of its author – fleeing confinement, desiring the spaces of freedom. At the same time, the prison itself is a double building; parts were rebuilt in the sixteenth century by architect Hernán Ruiz, a follower of Vitruvius. Its façade recalls, in some aspects, the Vatican Palace, which is also evoked in the prologue. Thus, structures of plurithmia and dysrithmia become a key feature of Cervantes' novel as one architecture hides another and as their foundations become unstable. The episode of the windmills reveals not only its infernal and anthropomorphic structures but also triggers consideration of a giant in terms of a Vitruvian man. The heated conversations between Don Quixote and Sancho on the reality that each one sees may problematize what today we call "safe spaces" and lead us to the transformation of space (dangerous adventure) into a place where friends can challenge each other without safety but in the comfort of their bond.

Chapter 4 turns away from the knight's adventures and focuses on four interpolated tales. Curiously, in all, windows (or their absence) play a central role as they become an architectural feature that allows for the contemplation of the openness of spaces outside, and, when left open, they also attract the dangers outside. Chapter 5 begins to explore the architectures of the second part of *Don Quixote* (1615), evoking first of all the classical architectures exuding eurithmia and then turning to composite and grotesque images drawn by the trickster Sansón Carrasco to further disorient the knight. Indeed, Don Quixote seems haunted by the statue of Victory in the Giralda tower, which turns into a "giantess," and by a chasm that evokes a hell-mouth. Only after "defeating" a lion that stands for the zodiacal sign of Leo, which corresponds to the chasm, is he able to move forth to an enigmatic structure – the home of Diego de Miranda – where he can attain a moment of peace and rest. Chapter 6 shows that the knight, unable to forget some of his difficult experiences, seeks to transform the Cave of Montesinos into a palace. And yet the palace hardly resembles the benefic abodes of the romances of chivalry. It calls upon the imprisoned Merlin. It takes on some of the characteristics of Nero's Golden Palace, long buried underground and rediscovered in the Renaissance. This is but the beginning of the knight's sufferings in the 1615 novel. We turn to other treacherous architectures: the Duchess's torture chamber, and the city of Barcelona where the knight is humbled and defeated.

The last three chapters are devoted to Cervantes' posthumous novel, *Persiles y Sigismunda* (1617). The first two books of this novel insert its copious tales into a world of darkness and illusion where civilization is tenuous, and culture menacing. Its architectures melt into thin air and leave behind nought but the darkness of desire, the urge for possession, and the gloom of the heterodox and the unearthly. Chapter 8 follows the pilgrims as they move from Portugal through Spain and France on their way to Rome. Here sacred architectures are set next to dangerous towers. A Veranzio woman emerges in contrast to the Vitruvian man. The last chapter contrasts the phantom architectures of the north with the sacred yet deceiving monuments of Rome. In his very last writings Cervantes presents us with alternate architectures for the Christian city, from an invisible villa to a vanishing ghetto; and from a Jewish home that welcomes Christian pilgrims to a church that is recreated to receive both Masimino, embodiment of the ancient epic that Cervantes seeks to displace, and the writer himself, who, leaving his book in this world, hopes to enter a sacred domain.

2 Temples and Tombs: *La Galatea*

La Galatea is the first work of fiction published by Cervantes, although
it was antedated by a series of plays that seem to have achieved some
success. A pastoral novel, it follows in the footsteps of a genre that
was popular at the time. The genre started with Sannazaro's *Arcadia* in
Italy and became even more popular with the appearance of Jorge de
Montemayor's *La Diana* (1559). Montemayor's novel had two sequels:
Alonso Pérez's *Segunda parte de la Diana* (1564) and Gaspar Gil Polo's
Diana enamorada of the same year. Other novels followed. The pastoral presents idealized shepherds in an idyllic environment and follows
their love laments, as many are ignored by those whom they love. For
some, this genre serves to highlight the poetry sung by shepherds; others see it as romans à clef with "real" people in almost ethereal beings
that have little to do with actual shepherds; others investigate its debt
to the ancient eclogues. Some even believe that the lack of interest in
their own subjectivity leaves some of these characters with little indi-
viduality, thus being assimilated or subsumed by nature. As the pastoral develops, the monotony of emotional laments is compensated by
the introduction of interpolated tales, and the pastoral of love becomes
the pastoral of the self (Poggioli 1959, 686–7; Cammarata and Laguna
2020, 37). What seems to be a constant, however, is the notion of topophilia, which Yi-Fu Tuan defines as "the affective bond between people
and place or setting" (1990, 4).

This chapter begins with a look at Cervantes' self-fashioning both as
a young author who can publish eclogues and follow Virgil's literary
career and as a writer who may have had Vitruvius in mind even in this
early pastoral, *La Galatea*. It then moves to the architectures of spring
and the ways in which art conjoins nature and the word to draw an idyllic environment, one that exudes topophilia. A section on contrapposto
emphasizes the novel's many antitheses. I then turn to hermitages and

churches as key to the novel, as they are contrasted with the temple. Although appearing to be the centre of harmony, placed in the middle of the novel, the wedding feast is surrounded by other elements that subvert its role and question the Platonizing perfection of the pastoral. Elements such as poison, plague, and drought endanger the notion of the pastoral as an intimate and safe place. The chapter ends with a marvellous vision among the tombs, one that further exposes the political subtext of this pastoral.

Virgil and Vitruvius

Published ten years after Cervantes' Italian sojourn (1569–75) and five years after his return from captivity in Algiers (1575–80), *La Galatea* is touted as a novel of youth, although the author would have been in his late thirties. At the same time, it is a work that plans ahead and hints at what is to come. Cervantes, like many other early modern writers throughout Europe, sets out "to think in terms of decades, perhaps generations [...] The master plan, like scaffolding, holds everything in place" (Lipking 1981, 79–80). His choice is to follow the Virgilian career. The *rota Virgilii* (Virgil's Wheel) became commonplace in medieval rhetoric. It distinguishes three styles (low, medium, and high) that correspond to the occupations of the protagonists of such works (shepherd, farmer, and warrior). It also includes the non-human animals that symbolize each group (sheep, cattle, and horses). This triple division is based on Virgil's three main texts, *Eclogues*, *Georgics*, and *Aeneid*. The three styles and three genres became the three steps in the literary career of a Virgilian poet. The poet should start with pastoral, in other words, the *Eclogues*, he should continue in the fields of the *Georgics*, and he should reach the climax of a literary career with a martial and imperial song – an epic poem such as the *Aeneid*. For example, William Kennedy explains how Petrarch's works, in spite of their frequent change in direction, seek to emulate the Virgil's Wheel.[1] Also, Patrick Cheney has discovered how the works of Edmund Spenser imitate this classical model, and Anne Lake Prescott has studied the poetry of Clement Marot and Du Bartas as sacred mirrors of these careers.[2]

Cervantes utilizes Virgil's Wheel to fashion himself as the ideal poet in tune with the ancients. Instead of following the career in verse, he turns to prose fiction. Obviously, his first work as part of this scaffolding is *La Galatea*, in which he announces in no uncertain terms his imitation of Virgil's career. Since this is not the main focus of this section, I will be brief, although the term *scaffolding* certainly points to construction and architecture.[3] In the prologue to his pastoral the "author"[4] confesses that he began this path somewhat late due to his many voyages and his captivity in Algiers. At the same time, he affirms that he is still entitled to write such a work "habiendo apenas salido de los límites de la juventud" (for when I was scarce emancipated from my youthful shackles; 1995, 156; 1892, x).[5] Alluding to the three Virgilian styles, he describes how a writer must start with the lowest form because these enrich his knowledge and ability and help him "para empresas más altas y de mayor importancia" 1995, 156; 1892, xi; with a view to higher aims and of more serious import). Following in Virgil's footsteps, the author explains that eclogues are a way not just to learn the humble style but also to start to ascend and comprehend higher styles and forms, including the highest, epic. Indeed, the eclogue or pastoral can hide elements of the high style. Thus, lower genres such as eclogues and georgics are often called audacious by Virgil (Coolidge 1965, 12).

Cervantes utilizes the same term to describe his *Galatea*: "he dado muestras de atrevido" (I have given proof of boldness; 1995, 157; 1892, xi). His move towards epic culminates in his posthumous novel, *Los trabajos de Persiles y Sigismunda* (*The Travels of Persiles and Sigismunda*). Cervantes claims that it was written as an imitation of Heliodorus. The *Aethiopica* is an ancient Greek novel that was rediscovered during the Renaissance. Alban Forcione explains: "Educated circles, from the early sixteenth century on, universally condemned the popular romances of chivalry [...] and seized upon the newly discovered *Aethiopica* of Heliodorus as an alternative of prose fiction" (1970, 85–6). Some even considered it an epic in prose. Michael Armstrong-Roche thus poses an important question: "the challenge that Cervantes set himself for his prose epic is itself epic: how to make a hero credibly heroic – and, notably, fit to govern a Kingdom – whose first priority is love?" (2009, 169). He concludes that even in this final Cervantine epic we can observe his audaciousness: "we can renew our appreciation of *Persiles'* freshness, complexity and daring by looking back to epic" (2009, 8). For Cervantes, then, Virgil's Wheel was used as scaffolding for his audacious edifice of fiction. He would begin with pastoral and end with epic. But if each genre had its style, object, and non-human animal, did it also have its architecture? In other words, were there specific architectures that were typical of different genres? Did Cervantes utilize them within his edifice of fiction?

In pastoral, nature is essentialized and perfected;[6] it even takes on the emotions of some of the characters in the manner of a pathetic fallacy. Joan Cammarata and Ana Laguna explain that "[r]ather than acting as a witness to or a mediator of these suitors' desire, nature – the valleys and the beech trees – appears as a metonymical substitution for all such human subjects [...] at odds with any individual differentiation" (2020, 38). While nature is perfected, however, human beings tend to love the wrong person. Thus, there is little of the individual self, and the landscape is dotted with lamenting shepherds and shepherdesses. It is as if these novels at times seemed to include a plot as pretext for the verses or even for the philosophical or Neoplatonic context. The pastoral often minimizes architecture so as not to disrupt the ambience of the work. The shepherds' huts are often but a feature of the landscape, a small place to retire at night in a world where perpetual spring disallows inclement weather or other dangers. However, emotions are the tempests of nature in these pastorals. Here the most beautiful woman in the region is often at the centre of the many laments. The main plot is often as static as the landscape, a vision of sunny pastures in an ideal climate. The days alternate striking sunrises, noontime in the shade, and melancholy sunsets.

At first it appears that Cervantes closely imitates other pastorals. *La Galatea*'s architectures are mostly cosmic, revealing natural beauty with its main feature being the river Tagus and the many little streams in the vicinity, which often trigger the shepherds' memories and songs. Springs, forests, gentle hills, and plains define the landscape as the shepherds guard their sheep. These are accompanied by numerous images or symbols taken from the natural world: the elm and the vine as images of love (1995, 267; 1892, 72); and the willow as image of orphic poetry (1995, 245, 399, 410; 1892, 55, 173, 180). This harmony recalls the eurithmia of Vitruvius' architecture, as Cervantes constructs a place that seems to seek symmetry and perfection. The landscape is dotted with small *cabañas* (huts or cabins) that are barely separate from nature and where shepherds abide, a kind of organic architecture in miniature that would be echoed in the twentieth century by Frank Lloyd Wright. Wright's conception of nature flowing in and out of buildings, of houses that appear to grow out of the natural environment, echoes the Cervantine pastoral.

Cervantes' pastoral also evokes the development of buildings in *The Ten Books on Architecture*, and Vitruvius makes the point that early buildings, such as those in this pastoral, are closer to nature: "Some made them of green boughs, others dug caves on the mountain sides, and some, in imitation of the nests of swallows and the way they were built, made places of refuge out of mud and twigs. Next, by observing the shelters of others and adding new detail to their own inceptions, they constructed better and better kinds of huts as time went on" (1960, 38). In the novel there are twenty-eight mentions of *cabañas*, mostly indicating a place to shelter for the night and a place to rest and sleep. At times, a shepherd or shepherdess meets another at the door of his or her hut or invites a friend inside. Although never stated, the *cabañas* give the sense of minimal size. At one point these huts are called "pajizas cabañas," their straw material recalling the boughs and twigs mentioned by Vitruvius. Cervantes also points to small villages, seldom described, that take on some importance as feast days approach and those living in the surrounding areas come to prepare and celebrate the event.

Key to *La Galatea* is a rustic wedding at a temple, towards the end of the third book. The work never describes the wedding or its rites, whether pagan or Christian. All we discover in the dozen mentions is that appropriate sacrifices are celebrated. Nothing is said of the temple's altars, columns, or doorways, eliding Vitruvius or early modern architects from such scenes. As with the huts, the temples seem close to nature, as shepherds bring flowers and boughs to decorate them on feast days. There is also a wide plaza in front of the main temple in the third book, where those arriving or departing congregate under the shade of four ancient and lush poplar trees. These trees may lend the place a mythic aura because numerous transformations of nymphs into poplars are recorded in ancient mythology, from the Heliades to the Hesperides. It is appropriate that the Heliades, as daughters of the Sun, bring shade in the heat of the day. They thus point to the central architectural feature in the pastoral world of *La Galatea*, the cosmos itself: the four elements that come together and mix in different ways to create, uphold, or destroy (1995, 424, 442; 1892, 188, 197); and the vast fabric of the universe with the sky as earth's ceiling. Thus, "la belleza que en los estrellados cielos y en la máquina y redondez de la tierra, contemplaban, admirados de tanto contento y hermosura" (attracted by beauty as in the starry firmament, and the machine and rotundity of the earth, to contemplate, wonderstruck with its much symmetry and beauty; 1995, 439; 1892, 195) led the ancient philosophers to glimpse at the first cause, at divinity itself. This is in many ways the architecture of eurithmia evoked by Vitruvius: "The heaven revolves steadily round earth and sea on the pivots at the end of its axis. The architect, at these points was the power of Nature, and she put the pivots there, to be, as it were, centres, one of them above the earth and sea at the very top of the firmament, and even beyond the stars composing the Great Bear" (1960, 257). The twelve signs of the zodiac also revolve around the earth; six signs of the zodiac are always in the heaven above (258). While they revolve from east to west, the seven planets "pass through the signs in just the opposite direction" (258). Sun and moon preside day and night, often appearing in the guise of mythological sunrises in Cervantes' *La Galatea* (1995, 204, 225, 328; 1892, 27, 40, 119), and as Diana or a luminous chariot of stars lighting up the darkness (1995, 182, 188, 249, 468, 476, 480, 502; 1892, 11, 16, 59, 215, 223, 226, 243). Although Vitruvius, in discussing the sun's path throughout the year, points to the seasons, it is as if the characters in *La Galatea* inhabited a land that recalls perpetual spring. They may allude to winter metaphorically as a time that never comes or a "space" where they are rejected by the beloved (1995, 177, 235, 335, 410; 1892, 8, 47, 134, 180), but at the same time, as they play their rustic instruments, they intuit the music of the spheres.[7] Again, the harmony of eurithmia pervades.

The Vitruvian architecture is most clearly perceived, however, in the relation between the beauty of the human body and the beauty of objects such as buildings and art works. In future chapters I will discuss in more detail the Vitruvian man, but for now let us recall that for the ancient architect, the proportion, symmetry, and measure of the temples to the gods derived from the human body, which demonstrates corporeal perfection through the "perfect" geometrical form of the circle, which has its centre in the navel and the circumference formed through extended limbs, thus touching fingers and toes (Vitruvius 1960, 73). In *La Galatea*, Cervantes, although veering away from this exact notion to one of the human being as microcosm, still emphasized the Renaissance's laudation of human perfection. Tirsi, who told that even the ancients were wonderstruck at the cosmos, goes on to confirm that beauty is also in man: "Pero lo que más admiró fue la compostura del hombre, tan ordenada, tan perfecta y tan hermosa, que la vinieron a llamar mundo abreviado" (Yet what much excited astonishment and reflection was the sight of man, so constructed, so perfect, and beautiful, that he was styled a world of himself; 1995, 439; 1892, 196). Rejecting the goodness of human love, Lenio perceives two equal beauties: "la belleza corporal en cuerpos vivos [...] la parte corporal no viva consiste en pinturas, estatuas, edificios" (corporeal beauty [...] the other beauty of corporeality is not animate, consisting in pictures, statues, edifices; 1995, 418; 1892, 185). As opposed to the simple comparison of temples and bodies, here Lenio chooses the inanimate beauty in art and architecture as superior because it can be loved without the kind of passionate desire that can lead to tragedy and disaster. Although here, as Geoffrey Stagg has argued, Lenio seems to be evoking Equicola's ideas (1959, 272), in later texts Cervantes will reveal a much closer meditation on the Vitruvian man, even going so far as to contrast him with what I have labelled as the "Veranzio woman" in the *Persiles*.

Primavera's Dissonance

The idealizing of classicism, with evocation of Graeco-Roman deities, gives *La Galatea* a sense of artful creation. It is as if the text became a series of visual moments that exhibited images like those of the many mythological paintings found in Renaissance Italy.[8] Indeed, we will see how Cervantes carefully inserts art as fragmented or dramatic ekphrasis to show portions of a painting or to make a specific painting come to life when figures start moving this way or that. Music and song also pervade the landscape, creating a most sensual and appealing texture that is meant to soothe. At the same time, the pleasure derived from beauty hides, according to Javier Irigoyen-García, a political agenda, serving to "promote a homogeneous conception of national identity" (2014, 25). This homogeneity makes it what we would label today "a safe space," where the most fragile of selves can shelter away from discordant notes or trigger words in a world that is as unreal as the utopia that some seek to create. Unfortunately utopias tend to be univocal, with readers placing or imagining themselves at the top of the ladder of a Platonic society that rules on what is right or, in the case of Tommaso Campanella's *The City of the Sun*, accepting the premises of the new space that organizes knowledge to enable power over a subject. The benefic power of utopias disallows dissent and censors what is outside or beyond them.

While there is perfection all around them, the shepherds in *La Galatea*, wanting to partake of universal love, always encounter obstacles to their desires, thereby suffusing the work with a melancholic aura. Indeed, the novel begins with a poem of lament (Cervantes 1995, 165; 1892, 1). This sadness is echoed by the fields and by the hills as if nature could mourn for a love not attained. Here the beautiful Galatea is desired by two shepherds, Elicio and Erastro. Such is the harmony of this pastoral place that the two can play their instruments in concord: "acordemos nuestros instrumentos" (let us unite our instruments; 1995, 175; 1892, 7). Even this concordance, although perhaps soothing to readers of *La Galatea*, is dissonant when contrasted with the actual countryside at the time. In addition, the dangers of this pastoral place at times surface in the narrative, but just as hints of a mightier and more threatening nature. In the words of Yi-Fu Tuan, topophilia turns to topophobia, a physical and mental landscape of fear and anxiety (1979). We have already noted the fleeting references to terrifying winters, which could create a hidden dysrithmia in the work. In addition, the dogs must guard the sheep against "los carniceros dientes de los hambrientos lobos" (the fleshy teeth of hungry wolves; Cervantes 1995, 171; 1892, 6). While discussing the pains of love, Erastro refers to other dangers for his flock: "no hallen en el verde prado para sustentarse sino amargos tueras y ponzoñosas adelfas" (they find not herbs enough to support them, but bitter *tueras* and venomous oleanders; 1995, 173; 1892, 6). Oleander is a most poisonous flower that affects both dogs and sheep. Thus, the beauty of the pastoral can hide threats, although these are never fulfilled in the novel. Not long after the publication of *La Galatea*, Hernando de Soto utilized this beautiful but poisonous flower in his *Emblemas moralizadas* (1599), including it as a representation of deception: "De la adelfa y de su rosa / Es el engaño increíble / Que a la vista es apacible / Pero al gusto venenosa" (Of the oleander and its rose, deception is incredible since to the sight it is gentle but to the taste, poisonous; 1983, 33). Javier Lorenzo Domínguez points out that this notion also appears in Lope de Vega (2017, 484–98). Although in Soto and Lope the allusion incorporates misogyny, as the oleander is compared to the venom of a beautiful woman, in Cervantes it stays within the landscape. It does not even manifest there but remains as a latent threat. The inhabitants seem "sheltered in place," seldom needing to leave their protected areas. At the same time, Cervantes differentiates the places of pastoral with the spaces outside. A series of interpolated stories, four main ones and two of shorter length, weave in and out of the main plot.[9] These often take place beyond the pastoral realm. Marsha Collins asserts: "Overall the community by the Tagus, as Arcadian communities tend to do, live quiet lives of little action [...] but the interpolated romances explode and disrupt the relative peace and bring with them nonstop adventures, many of them adventures with life-death stakes on the outcome" (2016, 149). As these adventures spill into the harmonious countryside, they bring about unexpected conflicts and even murder.

Perhaps the novel was not quite as successful as other pastorals of the period, because it dashed readers' expectations. It is one thing to discreetly point to dangers inside; it is quite another to depict humans as bloodthirsty as wolves. It is one thing to postpone the first appearance of the beautiful Galatea in the novel; it is quite another to have her appear at the end of the first interpolated tale in the novel – a tale that begins with the brutal murder witnessed by Elicio and Erastro.[10] By his daring and experimentation, Cervantes may be turning against the univocal lyricism of the pastoral and towards new forms, thus disorienting the reader who would prefer generic limits in fiction. Elicio, one of the witnesses to this first murder, leaves his hut that evening. He does not do so because the event has triggered fear or anxiety in him. Rather, his reaction is based on other motives, mainly love and a pastoral "of melancholy and solitude" (Poggioli 1959, 686). In his pursuit of solitude he journeys to the "espesura de un espeso bosque" (thick of a wood; 1995, 182; 1892, 11) where he searches for an appropriate place to lament his unrequited love for Galatea. It is worth noting that he is almost mono-maniacal in his laments. It is as if he had totally forgotten the brutal murder. And yet the forest at night might be lugubrious enough to recall his recent encounter with violence. At the same time, this somewhat threatening space contrasts with other natural forces that surround him and slowly transform his route into place. Elicio moves along with a soft wind ("un templado céfiro"), smelling the sweet scent of flowers: "olorosas flores que el verde suelo estaba colmando" (the fragrant smell of flowers which were concentrated there; 1995, 182; 1892, 34). But instead of finding the longed-for solitude, Elicio runs into Lisandro, the assassin who has also chosen this site for his lamentations. Elicio has entered the spaces of danger, even so close to his pastoral hut.

For George Camamis, there are a number of key elements here that reveal that the description is a partial ekphrasis of Botticelli's *Primavera* (see figure 2.1): "A thick dark wood, Zephyr blowing his wind and the green ground covered with sweet smelling flowers" (1988, 189). Furthermore, when Elicio wants to step forth to join Lisandro in a clearing in the woods, the latter adopts a specific pose: "estaba con el pie derecho delante y el izquierdo atrás y el diestro brazo levantado a guise como de quien esperaba hacer algún recio tiro" (stood with his foot advanced, and the left hand behind, and the right raised as if to make a cast; Cervantes 1995, 187; 1892, 15).

Camamis explains: "Cervantes has actually reproduced exactly the figure of Mercury in Botticelli's *Primavera*" (1988, 190). The Cervantine ekphrasis finds completion towards the end of the novel, in the sixth book. As the shepherds move towards the Valley of the Cypresses, they discover a place akin to the Elysian Fields. The description includes four main elements from Botticelli's painting, the figures of Primavera, Venus, Zephyr, and Flora: "Aquí se ve en cualquiera sazón del año andar la risueña Primavera con la hermosa Venus en hábito sucinto y amoroso, y Céfiro que la acompaña, con la madre Flora delante, esparciendo a manos llenas varias y odoríferas flores" (Here we observe, in each season of the year, that the laughing spring unites with the lovely Venus, in short and amorous garment, and Zephyr, the companion with Flora; Cervantes 1995, 542; 1892, 277).

For Camamis, then, Venus is akin to Galatea herself – and we recall that elsewhere in the novel she is accompanied by the three Graces. Thrice in the pastoral Galatea is associated with the myrtle, a tree that surrounds Venus in the painting (Camamis 1988, 194). For Camamis, Galatea has little to do with the nymph in Raphael's fresco *The*

Figure 2.1. Sandro Botticelli, *Primavera*, ca. 1477–82. Uffizi, Florence, Italy. Alinari Archives/Art Resource, NY

Triumph of Galatea, where she is loved by Polyphemus but disdains and moves away from him – a model that was proposed by Edward Dudley (1995, 27–45). I would argue that Cervantes' Galatea not only refers to *Primavera* but actually embodies a clash between two models, two paintings located in the loggia of the Villa Farnesina in Rome. While Raphael's work shows the happy yet fleeing Galatea, Sebastiano del Piombo's work portrays Polyphemus, the giant who loves Galatea (De Armas 2000, 33–48). For our purposes, however, what is important is that each of these paintings represents a very different site: the menacing spaces of Sebastiano join the more joyful yet still dangerous seascape of Raphael. In the *Primavera* we come much closer to the feeling of place. The place is spring itself, with the goddess Flora distributing countless flowers while Venus/Primavera watches with approval as the three Graces dance in a beauteous site, protected by a forest in the background. In one corner we have the figure of Zephyr with its benefic and soft west winds; in the other we encounter Mercury playing with some clouds in the sky and representing the rains necessary for fruition or the end of spring. If Cervantes knew this painting, then it makes perfect sense to see Lisandro in Mercury's pose. The clouds that symbolize the end of the springtime of perfection are indeed reflected in Lisandro, a man who, albeit a victim, has polluted the spring of pastoral with spilled blood.

Theatre

There is another place within the pastoral that merges the rustic scene or architecture of *Primavera* with the text. Lisandro, we are told, stands in a round opening in the woods that is "a manera de teatro" (like a theatre; Cervantes 1995, 187; 1892, 15). As if this were a theatre from ancient Greece or Rome, Elicio not only sees the circumference of the performance area in these buildings (Vitruvius 1960, 146) but clearly hears Lisandro's laments for his now-dead beloved. Voice, as Vitruvius argues, increases its power through the application of the theory of harmonics in theatre (1960, 139). In a long poem Lisandro imagines his beloved's soul ascending to the heavens and wishes to join her. His speech recalls the role of Hermes/Mercury in mythology as a psychopomp or guide of the souls to the afterlife. It melds with Botticelli's painting as Mercury points upwards and as Lisandro longs for the perpetual spring above. In addition, Hermes/Mercury often appeared in ancient plays, such as in Euripides' *Helen* and *Ion*, and his statues graced a number of temples, mainly in Arcadia, thus recalling the setting of Cervantes' pastoral. Vitruvius notes that these temples could be circular (1960, 122), thus recalling the "theatre" where Lisandro laments. Indeed, Hermes/Mercury was often portrayed as a shepherd, thus belonging to Arcadia. Carrying a ram around his shoulders, he walked the walls of the city to save it from the plague. As a god of boundaries, Hermes/Mercury delineates the place for Cervantes' pastoral setting, giving it protection from the plague, thus affirming it as a shelter or place akin to the *Primavera*.

Mercury as healer also embodies notions of architecture. Gaspar Gutiérrez de los Ríos, for example, claims that medicine is as much of an art as architecture and painting: "Efectivas llama aquéllas, adonde del hazer nace alguna obra visible, como son la Medicina, Architectura, Escultura y Pintura; en las quales, el curar produze de sí un cuerpo sano, el del edificar forma un edificio, y el de pintar y esculpir, la diversidad de formas, figuras e historias que vemos pintadas y relevadas." (Effective are those who make a visible work, such as medicine, architecture, sculpture, and painting; in which healing produces a healthy body, building forms an edifice, and painting and sculpture create a diversity of forms, figures, and histories that we see as painted and sculpted; 2000, 31.) Thus, in the figure of Lisandro/Mercury, along with its theatre or temple, we have the fusion of several arts from medicine to architecture to sculpture. To these we must add painting since the figure of Mercury seems to derive from Botticelli's *Primavera*.

The complex setting leads us to inquire whence Lisandro had come. After all, it appears that he lives nearby the pastoral but sufficiently apart in a town that would not contaminate the setting. Curiously, as he begins his tale of misfortune, Lisandro states that he comes from the shores of the Betis River. Using its roman name, he clearly erases its contemporary name of Arabic origins, the Guadalquivir (meaning "the great river"). The Betis was navigable in the early modern period from Cádiz up to Seville and even up to Córdoba. Seville had grown exponentially as it became one of the most important and wealthiest ports in Europe owing to its trade with the Americas. Although Lisandro, when he tells his story, claims to be from a "village," the statement may conceal veiled references to Seville. Renowned for its tremendous wealth, it was also known for its crime and violence. It is no coincidence that Cervantes sets one of his picaresque tales, *Rinconete y Cortadillo* (Rinconete and Cortadillo), in this city. Seville is also the place where Cervantes was imprisoned, a main feature of the beginning of *Don Quixote*. Numerous books, following Mary Elizabeth Perry's pioneering account, have dealt with crime in this bustling city. Perry points to the symbiotic relationship between the upper classes and the underworld (1980, 74), and Cervantes weaves it into his narrative. Ruth Pike highlights that, although most criminals were thieves, those imprisoned were, in the majority, guilty of homicide. Indeed, nobles were as responsible for murders and assaults as was the underworld. Their many rivalries resulted in numerous assassinations (Pike 1975, 5–6). Thus, it is quite possible to envision the tale told by Lisandro as something that could have taken place in Seville. In 1581, four years before the publication of *La Galatea*, a complaint was sent to Philip II concerning the mismanagement of an epidemic that had swept the city that year and the previous one. Although at times labelled *catarro* (catarrh), the epidemic was also characterized as a *mal de peste* (plague) (Wilson Bowers 2013, 89). The complaint also pointed to "a crime wave, including thieves breaking into houses and an unusual number of deaths" (89). Pointing to specific officials, the complaint probably stemmed from fights for control in the city. The plots and counterplots among the two ruling families in Cervantes' tale, albeit borrowed from Matteo Bandello, the source of Shakespeare's *Romeo and Juliet*, could well be adapted to point to a city in turmoil.[11] Furthermore, Lisandro's tale points to the particularly heinous nature of his rivals. Ruth Pike states: "Crimes perpetrated at night or in uninhabited or sparsely populated districts were considered particularly heinous because such conditions lessened the ability of the victims to defend themselves or receive assistance from others" (1975, 9). Readers would then see Lisandro's attacker as particularly malevolent. As for the manner of death, "sword and knife wounds caused the largest percentage of deaths" (1975, 9). This once again points to Lisandro's tale as very plausible. Cervantes thus presents the dangers of a city on the Betis River as spilling into the pastoral narrative. Not only murder but perhaps even some kind of plague could infest the safe places of narrative. Topophilia is shaded by topophobia, while eurithmia turns to dysrithmia. Lisandro, in the posture of Mercury as healer, would represent space and place, city and pastoral, illness and cure, topophilia and anxiety, violence and safety. The temple in the forest is a site of antithesis.

The temple concretizes the many oppositions, while the figure of Lisandro in contrapposto evokes a series of striking poses in this novel that echo the "artes extremadas" (excessive arts) that according to Dámaso Alonso are related to mannerism (1971, 386).[12] As David Summers reminds us, *contrapposto* derives from *contrapositium*, the rhetorical device on antithesis (1977, 339). Turning to this specific scene, Patricia Zalamea argues that Lisandro, as he stands in this manner , points to disruption: "diera aviso de que la narrativa pastoril está por interrumpirse de una forma no convencional, puesto que unas escenas violentas – que contrastan con el idilio pastoral – están por relatarse

(2018, 349; gives notice that the pastoral narrative is about to be interrupted in an unconventional way, since violent scenes – which contrast with the pastoral idyll – are about to be narrated). Indeed, there are a number of antitheses that can be envisioned here. The anticipation of happiness as Leónida accepts to marry Lisandro in the next village contrasts with the dreadful ending; the savage happiness of Crisalvo bearing the news that he has killed Silvia contrasts with the fact that she is alive; and Lisandro's soft and touching love becomes the antithesis of his savage murder of Carino. Thus, the figure of Lisandro/Mercury in contrapposto represents the many antithetical elements that bring about a murder in a pastoral setting. At one point Lisandro laments his trust in the astute and treacherous Carino: "¡Ay, mal aconsejado Lisandro!, ¿cómo, y no sabías tú las condiciones dobladas de Carino?" (Oh evil-counselled Lisandro! Know you not the double conditions which bound Carino?; 1995, 198; 1892, 22.) This double condition is nothing more than an extreme contrapposto, a mixture of apparent sincerity and hidden treachery, a harmonious front antithetical to its inner will, readying to attack. The village (Seville) becomes a noxious space, filled with treachery, spies, false friendships, and contending families. It is part of a landscape of fear that Yi-Fu Tuan bemoans. The buildings into and out of which the characters of the tale weave represent the anxious, fearsome, and noxious urban setting that shepherds flee. These edifices of doom are barely described (as in an ellipsis), perhaps hiding the urban architecture of Seville, their phantom presence haunting the places of pastoral. The pastoral itself embraces Lisandro, whose lovelorn and guilty figure haunts the idyllic landscape, searching for a lost love and redemption. His is a tragic play whose setting is Seville and whose performance is riddled with antitheses.

Hermitage

The third interpolated tale in the *Galatea* begins in the second book and continues, highly fragmented, throughout the novel.[13] A group of shepherds stop close to an old hermitage: "una antigua ermita que en la ladera de un montecillo estaba, no tan desviada del camino que dejase de oírse el son de una arpa que dentro, al parecer, tañían" (an ancient hermitage, which had its site on the side of a hillock, not so remote from the path but that a harp was heard; Cervantes 1995, 268; 1892, 72). Although it seems an inviting and secluded place, Erastro explains that the new inhabitant of the hermitage is a young man who arrived some two weeks earlier and lives a rather austere life: "tanta soledad y estrecheza" (so much solitude and a so confined state; 1995, 268; 1892, 73).

As they hear him playing the harp, the curious group moves towards the building to meet him and listen to his story. As they do, they hear him complaining and lamenting of Timbrio and Nísida. Upon entering, they discover that he has fainted while singing. Sitting upon a stone, he appears thusly: "Estaba con la cabeza inclinada a un lado, y la una mano asida de la parte de la túnica que sobre el corazón caía, y el otro brazo a la otra parte flojamente derribado" (His head was leaning on one side, and his hand rested on that portion of the tunic which covered his heart, while the other arm fell down loosely by his side; 1995, 272; 1892, 76). This detailed description shows him helpless but with a hand on his heart. Such a gesture points to love, and the viewers may ask if it pertains to the love of God or to a secular passion. The names he has been invoking move us away from the sacred and towards the profane. Slowly he recuperates and tells his tale. His name is Silerio and he is from the city of Jerez, and thus the action moves from a pastoral setting to a city. There he sought to become best friends with Timbrio, and he fulfilled his wish, so much so that they were called by all "los dos amigos" (the two friends) as they spent all their time together: "los mozos años pasábamos, ora en el campo en el ejercicio de la caza, ora en la ciudad en el del honroso Marte" (did we two with incredible satisfaction pass our adult years, now in the chase, now in the city, honoured by Mars; 1995, 275; 1892, 77).[14] A question of honour forces Timbrio to leave the city for Naples. Silerio cannot follow him right away because he is ill. The closeness of the two friends becomes obvious from the start, as it is a question of health that prevents them from travelling together. But when Silerio does follow, he finds his friend in a small Mediterranean town, condemned to die. Silerio saves his friend, and then Timbrio seeks to save Silerio. Thus the story underlines one more key point in the typical tale of the two friends: the selfless desire to sacrifice one's life for the other. But once again they lose each other during the journey.

Once Silerio arrives in Naples, he discovers that his friend is ill. The malady, he finds out, is one of melancholy because Timbrio has fallen in love with Nísida. At once, Silerio strives to find ways to bring the two together, but, of course, given the mimetic desires of the friends, Silerio ends up also falling in love with Nísida. Countless emotional scenes, wrenching tears, secret sacrifices, and plot reversals follow as the two become closer and yet paradoxically more distant as they set the test of their friendship through the love of one woman. In one instance Silerio searches for Timbrio and finds him in a strange posture, face down on the bed and crying. Timbrio lies to Silerio and tells him he is not in love with Nísida. Rather, he is in love with her sister, Blanca (1995, 298–9;

1892, 96). Intimacy is constantly broken as each refuses to tell the full truth to the other. As we follow the two friends and the woman they love, we discover that fainting is a common response to their plight.

Three elements are of particular interest to our study of Cervantes' architectures: first, the strange poses and fainting spells; second, the importance of hermitages, churches, and chapels; and third, the presence of temples. While the temples within pastoral seem pagan in nature and evoke Vitruvius, those in the tales "outside" of pastoral are Christian chapels and churches. We have seen how contrapposto takes on the meaning of antithesis. Silerio's pose, which includes a fainting spell, and a later one assumed by Timbrio, echoes Jacopo Pontormo's *Deposition from the Cross*, and the serpentine contours that so often characterize Pontormo's work represent the suffering that each must endure to preserve a perfect friendship, as each of them appears to be in love with the same woman. At the same time, Cervantes utilizes a serpentine manner of interpolation in this third story, the tale coming in and out of the work, undulating, showing itself and disappearing as if reflecting the architecture of Francesco Borromini's Church of Saint Charles at the Four Fountains in Rome, which was built a half century after Cervantes' pastoral. Its non-classical manner reflects how Cervantes, albeit following the traditional story of the two friends, injects it with unexpected aspects, as the love of the two friends is put on trial time and again, creating moments of bliss and torture.

During the Renaissance there was a cult of male friendship that brought together two noble youths. This bond was sacred and was to last throughout their lives, being as important as family ties. Juan Pablo Gil-Oslé asserts: "En el discurso europeo de la amistad, que bebía de la *Ética Nicomáquea* de Aristóteles y de *De Amicitia* de Cicerón, la intensidad de esta unión entre los amigos ideales es tal que alcanza el estatuto de sagrada ley. En su calidad de sagrada unión, el compromiso en la amistad se caracterizaba por su carencia de límites, por encima de los deberes familiares y conyugales." (In the European discourse of friendship, which was influenced by Aristotle's *Nicomachean Ethics* and by Cicero's *De Amicitia*, the intensity of this union between ideal friends is such that it reaches the status of sacred law. As a sacred union, the commitment to friendship was characterized by its lack of limits, above family and conjugal duties; 2013, 17.) From Montaigne to Shakespeare it was extolled as one of the highest of human bonds, even above heterosexual marriage.[15] At the hermitage Silerio's verses are sung to the sound of a harp – an instrument connected to the sacred – and contain phrases such as "Yo como puedo, buen Señor, levanto / la una y otra palma / los ojos, la intención al Cielo santo" (I, my good Lord, as I can, elevate / the one and other palm, / my eyes intent on the all sacred sky, / by which my soul doth hope; 1995, 272; 1892; 75). Famous psalms indicate that the faithful should raise the palms of the hands to the heavens (Psalm 63) and that they should elevate the eyes (Psalm 121). In the hermitage Silerio is bemoaning loss but singing of the sacrifices needed to achieve perfect friendship, a relationship that is pleasing to the deity. In the midst of the tale, Silerio, while searching for his friend, finds himself in a small coastal town and faced with an immense raised crucifix, a town crier, and a bandit condemned to death:

> [L]o primero en que puse los ojos fue en un alto crucifijo y en mucho tumulto de gente, señales que alguno sentenciado a muerte entre ellos venía, todo lo cual me certificó la voz del pregonero, que declaraba que, por haber sido salteador y bandolero, la justicia mandaba ahorcar un hombre, que, como a mí llegó, luego conocí que era el mi buen amigo Timbrio, el cual venía a pie, con unas esposas a las manos y una soga a la garganta, los ojos enclavados en el crucifijo que delante llevaba, diciendo y protestando a los clérigos que con él iban, que por la estrecha cuenta que pensaba dar en breves horas al verdadero Dios, cuyo retrato delante los ojos tenía, que nunca en todo el discurso de su vida había cometido cosa por donde públicamente mereciese recibir tan ignominiosa muerte; y que a todos rogaba rogasen a los jueces le diesen algún término para probar cuán inocente estaba de lo que le acusaban. (Cervantes 1995, 277)

> ([T]he first thing that struck my eyes was a crucifix, and much people, a sign that some one sentenced to death was on the way, which the voice of the town-crier confirmed, exclaiming, that being a highway robber and a brigand, justice ordained that he should be hanged. As I advanced towards the supposed culprit, in a twinkling I recognized my dear friend Timbrio, who onward came, his hands in fetters, a close garment to his neck, and eyes rivetted on a crucifix, which was before him, disputing with the priests who accompanied him, and alleging, by the name of that God in whose presence he should quickly be, whose effigy he bore before him, that never in his life had he committed an act for which he deserved public execution, and he supplicated all to petition the judge to give him time to prove his innocence.) (Cervantes 1892, 78–9)

Silerio stares at the scene without moving, as if he were a marble statue. Although he almost faints, his "alterada sangre" transforms him. In a choleric fit of bravery he is able to save his friend, who finds sanctuary in a church. The town, now angry at Timbrio, wants to sacrifice him. The scene at the hermitage mirrors the scene at the church. In both, the crucified Christ embodies the sacrifices that must be made by perfect friends. It can be argued that the church saves the two friends from the dangers of the space outside, while at the same time they save each other, the bond between them becoming a soothing "place." In other words, place is a site for comfort, intimacy, and protection. The bond between Timbrio and Silerio fulfils the desire for place, for sheltering from the dangers outside. The architectural place is thus transformed into an emotional and corporeal place that brings together the two friends.

The church becomes a marker of the sacredness of their bond as they vie to save each other. Very much like the hermitage, it is a place of refuge and a marker of Christian sacrifice. In other words, these are places in the sense that they provide safety, while triggering devotion and redemption. At the same time they are "spaces" of danger where Christ's sacrifice serves as an example for friends to sacrifice their lives for each other. Other architectures impinge upon the text, but what is important here is that Silerio's tale is interrupted when a large crowd playing musical instruments passes by, including Daranio crowned with a wreath, as all delight in his impending marriage. If hermitage and church point to selfless sacrifice, the temple where all the shepherds are to meet takes on different connotations. It is a mythical place, the centre of a pastoral land that shelters the shepherds from the outside.

Temple

In the serpentine tale of Timbrio and Silerio a chance attack by Turks actually saves them. They can then escape a town that wants to claim one of their lives. This sudden menace from the outside, this space of danger, recalls that, as Javier Irigoyen-García has pointed out, Moriscos were often involved in shepherding, an element missing from all pastorals: "the pastoral frame aimed at erasing the Moorish legacy from the perception of Spanish landscape" (2014, 158). In so doing, pastoral sought to present a homogenous Spanish identity made up of Old Christians who would then be shepherding their flock as the Spanish empire grew into a uniform Christian land that sought to erase others. Just as sheep had to be culled to preserve the whiteness and purity of Merino wool, the empire also sought to preserve the purity of the blood of its inhabitants.

If this key element was erased, what else did pastoral eliminate? In later chapters we will discuss the relation of ellipsis with the geometry of the elliptical. At this point, Cervantes is still developing this vision, which will concretize with the discovery in 1609 of Kepler's elliptical orbits. Here, however, the elliptical, with its double centre, is still being developed. At the same time, we can point to a pastoral centre that is displaced at times by outside concerns. First of all, readers contemporaneous to *La Galatea* were being confronted with one of the four catastrophic periods of what is now called the Little Ice Age and which alternated heavy rainstorms and great periods of drought. Many deaths were caused by drought. Although the three great plagues of the period were yet to arrive in Spain, occurring in 1597–1602, 1647–52, and 1676–85, other epidemics had either just passed or were occurring elsewhere, as Spain and other parts of Europe were constantly threatened by catastrophic events.[16] And, although Irigoyen-García underlines the purging of the Moorish elements from the pastoral, he does not deal with a real danger at this time: the constant attacks and kidnappings by pirates not only in the Mediterranean but throughout the Spanish, French, and Italian coasts. As they conjoined with the threat of different diseases, these two dangers outside were transformed into grotesque marvels.

Paul Barolsky, in a study of Benvenuto Cellini's autobiography, has underlined the way in which such events caused both fear and wonderment. Cellini tells how he fell victim to the plague in Rome and, upon recovering, thanked God for this miracle. "As therapy, he rode to the seashore to collect stones, snails and shells for his collection of marvels" (Barolsky 1993, 42). Just as he was starting to enjoy himself, he was attacked by Moors. Barolsky asks if his miraculous escape, as his pony jumped evasively, could be a "poetic embellishment of the account of how he escaped death by the plague?" (1993, 42). We may wish to consider Cervantes' pastoral novel as one such poetic embellishment, as an "escape" from the many threats that were being faced in this particularly dangerous period. While the serpentine plot of the two friends surfaces here and there, always presenting new dangers and new unusual poses, the dangers inside the main plot of the novel continue to be unveiled.[17]

La Galatea was dedicated to Ascanio Colonna, who was named cardinal in 1586, the year after publication of the pastoral novel. The dedication has much to do with Cervantes' wish to return to Italy. Having spent years of his youth in the area, he would have known of the many threatening pandemics and diseases. For example, the plague of 1576–7 killed fifty thousand people in Venice (Lindemann 1999, 41). Malaria, which some contemporary researchers consider to be one of the causes of the fall of the Roman Empire, arrived in the coastal marshes of Italy and brought about countless deaths. The port of Ostia was at first spared due to the salinity of its waters, but later succumbed (Sallers

2002, 86–7). The pastoral beauty of the Roman Campagna hid its deadliness, particularly in the summer months (235–61). During the sixteenth century the swampy areas around Rome, and part of the road between Rome and Naples, killed many with what at the time were considered to be the miasma or vapours from the swamps; it was not known that the disease was propagated by mosquitoes. Cervantes, who abided in Rome for a time and then travelled from Rome to Naples, would have known of the deadly disease.

The dreaded *cocoliztli* struck the Viceroyalty of New Spain three times during the sixteenth century: 1520, 1545, and 1576. It decimated both the Indigenous and the Spanish inhabitants and infected, among others, Bernardino de Sahagún, the well-known Franciscan friar whose interest and knowledge of Mexica culture was unparalleled at his time (Prem 1991, 20–48). Cervantes, who, in addition to desiring to return to Italy, sought to migrate to America, must have been very conscious of the danger. In the sixth and last book of *La Galatea*, he lists some one hundred poets, in the "Canción de Calíope" (Calliope's song). Their names are placed in the poem in relation to the river that represents their region in Iberia, such as the Tajo, Betis, Tormes, Pisuerga, Ebro, and Turia. This song of praise for poets, many of them unknown today, contains a list of fourteen bards from America, including the famed Francisco de Terrazas (1525?–1600?), who survived two of these epidemics. Curiously, Terrazas' work tends to question to some extent the excluding imperial policies of the empire. He decries that peoples of Spanish descent born in America (criollos) were treated as inferior to those born in Spain. He was brought to the Inquisition for questioning, and in a fragmented and incomplete poem dealing with the conquests of Hernán Cortés he often criticizes the conqueror's attitude towards his companions.[18] At least in this one instance, then, Cervantes praises a poet who did not conform to the norms of his times and who survived both the dangers outside and the threats of the powerful. If, on the one hand, Cervantes creates a place of harmony in his pastoral, on the other, he also questions this place and finds that it can be a contentious space. Unrequited love, although a common topic in pastoral, assumes here a more dangerous and threatening aspect, perhaps pointing to the environmental and medical threats of the period.

The very end of the third book is considered to be the culmination of the first half of the novel, with a wedding at a rustic temple. This edifice contrasts with another architecture that signals the end of the novel, the tombs that surround the exequies in honour of Meliso.[19] Placed almost at the centre of the novel, the celebrations for the wedding of Daranio and Silveria shadow the true sacred centre, the hermitage and the church. The temple exhibits its adornments and ostentatiously claims the centre with its openness; it claims an artful nature with a mix of flowers, tree branches, and stone. But its surroundings belie its placement. The temple, which, through a rustic wedding proclaims perfection and harmony, is besieged. The narrative stops to present a list, a kind of epic catalogue of suffering shepherds: "el triste Orompo, el celoso Orfenio, el ausente Crisio y el desamado Marsilio" (the mournful Orompo, the ardent Orfenio, the absent-minded Crisio, and the disenamoured Marsilio; Cervantes 1995, 337; 1892, 126). It is followed by the song of Lenio, a shepherd who does not believe in love. Accepting the marvellous power of the god, he hopes the newly married couple can enjoy the springtime of love – "la agradable eterna primavera" (the charming, grateful, never-ending spring; 1995, 342; 1892, 129) – thus echoing the eternal springtime of pastoral. But he slowly becomes enraged, knowing all the perfidious tricks of Eros, which often lead to "infernal rabia celosa" (infernal low-born jealousy; 1995, 343; 1892, 130). To further destabilize this moment, the four suffering shepherds from the epic catalogue propose to sing an eclogue that they have composed in honour of their friend Daranio and his wedding. Ironically, the verses by Orompo, Marsilio, Crisio, and Orfenio within the eclogue deal with each of the shepherd's misfortunes in love (1995, 346–68; 1892, 131–50). The first, about the untimely death of Listea, Orompo's beloved, is filled with images of blood, poison, pain, and torment; the last, filled by jealous rage, is sung by the jealous Orfenio. Damón judges that Orfenio is the unhappiest of the four: "ninguno fatiga tanto al enamorado pecho como la incurable pestilencia de los celos" (nothing so disturbed the enamoured breast as the incurable rage of jealousy; 1995, 369; 1892, 150). The term *pestilencia* is related to the black plague. In his treatise on the plague Juan Jiménez Savariego asserts: "Peste no se dice ninguna enfermedad por su esencia, sino por el modo pestífero que toma la enfermedad (The plague is not thus called because of its essence, but for the pestiferous aspect of the illness; 1602, 5v). Jealousy, we are told, is as ill smelling as the plague.

Thus, a perfect environment hides the worst of epidemics. Death enters Arcadia both through the death of Orompo's beloved and through Orfenio's image of jealousy as a plague. The marvellous in the pastoral is located within this opposition of beauty and dread.

Tombs

In book 3 the temple serves as centre, as shepherds from the surrounding area converge for a wedding.In book 6, however, an old wise man who acts as priest conducts the shepherds to the Valley of Cypresses where they will celebrate exequies by Meliso's tomb. In a marvellous geography that seems to bring together rivers from Iberia, Italy, and the classical world, Elicio brings up once again the evocation of springtime, reminiscent of the feast of the Floralia in Ovid's *Fasti*, a May festival dedicated to Flora, a goddess who enjoys "perpetual spring" (Ovid 1989, 5.207), creating a landscape filled with flowers in the company of the Graces. The environment also recalls Botticelli's *Primavera*, cited earlier, which includes the figures of Primavera, Venus, Zephyr, and Flora. Even a reference to Garcilaso evokes here the four tapestries of his third eclogue, all of which tell a tragic tale: the death of Eurydice; Apollo pursuing Daphne, who is then turned into a Laurel tree; Venus' love for Adonis, who will soon die in the hunt; and the death of Elisa, beloved of Nemoroso. Again, death and the marvellous come together as the pilgrims approach the valley. It is as if, once again, Cervantes is seeking to paint over the horrors of death at a time of climate instability, wars, and epidemics, using the most endearing myths that were often the subject of vast and absorbing mythological paintings. We need only recall Titian's *Venus and Adonis*, a prized possession of Philip II, which depicts the moment in which Adonis decides to go hunting and must leave Venus behind. She holds on to him, knowing that this hunt will be his last.

Thomas Puttfarken explains that a number of mythological paintings by Titian, while explicitly erotic, also contain a tragic component that is hidden or mitigated. *Venus and Adonis*, for instance, presents us a pastoral landscape, a new Arcadia, where the couple is consumed by affairs of love and of hunt. But there is in the background a definite sign of what is to come: the death of Adonis, and Venus' tears for her beloved. *Et in Arcadia ego* – even in Arcadia do we find death. For Puttfarken, Adonis' tragic hubris is to be found in his disdain for Venus' love and his determination to go hunting in spite of her pleas and lamentations (2005, 164). Sent from Venice to Madrid in 1554, Titian's painting could certainly be seen as part of the marvels that hid the horrors of life. Venice was decimated by plagues throughout the fifteenth and sixteenth centuries, and a new set of victims' remains was recently discovered in an island used for quarantine in the Venetian lagoon. Sixteenth-century epidemics were deadlier than earlier ones, with five hundred deaths per day (Valsecchi 2007). I would argue that both Titian and Cervantes considered death a marvel, the ultimate marvel experienced by a human being in this life, as they sought to surround it with the marvels of living in the most perfect environments.

Cervantes reveals, next to mutability and death, the artful perfection of nature, where even the trees are "puestos por tal orden y concierto que hasta las mesmas ramas de los unos y de los otros parecen que igualmente van creciendo" (so beautifully arranged that their boughs interwoven so did grow; 1995, 543–4; 1892, 278). These very trees establish walls and streets in the city of the dead. At the very centre of this valley we encounter "una artificiosa fuente de mármol fabricada, con tanta industria y artificio hechas, que las vistosas del conocido Tíbuli y las soberbias de la antigua Tinacria no le pueden ser comparadas" (an artificial fountain, fabricated of white but precious marble, and so artfully constructed that the rarities of the renowned Tivoli and the grandeurs of ancient Sicily can scarce hold comparison; 1995, 544; 1892, 278). Here Cervantes deviates from a true ekphrasis, the description of an object, to use allusiveness instead. By turning to Tivoli, he is asking readers to recall one of the most amazing gardens of the Renaissance. Built by Cardinal Ippolito d'Este when he was made governor of this town situated near Rome, the gardens were famous for having the tallest cypresses in Italy (Shepherd and Jellicoe 1993, 13). But, most of all, the gardens at Tivoli were famous for their waters, which flow throughout this immense garden and often burst forth in striking fountains. Water is also central to this new garden city of the dead. Here we find "claros y frescos arroyos de limpias y sabrosas aguas" (brooks of clear and salubrious water; Cervantes 1995, 544; 1892, 278). Cervantes cleverly makes of this imagined valley a site that surpasses one of the great marvels of Italy. However, there is a hidden reason that Cervantes picks Tivoli. This place, with its benefic winds in the hills surrounding Rome, had been used ever since the time of the Roman emperors by citizens fleeing the city during the heat of summer, a time that also brought illnesses such as the then deadly malaria. Most famous of all was Hadrian's Villa, whose remains Ippolito d'Este plundered to construct his own edifice. Thus, we are faced once again with a secure and joyful place for the living that wards off the dangers outside, and with an architectural and engineering splendour that seeks to obviate the spectacle of death.

Cervantes compares the fountain at the centre of the Valley of Cypresses with yet a second one, in Tinacria, the poetic name for Sicily. Although Tinacria is famous for its fountains, it is possible that one stands out for its mythical tones. Cervantes had already prepared us for this allusion when he mentioned the river Alfeo as one of three classical streams. Alfeo pursues Arethusa, who, refusing to accept his advances, is turned into a spring. He then transforms himself into a river so that his waters can commingle with hers. This story is told in the *Silva de varia lección* (A miscellany in several lessons), a work that Cervantes knew well, and it also appears in a number of classical texts.[20] In his tenth eclogue Virgil invokes the Sicilian muse who inspired Theocritus: "This now, the very latest of my toils, / Vouchsafe me, Arethusa!" (vv. 1–2). Theocritus, in turn, recalls in his first *Idyll* that Daphnis, before dying, says his goodbyes to Arethusa's spring. Thus, we can see how Arethusa is related to elegies written for the dead, as well as to the Muses – the latter soon to make an appearance in Cervantes' pastoral.

The white marble of the Cervantine fountain takes us to the houses of the dead, the tombs in the valley: "cual de jaspe y cual de mármol fabricadas, en cuyas blancas piedras se leían los nombres de los que en ella estaban sepultados" (some of jasper, some of wrought marble, and on white stones are visible the inscriptions of those interred within; Cervantes 1995, 545; 1892, 279). While the huts of the shepherds can barely be distinguished from the landscape, the homes of the dead are resplendent. This recalls the discussion in favour or against the building of sepulchres, as found in Diego de Sagredo's *Medidas del romano*. Eschewing the Erasmian point of view, Cervantes glorifies the building of elaborate tombs. Perhaps the most ornate is that of the shepherd Meliso: "de lisas y negras pizarras y de blanco y bien labrado jaspe parecía" (of polished and dark stones, and made of white and well-chiseled alabaster; 1995, 545; 1892, 279). After some sacred rites performed by the wise old man Telesio, he briefly praises Meliso's life and virtues as well as his many accomplishments. As if this were not enough, an elegy is dedicated to Meliso and sung by four of the shepherds, placing him in the heavens and praising his many accomplishments such as that of ambassador to Venice (1995, 551; 1892, 283). His poetry is also lauded as he is presented among the nine Muses, who then break into tears at his death (1995, 551–2; 1892, 283–4). Soon thereafter, the shepherds and shepherdesses retire to sleep but are suddenly awakened by a strange and wondrous fire appearing on top of Meliso's tomb. Calliope, Muse of epic poetry, emerges unscathed from this blaze. Her appearance here has to do with Meliso's persona in the novel.

His is the poetic name given to Diego Hurtado de Mendoza (1503–75), a writer who spent most of his life in Italy, was famous for imitating Virgil, and was versed in Latin and Greek as well as Hebrew and Arabic.[21] Labelled as a canonizing moment by Pedro Ruiz Pérez (2010, 417), these scenes in the pastoral render homage to one of the great poets, humanists, politicians, and diplomats of the sixteenth century, who served as governor of Sienna and ambassador to Venice and to the Council of Trent, someone who towards the end of his life and in spite of all his merits, quarrelled at court and was exiled to Granada, where he spent the last seven years of his life. Cervantes must have admired his Italian sojourns, something for which he longed, and he would have understood the quarrels at Court because, in spite of his role in the battle of Lepanto, he was never able to obtain many favours from Philip II. If pastoral, as Irigoyen-García asserts, serves to hide the Morisco presence in Iberia, Cervantes, while hiding the Moorish, still foregrounds the plight and battle of the Moriscos. After all, Hurtado de Mendoza penned a book about the Morisco revolt of 1568, *Guerra de Granada* (War in Granada), which was not published until several decades after his death. As Juan Varo Zafra makes clear, it is a deeply elegiac account of the fall of Granada and the fall of the Moorish nobility in Spain; the book realistically portrays with terrible honesty all the horrors unleashed by greed and the desire for power, as well as the mistakes made by both sides in this war.[22]

La Galatea, a work that seems to keep getting lost among the works of Cervantes and among the pastorals of the period, is in reality a remarkable work, one that utilizes art and architecture to present what at first may seem to be a splendid vision of the beauties of culture and empire during the times of Philip II. In reality, the novel is very different from what it appears to be. The safe places of pastoral are constantly invaded by the outside and are contrasted with a reality that mocks the text. Antithesis finds in contrapposto its perfect image, as the figure of Lisandro/Mercury both pollutes the landscape and cleanses it, designing a temple in the forest and standing for health, plague, and violence. Lisandro's tale, although appearing to take place close to the pastoral enclosure, may well point to Seville, a city of many dangers. The very centre of pastoral, the temple where the wedding occurs, is a problematic space that differs from places of safety and sacrifice, the hermitage and the church, where perfect friends find shelter as they strive for the ideal. Subtly contrasting the place of pastoral with the space of empire, Cervantes carefully shows that the wonderments of art are often built out of the dread of plague; that the temples of light are constructed around the suffering of its people, its shepherds; that the fertility and bounty of springtime hide a period of environmental uncertainty; that the memorable waters of pastoral evoke the many droughts of the period; and that the building of empire, of its cities, does away with a sense of place and brings out the dangers of chaotic space. The one architecture that is true is that of the resplendent city of the dead, of the tombs in the Valley of Cypresses. Only here can Calliope sing of many unheard voices; only here can an ancient priest praise Diego Hurtado de Mendoza, who dared to speak truth to power; only here can we mourn for a lost

Granada, a place of great and varied cultures. If Cervantes is yet in the springtime of youth and his work is an eclogue, it is one that dares to rise above, pointing to the dangers outside pastoral and to the epic life of Hurtado de Mendoza, the life of a humanist brought down by the mistaken policies of his king.

3 Unstable Architectures: *Don Quixote*, Part 1

The first part of *Don Quixote* contains few striking architectures, or so it would appear. After all, there were not many imposing buildings in the rustic areas of La Mancha. Some are imagined by the knight. Others are well hidden in the text, and a number of them exhibit a metamorphic nature that will make them unstable, as if we could pass from one to the other in the blink of an eye or in the twist of a sentence. Thus, this chapter points to the capriciousness of design, the magic of mutability, the instability of edifications, and the metamorphoses of structures. This uncertainty in building and design also encompasses the idea of the home, now imperilled; the solidity of the tower/mill, now shaken; the construction of a small inn, now threatened by occupancy; and the transformation of this very inn into a palace/castle, much more ample and luxurious than it would appear. The chapter ends with a double glimpse at a cosmic design.

There is no question that this chapter may appear choppy, metamorphic, and dizzying in its many visions. But it must be so, as we follow the knight's unstoppable imagination and the narrator's somewhat antagonistic prose. Eurithmia is hardly to be found in this chapter. While the text portends to the simple and linear, it hides an architectural instability that mirrors the deep anxieties and crazed visions of the knight. Don Quixote bends reality, and the narrators follow suit. Or perhaps it is vice versa, or perhaps they are intertwined as if palaces and prisons, chaotic madness and pervasive lucidity, go hand in hand.

It should not surprise us that one of the most fascinating and complex architectures appears in the very prologue to the novel, because the paratext was most likely written after Cervantes had completed the novel and could envision his shimmering edifices. Here we encounter a prison that by the magic of an allusive narrative becomes a palace, while the action actually takes place in the author's study, as a friend appears and they engage in conversation. These three spaces seem almost unconnected, as if we were looking at the stairs to nowhere in Piranesi's prints in *Carceri d'invenzione*. The nowhere, then, is found in this disjunction of spaces and places, with their ability to change as if by magic. This is indeed what the knight does: he goes nowhere outside of La Mancha, remaining in a closed space that is imagined as the immensity of the geography of chivalry. It is important, therefore, to open our awareness to the cuts and transformations and to the magic of a narrative that, like the mind of the knight, is forever changing in its design and architecture, providing the reader with unexpected vistas that shimmer, shrink, disappear, or expand in unexpected ways.

As the novel begins, the reader may become aware of a cosmic architecture as well as a claustrophobic ambience in the gentleman's abode. Doors and windows acquire new significance, while the books in Alonso Quijano's study become windows to another world. Somehow, it feels like an imperilled home, which he has to abandon as if he were haunted by his past and menaced by his household. Although he seeks the dangers outside, he seems relieved to flee the imperilled home. As the knight ventures into the dangerous spaces outside, he discovers windmills/giants that may mock the Vitruvian man, and an inn whose occupancy and architecture are always fluctuating as if it were being constructed over and over again and as if it were stretching its very walls to accommodate more and more guests. The inn transformed into a castle by the knight's imagination is much more than that – an ancient city, a window to the heavens, an Italian villa with ceiling frescoes. As we quickly skip over a series of adventures, as well as the labyrinth of Sierra Morena, we reach the final section of the 1605 novel. The enchanters whisper into the knight's ears, and the sounds seem to echo all the way to the heavens, calling for cosmic harmony. His improvised jail also echoes beginnings, returning us to notions of incarceration. We end as we began, with jails turned into palaces and back again, and with a study of melancholy, now out in the open.

A Mutable Structure

In 1916 the city of Seville commemorated the third anniversary of Cervantes' demise, with, among other events, the placement of seventeen plaques or tiles throughout the city, which pointed to specific places mentioned by the author in his works. These attest to Cervantes' concern for the cityscape during the many years he resided there. The plaques were placed from the Church of the Annunciation to Sierpes Street. Indeed, both of these sites owe much to Hernán Ruiz the

Younger (1514–1569). He improved on the original designs of the Church of the Annunciation, beginning the project around 1565, and he also worked on the Royal Jail in Sierpes Street in 1569. Ruiz was the most important architect in Andalucía during this period, his influence spanning from Córdoba to Seville and from Cádiz to Huelva. One of his early works was the baptistery of San Nicolás de la Villa in Córdoba, where he had already shown his technical expertise (Alfredo Morales 1996, 12). Having travelled as a young man to Seville with his father in 1535, Ruiz "descubrió todo un cúmulo de posibilidades, una ciudad pujante, capital del Nuevo Mundo, en la que su incontenible ambición podía resultar satisfecha" (discovered a myriad possibilities, a bustling city, capital of the New World, in which his irrepressible ambition could be satisfied; Alfredo Morales, 1996, 11). Later in life he turned to this bustling city and worked, for example, on the city gates (the gates of Goles, Jeréz, and Macarena), the city hall, and the Hospital of the Five Holy Wounds. Most of his energy, however, was directed during the last years of his life to the cathedral of Seville. Everywhere he turned, Cervantes would have seen edifices by this famed architect. Considered one of the key figures of the period, according to Alfredo J. Morales, Hernán Ruiz "supo unir la práctica arquitectónica a la especulación teórica" (was able to bring together architectural practice with theoretical speculation; 1996, 6). His vast library included works by Alberti and Dürer, and he even attempted a partial translation of Vitruvius' treatise. Cervantes would not have failed to note the importance of this architect and his many constructions.

Curiously, it is not one of his most famous works that interests us in this section. Instead, it is the first one mentioned in print by Cervantes. The prologue to *Don Quixote*, although it begins in the author's study, is shadowed by the very first lines of the text, which point elsewhere. The turn of a sentence turns the reader's attention to a different architecture, as if it coexisted with the first. The "author," addressing the reader, laments that his book or child is not as wise and handsome as he would have liked. It is dry and whimsical because the novel was not conceived in a pleasant location. Rather, "se engendró en una cárcel, donde toda incomodidad tiene asiento y donde todo triste ruido hace su habitación" (born in a prison, where every inconvenience keeps its residence, and every dismal sound its habitation; Cervantes 1978, 1.50; 2008, 15).[1] While the prologue takes place in the writer's study, the reader is consumed from the start with the image of a difficult artistic birth. It is of little consequence at this point that a friend comes in to offer advice. The comical aspects of the (fictive) friend's counsel do not detract from the first important architecture in the novel, the jail, a walled-in space of confinement and discomfort. This initial architecture, I would argue, is present as a marker of Cervantes' own biography and becomes an important context not just in the prologue but throughout part 1 of the novel. By telling us of the origins of the novel, the author invites the reader to discover the many aspects of plot and characterization that could have originated here. In one sense, the Royal Jail of Seville becomes a trigger of memory, which leads us to imagine the jail as a site of creation.

Cervantes was incarcerated in the Royal Jail of Seville, one of the most infamous buildings in Spain, spending approximately three months in this dangerous space, from September to December 1597. Accused of tax fraud, he was eventually released.[2] He was left, however, with a sense of what Yi-Fu Tuan calls topophobia, an anxiety related to his relationship to place. His contemporaries would have known many horrifying tales about this prison. Indeed, Philip II, when he visited Seville in 1570, stopped in front of it, amazed at the loud and varied cries and laments and the unbelievable noise that emanated from the building on Sierpes Street, almost at the very centre of the city. (See figure 3.1.)

When Cervantes was taken to the prison, it would not be the first time he would have noted its impressive façade. Although mainly devoted to sacred architectures, Hernán Ruiz accepted the commission to modernize the Royal Jail in 1569, during the last year of his life. He added a new façade to the three-storey building, which now had its main entrance on Sierpes Street, almost adjacent to the city's main plaza of San Salvador and surrounded by imposing buildings such as the city hall and the Convent of San Francisco. It was as if the Royal Jail, with its new look, could compete with sacred and administrative edifices, showing its face but hiding its tumultuous interiors. Close to the entrance were all the new areas, with administrative offices, rooms for the chief jailer, and dormitories for the guards. There were spacious cells here for more affluent prisoners, although members of neither the nobility nor the clergy were ever confined in this jail; they were imprisoned in their own places or in special locations. The majority of the prisoners at the Royal Jail abided beyond these more tranquil spaces. They could hear mass, which was held in the chapel at the other end of a main corridor (Copete and Vincent 2007, 261–86). There was also a small room with an altar for prisoners condemned to death, who would remain there for three days before execution in the company of a priest (Copete and Verger 1990, 106, 114). Even in the last days of their lives these prisoners were not given any freedoms. Instead, the priests and functionaries sought to imprison their minds, so that they would follow correct religious principles, rather than to search for ways to ensure

Figure 3.1. Juan Navarro, *Façade of the Royal Jail in Seville*, 1716. Alamy Stock Photo

clemency or justice in their sentence. It was equally true, however, that before their death some prisoners could be accompanied by their favourite prostitute and other women from the brothels.[3] This is not to say that exceptional individuals did not try to assist the prisoners. A Jesuit, Pedro de León, devoted himself to helping prisoners from 1578 to 1616. His memoirs give a more intimate view of this prison. Indeed, he established a Cofradía (Confraternity) to help the incarcerated. An indefatigable figure, he walked all quarters of the city of Seville, asking for alms for these prisoners. María Velázquez de Castro explains: "Con el dinero recaudado pagaba deudas y agravios de los presos, a algunos de los cuales libró de sentencias como ir a galeras, azotes e incluso la horca" (With the funds collected he would pay the debts and grievances of prisoners, some of whom he freed from sentences such as going to the galleys, whipping and even the gallows).[4]

Father León discusses, among other architectural elements, the three main doors to the jail in chapter 29. At the first or golden gate an official checks the prisoners' status and the amount of money they have available. In a most apt metaphor, the door was said to be golden: "porque para contentar al alcaide y porteros de la puerta de la calle es menester todo eso y más" (because in order to please the mayor and the doormen of the street door, all of that and more is necessary; León 1981, chap. 29). Mary Elizabeth Perry explains: "If he had little or was not well known, he was sent upstairs to the copper door, to enter the section which took the left-overs from the golden door" (1980, 76). The silver door locked in those who were the greatest threat to society.

Over the main door was the coat of arms of Seville, depicting in the centre Ferdinand III of Castile – who had taken back the city from the Muslims in 1248 – surrounded by the archbishops Isidore and Leandro. An inscription detailing those responsible for the work was also to be found by the main entrance. Above, corresponding to the second and third floors, the façade exhibited the coat of arms of Spain, held up by two lions rampant (standing on their two hind feet with forefeet in the air). A niche containing the figure of justice, portrayed as usual with sword and balance, stood above the three floors of the façade, flanked by Fortitude and Temperance (Copete and Verger 1990, 113; Falcón Márquez 1996, 160). Mary Elizabeth Perry comments on the irony of the symbol of justice: "The prison was an agency of coercion, forcing people to obey the laws or suffer the penalties. It was a tool of cultural domination, a symbol of authority that permitted a ruling oligarchy to pose as the legitimate source and guardian of justice" (1980, 86). Some of these images would enter into the construction of Cervantes' novel to remind the reader that *Don Quixote* was conceived in this prison.

The imposing entrance sought to silence the cries inside and to create a modicum of eurithmia based on beauty and harmony. Let us recall that Hernán Ruiz composed a partial manuscript on architecture, wrote on geometry, drew many buildings, directed countless architectural projects, and prepared a rough translation of the beginnings of Vitruvius' text.[5] Thus, the front part of the building contrasted with the rest: the remnants of the medieval architecture, and those sections that were noisy, dirty, and chaotic. It is curious that in a chapter devoted to the "Treasury, Prison and Senate House," Vitruvius ignores the prison. Instead, he focuses on the senate house, explaining how "to capture the voice of men engaged in discussion" so that it would "be intelligible to their listeners" (1960, 137). Such intelligibility was not a main characteristic of the jail, where loud cries would mark the hours. Even though the jail was quite small, some claim that a thousand prisoners were there at any one time. Jean Canavaggio asserts that it was "a veritable monster where almost two thousand detainees resided permanently" (1990, 172). There were people not yet condemned, along with all sorts of criminals, from murderers and rapists to petty thieves and debtors. Many were there awaiting execution, and the death sentence was applied to numerous "criminals" including "sodomites" (Copete and Verger 1990, 108).[6] A number were condemned to be sent to the galleys, because the empire was always in need of people to row and work on the ships. As María Paz Alonso Romero states, the site was an example of "a mechanism to produce condemnations and not a gauge of the worth of individuals facing the State's *ius puniendi*. The republic's sacrosanct right for vengeance is elevated far above any respect for the rights or interests of human beings" (1982, 206).

As the first architecture in the novel, the jail acquires primacy and significance. Very much like other writers such as Lope de Vega, the Cervantes character in the prologue self-fashions and creates what Antonio Sánchez Jiménez refers to as a *persona*.[7] From the start the author hints at being maddened by the many thieves and murderers roaming the prison. He can thus conceive of a character maddened by opposite figures: idealized knights in romances of chivalry. Cervantes' evidence that justice was far from present in the chaos of the prison is transformed into Don Quixote's quirky quest for justice. As the readers continue to pursue the mnemonic superimposition of spaces or places proposed by Cervantes' persona, they may ponder the relationship between the jail and several adventures in the 1605 novel. I am not arguing that the novel is affected by history and its artefacts or architectures but that the architectures in the novel reflect upon the social conditions of the times, "becoming an agent in constructing a culture's sense of reality" (Howard 1986, 25). As a war veteran and a captive in Algiers, Cervantes introduces the jail so that we can recognize that there are many histories in history, that it is not monolithic. The din of voices at the Royal Jail of Seville may be covered over by Vitruvian harmonies (a kind of universalizing history), but the voices need to be accounted for in other "histories" such as different episodes in this particular novel. The closed spaces of the jail open up spaces in the text for the readers' reflection.

As the knight hears the boy's laments, he concludes: "Estas voces, sin duda, son de algún menesteroso, o menesterosa, que ha menester mi favor y ayuda" (These are doubtless the cries of some distressed person, who stands in need of my protection and assistance; Cervantes 1978, 1.4.95; 2008, 37). While Cervantes may have run into many in need at the prison, the presence of so many thieves and delinquents may have led him to wonder if the person lamenting was merely pretending. As opposed to the way he himself might have acted in prison, Cervantes configures Don Quixote in this first adventure as someone who judges Andrés, a shepherd who is being punished for losing track of the sheep, merely by the appearance of what is taking place. It thus revervses Cervantes' likely wary disposition in prison. But we may also hear the disillusioned Cervantes whispering that the knight has become a mirror of the uniform kind of justice that he witnessed at the prison in Seville.[8] At the inn, when Don Quixote does not recognize the prostitutes who help him as such, we may be reminded of the way in which these brave and caring women accompanied condemned prisoners to their death. Thus, Cervantes, through the knight, grants them the titles of "doña Tolosa" and "doña Molinera" (1978, 1.3.94; 2008, 37).

The episode of the two armies or flocks of sheep, in addition to its classical echoes, may recall a common occurrence at the prison, yet another site for the game of memory triggered by the allusion to the jail in the prologue. The patio there was known for its fights and duels with knives, pointed sticks (*pastorcillos*), swords, and other weapons smuggled daily into the prison. Once the "polvareda" (dust) of a fight had cleared, as described by Pedro de León, officers of the law could find no one except the dead and wounded (León 1981, chap. 31). In the novel, a "grande y espesa polvareda" (great and thick cloud of dust; Cervantes 1978, 1.18.218; 2008, 127) alerts the mad knight that an army and then a second one are approaching. As the knight ascribes grandiloquent names to some of these imaginary fighters, Cervantes may have been satirizing the picaresque scuffles in the *polvareda* of the prison. The episode of the galley slaves again demonstrates how Don Quixote administers justice only by appearance, not fully understanding the language of the prisoners. The knight looks at them in chains: "ensartados como cuentas en una gran cadena de hierro, por los cuellos, y todos con esposas a las manos" (strung like beads in a row, by the necks, in a great iron chain, and all handcuffed; 1978, 1.22.265; 2008, 163). Such shackles would have reminded Cervantes of the many who were accused of major offences and were not only kept in a cell but also shackled hands and feet at the Seville prison. While in some ways Cervantes' text elicits compassion for the galley slaves, he also points to many verbal tricks that derive from the language he heard in prison. At the same time, in freeing them, Don Quixote is actually going against the justice of the king, as the guards warn him. With the growing needs of the empire, more and more prisoners were sentenced to serve as oarsmen in ships.[9] Whatever Cervantes may have felt or believed about the justice provided to galley slaves, he nonetheless shows Don Quixote battling the guards. Consequently the knight, following Sancho's advice, must hide in the mountains of Sierra Morena. Thus, as Roberto González Echevarría explains, "Don Quijote is the first hero in the Western tradition to be a fugitive from justice" (2005, 61).

The lack of free food at the jail and the fact that prisoners had to pay for whatever they ate (Perry 1980, 77), unless it was brought to them by family or friends, is perhaps echoed in Don Quixote's desire to fast and stay up nights, thinking of his beloved. Cervantes could well be replicating his own experience – hungry, unable to sleep for all the noise and cries, while imagining his knight roaming the countryside. If we continue this mnemonic game, this superimposition of spaces, we may ponder if the name Venta or inn given to the room where new prisoners had to pay money to be in the Royal Jail in Seville could also reflect a situation in the novel. Although Don Quixote claims that no knight pays for his stay at a castle/inn, the knight's refusal to pay for his stay at an inn could be seen as Cervantes' reaction to having to pay at the chamber called Venta in the prison. It could even be argued that the three main gates at the jail, in gold, silver, and copper (plus a gate of iron), could have had an impact on the knight's speech about the Golden Age of humankind. After all, he bemoans the greed of his times, which he locates in the Iron Age, and claims that the age of gold had little to do with the metal: "no porque en ellos el oro, que en nuestra edad de hierro tanto se estima, se alcanzase en aquella venturosa sin fatiga alguna, sino porque los que en ella vivían ignoraban estas dos palabras de tuyo y mío" (not because gold (which in this our iron age, is so much esteemed) was to be had in that fortunate period without toil and labour; but because they who then lived were ignorant of these two words, *meum* and *tuum*; Cervantes 1978, 1.11.155; 2008, 77). It may well be that Cervantes became acquainted with Father Pedro de León and his good deeds at the jail. His selflessness may have helped one imagine a better age. Much more could be said in terms of Seville's prison as a trigger for Cervantes' novel, but it is time to move to other features of the prologue that are at play with the prison.

Although many other elements could be added to this initial mnemonic game triggered by the prologue, we must forge ahead because the prologue quickly creates a second puzzle for the reader. Slowly but none too surely we discover the mutability of Cervantes' architecture and the superimposition of spaces. We have yet to truly visualize the author's study when we are led in a direction that evokes the opposite of the jail. The Cervantes character of the prologue bemoans the fact that his novel was born in jail, rather than in the most benefic of sites for writing poetry: "El sosiego, el lugar apacible, la amenidad de los campos, la serenidad de los cielos, el murmurar de las fuentes, la quietud del espíritu son grande parte para que las musas más estériles se muestren fecundas y ofrezcan partos al mundo que le colmen de maravilla y de contento" (Whereas repose of body, a desirable situation, unclouded skies, and above all, a mind at ease, can make the most barren Muses fruitful, and produce such offspring to the world, as fill it with wonder and content; 1978, 1.50; 2008, 15). This inspiration allows him to compose such works that deserve a place in Parnassus, the home of the Muses and a site that was very much in vogue. The Royal Jail with its chaos and noise is transformed into a place of quietude and solace. Topophobia suddenly turns into topophilia. But this outside within the inside is further destabilized by its allusive frame. Images of the great bards abiding on this exalted mountain were by now a common staple of poets, painters, and academicians, going back to Raphael's famous painting at the Vatican.[10]

In this second game, one of allusive superimposition of spaces, the fictive Cervantes exhibits the four great frescoes painted by Raphael for the Stanza della Segnatura at the Vatican Palace (De Armas 2006, 34–40). This move from prison (through the luminescent outside of Parnassus) to palace is never made explicit in the text. It is up to a learned reader to make the connection, as if inside of Piranesi's jail this new inmate or reader, in a whimsical prologue, seeks to move from one space to another through the nowhere bridge of art. What I failed to point out in an earlier study was that this tenuous pathway allows us to view the clever juxtaposition of prison and Vatican Palace, two salient edifices of the times, two buildings that Cervantes "visited," but each standing as the antithesis of the other. One stood for the glory of religious power, and the other for the punishment of those who infringed the laws of the state. And yet both are brought together in the prologue. Cervantes' ekphrasis of Raphael's *Parnassus*, with its murmuring springs, serves as contrast to the one water source available to prisoners in the patio of the Royal Jail of Seville. It is as if Cervantes were imagining Piranesi's *The Well*, the thirteenth plate of the first edition of *The Prison*, where grandiose stairs and edifices surround a well and in which human figures seem beaten down and doomed, thereby signalling anxiety, oppression, and the denigration of the human even while surrounded by a magnificent palace and an enticing well. (See figure 3.2.)

Numerous harsh and hasty sentences were issued at the prison, but the Hall of Signatures at the Vatican only produced carefully thought-out missives and decrees; their impact is indeterminate in Cervantes, as prison shadows palace. No artworks were seen in the interior of the jail – except for the chapel's altar. The tranquility and serenity of Parnassus becomes the agitation and constant jostling and anxiety of the jail, while the pleasant pastures become a muddied and smelly prison yard. The smells of the prison and its "corrupt" air recall two major causes of the plague during the period. Juan Jiménez Savariego emphasizes the link between corrupt air and the plague (1602, 13v, 15r, 15v). Indeed, the first of the three great plagues to devastate Spain came to the peninsula in 1597, the year in which Cervantes was jailed. It is quite possible then,

Figure 3.2. Piranesi, *The Well*, plate 13 in *Imaginary Prisons*, 1761. The Art Institute of Chicago. Open access, public domain

that he, like those who wrote treatises on the subject, related plague and prison. Jiménez Savariego affirms that at such times it was necessary to "las cárceles limpiarlas de gente inútil y enferma" (clean the prisons of useless and sick people; 1602, 120r). The prologue sets to clean and purify the prison through images of the Vatican Palace. At the same time, the Vatican becomes "infected" by the prison, its lavish decorations contrasting with the hunger of the people.

Yet another fresco in the Vatican stanza connects with the author, his character, and the prison. *The Cardinal Virtues* show at the right-hand side of the fresco a feminine allegory holding a bridle in her hand, which would reflect how a knightly spirit controls the equine passions. The prologue praises the temperance of Don Quixote as the "chastest" of lovers, but he does not always control Rocinante. Indeed, the horse even exhibits his lack of chastity while pursuing the Galician mares. Upon entering the prison, Cervantes would have seen above the façade an image of Temperance, along with two of the other cardinal virtues. Did this figure remind him of Raphael's fresco, which he would have seen in an earlier sojourn in Italy? The prologue further refers to Don Quixote as "el más valiente caballero" (the most valiant knight; Cervantes 1978, 1.58; 2008, 20). He thus embodies Fortitude on the left-hand side of Raphael's fresco. This virtue as a "pet lion and a leonine boot ornament" (Jones and Penny 1983, 80) recalls Don Quixote's famous adventure with the lion (Cervantes 1978, 2.17). It also echoes the prison façade with lions rampant as well as the figure of Fortitude on the opposite side of Temperance, both facing the central image of Justice. Justice, although missing from the fresco, is portrayed in the ceiling above, much like the figure in front of the prison. The question of Cervantes, Don Quixote, and justice is thus foregrounded through the juxtaposition of two contrastive edifices.[11]

A Study in Melancholy

These two buildings, Vatican Palace and prison, as well as some of their images, not only serve to strengthen important themes and significant motifs in the work but also impinge on the way the author wishes to portray himself in the prologue. When Cervantes published the first part of *Don Quixote*, he was already in his fifties and he was still a fairly unknown writer whom some may have remembered from his early plays (now overshadowed by Lope de Vega's popularity) or from a pastoral romance that was never successful. Cervantes quite carefully exploits not being part of the inner circles of literati, of those who thought of themselves as members of Parnassus.

We now find Cervantes' persona in his study, the third architecture of the prologue. Let us begin with a crucial moment, the portrait of the author. The fictive author depicts himself at the moment when he despairs of writing the prologue and adorning it and his book with the much coveted biblical, poetic, and philosophical authorities of antiquity: "Muchas veces tomé la pluma para escribille, y muchas la dejé, por no saber lo que escribiría; y estando una suspenso, con el papel delante, la pluma en la oreja, el codo en el bufete y la mano en la mejilla, pensando lo que diría." (I often took pen in hand, and as often laid it down, not knowing what to say: and once upon a time, being in deep suspense, with the paper before me, the pen behind my ear, my elbow on the table, and my cheek on my hand, thinking what I should say; 1978, 1.51–2; 2008, 15–16.) The text draws upon the traditional pose of the thinker, most often considered as a melancholy figure. We need only remember the pensive image at the very centre of Raphael's fresco in the Stanza della Segnatura, *The School of Athens* (see figure 3.3). He also has his hand on his cheek and has paper in front of him. Raphael's fresco depicts a double image, that of the philosopher Heraclitus and that of Michelangelo, both known for their melancholy. As we know, "from the sixteenth century onwards, there are frequent references to the melancholic disposition of artists in relation to their exceptional talents" (Van den Doel 2010, 108).[12] Michelangelo in both his artistic and poetic endeavours depicts himself in this way, and his biographers pick up on his qualities of solitude, whimsy, and inspired genius, which derive from his temperament.[13] It is thus not surprising to find that the Cervantes of the prologue is alone in his musings and has produced "un hijo seco, avellanado, antojadizo y lleno de pensamientos varios" (a child, meagre, adust, and whimsical, full of various wild imaginations; Cervantes 1978, 1.50; 2008, 15). His child or book is dry because the melancholy humour shares two qualities, dryness and coldness. This quality and temperament echo not only those of the author but also those of his main character. From the very start of the novel we discover that Don Quixote's brain has dried up from too much reading. The knight's emaciated body is also a reflection of his dryness.

In addition, the text may well draw from Sagredo's *Medidas del romano*. Picardo, when he visits his friend, always encounters Lampeso at work. He thus warns him: "La mucha continuación de estudios engendra melancolía; y la mucha melancolía incita y mueve enfermedades" (The continued pursuit of studies breeds melancholy; and much melancholy incites and creates illnesses; Sagredo 1526, 2r). He emphasizes that strenuous work of the mind increases melancholy and shortens a person's life: "con él se muelen los huesos y se fatigan las carnes y se acorta la vida" (with it bones grind and flesh fatigues and life shortens; 1526, 2r). In the prologue to *Don Quixote*, Cervantes sits at work as his friend comes to visit. As if modelled after the author with his melancholy, the knight is depicted as lean, sickly, and lacking agility.

Melancholy figures were known to suffer from visions, be they celestial or demonic, providing ecstasy or severe distress. Thus Cervantes shows his child or book as filled with extravagant fancies, which at times seem closer to the demonic than to the celestial.[14] Invoking Cornelius Agrippa, Robert Burton claims that "melancholy persons are most subject to diabolic temptations and illusions and most apt to entertain them" (1938, 175). While the melancholy author writes of his fancies, his child is equally eccentric, a knight-errant who is almost mad. Paradoxically, it is the madness that makes us laugh. Towards the end of the prologue we encounter one more advice from the elusive friend: "Procurad también que, leyendo vuestra historia, el melancólico se mueva a risa, el risueño la acreciente" (Endeavour also, that, by reading your history, the melancholy may be provoked to laugh, the gay humour be

Figure 3.3. Raphael, *The School of Athens*, fresco, detail of central section, ca. 1510–12. Philosopher: Heraclitus and Democritus. Character: Michelangelo Buonarroti. Stanza della Segnatura, Stanze di Raffaello, Vatican Palace, Vatican State. Scala/Art Resource, NY

heightened; Cervantes 1978, 1.58; 2008, 20). Thus, melancholy madness can trigger laughter. By juxtaposing the melancholy with the jovial, the friend provides yet one more clue to the author's condition. Jupiter, as the most benefic of Ptolemaic planets in ancient and Renaissance astrology, was countered by Saturn, the most malefic.

We know from the extensive labours of Klibansky, Panofsky, and Saxl that the conflictive nature of melancholy actually derives from Saturn, a planet that was said to rule melancholy but was also considered the most malefic of celestial bodies. Cervantes tells us that his book was born in a prison, and imprisonment is one of the more often cited consequences of a saturnine influence (Klibansky, Panofsky, and Saxl 1964, 11).

The Renaissance's depiction of the visionary artist, poet, and scholar owes many of its iterations to Marsilio Ficino. The Renaissance philosopher and translator of Plato was most concerned with Saturn, a planet that featured prominently in his horoscope. Saturn was not only on the ascendant, the most important place in a horoscope, but also in Aquarius. Ruth Clydesdale, who has studied the astrological component of Ficino's letters, explains that Aquarius, being one of the two Saturn's houses, "is therefore able to express itself in a particularly powerful way" (2011, 123). I would add that Aquarius is the nocturnal house of the seventh Ptolemaic planet, thus further increasing its shadowy presence. In one of Ficino's letters we find a clue to his future path: "I shall, in agreement with Aristotle, say that this nature itself is a unique and divine gift" (Ficino 1975, 34). Thus, to counterbalance this planetary influence Ficino wrote *Three Books on Life*, publishing it in 1489. It was a bestseller, an immensely popular work, with nearly thirty editions published through to 1547. The book included many ways to remedy the excesses of melancholy and the baneful influence of Saturn. Sagredo's *Medidas* also point to such remedies but often those of a much more mundane character. Citing Cato, one of the names that the friend wished to have inserted in Cervantes' prologue, Picardo advises Tampeso: "No sin causa el viejo Catón manda entremeter placeres a vueltas de los cuidados" (Not without reason does old Cato mandate blending pleasures with cares; Sagredo 1526, 2r).

Ficino's treatise was also meant to reinstate the positive aspects of the seventh planet. As the highest of planets in the Ptolemaic cosmos, Saturn would, of necessity, provide the highest gifts to the human being, although such rewards would be balanced with suffering. In *De vita* the philosopher affirms that the child of Saturn is "an individual set apart from others, divine or brutish, blessed or bowed down with the extreme of misery" (Ficino 1989, 251). Clydesdale asserts that, for

Ficino, "the solitary man given to deep thought is ideally placed to contemplate the divine and hence Saturn can elevate his chosen ones 'to the heights above their physical strength and the customs of mortals'" (2011, 125).[15] Needless to say, Don Quixote is most certainly someone lacking the physical strength needed to carry out his chivalric visions. And there are instances in the novel where he is indeed helped by Saturn (Fajardo 1986, 233–51; De Armas 2011, 162–80). Through Ficino, the seventh planet became for some not only a destructive force but a symbol of the new artist or writer who suffered Saturn's melancholy in order to receive its most precious gift, wisdom, which was to be wrenched out of madness, one of the planet's worst effects.

As someone outside the literary centres of his time, the Cervantes character seems to "cancel culture," to stand against all the authorities present and past and all the well-recognized ways of joining the network of those who wish to be seen as part of Parnassus. In reality, Cervantes consciously crafts a new persona for himself. He may be rejected by Apollo in Parnassus; he may not be under the influence of a solar ruler and his court. He need not be part of the great masses of poets who cluster around the Sun. Instead, he is a solitary figure who writes under Saturn. He may not be the most acclaimed writer in his own time, and he may not hold favour at court, but as an individual apart he can write of the extravagant fancies of a would-be knight. Cancelling culture is simply a way of fabricating a new culture, one that may be wiser than the one before, or one that is filled with trivial word and mind games that can unfortunately lead to Newspeak. The prologue, then, chooses the former and sets up the way in which Cervantes wants to be viewed, as a solitary artist, as one who had to endure untold sufferings, including incarceration, in order to reach a new inspired wisdom, one that may be presented in a dry and whimsical manner but has a dark and shadowed power that can eclipse the writers of Parnassus. Cervantes writes from Seville's Royal Jail a novel that may be funny, fragmented, and monstrous, but it hides a greater wisdom perhaps than does even the Vatican Palace with its visions of Parnassus.

While he begins to write his novel in prison, the actual scene between the author and the friend takes place in the study in his own home, where the writer continues to be afflicted by melancholy. Frustrating those who seek a uniform message, the prologue may be presenting a shadowed vision of the eurithmia of the classical tradition. The triple architecture of the prologue – the prison, the study, and the palace – destabilizes the opposition between space and place, as one merges with the other. Danger, expansiveness, and solace seem to confuse expectations. The prologue also constructs an impossible architecture that is constantly rebounding back and forth, from the chaos of the jail to the quiet solace of the study, and from the grandeur of the palace with its many voices of power to the spaces of the prison with its cries for help and its constant dangers. As different visions and revisions of the prologue arise through its changing architectures, the very dysrithmia of the images may coalesce in the study. There the author takes up the pen and writes a proverb: "Debajo de mi manto al rey mato" (Under my cloak, a fig for the king; Cervantes 1978, 1.57; 2008, 15). In his own house he can do as he pleases. He can invent ways to confront and confuse the centres of power: the religious dogma of the Vatican, the civic punishment of the jail, and perhaps even Vitruvian architecture. After all, Hernán Ruiz created a harmonious façade to a chaotic building. How could Cervantes forget the image of Justice towering above the jail? Or how could he discard the image of a king and two saintly archbishops in a place that questioned authority through uncaring chaos? The prologue's mocking of authority, then, has its source in a deceiving façade. At the same time, the rejection of Vitruvius' authority through dysrithmia can well be a strategy to open the text to multiple meanings, to open the buildings to numerous uses.[16]

The Imperilled Home

Gaston Bachelard, as has been noted, once claimed that the home represents our "protected intimacy" (1994, 3), that such architectures bring comfort and trigger the benefic imagination as we recall its wardrobes, chests, and corners. Yi-Fu Tuan would make it the epitome of topophilia. If we turn now to the first part of *Don Quixote*, we come across Alonso Quijano's home. It is a place of safety and imagination. And yet, if we recall that the novel and its protagonist were conceived in a prison, then the walls of the house may trigger feelings of confinement rather than safety, and the people within, albeit seeming to appreciate the timeworn gentleman, may appear somewhat suspicious and threatening. In addition, some of the objects within, although intimate to the gentleman's thinking, conspire against him, or so others believe. For Benito Gómez, a key concept in Cervantes' novel is "Fleeing the House" (2016, 112).[17] Very close to the feeling of safety at home is that of constriction and repression (2016, 116), and Gómez equates Quixote's departure with seeking a new identity and a newly acquired freedom from social conventions. In other words, the gentleman, Alonso Quijano, could be seeking the liberating spaces evoked by Yi-Fu Tuan.[18] So, let us examine this abode more carefully.

From the very start we can perceive the home as a place of regimented events and safe repetitions. Days of the week are often marked with a particular dish that the housekeeper serves him, such as lentils on Fridays and culminating with a small pigeon added on Sundays. Describing the one sentence in the text that summarizes the gentleman's weekly meals, Carolyn A. Nadeau asserts: "This single phrase [...] confirms the relationship between food and social inclusion and exclusion [...] It accentuates the religious mores that guided a country's eating habits and sought to unify Spain under one religion" (2016, xvi). There seems to be little room for deviation in his humdrum existence, even in terms of food. Although Alonso Quijano is an hidalgo, there is little in his home and surrounding property to keep him entertained, otium being his main pursuit or enemy. The imprisoned Cervantes had to watch out for dangers at every turn during his confinement, but there seems to be nothing that breaks the tranquility of the gentleman's home. To alleviate the situation he engages socially with master Nicholas, the barber, and with the priest of the village, who exhibits his learning, having taken his degrees at Siguenza, a minor and rather forgotten university.[19]

The actual architecture of the house is less haphazard than that of the prison, but we may imagine that the jail's chapel is transformed into the gentleman's library, and that the chapel's sermons are transformed into chivalric allocutions, letters, and descriptions of battles. The gentleman's home seems to be two storeys high, the library being in the floor above. All images make it a typical house of the period. While the patio and places for storage were downstairs, the upstairs was often flanked by a gallery that was held up by classical columns, in most cases Corinthian (Parra Luna et al. 2005, 119). There is no mention of there being such columns in Don Quixote's home, because it is not to be an example of eurithmia. The actual architecture of the home seems less important than the way in which the chapter is constructed, centred on Pythagorean quaternities: everything is described in sets of four, thus recalling elements, humours, seasons, and other quaternities.[20] But their careful balance is violated by the owner. He has sold three quarters of his estate to buy books, thus engaging in pursuits that go against his earnings and status. Rather than building upon a secure place, he indulges himself in imagining dangerous spaces. While the house is a secure container that keeps away dangers, books are also containers, but they enclose the dangers sought by Alonso Quijano, if only at first for the pleasure of imagining daring battles in the comfort of his home. Just as he chooses two books of chivalry, he also favours two of the four humours: the eponymous protagonist of *Belianís de Grecia* (*Belianís of Greece*), covered with scars, represents his choleric disposition; and the novels of

Feliciano de Silva, possibly the *Amadís de Grecia* (*Amadís of Greece*), point to his melancholy. There are other dangers that are well hidden in the home. He discovers, albeit quite rusted, the different parts of the armour belonging to a great-grandparent. Thus, they derive from the fifteenth century. Curiously, he locates them in a corner or *rincón* (Cervantes 1978, 1.1.75; 2008, 23). According to Sebastián de Covarrubias, this term refers to a place "donde de ordinario no llegan directamente las luces: y así se toma por lugar escondido y oscuro" (where ordinarily there is no direct sunlight; thus it is conceived as a hidden and dark place; 1943, 911). What mysteries are the armours hiding? Nothing is ever said regarding Don Quixote's prehistory; we know nothing of his family, nor do we know his name for certain. The corner then serves not to reveal but to hide knowledge from the readers. It is a place of mystery, echoing the mystery of the gentleman's desire to leave the house.

While Don Quixote's madness consists in breaking the boundaries between fiction and reality, it impels him to go beyond the boundaries of his home in order to seek adventure with its inherent dangers. He embodies in many ways the dangers faced by his creator – the confinement of the jail and the free spaces as Cervantes, a collector of taxes, roamed through Andalucía.

Alonso Quijano, now as Don Quixote, departs his home during the wrong season, summer being too hot to wear armour, and during the autumn of his life, chivalry being the occupation of youth and spring. By Cervantes' breaking down of the architecture of quaternities through excess, the crazed knight seeks spaces for freedom and folly. He also seeks danger, "deshaciendo todo género de agravio, y poniéndose en ocasiones y peligros" (redressing all kinds of grievances and exposing himself to danger on all occasions; Cervantes 1978, 1.1.73; 2008, 23). After being repeatedly defeated in these spaces, he returns home, which suddenly becomes a place to restore his powers, but he reacts to the home as claustrophobic and flees again.[21]

Even though Bachelard turns to the house as a felicitous space, others speculate that it may harbour "spaces of hostility" (Klooster and Heirman 2013, 5). At the very inception of the novel there seems to be a harmonious atmosphere in the house, but this turns out to be deceptive. The priest and the barber, and even the housekeeper and the niece, conspire against Alonso Quijano's desire to imagine. After his first and brief sally they see his books as counter to the safety of the owner of the home, and thus they turn the home into a place of contention. The priest leads an inquisition of Don Quixote's books, as if they were heretical bodies, having them thrown out the window: "Tomad, señora ama; abrid esa ventana y echadle al corral, y dé principio al montón de la hoguera que se ha de hacer" (Take him, mistress housekeeper, open yon casement, and throw him into the yard, and let him give a beginning to the pile for the intended bonfire; Cervantes 1978, 1.6.112; 2008, 48). We learn several things from this statement: first, that Don Quixote did not seclude himself in a hermetic space but could enjoy the outside from his window. This may well mean that he could open it, yearning for the danger outside, while at the same time containing in his mind a series of chivalric adventures that would burst open and lead him to imaginary battles in his rooms. Yet, not once does the narrator state that he looks out the window. The *ventana* is only mentioned when used by his so-called friends to toss out his books, not only sending them to the danger outside, to which they think they belong, but also burning them, destroying them, subjecting them to the ultimate danger. It is as if the gentleman were not ready for outside spaces until he has filled his memory with the spaces of chivalry. Only then does he feel capable in his madness of seeing what the dangers outside truly are. Through the art of memory he will be able to place correct chivalric adventures in what may appear to be rustic buildings or events.

The first two chapters of *Don Quixote* foreground an architecture of cosmos, that is, an architecture that serves to create the building-blocks of the novel, rather than detailing the architecture of the home. While the term *window* is used four times (as a quaternity) when dealing with the inquisition of books, there is only one other opening mentioned, "la puerta falsa de un corral" (a private door of his backyard; 1978, 1.2.79; 2008, 26), through which he sneaks, dressed as knight in order to seek adventures for the first time. In a sense, then we can claim that the ancient deity Janus is at work as the knight departs. As god of doorways and beginnings, Janus presides over thresholds and doors, and home doors are particularly within his purview. As Don Quixote departs by a hidden door, he does so in July, the beginning of the second half of the year, thus mimicking and inverting Janus, who presides over January and the beginning of the year. Although his festival was marked with gift-giving, here Don Quixote shuns company and leaves alone. Yet, Janus is a most fitting god for the architecture of cosmos. We read in Ovid's *Fasti* that he was part of chaos, and only when the four elements separated did he become one god: "And even now, small index of my erst chaotic state, my front and back look just the same" (1989, 1.113–14). He is the porter or gatekeeper: "and just as your human porter, seated at the threshold of the house-door, sees who goes out and in, so I, the porter of the heavenly court, behold at once both East and West (1.137–40).[22] The closing of the doors to Janus' temple occurred during the time of Augustus to signal the arrival of a new Golden Age and a time of peace. Here, Don Quixote opens rather than closes the door because he must restore and bring back a more perfect age. The fact that he uses the back door undermines his quest.

Upon Don Quixote's return, we discover more details regarding his house. The knight's room is upstairs, and there we see a separate room containing his library. Doorways once again take on an almost godly aspect, as the entrance leading to the room that housed his library has been walled up by the conspirators. The knight cannot find his books, which are no longer in the walled-in library; many of them have been burned. The inquisition of books has been his friends' way of "cancelling culture." Rejecting the ideal of chivalry, they seek to render void a whole set of "antiquated" structures and beliefs that render Don Quixote "mad." A contemporary controversy may shed light on this practice and vice versa. Adam Robbins from the University of Pennsylvania explains: "Cancel culture is a social climate characterized by hostility to unfashionable ideas and a willingness to act aggressively to ensure they are never heard at all" (Murante 2020). There is no question that Don Quixote's household has acted aggressively in order to make him forget. What his four friends and conspirators (yet another quaternity)[23] do not realize is that the library as container is now even more dangerous in the sense that it is contained in the knight's mind, where through memory and imagination he can transform these ideals and make them his own. In today's world we seek to differentiate between inquisition and cancellation, but they both use censoring methods and are much the same in their results, instilling fear in the pliable and pride in the initiated and "orthodox."

Joseph Murante from Seton Hall states: "College students have all experienced this: a lecture hall that stays silent even as the professor tries to provoke discussion and debate on controversial issues. How can we hope to generate a diversity of ideas if we fear retaliation for any dissent? So long as the threat of lifelong condemnation hangs over our heads, we can't" (2020). Don Quixote seems blind to condemnation, never remaining silent, always expressing his point of view. He can be regarded, in some ways, as a model for our silenced and cancelled culture. It is as if only the mad can speak, and this is also the case of *El licenciado Vidriera* (The Glass graduate). In addition, the priest and the barber justify their violent behaviour as a response to Don Quixote's madness. In this they might take umbrage at what Robbins has to say: "The prevailing belief used to be that good ideas win out over bad ones via rational persuasion and the combat of argument. Cancel culture, by contrast, objects to the very idea of discourse, opting to silence rather than refute those who differ" (Murante 2020). But isn't the whole purpose of the novel to present both the comic and outrageous and the heroic and determined sides of the protagonist? John J. Allen's old question, "Hero or fool?" (1969, 6) is still a basic one, the answer being a paradoxical affirmative. We do not read the novel simply to laugh at Don Quixote; we detect much more in his impulse to recreate society, one mirrored in the past. His memory fuelled by his imagination, and vice versa, leads him to reimagine dangers any way that he pleases when he leaves, now with a squire, for the second time.

From the start of the novel, then, space and place become problematized. If the home is security, it is also stagnation, incarceration, and cancellation. The objects within the home may trigger positive memories, but they may also contain images of freedom. As the would-be knight recalls his books in a confined environment, he sees his home as a trap when he seeks the spaces of danger that he already carries within himself, spaces that are also related to humoral imbalances and wrong seasons. In addition, they are related to hidden corners where ancient armour can be found, concealing the deeds or disasters of his family. Having opened Janus' secret door, the one that leads to war, the knight and his squire must be prepared for the many dangers ahead. The knight is both a hero and a fool because he counters the culture of his circle. He must thus leave the house and expand the circle, even if the new circle threatens his own survival.

Windmills

The windmills are the first major hostile architecture that the knight faces after leaving his home during his second sally. By this I mean that in the previous episodes he fought people, but here he comes up with his first threatening edifices. In the initial "part" of the novel as Cervantes conceived it, comprising eight chapters, there are four episodes. The fourth chapter contains his first two adventures, in which he fights his foes alone, and the eighth chapter describes the next two adventures, in which he now fights his foes, having a squire to share (or oppose) his deeds. The episode of the windmills, in the eighth chapter, is the first in which he shares his view of the battle against the "enemy" (windmills/giants) with Sancho Panza. For centuries it has been regarded as the single episode among many that can represent the substance of the knight's quest. In the introductory poems to the volume Cervantes fashions himself as an "español Ovidio" (*Spanish Ovid*; 1978, 1.64).[24] The ease with which thirty or forty towering windmills, their sails turning, can suddenly appear around the bend and, in their surprising presence, become giants in the mind of the knight surpasses and transforms many of the ancient metamorphoses.[25] In Ovid, metamorphoses usually move downwards, that is, from a divine, semi-divine, or human figure to the animal and plant world. In Don Quixote's mind, they move upwards from inns to castles, from prostitutes to ladies, and from peasant women to princesses (De Armas 2014, 277–90). Rarely, however, do they move from inanimate to animate. A key exception is the episode of the windmills.

Very much like the metamorphic games played by the Cervantes figure in the prologue, here the knight (together with his squire) is caught in transformations. Giants, the preferred antagonists of heroes in chivalry, were at times compared to towers (Redondo 1998a, 339). Invoking Sebastián de Covarrubias, Redondo recalls a saying: *"armar torres de viento* es dejarse llevar de pensamientos vanos e imaginaciones locas"* (*to construct towers in the wind* is to allow vain thoughts and crazy imaginings to take hold of us; 331). Sancho, somehow aware of the power of the word, the power of metaphor, tells his master after the episode is over: "¿no eran sino molinos de viento, y no los podía ignorar sino quien llevase otros tales en la cabeza?" (they were nothing but windmills; and nobody could mistake them, but one that had the like in his head; Cervantes 1978, 1.8.130; 2008, 60). Like towers in the wind, windmills and their smaller cousin, pinwheels, were considered images of mental challenges and in particular madness. Velázquez, for example, painted Philip IV's court jester Juan de Cardenas, called Calabazas (gourd or simpleton), with a pinwheel in his left hand.[26] The painter further highlighted his physical and mental frailties by depicting him with a misshapen foot, undersized head, and crossed eyes to indicate his physical and mental frailties.[27] To rephrase Terence Cave (1976, 5), things, in the guise of metaphors, inhabit words. Here the madness of Don Quixote takes the form of windmills, while he transforms them into giants.

While knight and squire play with transformation, the narrator seeks to undermine this comic or fearful vision: first, by denying ekphrasis and thus restricting the visual nature of the scene; second, by underplaying the giant(s) and thus making it more difficult to visualize; and third, by having the knight deny that there is an architecture of danger here. The chapter begins with an unexpected image: "En esto, descubrieron treinta o cuarenta molinos de viento que hay en aquel campo" (As they were thus discoursing, they perceived some thirty or forty windmills that are in that plain; Cervantes 1978, 1.8.128; 2008, 59). For Don Quixote, these structures should have evoked architectures akin to the romances. He could have turned to hundreds of descriptions of castles, towers, and magical buildings. Indeed, why not think of an immense and magical castle with some thirty or forty towers? Instead he radically transforms them into giants. They are only described as "desaforados" (monstrous; 1978, 1.8.128; 2008, 50), a term that is difficult to translate because it relates to something or someone that is monstrous, wild, lawless. If we are to look for a more apt description from Sancho, who corrects the knight, telling him that they are windmills, we do not find it: "no son gigantes, sino molinos de viento, y lo que en ellos parecen brazos son las aspas, que, volteadas al viento, hacen andar la piedra del molino" (those which appear yonder, are not giants, but windmills; and what seem to be arms are the sails, which, whirled about by the wind, make the millstone go; 1978, 18.129; 2008, 59). What Sancho describes is the technology of the windmills. He also tries to understand and explain to the knight why he views them as giants. It must be because the sails that are moving may seem like the arms of a huge being. Nowhere in the scene are the windmills fully described, so we are left astonished not at what we see but at what the characters must be seeing – two very different things. This denial of ekphrasis leaves an opening for the readers to construct their own image. The myriad illustrations of this scene are then a way to fill a gap, to bring out a structure from very few words. The denial of description, a kind of ellipsis, then, has spurred the imagination of many, perhaps because the metamorphosis here indicated is so easy to visualize.

The second way in which the episode seems to undermine the sense of familiarity and visualization is in the naming of the giant. Readers of the prologue would remember that the friend counselled the fictive author not just to include general words such as *rivers* or *giants*, but to select a specific one so that a note could be added and the prose appear more erudite and less simple, or "naked." In terms of giants, the friend recommended Goliath, and this would have been the perfect example here because Don Quixote would be a new David fighting the philistine.[28] Instead, the narrator picks a more obscure giant, depriving the reader of the pleasure of linking the episode with the prologue, and making it more difficult to visualize. Yet, in spite of the more recondite identification, this second giant seems better suited for the episode. As Don Quixote charges the windmills, a wind sets the sails of the windmill turning, and the knight exclaims: "Pues, aunque movais más brazos que los del gigante Briareo, me lo habéis de pagar" (Well, though you should move more arms than the giant Briareus, you shall pay for it; 1978, 1.8.130; 2008, 59). Briareus was one of the three hundred-handed or hundred-armed giants, offspring of Sky and Earth, who were born close to the beginning of time. Due to his great might, Briareus was given the task of guarding the Titans in Tartarus. Although more recondite an allusion, Briareus also lends the episode a more sinister character because Dante chose him as one of the beings imprisoned in hell for all time.[29]

The third way in which Cervantes appears to undermine his narrative is by refusing to include an architecture of danger. After all, as opposed to the home and the inn, this is the first major building in the novel that portends danger – there are thirty or forty of these edifices (or perhaps just one with many towers). Yet, Don Quixote transforms windmills into giants, disallowing the numerous marvellous architectures of the romances. Perhaps this is a signal that architectures in the novel can be expanded to include the anatomy of humans and giants – and, as we will see in part 2 of the novel, the grotesque can be perceived in both. We have already mentioned that giants are analogous to towers: "tan grandes como torres" (as big as large steeples; 1978, 2.1.50; 2008, 477). In the case of the windmills the reference to Briareus could be quite apt given his many hands or arms that correspond to the turning sails of the windmill – although I have never encountered an illustration or painting that seeks to incorporate this image of a hundred-armed windmill.

French painter and illustrator Édouard Léon Louis Warschawsky, who went by the artistic name of Edy Legrand (1892–1970), illustrated the works of Dante, Shakespeare, Virgil, and many others. He even created one of the first books for children in which illustrations were more important than words: *Macao et Cosmage* (1919), a fable about the arrival of civilization at a paradisiacal place. He participated in the first exhibition of engraved works at the Art Institute in Chicago in 1928, together with Picasso, Matisse, and Derain, winning honourable mention.[30] It should not surprise us that later in life he turned to *Don Quixote*, producing images as memorable as those of his early children's book, but in this case majestic, mysterious, and captivating.

For the episode that concerns us, we can view the giants arising out of the windmills (see figure 3.4). If we look closely at the arms or sails of the first giant, they seem to form a circle whose centre is the navel, although slightly to one side. These two notions – the substitution of a building for a gigantic human, and the navel as the centre of a circle – bring to mind Vitruvius, who argues that symmetry is central to building and that it is based on proportion, "the correspondence among the measures of an entire work" (1960, 72). In order to understand symmetry and proportion in temples, he calls for an understanding of the proportions of the human body, which he describes in detail: "For the human body is so designed by nature that the face, from the chin to the top

Figure 3.4. Unknown artist, *Don Quijote se lanza al camino de la Caballería Andante*. Illustration inspired by Jacques-Valentin Radigues (ca. 1670–1746), based on Charles-Antoine Coypel (1694–1752), ca. 1746. Biblioteca Nacional de España. Open access, public domain

of the head to the end of the lowest roots of the hair, is a tenth part of the whole height" (1960, 72). Diego de Sagredo specifies how many heads are needed to form the human body, correcting Vitruvius: "hombre bien proporcionado se puede llamar aquel que contiene en su alto (según Vitruvio) diez rostros […] Pero los modernos auténticos quieren que tenga nueve y un tercio." (We can call a well-proportioned man he who is ten faces in height (according to Vitruvius) […] But the moderns want him to have nine and one-third; 1526, 4r.)

More importantly, Vitruvius was making a truly revolutionary finding for the Renaissance. Toby Lester explains: "Ancient thinkers had long invested the circle and the square with symbolic powers. The circle represented the cosmic and the divine; the square, the earthly and the secular. Anyone proposing that a man could be made to fit inside both shapes was making a metaphysical proposition: The human body wasn't just designed according to the principles that governed the world; it *was* the world, in miniature" (2012, n.p.). Indeed, the Vitruvian ideal echoes the new conception of humankind during the Renaissance, one that was most clearly articulated by Giovanni Pico della Mirandola in his *Oration on the Dignity of Man*, first published in 1496: "But when this work was done, the Divine Artificer still longed for some creature which might comprehend the meaning of so vast an achievement, which might be moved with love at its beauty and smitten with awe at its grandeur" (1956, 5). This creature would share what all other creatures had and, using his free will (7), could descend into the lowest matter or ascend towards the angels and even towards God himself through the use of the intellect. Pico then asserted that man was a protean figure, capable of every possible metamorphosis (9). It could well be that many of Don Quixote's comical transformations are but an echo of Pico's image of the human being, and his windmill episode a commingling of the Vitruvian man and Pico's vision.

It is from the Roman architect that Leonardo da Vinci drew his *Vitruvian Man*, knowing the ancient architect's assertion that a square could be formed from a man with arms outstretched, while a circumference could be sketched using a human's navel as the centre and going around his hands and feet when they were extended (Vitruvius 1960, 73).[31] Around 1490, Leonardo prepared his drawing with plenty of annotations. The discovery by Claudio Sgarbi of a manuscript of Vitruvius' text with 127 illustrations has shown that Leonardo was not the first one to draw the Vitruvian man (1993, 31–51). Giacomo Andrea da Ferrara appears to have been the first to attempt it, and he must have discussed his theory with Leonardo, who annotated at a dinner with him in that year. Giacomo Andrea's drawing is imperfect because he fails to include the two positions described by Vitruvius as applied to the circle and the square (Lester 2012; Sgarbi 1993, 40–4). Sgarbi claims that this human being stands between medieval visions of men and the new Renaissance ideal: "The executor of the drawing knew he could not simply borrow the medieval Everyman: a fragile body of a man around whom a wheel of fortune revolves" (Sgarbi 1993, 45). Nor could he present the crucified Christ, because his image did not follow "set geometrical patterns" (35). Perhaps there may be something of a Christ here, in the eyes closed, the arms extended, and the absence of perfect beauty that would serve as analogy for the temple. So, Giacomo Andrea's drawing was a work in transition, not yet reaching the perfectibility of the classical ideal. Many illustrations of the Vitruvian man in architectural manuals of the period would follow, including texts by Fra Giovanni Giocondo (1511), who in his edition of Vitruvius

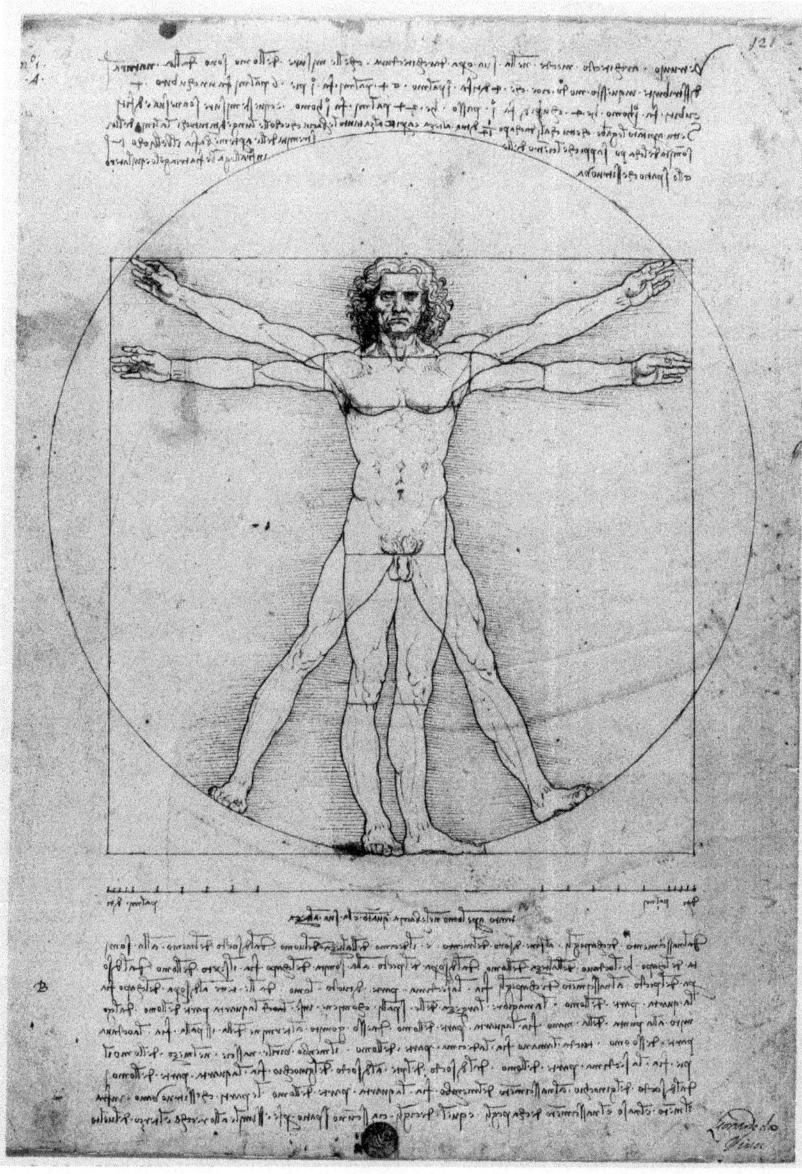

Figure 3.5. Leonardo da Vinci, *Drawing of Ideal Proportions of the Human Figure According to Vitruvius' 1st Cent. A.D. Treatise* De Architectura (called *Vitruvian Man*), ca. 1492. Alinari Archives/Art Resource, NY

used two images, one for the square and the other for the circle.[32] As opposed to some of the Apollonian figures before him, Francesco Di Giorgio Martini (1525) transformed the anatomy into a more Dionysian and rounded figure within a circle.[33]

In Cervantes, then, the knight might be attacking either an infernal giant or a Vitruvian man of very large proportions, one who, as in Edy Legrand's illustration, uses only his arms (and not his lower extremities) to create the circle of perfection and whose whirling sails recall the many-armed Briareus. Let us return to Dante who chose Briareus as one of the beings imprisoned in hell for all time.[34] In the *Inferno* the poet asks Virgil to show him "the enormous one, Briareus" (1980, 31.99). He is shown Anteus but denied the sight of Briareus, who is further down in the pit and "is bound up and just as huge as this one / and even more ferocious in his gaze" (31.104–5). Such is his fame in the underworld that an effigy of him can be located in the *Purgatorio* as one of thirteen sculptures that exhibit pride (Dante Alighieri 1982, 12.28–30).

Dante "provides a variety of precise details which would enable the curious reader to calculate the giants' size. Thus, Nimrod's head is as big as the huge bronze pine cone which is still displayed at Saint Peter's in Rome;[35] moreover, the distance from his navel to his shoulders is thirty hands (*gran palmi* or spans) […] Ephialtes [36] is bigger than Nimrod, as is Briareus" (Kay 2002, 17). Using this data, Richard Kay, calculates the size of Dante's giants, utilizing "a canon of human proportions […] given by Vitruvius in his *De architectura* 3.1.2" (18). I would then ask: can a giant have perfect proportions and symmetry as demanded by Vitruvius? Can giants imitate human proportions since their temperament and actions in the chivalric romances are most often highly immoderate, violent, and destructive? Did Cervantes' interest in giants and his reading of Dante and Vitruvius lead him to similar reflections?

In his commentary on Vitruvius, Daniele Barbaro asserts: "What delights and pleases us, and not something else, does so because it contains proportionate measurements and moderate temperament" (cited in Cellauro 2004, 317). He compares the perfectly proportioned architecture of the temple not only with the human body but also with a person's moderate temperament. Again, are giants simply humans who are bigger but lack the appropriate temperament? After all, Michelangelo's *David*, a gigantic statue, shows the beauty of symmetry and proportion. Paradoxically, the Florentine statue was to depict David confronting a giant, but Michelangelo depicts the biblical figure as a giant. Other than a great feat arising from a single block of marble, the David represents his powers as akin to those of ancient gods. Christopher Scott McClure asserts: "Statues of this size in ancient times were also reserved for depictions of gods or demigods" (2016, 113). It would not have escaped the artist that his statue was commonly referred to as the giant, even though it depicted a man fighting a giant. It also made Michelangelo into a giant of an artist. Hibbard affirms that "[t]his is the first wholly successful union of antique inspiration with the new Florentine celebration of man; and from the time of its unveiling it was understood as the beginning of a new epoch in art" (1974, 56). Well aware of the Vitruvian man, Michelangelo crafted a perfectly proportioned gigantic figure of a man. I would say that, for all this talk of giants, it would go against the times to view Michelangelo's *David* as a true giant.

My point here is that by appearing to undermine the dangerous architecture in his narrative, Cervantes is actually expanding architecture into anatomy and vice versa following the *Ten Books on Architecture*. The circle made by the rotating sails of the windmill recall the Vitruvian man and place the giant not just as a wild creature but as a human of large proportions whose many extended arms may fit within the circle. Is Don Quixote assailing a monstrous deformation of the ideal of the Vitruvian man? Is he turning against the "desmesurado"? For those who would reject such a notion out of hand, I invite them to peruse the episode of the "giantess" in part 2, one that is clearly influenced by the Vitruvian man. Turning to the knight, I would say that he is certainly not a new David, although he might wish to be so. In his defeat he is shown as a man lacking moderation and thus outside of the Vitruvian circle. Very much like the prison episode, here the theories of the ancient architect serve as scaffolding for theories and architectures that respond to Renaissance images and notions, though falling short of admiring the giants in their eternal incarceration.

The circle continues to spin, raising Don Quixote as his lance is caught in the sails, and then plunging him to the ground with Rocinante. In a sense, the adventure shows him as an eccentric figure that could fall outside the Vitruvian circle of perfection. But there is another circle, a very intimate one, a circle of friends that includes only Don Quixote and Sancho. This is the first episode in the novel that follows what Ian Watt has found to be a recurring pattern in the knight's adventures: "a visual stimulus, a misinterpretation of the stimulus by Quixote in terms of his chivalric compulsions; a realistic correction by Sancho Panza" (1996, 64). Sancho's "realistic corrections" will continue throughout the novel, although at times he is carried away by the knight's zest for adventure. In many cases, what seem even more important than their quest are the conversation and at times the acrimony between the two. They laugh, they fight, and their reasoning and responses become so intertwined that it is impossible to conceive of one without the other.

Knight and squire have left their homes in order to partake of adventure; thus the spaces around them can be viewed precisely as those of expansion and danger. They expand their knowledge of the land, but more importantly they expand the knowledge of each other, their beliefs and emotions, and what makes them human. This expansion carries with it a bond as they often come together, the squire helping his master to recover from his mishaps. Space, in a way, becomes place. Their familiarity with each other, their bond, makes adventures less dangerous, or at least less lonely because now Quixote has a spectator (in addition to the almost otherworldly enchanter who can write of all his deeds and does not communicate with his subject). The windmills episode, which started in what for the knight was a dangerous space, ends as Sancho runs to help the fallen knight. While they get on their mounts and move away from the space of disaster, they restart their conversations. Space has now become place. The two together form a kind of union that upholds comfort and leisure, an ambulant home where the two can look after each other. This safe place is much different from today's "safe spaces," for knight and squire are not averse to having heated discussion on controversial topics. Perhaps there are terms that "trigger" some of the controversies, but these discussions are always relished as part of a way to explore the world of ideas in the reduced space of La Mancha.

Occupancy at the Inn

Ronald Paulson defines the inn as one of the "basic metaphors of eighteenth-century fiction" (1984, 200). He goes on to say, "The inn was also a place where inhibitions could be left behind or stripped away, true or new identities revealed" (200). Indeed, it is a place for solace and solitude, for storytelling and bragging, for coincidence and anagnorisis, for rowdiness and drinking, for gambling and sexual licence. A century before the English novel exploited the inn as a liminal space, somewhere between the inside and the outside, somewhere between the place of home and the public space, Cervantes had already provided *Don Quixote* as model. The inn is the most common edifice in the 1605 novel. Part 1 of the novel itself fully relies on the inn, since it is here that people gather for numerous purposes. Indeed, the inn is in many ways the ancestor of today's hotels, which, according to Robert A. Davidson, have much to do with "occupancy," that is, the "space-over time-equation" (2018, 4). The longer stay, Davidson argues, "allows for increased contact with staff [...] creating the potential for formal or informal relationships" (5). The inn, in Cervantes, fosters a closer relationship with staff because it is a small building, with a very limited number of rooms and very few staff, the innkeeper, his family, hangers-on such as prostitutes, and limited service personnel. In Cervantes' inns we see how quickly staff and travellers establish a relationship.

In today's world the lobby becomes the very site of liminality, standing between the spaces outside and the privacy of the rooms in which travellers can achieve a modicum of safety and comfort, such as "sleeping, dressing and having sex" (Davidson 2018, 5), whereas at the inn the common room where food and drink were served functioned as that site. In modern hotels rooms tend to be private, for those who reserve them, be it an individual, a family, colleagues, friends, or intimate partners, but, given the exigencies of the inn, more than one traveller, who might not know the other one, usually had to stay in the same room. We need only remember one of Cervantes' *Novelas ejemplares* (*Exemplary Novels*) entitled *Las dos doncellas* (*The Two Damsels*). Arriving at an inn five miles from Seville, a guest wishes a room to himself but is told that the inn only has a room with two beds, and if someone else comes, he is bound to rent it. The guest insists, paying a large sum for his privacy and locks himself in the room. In spite of the short conversation with the innkeeper and his wife, gossip starts immediately as they and other guests discuss his beauty, munificence, and desire for privacy. A second guest arrives and, being told of the lack of occupancy, seeks to negotiate, offering "si el entrase a dormir en la otra cama y le daría un escudo de oro" (if he could go into the room and sleep in the other bed, he would offer a gold coin; Cervantes 2015a, 478). The greed of the innkeeper is aroused, and the action of the tale surges.

Turning to the first part of *Don Quixote*, we encounter two inns, an early one and a second one hosted by Juan Palomeque. The number of people who meet and lodge at the latter inn is astonishing, particularly as the action progresses towards the dénouement. The architecture of the inn, though somewhat clarified in the early chapters, always seems very confining, thus augmenting pleasure and disharmony at different times. In the later chapters, as more guests arrive, it is as if the building had become an ill-tuned accordion, inflating in size and allowing more guests to stay, as unexpected encounters, reconciliations, more confusion, and discordant voices emerge, always straining the question of occupancy. In chapter 37, once a number of those present have been reconciled, Don Fernando orders a large meal for all:

> [S]entáronse todos en una larga mesa como de tinelo, porque no la había redonda, ni cuadrada en la venta, y dieron la cabecera [...] a don Quijote, el cual quiso que estuviese a su lado la señora Micomicona, pues él era su

aguardador. Lugo se sentaron Luscinda y Zoriada, y frontero dellas don Fernando y Cardenio, y luego el cautivo y los demás caballeros, y al lado de las señoras el cura y el barbero. Y así cenaron con mucho contento. (Cervantes 1978, 37.464)

([T]hey all sat down at a long table, like those in halls, there being neither a round, nor a square one, in the house. They gave the upper-end and principal seat [...] to Don Quixote, who would needs have the lady Mico-micona sit next to him, as being her champion. Then sat down Luscinda and Zoraida, and opposite to them Don Fernando and Cardenio, and then the stranger and the rest of the gentlemen and next to the ladies sat the priest and the barber: and thus they banqueted much to their satisfaction.) (Cervantes 2008, 337)

Occupancy seems to be at the maximum, straining the abilities of the inn, and yet the crowded space creates a scene of conviviality where Christians and Moors, captives and freemen, eloquent madmen and ladies versed on the chivalric, individuals from the elite to the rustic, noble ladies and daughters of rich peasants, can all dine together and enjoy each other's company. It is precisely the centripetal force cre-ated by close quarters and excessive occupancy that gives moments such as these their ability to charm a public that lives among social restrictions.

As for the rooms at the inn, they seem to be as scarce as they are in the beginning, although the narrators try to be rather circumspect about it. Again the pressure due to occupancy enables acts of graciousness and generosity. First Dorotea and then Luscinda invite the newly arrived Moorish woman (Zoraida/María) to stay in a room they are sharing (Cervantes 1978, 1.37.462; 2008, 335–6). The inn as prelude to the mod-ern hotel serves one more purpose, as defined by Robert A. Davidson, that of (incipient) "transculturation" (2018, 3). Adventures of captivity are narrated next to tales of the Indies; chivalric romances are inter-twined with distant geographic spaces; and unexpected compromises, pointing to cultural and class relaxation, are made possible. The "baci-yelmo" (barber's basin/helmet) is thus born at the inn.

The compression of space and occupancy is a kind of pressure cooker that brews a new and more open place of community. Cervantes points out that the inn is still under construction, thus it is a site not fully formed; rooms are allotted to different groups, and the number of such places is never fully defined. As it turns out, the *camarachón* or loft that, as will be discussed in the next section, is the location for the comic and cosmic bedroom farce between Don Quixote, the muleteer, and

Maritornes is now being readied for the ladies – a very cramped space for Spanish aristocrats and women from Algiers to share (Cervantes 1978, 1.38.472; 2008, 343). In the later chapters Clara joins the women and is wakened by Dorotea, who asks her to listen to admirable harmonies of a song outside, which is the beginning of yet another tale. As for the men, the narration is even less clear: "Recogidas, pues, las damas en su estancia, y los demás acomodándose como menos mal pudieren, don Quijote se salió fuera de la venta a hacer la centinela del Castillo, como lo había prometido" (The ladies being now retired to their chamber, and the rest accommodated as well as they could, Don Quixote sallied out of the inn to stand sentinel at the castle gate as he had promised; 1978, 1.43.521; 2008, 386). We will leave readers to ponder on Cervantes' ellipsis here. How did friends who had just reconciled share a space? Was a bedroom made available to Don Fernando, son of one of the great nobles of Andalucía? Where did the former captive find his "place" of rest?

This night of relative peace, however, is followed by a day of contention as more guests and other visitors arrive at the inn while others seek to depart, thereby confusing and increasing occupancy. First, four servants arrive at the inn from the court, sent by the father of a fifteen-year-old youth, Luis, who has left his side. As it turns out, the singing muleteer is none other than this youth, who is enamoured of Clara. The judge, Clara's father, tries to settle this question: "oyeron grandes voces a la puerta de la venta, y era la causa dellas que dos huéspedes que aquella noche habían alojado [...] habían intentado irse sin pagar" (they heard a great outcry at the door of the inn, and the occasion was, that two guests who had lodged there that night [...] had attempted to go off without paying; 1978, 1.44.535; 2008, 399). These guests, unknown to the reader, further confuse occupancy and lead us to review the architecture of the inn to determine where they may have slept. As if the double commotion were not enough, a new guest arrives at the inn, a barber who happens to be the very same one whom Don Quixote had deprived of his basin (thinking it Mambrino's helmet) while Sancho had taken the "aparejos del asno" (the ass furniture; 1978, 1.44.539; 2008, 401). To add to the tensions at the inn, three troopers of the Holy Brotherhood who are charged with keeping order in the countryside have also arrived (1978, 1.45.543; 2008, 405). They hardly understand why many of the guests agree with Don Quixote that the barber's basin is a helmet. They are intent on apprehending and taking away Don Quixote because he is on their list as robber and highwayman. We can hardly count how many people are now amassed at the inn, and many with conflicting purposes. I would argue that this is the climactic point in the novel, the moment of greatest confusion and one where the inn is a dangerous space with many struggles and confusions. As such, it brings out Don Quixote's voice, which had been attenuated for over twenty chapters. In a surprising turn, the knight views the scene as a contest narrated in the *Orlando furioso*, in which the Saracens, at the point of taking Paris, are confounded by Discord, a figure brought to their camp by the Archangel Michael. The many fights that break out in the Saracen camp are re-envisioned by Don Quixote as taking place at the inn; thus the inn takes on the shape of a triple architecture: inn, castle, and Agramant's camp. Looking around, the knight orders the disorderly scene:

> De modo que toda la venta era voces, llantos gritos, confusiones, temores sobresaltos, desgracias, cuchilladas, mojicones, palos, coces y efusión de sangre [...] se le represento en la memoria de don Quijote que se veía metido de hoz y de coz en la discordia del campo de Agramante, y así dijo [...], 'Mirad como allí se pelea por la espada, aquí por el caballo, acullá por el águila, acá por el yelmo, y todos peleamos y todos no nos entendemos.' (Cervantes 1978, 1.45.544)

> (Thus the whole inn was nothing but weepings, cries, shrieks, confusions, fears, frights, mischances, cuffs, cudgellings, kicks and effusion of blood [...] it came to Don Quixote's fancy, that they were plunged over head and ears in the discord of king Agramante's camp, and therefore he said [...], 'Behold how there they fight for the sword, here for the horse, yonder for the eagle, here again for the helmet; and we all fight, and no one understands one another.') (Cervantes 2008, 407)

The proliferation of actions at the inn and the many different sentiments and contentions point to the many people massed in one place, which Don Quixote, as if he were an architect or an adept at the art of memory, "places" in different locations, each based on one of the items over which the Saracens fought, turning on their own and forgetting the siege of Paris. To the sword, horse, and eagle Don Quixote adds a helmet, which could very well have been one of the objects of contention. I find this one of the most fascinating chapters in the novel because Don Quixote thinks of himself not as a Christian knight but as a Saracen, and when he does, he recovers his voice and is able to command others to stop the contentions and confusions at the inn (De Armas 2011, 146–61)

But now it is time to go back to the representation of the inn as castle and palace in some of the early chapters of the novel.

Lucretia's Castle

Already in chapter 2 of the novel, the knight has arrived at an inn that he clearly pictures as a castle: "era un Castillo con sus cuatro torres y chapiteles de luciente plata, sin faltarle su puenta levadiza y honda cava" (a castle, with four turrets and battlements of refulgent silver, together with its drawbridge and deep moat…; Cervantes 1978, 1.2.82; 2008, 28). The chapter is one of the more delightful parodies of chivalry since, with the aid of the picaresque innkeeper, who follows Don Quixote's humour, every event and every architecture is related to these fabulous castles. The prostitutes become ladies, the rustic meal becomes a banquet of delicacies,[37] the innkeeper becomes a Castellano, with its comic equivocation – the knight referring to the lord of the castle, and the innkeeper thinking that Don Quixote refers to someone from Castile. As there is no chapel where he can watch over his weapons all night before he is an armed knight in the morning, he is offered, if not the courtyard of the castle, at least the corral at the side of the inn. Here a well and a trough for water serve as a kind of altar for his vigil. We need not enter into the details of his fight with the muleteers, or extol the innkeeper's excellent advice to the knight.

The scene is set, and when the knight sallies forth a second time with Sancho Panza, we, together with Don Quixote, can easily imagine Juan Haldudo's inn as a castle. Although this is an obvious parody of the romances of chivalry, the pastoral is not far behind. In the sixth chapter, as the priest and the barber are purging Don Quixote's books, they discuss in detail Jorge de Montemayor's *La Diana*. The priest objects in particular to the magic waters and to Felicia's palace. Recently Benjamin J. Nelson has discovered that the palace is modelled after the Count of Cobos' palace in Mérida, which was a composite building, including parts of an ancient temple to the goddess Diana (2017, 247). It is not inconceivable that Cervantes, fond of double and metamorphic building, had this particular site in mind for the inn/castle and other buildings. After all, the temple was modelled after Diana's temple at Ephesus, one that is constantly praised by Vitruvius (Nelson 2017, 147; Vitruvius 1960, 198).

Although exhausted and beaten by the Yanguesan carriers over Rocinante's desire to meet their mares, the pair can still bicker over the kind of building they are approaching: a castle, said Don Quixote; an inn, argued Sancho. By then the pair may have forgotten that Don Quixote, upon his arrival at the inn, is barely riding, not on Rocinante but on Sancho's ass. The knight had stated that this was far from a humiliation for him, recalling classical mythology: "Porque me acuerdo haber leido que aquel buen viejo Sileno, ayo y pedagogo del alegre dios de la risa, cuando entró en la ciudad de las cien puertas iba, muy a su placer, caballero sobre un muy hermoso asno" (for I remember to have read that the good Silenus, governor and tutor of the merry god of laughter, when he made his entry into the city of the hundred gates, went riding, much to his satisfaction, on a most beautiful ass; Cervantes 1978, 1.15.196; 2008, 109). Don Quixote is conflating his myths in order to acquire the authority of Silenus. Although it is true that Silenus, often drunk, rode on the back of a donkey, it was Bacchus who was associated with Thebes.[38] Bacchus was actually born there, but the inhabitants, not accepting his divinity, cast him out. Later the city did become the principal Greek centre of the god's cult. The inn/castle is thus contaminated by the myths of a very ancient city. Thebes was also the location of the Oedipus story and the epic conflict between his two sons, Eteocles and Polynices, which resulted in the death of the two brothers.[39] Thus, by entering the gates of the city, that is, the gates of the inn, the knight is subjecting himself to a conflictive architecture, one of confusion and even murder.

William Hogarth (1697–1764), who did a number of illustrations of *Don Quixote*, uses the stagecoach as a metaphor for life, and the inn as a stopping place in our journey.[40] But it is a pause filled with different kinds of activity. Turning to Henry Fielding, an imitator of Cervantes, Hogarth depicts a country inn yard (figure 3.6), where much of the goings-on in Cervantes' inns are replicated, such as in the bill that the rotund innkeeper presents to a well-dressed traveller who thinks it immoderate – recalling Don Quixote's refusal to pay his bills to the castle keeper. Hogarth also portrays the amorous farewell of traveller and chambermaid behind the innkeeper and guest. She is not moved by her mistress's voice or bell. We are reminded here of the episode that will be key in this section, the assignation of Maritornes and the muleteer, which is disrupted by the amorous Don Quixote, and the chaos that ensues. Much more than in modern hotels, the occupancy need not be long for the relationships between the staff and the guests to be heightened.

Although little is said of the architecture of the inn, we know that rooms are limited, and, as exemplified in *Las dos doncellas*, guests who do not know each other are often placed in the same room. Here, Don Quixote is settled in a "camaranchón" (garret; Cervantes 1978, 1.16.198; 2008, 111), something less than a full room that in the past had been a hayloft. Such a small space has to accommodate not only the wounded knight but also Sancho and a muleteer who is already lodging there in a bed that is a bit nicer than Don Quixote's. That night, as he sleeps

Figure 3.6. William Hogarth, *The Country Inn*, 1747. The Metropolitan Museum of Art, New York. Open access, public domain

in the room with Sancho and the muleteer, Don Quixote has his eyes wide open, thinking of an amorous adventure. He is afraid – or perhaps wishes – that the daughter of the lord of the castle will come in and offer herself. The description of his eyes "tan abiertos como liebre" (as wide open as a hare; 1978, 1.16.202; 2008, 114) is an image of sexuality: hares were considered to be the one of the creatures of Venus because both goddess and creature were constantly desiring erotic unions. Instead, Maritornes, the Asturian maid, enters the room in search of the muleteer, with whom she has an assignation. Once again, the separation between guests and staff is broken, this time for sexual purposes. Unfortunately the muleteer's bed is in the back, and she must make her way past two other beds, those of Don Quixote and Sancho. As soon as she enters the room, the knight hears her, sits up in bed, and extends his arms towards her: "el cual la asió fuertemente de una muñeca, y tirándola hacia él, sin que ella osase hablar palabra, la hizo sentar sobre la cama" (he caught fast hold of her by the wrist, and pulling her towards him, she not daring to speak a word, made her sit down on the bed by him; 1978, 1.16.203; 2008, 114). The double description is one of the finest in these chapters, allowing us to view both the rather unattractive maid and the beautiful princess whom Don Quixote envisions. In fact, the idealized image and the gesturing that takes place seem to imitate Titian's famous painting *The Rape of Lucretia*. The painting came into the possession of Philip II in 1571.[41] Maritornes' hair becomes as golden as that pictured by Titian. Lucretia's arms in the Italian canvas are adorned with bracelets that could fit the double description in the novel: they are encrusted with glass beads (jewels) and confused with fine pearls from the Orient. In Titian's painting, Lucretia attempts to disengage herself from the threatening Sextus. With one arm she pushes him away, while he holds on to her other arm. Maritornes also battles the knight while he perseveres in his attempts to hold her down, "la moza forcejeaba por desasirse y don Quijote trabajaba por tenerla" (the wench strove to get from him, and that Don Quixote laboured to hold her; 1978, 1.16.204; 2008, 115). Finally, the painting shows a figure at the foot of the bed, a slave watching the scene. This voyeur also appears in the novel. The mule carrier who was awaiting Maritornes' visit, on seeing her with Don Quixote, "se fue llegando más al lecho de don Quijote" (drew nearer and nearer to Don Quixote's bed; 1978, 1.16. 204; 2008, 115). In some ways, then, Don Quixote is moving beyond his chivalric character. He claims that he will be chaste and love only Dulcinea, but at the same time he refuses to let go of the would-be daughter of the lord of the castle.

Although Titian's painting has as theme Lucretia's chastity, it also displays Lucretia's body. The slave's presence and her pose are, as Ian Donaldson states, "an invitation to male voyeurism," which "hint at a central conflict in purpose" in the work (1982, 20). On the one hand, she is a symbol of chastity; on the other, she is displayed as a Venus, with pearls as the jewels of the goddess, and her nudity and the lushness of her couch suggesting the desires of Venus. In Cervantes' novel the mule carrier and the reader are thus implicated in this kind of viewing. Of course, the farcical aspects of the episode relieve much of the sexual tension of the painting. At the same time, an assignation with Maritornes would have done much to soothe Don Quixote's anxieties over his vigour and potency, the knight having lost so many battles. Maritornes would have been the balm that would have mollified him, while shattering his ideal love for Dulcinea. Instead, the scene becomes a farcical battle involving the Holy Brotherhood. The immobile Don Quixote, whose bed had collapsed when he was attacked by the muleteer, is at one point considered a corpse, as light is brought in to search for an assassin. Most of the action takes place in darkness, and the inn is hardly described: there is mention of a door into the small bedroom and of the rooms of the innkeeper, the justice official, and Maritornes.

Once the official from the Holy Brotherhood has demanded that the gates of the inn be closed so that a search can be made for the murderer, all escape to their own beds or rooms in order not to stand in the light of justice.

What makes this scene memorable is both the chiaroscuro of the setting and the swings in tone from suspense to farce, from chivalric adventure to holding a woman against her will, and from erotic desire to comic fights and the suspicion of murder. The setting may get lost somewhat, except for the doubling of the architecture, inn/castle, and perhaps the tripling, inn/castle/ancient city. We are left with the question of why Thebes. It may be that the supposed murder of Don Quixote points back to the city's tragic past, but this is too tenuous a thread and it does not take into account other clues given in the episode, such as the arrival of the knight and squire as Silenus and Bacchus. A more likely solution can be found at the end of chapter 17. After drinking the potion of Fierabrás and recovering from the many contretemps in a haunted inn, Don Quixote departs, refusing to pay and invoking once again his books of chivalry. When Sancho tries to do the same, some of the more picaresque figures at the inn decide to teach him a lesson and toss him up and down on a blanket. On hearing the cries of his squire, the knight attempts a return, to no avail: "llegó a la venta, y hallándola cerrada, la rodeó por ver si hallaba por donde entrar" (he came up to the inn; and finding it shut, he rode round it to discover, if he could, an entrance; 1978, 1.17.214; 2008, 124). With the gates closed and the walls (and his wounds) preventing him from entering, Don Quixote has to observe his squire bemoaning his fate as he flies up in the air: "ni el volador Sancho dejaba sus quejas" (nor did the flying Sancho forbear his complaints; 1978, 1.17.214; 2008, 124).

The inn thus resembles a city whose gates have been closed, and the knight cannot enter. Eventually the merrymakers tire, and Sancho is allowed to leave as the gates are fully opened: "abriéndole la puerta de la venta de par en par" (the inn gate being thrown wide open; 1978, 1.17.215; 2008, 124). Since ancient times the gates of mythic cities, and Thebes in particular, have each been assigned to one of the seven planets. Nonnus of Panopolis, a poet from Upper Egypt who flourished during the Roman Empire, wrote an epic poem in forty-eight books, the *Dionysiaca*, which tells the life of Dionysus/Bacchus. In the fifth book he describes the founding of Thebes by Cadmus and how he dedicates each of the seven gates to one of the planets: "He dedicated seven gates, equal in number to the seven planets. First towards the western clime he allotted the Oncaian Gate to Mene Brighteyes, taking the name from the honk of cattle, because the Moon herself, bullshaped, horned, driver of cattle, being triform is Tritonis Athene" (1940, 5.67ff). This reference thus brings together the allusion to Bacchus and the gates of Thebes, adding a new component, the seven spheres. A new architecture is added, that of the heavens. Looking back on the text, we can ascertain that this fourth architecture has already been suggested. Roberto González Echevarría, with unerring insight, veers away from the "bedroom farce" at the inn and points out that the roof in the small room where Don Quixote, Sancho, and the muleteer are lodged, has holes in it, becoming an "estrellado establo" (starlit stable) and permitting those sleeping there to gaze at the heavens (2019, 42, 82). There is indeed here a comic response to the cosmic, or vice versa. We may have a parody of the astrological ceilings that decorated many of the famed Italian villas and palaces of the Renaissance. In Rome, for example, we think of the scenes of the Sala di Galatea in the Villa Farnesina, and those of the Stanza della Segnatura or the Sala dei Pontefici in the Vatican Palace. Is Cervantes once again painting his novel with brush-strokes derived from his Italian sojourn? Is he reconstructing the inn as Lucretia's palace? Or perhaps we think of Tycho Brahe's observatories, Uraniborg and Stjerneborg. From the latter's cellars he could have a more accurate view of the heavens and thus develop his messy yet insightful view of the cosmos, an architecture that, although based on so many computations, appears to be improvised and eccentric.

The knight's relation to the heavens is a complex one: "El duro [...] lecho de don Quijote estaba primero en mitad de aquel estrellado establo" (Don Quixote's hard [...] bed stood first in the middle of that illustrious *starlit* loft; Cervantes 1978, 1.16.201; 2008, 113). The text shows not only that the knight is staring at the heavens through the holes in the roof but that his eyes are not closed. He is like a hare, one of the animals dedicated to Venus. Thus, he is under the influence of this planet and its very specific gate at Thebes. What occurs at the inn, then, has much to do with the planet of desire. But it is a planet that is obstructed by a jealous god. In chapter 15, Don Quixote assured us that the god of battles was punishing him (1978, 1.15.192). Mars, desiring Venus, is forever jealous of her other lovers; thus, he kills or has Adonis killed. At the inn the muleteer, under the influence of Mars, causes havoc as he comes to believe that Maritornes is rejecting him for Don Quixote. In a truly comic and cosmic tour de force Maritornes then becomes a new Venus, now "painted" in a grotesque manner. Even though she is the object of men's desires and the object of contention, her last action makes her the shining star in the episode, the morning star that will bring a new light to the events. The compassionate Maritornes brings water for Sancho to drink after he has been tossed into the heavens (yet another planet whose identity is not revealed). On his rejection of the water, Maritornes buys him some wine, the perfect beverage that ends the episode and brings together Silenus, Bacchus, and Venus, gods that stand often in opposition to Mars. The inn has been revealed as a space of contention. Its architecture is forever changing, becoming a castle, an ancient city, an Italian villa, and even an observatory from which we can perceive the influences and architectures of the heavens.

Prison/Castle

Towards the end of the novel, in chapter 47, the priest and the barber, along with many of Don Quixote's new acquaintances at the inn, believe that they must take the knight home for his health and well-being. After all, he had emerged from the penitence at Sierra Morena looking very yellow and sickly. They construct a cage with wooden bars on top of a cart and shut him in; it is then yoked to some oxen. This new form of incarceration echoes the very beginning of the novel where the author, rather than the protagonist, tells us that he conceived of the novel while he was incarcerated at the Royal Jail in Seville. This biographical trace may well be part of what has been called Cervantes' trauma, his imprisonments, from Algiers to Seville. Don Quixote, at first, shows discomfort. He thinks of countless examples in books of chivalry where knights are transported by enchantment, but this happens as they are enclosed in dark clouds, carried in chariots of fire, or flown by winged hippogryphs. But in the end he is content to acknowledge that in modern times such a new type of conveyance could be part of the chivalric world.

Yet, it turns out that Don Quixote is not the only one who has been tricked into an ambulatory jail. All those who partake of these deceptions are themselves tricked by the gods. This means of transport recalls an image from the heavens. Ever since antiquity, planetary gods have been depicted riding in chariots led by the animals assigned to them. Venus, for example, is often seen in a chariot drawn by either doves or swans.[42] Renaissance Latin versions of treatises by Albumazar (Abu Ma'shar), the famed astrologer from Baghdad, depict Venus with doves. She is also presented thusly on the cover of the seventeenth-century Spanish translation of Boiardo's *Orlando inamorato*, as well as in numerous Renaissance paintings, including one by Pietro Perugino at the Collegio del Cambio in Perugia.[43] In order to allude obliquely to what is transpiring, a prophecy is intoned by the barber, who is disguised as an enchanter, in which he speaks of Dulcinea as "la blanca paloma tobosina" (the white Tobosan dove; 1978, 1.46.555; 2008, 416).

Here the common image in ballads of the time of the hunt of love in which the man pursues his beloved, a white dove, is conflated with the chariot of Venus (Rogers 1974, 144).

While Dulcinea may be viewed as conducting Venus' chariot, the cart in which Don Quixote rides represents quite a different planet. The passage tells that it is being pulled by oxen, described as "perezosos y tardíos animales" (lazy, heavy animals; 1.47.556; 2008, 418). The quality of slowness is again underlined when the text refers to the "el paso tardo" (the slow pace; 1.47.560; 2008, 421) of the animals. These attributes belong to Saturn, who was viewed as the farthest and slowest of planets in Ptolemaic astrology. He was said to be the most malefic of planets, responsible for delays and incarcerations. Thus we find Don Quixote in his cage, delaying his chivalric quest. Indeed, Saturn was often portrayed in a cart drawn by slow and slothful oxen. The ox-drawn Saturn can be found in works as different as Boccaccio's *Genealogy of the Gods* and Baccio Baldini's account of a Medici wedding in Florence in 1565 (Fajardo 1986, 249).

Even though Don Quixote struggles to amplify the scene and turn it into an ancient chivalric adventure, he seems to be aware that somehow his enchantment has to do with a malefic planet. When he is unable to free yet another captive (a statue of the Virgin in procession), he accepts his place in the heavenly cart, stating, "[S]erá gran prudencia dejar pasar el mal influjo de las estrellas que agora corre" (it will be great prudence in us to wait until the evil influence of the stars which now reigns, is over-passed; Cervantes 1978, 1.52.601; 2008, 456). In Cervantes' text, Don Quixote is trapped by Saturn, by the planet of melancholy. And thus he should be, for Saturn often signifies imprisonments. This new celestial prison reverts back to beginnings. At the same time, it points to further incarceration – the novel will end when Don Quixote, in this cart, reaches home, a place he sought to escape.

So far we have witnessed a rustic cart turned into an icon of Saturn, as the construction of a confined space in a cart has metamorphosed into an architecture of the celestial spheres. While the characters built the first structure, and the narrator allowed us to intuit a second, now the knight provides a third architecture. On his way home he meets a canon from Toledo and has various conversations with him. The canon detests the books of chivalry, the basis of Don Quixote's "mad" adventures. The knight seeks to convince the canon that books of chivalry are actually cures against melancholy, which is the opposite of what the gentleman's friends and acquaintances believe, and what the novel seems to posit. In many ways, his discourse on the subject shows the wisdom of the saturnine, bringing together a series of cures as he narrates a fanciful romance. Upon coming to a horrific lake of dark and boiling water filled with serpents and other menacing creatures, the knight hears a voice from the centre of the waters telling him that if he wants to be rewarded with what lies beneath, he must throw himself in; then he will witness the marvels below, including "los siete castillos de las siete fadas" (the seven castles of the seven enchanted nymphs; Cervantes 1978 1.50.584; 2008, 441). In chivalric romances and in ballads these fay or fates are either three or seven: when there are three, the first two bestow blessings, while the last one lashes out with curses; and when there are seven, the first six are benefic, while the seventh is malefic.[44] Thus, the mysterious voice is of uncertain origin and can bring him good or evil, but the knight immediately jumps into the waters, a positive action since uncertainty is usually chastised in the ballads of the period.

Having passed through the horrors on the surface of the lake, the knight arrives in a land as beautiful as the Elysian Fields. Beautiful greenery, a placid stream, the song of colourful birds, all impress the knight, who comes upon two beautiful fountains. The first, in classical style, is made of marble and jasper. The second, embellished with images from the Renaissance grotesque, is crafted "con orden desordenada" (in orderly confusion; 1978, 1.50.584; 2008, 441). It may be that these fountains represent two types of fiction: the classical tradition and the romances of chivalry. It is as if the text emphasizes that the monstrous or disorderly nature of the latter can be held together by a different kind of order. These carefully crafted objects are but a first indication of human habitation. The knight is then faced with a marvellous castle "cuyas murallas son de macizo oro, las almenas de diamantes, las puertas de jacintos" (whose walls are of massy gold, the battlements of diamonds, and the gates of hyacinths; 1978, 1.50.585; 2008, 441). Don Quixote, in his description, emphasizes that in spite of the many precious materials that go into the making of this castle, its architecture is much more valuable. Once again, he may be pointing to novels of chivalry as a perfectly structured genre.

Once inside, the knight of Don Quixote's imagined adventure is treated to a banquet of the senses. Sight is foremost, as all he sees, including the beautiful maidens with elegant dresses and the perfect architecture, delights this highest of senses. He is bathed in warm waters that soothe the sense of touch. He is massaged with perfumed unguents and dressed in perfumed clothing, which enliven the sense of smell. A magnificent meal satisfies his sense of taste, while delightful music delights his sense of hearing. Don Quixote, then, stresses that the romances of chivalry, in spite of their many monsters and battles, contain architectures of healing, places where warriors and readers can heal and recover from the adventures. And these adventures also serve to improve the protagonist as well as the reader. Don Quixote summarizes for the canon all the virtues he has gained from the adventures: "soy valiente, comedido, liberal, biencriado, generoso, cortés, atrevido, blando, paciente, sufridor de trabajos, de prisiones, de encantos" (I am become valiant, civil, liberal, well-bred, generous, courteous, daring, affable, patient, a sufferer of toils, imprisonments, and enchantments; 1978, 1.50.586; 2008, 442). He then establishes an analogy between his ability to endure incarceration and enchantments and his being locked up in a cage. In a clever twist Don Quixote points to all that is good in the books of chivalry and applies it to his patience and perseverance in the cage. Indeed, by narrating and visualizing all that happened in the marvellous palace, the caged knight is self-healing, seeking to enjoy all the benefits of the castle in his cage. He even asserts that chivalry books "destierran la melancolía" (will banish all your melancholy; 1978, 1.50.586; 2008, 442). Instead of being a melancholy visionary as the cage portends, he asserts that the books balance the humours. Of course, he does not take into account his excessive reading.

Thus, the ending of the novel leads us once again to the opposition prison/palace (in this case a castle). It serves to remind the reader of Cervantes' own incarceration, asserting that such "adventures" befall a person under Saturn (whether author or protagonist) and that they can lead to a higher knowledge. In this case, the vision of a higher knowledge is a castle that serves to cure the knight. We may even conceive of Cervantes as recalling the adventures of his imprisonment in Seville and transforming them into comical passages that, together with the healing nature of the marvellous castle, allowed him to endure his incarceration, rising above it through the birth of one of the greatest novels in the modern world.

Don Quixote, part 1, is a novel that hides much of its architectures, while highlighting the few metamorphoses created by the knight: inn/castle and windmills/giants. In so doing, it subtly conducts the reader through shadowed scenes and magnificent edifices that are barely constructed. Metamorphoses are hidden through veiled references and allusive ekphrases. A Vatican Palace can rise out of the Royal Jail in Seville, while both are anchored in the writer's study; windmills can become giants, but their circular sails or wheels can point to the Vitruvian man, problematizing proportion and eurithmia. The inn becomes like an inflated accordion as more and more guests arrive, and the place becomes a space of contention and a building that can barely enclose so many guests. Occupancy and architecture become unstable. The inn as castle can also become a Renaissance villa with ceiling frescoes that portray the heavens – or even an observatory that views the architecture of the heavens itself. The novel's edifices are in a state of flux, reminding us of Ovid's *Metamorphosis*, an ode to change and transformation. Buildings seldom stand solidly in order to confront the dangers outside. These fluid architectures point to the changing nature of reality, to the impossibility of trusting the senses. They also point to the changing nature of all individuals and their relations to place and space, and to the desire for a place of safety, a place for healing at a time when even the heavens can no longer reassure us through the representation of a stable and benefic cosmos.

4 Windows: *Don Quixote*, Part 1

Apollo at Delphi, through the oracular utterances of his priestesses, pronounced Socrates the wisest of men. Of him it is related that he said with sagacity and great learning that the human breast should have been furnished with open windows, so that men might not keep their feelings concealed, but have them open to the view.

Vitruvius, The Ten Books of Architecture (3.preface)

After numerous failed adventures Sancho complains that the knight's "feats" have taken place in obscure and rustic places where the knight cannot gain fame.[1] He calls on Don Quixote to go serve a prince or an emperor. But the knight explains to him that this is not possible because he has yet to acquire fame. There seems to be a double bind here: the knight cannot acquire fame in his rustic lands where few (if any) knights, giants, or terrifying beasts abide.[2] As if to avoid this difficult dilemma, Don Quixote narrates to Sancho a mini-chivalric novel in which an idealized knight triumphs against all obstacles. Having defeated numerous enemies, this imagined figure attains great fame, and everywhere he goes people acclaim him. His reputation facilitates his entrance into a king's castle: "se parará de las fenestras de su real palacio el rey de aquel reino, y así como vea al caballero, conociéndole por las armas, o por la empresa del escudo" (the king of that kingdom shall appear at the windows of his royal palace; and, as soon as he espies the knight, knowing him by his armour, or by the device on his shield; 1978, 1.21.259; 2008, 158). The king then welcomes him and introduces him to the queen and their daughter. The princess will, of course, fall for such a valiant knight, and so on. However, no such window and no such castle are actually conjured up by the knight in the plains of La Mancha.[3] The inn as castle never becomes a place where Don Quixote's adventures are recognized. In addition, the quixotic inns do not seem to have exterior windows that would allow the prince to view him and call him in. Thus, the very window that Don Quixote finds as a crucial site for recognition is virtually absent from the narrative.[4] Although windows are missing from the chivalric episodes, the 1605 novel finds a unique way of inserting them in the interpolations rather than in the main action.

The seven interpolated stories seem to move away from the chivalric, focusing on desire, centring on looking, on being looked at, and on the gaze that detects beauty in the danger outside or that threatens the inside through these liminal spaces. These architectural windows allow us to peek into the windows of the human breast, as Socrates would have wished (Vitruvius 1960, 69). They also enable new ways of seeing and picturing, new complexities in amorous relations, and new ekphrastic depictions. These sites actually recall chivalric scenes now placed within *novelas*. In addition, one of the liminal openings may point to the Homeric epics, and another to a legendary tale in Herodotus' *Histories*. This chapter will view five windows in particular. First, we will look at Luscinda's open window and the forbidden gaze that comes from the outside. Second, we will search for the phantasmal windows of Anselmo's home in Florence. Third, we will turn to the many windows in Algiers, which serve as a contrast to the closed spaces of battle at the beginning of the "Captive's Tale." Four, we will exhibit the double window of Luis and Clara's epic tale of doom. Five, we will end with Leandra's window as a teichoskopia of the dangerous outside. While denying epic and chivalric windows to the knight, the novel, as a way of problematizing genre and showing the disruptions of this type of liminal space, foregrounds their importance when the knight is absent.

Before proceeding, it is important to keep in mind that windows and their coverings were still developing during early modern times. The term *ventana* derives from the Latin *ventus* (wind). Ever since ancient times windows, as an elevated opening in the walls to allow light and fresh air to enter, were very common. Covered with different materials for privacy or to prevent excessive cold or heat, they were one of the most common architectural traits in Spanish houses. Sebastián de Covarrubias makes a point of underlining the two main functions of the window: to bring light and to allow air to circulate in the building. In his dictionary of 1611 he also explains that "hacer ventana" (1611, 69v) refers to a time in the afternoon when women go to their windows, and gallants or suitors walk down the street to see them. He warns that this only happens in some cities, while elsewhere windows are hidden from the streets. This was one of the few liminal spaces that could be used by women, often confined to the home, to balance the security of the house with the dangers outside. We will see in this chapter that windows giving on to the street are at times carefully covered with different materials to prevent penetration of the male gaze, which was considered a central danger to women in a patriarchal society. We will also encounter windows that are wide open to the outside, as well as sheltered windows that are not necessarily sufficient precaution against the dangers outside. Although windows had different cloth coverings, as time went on, glass began to be used to increase the light coming in without having to worry about the weather. While it was appropriate to palaces and homes of the nobility, its use in less ostentatious homes came about slowly.[5] Often these coverings for windows consisted of small pieces of glass held together by lead, thus supporting the fragility of the material. A woman reads by the light of a window in Pieter de Hooch's *Woman Reading a Letter*, composed in 1664. Furthermore, the window itself can become a "painting" that pictures the outside, as frames within frames bring together art and architecture. This is a device that Cervantes favours.

It is curious that Cervantes emphasized windows in private homes rather than in public buildings. In this, he preceded the work of modern architect Frank Lloyd Wright. Jonathan Lipman asserts: "It is one of the most intriguing and significant aspects of Wright's long career that almost all of his public buildings were introspective and virtually windowless while his private works were extroverted and integrated with the landscape. Where the one, the urban monument, was predicated on an internal semipublic realm, illumined from above, the other, the private house invariably extended its enclosure, through continuous fenestrations" (1986, xi).

Although in this chapter we will encounter numerous windows in homes, such openings are less frequent in other structures envisioned by Cervantes. In a later chapter we will be able to visualize the Pantheon in Cervantes' careful description. As with Wright's public buildings, it is illumined from above. Windows are central in Cervantes' homes, but they never reach the openness of Wright. For the American architect, windows and other such structures open to a landscape filled with "Edenic promise" (Lipman 1986, xi), but, for Cervantes, the home often guarded one from dangers outside. Windows, then, while liberating, could also let in the menacing world that was beyond the home.

Rear Window

Alfred Hitchcock's 1954 thriller *Rear Window*, in which Jeff, confined to a wheelchair, spends much of his time looking out the rear window of his apartment at his neighbours' activities, particularly during a hot summer when they have their windows open, has been studied time and again as a film that focuses on voyeurism. The classic scholarly work on the subject is done by Laura Mulvey who utilizes the scenes of Jeff watching characters such as a dancer he calls "Miss Torso" or a single woman he calls "Miss Lonelyhearts," to elaborate her theory of the male gaze. Jeff, representing the patriarchy, encourages the male audience to repeat his role as voyeur and gaze at women, objectifying them.[6] The movie is quite conscious of its extended use of voyeurism, and Jeff's nurse, Stella, chides him for it. This is not the only film by Hitchcock that develops the figure of the voyeur. As Katrina Powers has pointed out, Norman, in *Psycho*, spies on Marion, using a hole in the wall that is hidden by a painting. It is not without significance that the work of art is the 1731 painting *Susanna and the Elders* by Willem van Mieris, in which the elders spy on Susanna as she is about to bathe. Thus, window, painting and voyeur come together in two films by Hitchcock that are not very far removed from the techniques and ambience of an interpolated tale in the first part of *Don Quixote*.

Some years ago, David Quint entitled a subsection of his book on Cervantes "Lucinda at the Window" (2003, 15). Here he connected an old chivalric tale to this amorous interpolation.[7] My own interpretation swerves away from Quint in order to emphasize that, while in the chivalric, kings and princesses look out the windows in order to witness battles, welcome knights, or obtain news of the world,[8] in the story of Cardenio and Luscinda, moments of scopophilia (using Mulvey's terminology) occur with greater intensity when one is looking in from the outside. Very much like in Hitchcock, paintings will also come to the fore as images of voyeurism.

Cervantes' scene, I would argue, reimagines a very different chivalric tale – a key moment in the *Amadís*, and one that is unique. In the chivalric novel, King Perión awakens from a dream to see his beloved Elisena coming scantily dressed to his chambers with her maid Darioleta: "y levantando la cabeça vio entre las cortinas, abierta la puerta de que él nada no sabía, y con el lunar [la luna] que por ella entraba vio el bulto de las doncellas" (and raising his head he saw through the curtains, with the door open, of which he knew nothing, and with the moon that through it shone, entered a group of damsels; Rodríguez de Montalvo 1987, 1.238). Cervantes preserves the light of the moon, the open drapes, and the scantily dressed woman[9] but transforms the scene from one that highlights woman's agency and desire to one that focuses on the male gaze. Cardenio, we are told, had known Luscinda since childhood, and they had been together until their age led her father to forbid Cardenio's entrance to their house. Cardenio then turned to the pen to express his blossoming feelings, to which she acquiesced. This growing love and its dream of fulfilment seem to be closely related to the "felicitous space" of Luscinda's abode. It is the home of childhood memories, which for Bachelard "comes forth from the earth, that lives rooted in its black earth" (1994, 111). Although never described in detail, her house is intimately linked to Cardenio's memories and desires. Here they met while they were children, and here he still meets her surreptitiously by the window now that their amorous passion is blossoming. Having asked her father for her hand in marriage, and readying to ask his own father for consent, he is told that he is to go and serve Duke Ricardo, one of the foremost nobles of Andalucía. The problems in this love begin to emerge when his rootedness and topophilia are disrupted.

Perhaps meeting her by the window was a small transgression, but one that is typical of most young people in love in the literature of the early modern period. Fra Filippo Lippi's *Portrait of a Woman with a Man at the Casement* (1440) shows how the man can look in on his betrothed (see figure 4.1). In the painting, her sleeve is embroidered with letters that spell *lealta* (faithfulness). Since Cardenio has not been granted permission to marry Luscinda, his look, though consensual, sidesteps the patriarchal system. However, once place is distanced and disrupted by his father's command to go and serve the duke, he will return a changed man. He will use the opening not for mutual conversation but for transgressive voyeurism.

Cardenio confesses his love for Luscinda to the duke's second son, Fernando, who seems to become his friend. On hearing of Luscinda's great beauty, however, Fernando wishes to see her. Rather than choosing a public place such as a church, Cardenio obliges in an immensely transgressive manner: "enseñándosela una noche a la luz de una vela, por una ventana por donde los dos solíamos hablarnos" ("showed her to him one night by the light of a taper at a window, where we two used to converse together"; Cervantes 1978, 1.24.296; 2008, 189). Luscinda's beauty is framed by a window that is located away from the street, possibly a rear window, and by a light, candle, or moon. She is in a state of undress and as such should not be viewed by another. One of the voyeurs, Fernando, we are told, "[v]ióla en sayo, tal, que todas las bellezas hasta entonces por él vistas las puso en olvido" ("She appeared to him, though in an undress, so charming, as to blot out of his memory all the beauties he had ever seen before"; 1978, 1.24.296; 2008, 189). While in the chivalric tale the maid had opened the drapes, in Cervantes' text Luscinda seems to have gone to sleep without closing her own drapes, not shielding herself from the dangers outside. But this is a very minor infraction when compared to those committed by Cardenio.[10] First, he trespasses on Luscinda's privacy without her knowledge and consent

Figure 4.1. Fra Filippo Lippi, *Portrait of a Woman with a Man at the Casement*, 1440. The Metropolitan Museum of Art, New York. Open access, public domain

and thus becomes a voyeur. Second, he compounds this error by inviting his friend to gaze upon her. The space outside intrudes upon a safe place inside; Cardenio brings the danger outside to the window and triggers Luscinda's and his own undoing.[11] A chivalric scene such as the one in the *Amadís* has been reconfigured. King Perión welcomes the danger from outside, the secret liaison with Elisena, as he gazes upon her by the light of the moon, but here Luscinda is asleep safely inside and does not sanction either candlelight or the intruding gaze.

No matter how brief the passage, it is clear that Cardenio has turned Luscinda into a beautiful object and the object of the male gaze and is thus encouraging his friend to engage in scopophilia. Commenting on a photograph, Annette Kuhn states: "The spectator can indulge in the 'lawless seeing' permitted by the photo's reassurance that the woman is unaware of his look" (1985, 30). Here the immediate gaze is even more intimate because the two friends are looking at a human being and not at an image. The text does not reveal how long the two friends gaze upon Luscinda's body. We can be sure that she is asleep and unaware of their look. The reader of the novel, in turn, can also gaze upon this image. The felicitous place of childhood memories has been transformed suddenly into the setting for erotic "art."

Victor Stoichita has documented the fascination with windows in early modern art. He explains: "Hornacinas, ventanas y puertas son fragmentos de realidad que se distinguen por su capacidad de delimitar un campo visual" (niches, windows and doors are fragments of reality that are distinguished by their capacity to delimit a visual field; 2000, 59). The framed space also resembles that of a painting. Windows within a painting foreground the delimiting of visual space and can be viewed as art within art, thus leading to what Stoichita labels a meta pictoric doubling (2000, 75). In Domenico Ghirlandaio's *An Old Man and His Grandson* (1480) a window opens onto the outside (no glass seems to intrude in our vision), thus framing a landscape. Cervantes inverts the common image of a landscape viewed from within, framing an interior scene as viewed from the outside. Perhaps aware of the reluctance of artists to paint a view to the inside, Cervantes enables the narrator to create this reversal, while turning the interior scene into an ekphrasis. As Luscinda has not closed the curtains, two would-be connoisseurs of beauty, Cardenio and Fernando, can admire her.

Cervantes' scene is an ekphrasis of a type of painting that could no longer be executed in Spain at the time. Following the strictures of the Council of Trent, art could not exhibit scenes that aroused lust. Indeed, as Ignacio López Alemany explains, the Lisbon artist in Cervantes' *Persiles* was careful to eliminate sensual scenes from his portrayal of the pilgrim's adventures in the North.[12] Here, however, Cervantes is more brazen, revealing what he should not in a succinct but telling ekphrasis. This brief scene also contains other significant traits related to the art of the period. Pierre Civil reminds us that during the Siglo de Oro a cloth, in the manner of a curtain that could be pulled back, often covered canvases considered erotic. Of course, these canvases predate the Counter-Reformation (1990, 39–49). The drapes on the left side of Titian's *Danae* or the ones that seem to be pulled back in his *Tarquin and Lucretia* could be a play on the uses of drapes to hide erotic art.[13] If even at the palace such works were considered dangerous, Luscinda's portrait given to us by Cervantes as uncovered indicts the artist-lover, for it is not even transformed into a mythical or legendary tale. Bette Talvacchi asserts: "The great license that mythological subject matter afforded sexual representation is a factor of crucial importance for understanding Renaissance conventions concerning the differentiation between acceptable and nonacceptable erotica" (1999, 46).[14] Cervantes' erotic art lacks the cloak of mythology, thus erring twice: first by disregarding Renaissance notions of the decorous and secondly by rejecting the strictures of the Council of Trent.

Not long before the ekphrastic passage, however, Cardenio had portrayed himself as a new Pyramus, denied entry into Thisbe's home (Cervantes 1978, 1.24.293; 2008, 186).[15] This allusion could well evoke the many romances of chivalry that exhibited the myth in tapestries or paintings.[16] The mythical ambience thus created permits and even encourages associations with other ancient stories. Cervantes may have had the tale of Giges and Candaules in mind when he was constructing the scene of voyeurism.[17] We may recall the tale as narrated in Herodotus' *Histories*: the king of Lydia was so taken with his own wife's beauty that he hid Giges, his bodyguard, in his rooms so that Giges could gaze upon his wife at bedtime. This time it is not a window but a door that induces the danger from outside. The king tells his bodyguard, "I will bring you into the chamber where she and I lie and set you behind the open door; and after I have entered, my wife too will come to her bed […] you will be able to gaze upon her at your leisure" (1990, 1.9.13). The unhappy result of King Candaules' invitation in Herodotus' ancient tale may well serve as warning to Cardenio, who shares the beauty of his would-be wife with a friend. Although a door allows Giges to penetrate a forbidden space, it is a window that serves to frame Cardenio's tale. The reader can return repeatedly to this "picture" and gaze at Luscinda, who inhabits the gendered inner spaces of the home and is now threatened by the male gaze. Cervantes has thus created a transformative ekphrasis of a painting that depicts a classical story.

Cervantes, however, has inverted the roles of Herodotus' characters. We come to think of Fernando as the assertive Candaules and of Cardenio as the tricked Giges. After all, even though Fernando is described as "mozo gallardo, gentil hombre, liberal y enamorado" (sprightly young gentleman of a genteel, generous, and amorous disposition; Cervantes 1978, 1.24.294; 2008, 187), we come to know, as Anne J. Cruz reminds us, "his amoral cunning and uncontrolled passion" (2005, 622). Fernando penetrates Dorotea's home and pierces with his lustful gaze Luscinda's window.[18] While, as stated, Giges uses a door rather than a window, the allusion to Herodotus also relates to Cardenio's tale in other ways. Herodotus' *Histories* serves to display an orientalist vision and portray one of a number of eastern monarchs as either abusive or demeaning to women, often behaving inappropriately. Jennifer T. Roberts asserts that this behaviour, particularly in the case of Candaules, "offered him a window into the character of the failed bogeyman of the Greeks, Xerxes himself. For in fact, two parallel treatments of the *topos* bracket *The Histories*: the impudence of Candaules and the impudence of the Persian king" (2011, 69). As the tragic protagonist of Aeschylus' *The Persians*, a possible model for Cervantes' play *La Numancia* (*The Siege of Numantia*), Xerxes stands as the Other whose tragic fate may trigger glee and strong condemnation. But these orientalist villains must be seen in terms of the self. In some ways, Cervantes may be showing how the tyrannical barbarians (Xerxes, Candaules, and Fernando), while triggering judgment, can also serve to mirror the self.[19] Since male readers may tend to identify with Cardenio, his behaviour can be a warning not to throw stones at glass houses or, in this case, at glass windows. Cardenio also shares an orientalist vision, and his Candaules-like obsession frames him.[20]

In a subsequent scene Luscinda leans out of a window to give a passer-by a letter for Cardenio; she leans out into the world outside to warn him of Fernando's treachery. Cardenio does not act in the out side world and does not attempt to save his relationship. Quite the contrary, he even goes to the place of Fernando and Luscinda's wedding but observes it from a window.[21] David Quint wonders why Cardenio does not "step out from behind the tapestry to stop Don Fernando from marrying Luscinda" (2003, 30). Forever a voyeur, a representative of the danger outside, he will not intrude in the ceremony but will watch for others' mistakes without taking into account his own.[22]

The Ghosts of Place

Windows are often meant to expand the places of safety inside by allowing a view to the outside. Cervantes goes against this notion at least twice in his interpolations. The tale of Cardenio and Luscinda takes place mostly outside, and the view towards the inside endangers

places of safety. *El Curioso impertinente* (*The Curious Impertinent*), however, transpires for the most part inside. Windows to the outside are
mostly missing, subtly creating a forbidding space, one where the
inside is no longer safe, that closes in on the inhabitants as if they
were locked in a gothic and nightmarish space.[23] Sensing danger, the
characters are trapped, never knowing what their passions will dictate and how they will hide or fulfil their desires. The place of home
is transformed into a space of danger. The home becomes something
akin to what David Spurr calls the "demonic spaces" in modern literature where the "instinctual violence of human passion […] require[s] a
space of secrecy to be fully unleashed" (2012, 75). More than that, this
secret space seems ghostly. As characters move about inside the home,
it is almost impossible to discern its inner structure. We are told very
little of its rooms, its doors, and its windows. One space is key: the
dining table where Anselmo, Camila, and Lotario often sit together, in
twos or alone. If characters come in or leave the house, we are never
shown a door. If Florence actually exists outside the walls of the home,
we are never made aware of the cityscape and its famous buildings –
there is not a single description of the city. Illustrators are blind to this
absence and often add such views. Tony Johannot, for example, shows
a panorama of the city with views that include the Duomo, the Palazzo
della Segnoria, and the Ponte Vecchio (see figure 4.2).[24]

The closest we come to viewing the city in Cervantes' tale is in Lotario's admonition that the wife must be guarded at all times: "porque lo
que no se hace ni concierta en las plazas ni en los templos, ni en las fiestas públicas, ni estaciones – cosas que no todas veces las han de negar
los maridos a sus mujeres – se concierta y facilita en casa de la amiga o
la parienta de quien más satisfación se tiene." ("For that which cannot
be done, nor concerted, in the markets, at churches, at public shows, or
assemblies (things, which husbands must not always deny their wives)
may be concerted and brought about at the house of a female friend or
relation, of whom we are most secure"; Cervantes 1978, 1.33.401; 2008,
280.) This suspicion as to what a woman may do triggers the impetus
to enclose women so that men may have greater control over her space.
Nerea Aresti, for example, argues that "[t]he Counter-Reformation in
Spain fostered an intolerant attitude towards any gender deviations,
increased control over women and encouraged their sequestration,
symbolized by the convent" (2007, 406). And yet the convent and other
such structures create masculine anxieties because men lose control
of women in spaces that the male cannot or does not enter. Thus, the
most effective way of male control is the home. These "espacios reducidos" (limited or contained spaces), a term coined by Valbuena Briones
around the middle of the twentieth century, are spaces better suited

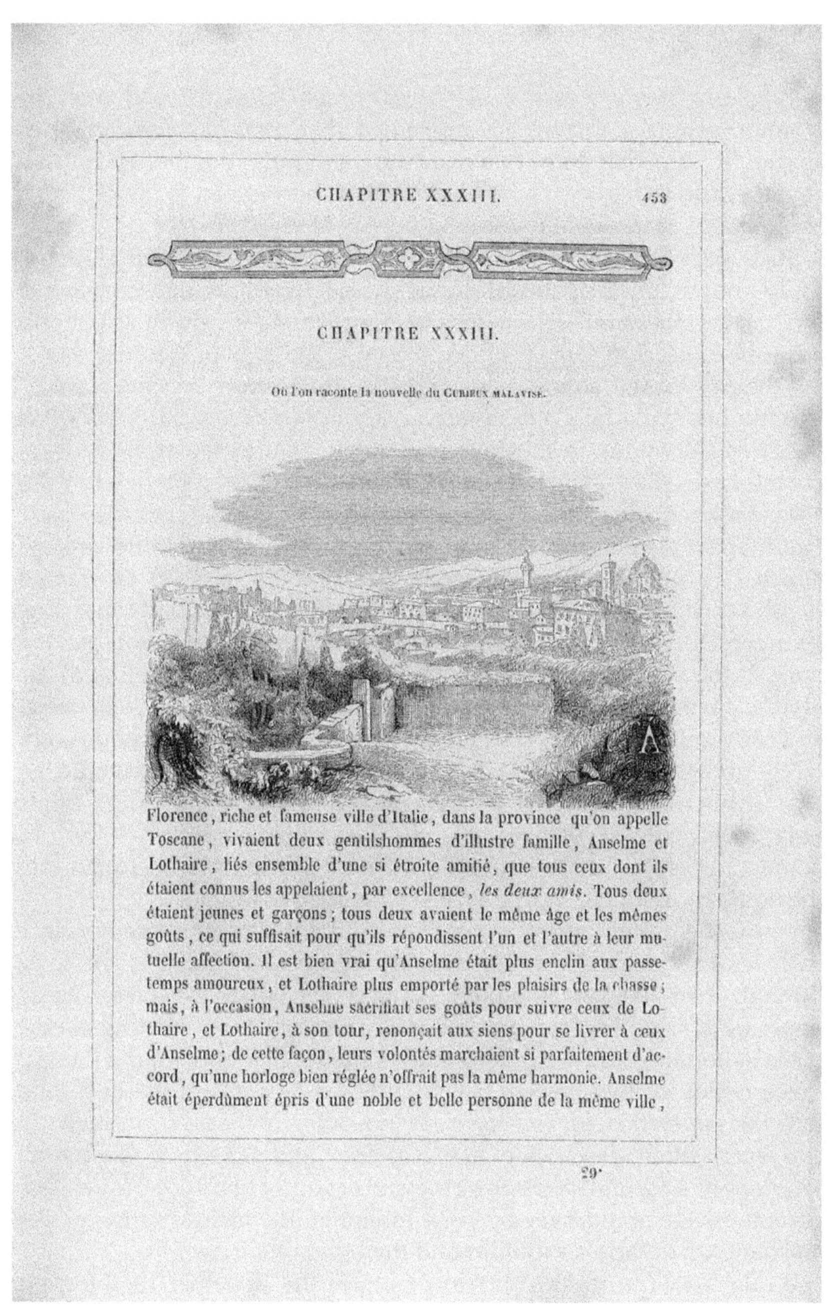

Figure 4.2. Tony Johannot, *El curioso impertinente,* in *L'ingénieux hidalgo Don Quichotte de la Manche,* 1836. Cushing Library Rare Books/Texas A&M University Libraries

for vigilance because parents, siblings, or husbands can watch over the woman.[25] Henri Lefebvre has explained that men have created such spaces "to establish dominion over it by assigning it a limited portion of space, and to reduce it to a 'femininity' subordinated to the principle of maleness, of masculinity or manliness" (1991, 377).

Such enclosed spaces, however, may seem out of place in Florence, a city known for its open vistas and spaces. Even Cervantes, in one of the *Novelas ejemplares*, *El licenciado Vidriera* (The Glass graduate), shows how one of his characters is quite pleased at the sight of Florence, praising the city for its "sumptuosos edificios, fresco río y apacibles calles" (sumptuous buildings, pleasant river, agreeable streets; 2015, 317). It is thus that Cervantes, in this tale, must write against the grain. Most of the tale takes place inside Anselmo's home, which seems a far cry from a Renaissance villa; only once are tapestries mentioned, but they have a utilitarian purpose rather than an artistic one. And a table, around which two or three of the characters sit, could suggest the famed Renaissance banquet, "a sign of perfect fulfillment" of body and soul (Jeanneret 1991, 15). However, this table intrudes in the action, having none of the splendour of a Renaissance banquet and much less of the mythical banquet of Cupid and Psyche. Lotario, Anselmo's best friend and constant companion, decides that he will only enter the home very rarely and then in the company of Anselmo, given that it would go against his friend's honour to spend much time with the bride. While Lotario seems to go beyond all sane counsel in avoiding his friend's home, thus espousing an extreme stance, Anselmo lures his friend into the home by demanding that he test Camila's faithfulness.

It is as if Anselmo were finding two different ways to share his place with his friend: first, through the testing and, secondly, if she fails, through their renewed intimacy because she would no longer be an issue. Both would have shared her in some manner, creating a new place of bonding. The situation seems a logical extension of the Renaissance notion of two perfect friends who always desire the best (and thus the same). It is, for some, a clear indication of the homosocial bond and even latent desire between Anselmo and Lotario.[26] Illustrators often show Anselmo as the desiring subject and Lotario as the desired, as in an image of intimacy by Tony Johannot in which Anselmo places one hand on Lotario's shoulder and the other on his arm.[27]

While Anselmo wishes to show Lotario that together they form a place, a locus of happiness, Lotario protests that Camila is herself a perfect place, so sacred that it cannot be sullied: she is a relic in a church and thus should be adored; she is a garden with beautiful flowers that should not be trampled upon (Cervantes 1978, 1.33.409; 2008, 287).

But Anselmo will view her as a dangerous space unless his best friend assures him of her faithfulness and thus of her place with him. Place as safety and comfort does not just belong to a particular site but can be created by sentiment. Just as Anselmo and Lotario had once elaborated place out of their friendship, now Anselmo challenges his friend to show him Camila as either space or place.

The house, which was to be the inviolable home of the married couple, loses what Bachelard calls its "protected intimacy" (1994, 3). The destructive passions unleashed in the house ricochet with verbal duels that bounce unexpectedly this way or that from its walls. Skipping questions, sensing danger, the characters are trapped, never knowing what their passions will dictate and how they will hide their desires. Rather than exhibiting a series of beautiful objects for the couple's pleasure, the house seems sadly empty, particularly of the feeling of love. It slowly acquires a kind of ominous atmosphere. According to the Finnish architect Juhani Pallasmaa, "[t]he ambiance or atmosphere of a room or an urban space is the overall feeling and tuning of the experience. It is a non-material or peripheral experience (a 'quasi-thing,' as Tonino Griffero calls the phenomenon) that tunes our minds in a specific way. We feel atmospheres immediately and without being conscious of the process" (Amudsen 2018). When we turn to a literary text, it takes more than just arriving at a page. Atmosphere can be built in one sentence, one paragraph, or a longer passage. It has to do with the very structuring of the room or the building, the adjectives that describe it, the images that surround it, the solidity or fragility of the structure, and how much it appears as a finished product or a ghostly site. And, of course, atmosphere goes beyond the architecture of the site to deal with human interaction, objects, the presence or absence of sounds, the uses of the senses, and so much more. Atmosphere is a feeling that, once created, clings to the walls, a "thing" that in the case of *El curioso* becomes paradoxically embodied in the ghost.

Once the testing of Camila starts, the action takes place around the dining table, and during Anselmo's first absence Camila invites Lotario to repose in her "estrado" (Cervantes 1978, 1.33.413; 2008, 291–2). This is a private site for the women in the houses of the period, in which cushions were used for rest and leisure, and women entertained other women. In a study on María de Zayas, Javier Irigoyen foregrounds the importance of the *estrado* as influenced by Moorish customs: "Ahora bien, a pesar de su plena integración en la cultura española, persiste una asociación de este espacio como propio de 'lo moro,' especialmente en textos literarios, asociación con la que Zayas parece jugar de forma consciente." (However, in spite of its full integration into Spanish culture, the association of this space with "Moorishness" persisted, in particular in literary texts, an association that Zayas clearly utilizes; 2016, 364.) In Cervantes, although it is never described, we can think of it as a symbolic space. When Camila invites Lotario to rest in her private spaces, she could be revealing a hidden desire and even an excessive and orientalized want. Curiously, Lotario had accused Anselmo of behaving like a Moor. Thus, this Italian abode takes on orientalized traits, a site in which a multitude of passions can be displayed.

In addition, the art objects of the city are infused into Camila, who in her hermetic silence becomes "una estatua de mármol" (a statue of marble; Cervantes 1978, 1.33.417; 2008, 295) that entrances Lotario as they sit in the closed-in home in a duel of silence and daring while Anselmo is away.[28] And Anselmo, who could be thought of as forming a "place" with his friend Lotario, begins to suspect him, not of adultery but of not testing his wife properly. Pretending to leave, he hides in one of the rooms of this ill-defined home and spies on them: "se encerró en un aposento y por los agujeros de la cerradura estuvo mirando y escuchando lo que los dos trataban" (shut himself up in an adjoining chamber, and stood looking and listening through the keyhole, how they behaved themselves; 1978, 1.33.414; 2008, 293). Once again, in this phantom house few things materialize. We know that the room in which Anselmo hides must be adjacent to where Lotario and Camila are sitting, that is, at the table, but it is very difficult to imagine the architectural plan of the house. In addition, the door to this room is not even mentioned. There is only a description of the hole in the key lock through which he can see. Thus, the phantom door is unimportant, while the lock becomes crucial, pointing to Anselmo's tunnel vision. He wants to see his wife tested, no matter the consequences.

Anselmo then admonishes Lotario, and the friend decides that he must complete his task or else Anselmo, ironically, will not consider him a friend. Lotario becomes the enemy within the house, and Camila is turned into a fortress besieged (1978, 1.34.419; 2008, 296). In many ways, what we have here is one more instance of superimposed architectures, the doubling of an edifice. Within the house itself there is another fortress or castle, representing Camila. In a letter to Anselmo his friend warns him that he has left the castle unguarded: "parece mal el ejército sin general y el Castillo sin su castellano" (an army, it is commonly said, makes but an ill appearance without its general, and a castle without its governor; 1978, 1.34.418; 2008, 296). Cervantes, in many ways, is echoing and reversing previous architectures. If the jail can also be seen as a palace, here the home that encloses Camila can become a palace of pleasure, and while the inn can become a castle, a closed environment can be opened up, allowing for a human traffic that Lotario has condemned and that has transformed Camila into a castle or fortress. Battles from the outer world of danger are now inside, in a space more dangerous because it is contained. Sight arouses passion, and the art object is eventually rendered human: Camila eventually succumbs. A new balance is achieved as Anselmo mistakenly considers his wife to be faithful, his friend at home, and he now content.

It is the maid, Leonela, who is the cause of the unravelling of the many passions and deceits that circulate within the house. She reasons that although it is forbidden by Camila, she can bring her own lover to the house just as her mistress does with Lotario. Lotario sees him depart at the break of dawn. In this house haunted by desire, Lotario at first considers him to be a phantom.[29] Curiously we do not witness nor are we told how he enters the house, only that he leaves: through an open space, a window perhaps? Illustrators such as the Belgian artist René de Pauw reject the hermetic home and seek to open up the claustrophobic space (see figure 4.3).[30] But this is not in Cervantes. Lotario thinks that Camila has now taken up with someone new. She explains what happened, however, and as she convinces both Lotario and Anselmo that all is well, the home returns to some kind of equilibrium with Anselmo being happily deceived.

The interpolated tale, which takes up three chapters in *Don Quixote*, would seem to be a hermetic section in itself, never touching the main text. Yet, close to its end, and after the first secret opening into the outside has been discovered by Lotario, the text itself also opens up onto the main narrative. The priest stops his reading when Sancho dashes in asking for help because his master, Don Quixote, is fighting a giant. No one is surprised to learn that the knight has confused wine-skins for giants, as the innkeeper's supplies dwindle with every knife-thrust. Such a curious slash within the narrative, stopping the hermetic tale, actually reinforces the hermetic because the battle derives from Apuleius' *Golden Ass*, often considered a hermetic text, that is, one related to the mysterious Hermes Trismegistus.

Two strands come together. As an interpolated tale based on a myth of Cupid and Psyche within Apuleius' *Golden Ass*, *El curioso impertinente* acquires a hermetic flavour pointing to the hermetic tradition, a mode of thought based on the writings of the Egyptian priest Hermes Trismegistus. After all, Apuleius was said to have translated the hermetic *Asclepius*, and his novel ends with rites to Osiris and Isis. In order to link the hermetic interpolation with the main tale, Quixote's battle is actually an imitation of a scene in Apuleius' novel in which Lucius, coming home one night, battles three wine-skins that he describes as

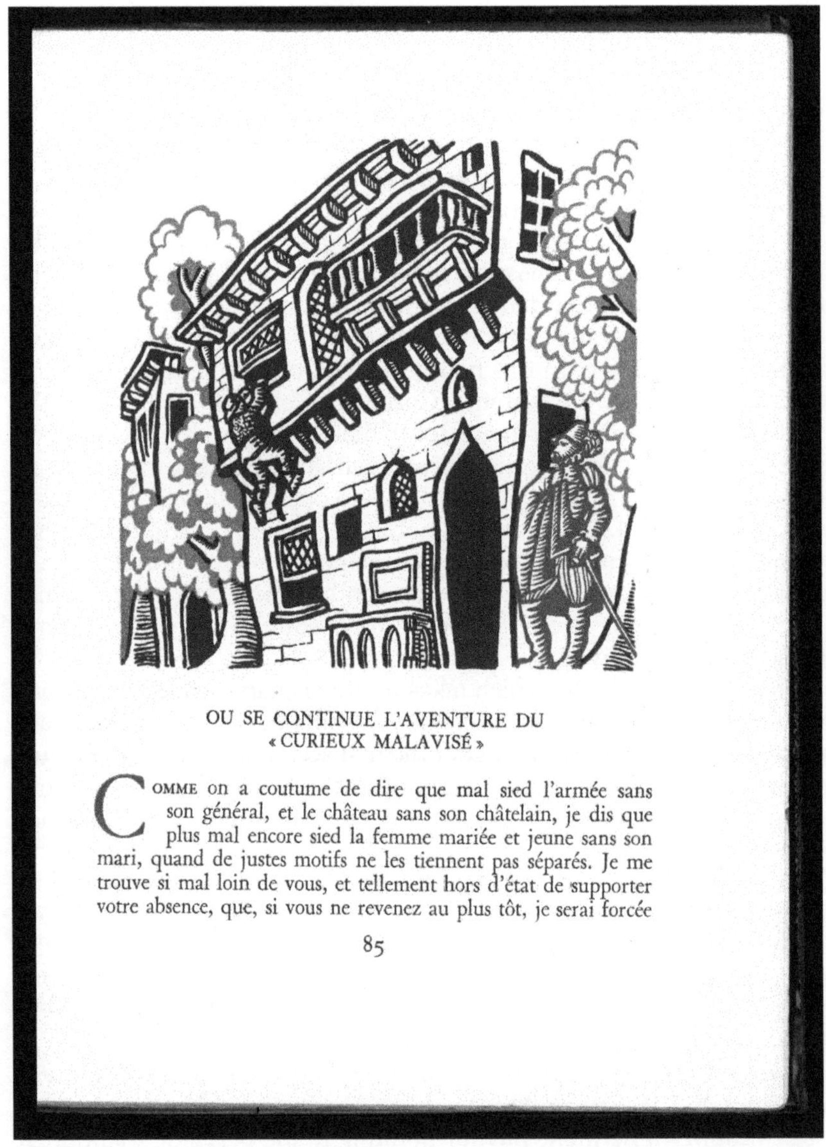

Figure 4.3. René de Pauw, *Lotario Observes a Man Coming Out of Anselmo's House*, in *L'ingénieux hidalgo Don Quichotte de la Manche*, 1947. Cushing Library Rare Books/Texas A&M University Libraries

giants (Scobie 1976, 75). Both Lucius and Quixote see themselves as heroes, but, not seeing correctly, they trigger laughter instead with their actions. In the tale of Cupid and Psyche and in Cervantes' *Curioso impertinente*, however, curiosity and the intuiting of what should remain invisible, be it a god or a secret passion, bring about great suffering (De Armas 2006, 193).

Once the wine-skins episode has ended and we return to the interpolated tale, it is Anselmo who now sees a man escape his solitary and hermetic home. This time we know that the escape takes place through a window.[31] The isolated reference to a window in Anselmo's home also serves to increase both the darkness inside and the hermetic ambience.[32] We still do not know the point of entrance, only how Leonela's lover departs. This double scene of leaving, witnessed first by Lotario and then by Anselmo, also points to the home as being the space of danger, a hermetically sealed abode that is ruled by a trickster god. We have come to the point at which all must leave it or die. Slowly, surprisingly, eerily, a few objects in the house seem to materialize but only to show Anselmo that something is amiss: "Acertó acaso, andando a buscar a Camila, que vio sus cofres abiertos y que dellos faltaban las más de sus joyas" (It accidentally happened, as he was searching for Camilla, that he found her cabinet open, and most of her jewels gone; Cervantes 1978, 1.35.443; 2008, 319). Anselmo had locked Leonela in a room, expecting her full confession in the morning. Hers is the most daring escape. Looking for her, Anselmo finds "unas sábanas anudadas a la ventana, indicio y señal que por allí se había descolgado e ido" (the sheets tied to the window, an evident sign that by them she had slid down, and was gone off; 1978, 1.35.443; 2008, 318–19). Now without a wife, without his best friend, and without servants, Anselmo locks the doors of the house and leaves. This is the first time that the narrative mentions the doors. Locked, the house once again becomes a ghostly habitation, the rumours of the passions unleashed there and the fate of its tragic inhabitants being reminders of its menacing presence. The window that shows nothing becomes a metonymy for the blindness of passion and for the inability to see beyond this evanescent space, a hermetic site, a container of its own dangers.

All four will perish in different spaces, as if the curse of this house haunted by desire still pursued them. Yet, even as they flee, no description of the city is to be found.[33] It is a tribute to Cervantes' consummate artistry and irony that this secret and dark architecture is placed among the brilliant sites of Florence, thus interpolating a hermetic phantom-like and tragic space into the midst of a space of openness, art, and beauty.

Of Windows and Fortresses

Not long after the telling of *El curioso impertinente*, other guests come to the inn, triggering a series of anagnorisis and the conclusion of the tales of Cardenio and Luscinda and Fernando and Dorotea. As if these many threads of storytelling were not enough, a woman, with a turban on her head and her face veiled (that is, a Moorish lady), arrives at the inn with a man who explains that he has been a captive in Algiers. Although Moorish, she has come because she wants to convert to Christianity and no longer wants to be called Zoraida, but Maria. The former captive then tells his tale of imprisonment and liberation, being helped by and himself helping Zoriada escape. Their whole interaction began through a small window:

> Digo pues, que encima del patio de nuestra prisión caían las ventanas de la casa de un moro rico y principal, las cuales, como de ordinario son las de los moros, más eran agujeros que ventanas, y aun estas se cubrían de con celosías muy espesas y apretadas [...] Y vi que por aquellas cerradas ventanillas que he dicho parecía una caña, y al remate della puesto un lienzo atado (Cervantes 1978, 1.40.486–7)

> (But to return. The courtyard of this prison was overlooked by the windows of a house belonging to a rich Moor of distinction, which, as is usual there, were rather peep-holes than windows; and even these had their thick and close lattices [...] And saw from one of those little windows I have mentioned, a cane appear, with a handkerchief tied at the end of it.) (Cervantes 2008, 354)

The handkerchief contains gold coins, and our captive thus realizes that the lady is being charitable to him. Her gestures and her making the small sign of a cross increase the mystery of the encounter.[34] Soon thereafter, an interchange of letters begins that has to be mediated by a renegade, given that the handwriting is in Arabic.[35] This casual mention of a renegade alerts us to the importance of this figure on the Barbary Coast. As Maria Antonia Garcés reminds us, in Cervantes' times, twenty-one of the thirty-five corsair captains were renegades from such places as Genoa, Murcia, Naples, and Venice. The very governor of Algiers at the time of the tale was a Venetian renegade (2009, 545–82). In Cervantes' tale the renegade serves as a go-between in this cross-cultural love affair. At the same time, he wants to obtain letters saying that he is a "good" renegade, one who is kind to Christians and wants to return home. Just as letters are used between Zoraida and the captive, letters will be used between the renegade and the Spanish authorities, establishing a double epistolary exchange. This opens the door to multiple perspectives. Alfredo Alvar Ezquerra and Fabien Montcher have argued: "If most historians during Cervantes's life solved the fragmentation of testimonies or their absence by privileging the political truth of their writing, Cervantes used the diversity of sources as a means to critique history writing. He presented many points of view based on many sources and witnesses and ceded to his readers the power to interpret the correct use of history and the degree of fiction in his writings" (2014, 30–1).

To further invite a plurality of perspectives, Cervantes creates a series of parallels that connect an Algerian tale with Spanish interpolations.[36] As in the tale of Cardenio, the window, however small, occupies an important place in the story. Called an "agujero" (hole), it thus recalls the spike-hole used by Maritornes, instead of a window, to fool the knight into thinking that she is the daughter of the lord of the castle who wants to hold one of his beautiful hands from a window (Cervantes 1978, 1.45.527; 2008, 391). Although Maritornes fools the knight and leaves him in suspense all night, Zoraida is in earnest and wants to escape to a Christian land.

The window is central to the Algerian tale, clashing with the prison in which the Spaniards are held. While we have noted that looking into windows can allow the danger outside to penetrate into a guarded place or home, we have also noted that windows allow those inside to enjoy the freedoms of the outside without danger. In the case of Zoraida, her window, rather than looking outside, looks onto the courtyard of a prison. A double imprisonment, hers as a Muslim who wants to be Christian, and his as a Christian captive who wants to return home, create a perfect cross-space of wish-fulfilment. They both will step into the danger outside in the hopes of arriving at a place, at sailing to freedom in Iberia. The window also represents how easily space turns into place, and vice versa, as different, clashing cultures seldom share the place. The captive bemoans the Algerian prison as a space of danger and confinement, while the Moorish lady looks upon it as a danger that may lead to her happiness. Windows proliferate throughout this narrative and seem to grow in size. It is as if the narrative called for a comparison between Spanish and Algerian windows as a liminal space or place from which women could yearn for freedom. As they are set to escape, the renegade and the captive arrive at Agi Morato's garden where "[e]staba la bellisima Zoraida aguardándonos a una ventana" (The lovely Zoraida was expecting us at a window; 1978, 1.41.501; 2008, 368). This is a moment of expansiveness and hope, in which the window onto the garden calls for the beauties of Spain. But just as this window inspires hope, it later arouses dread. Her father awoke "y sintiese el ruido que andaba en el jardín; y asomándose a la ventana, luego conoció que todos los que en él estaban eran cristianos" (and, hearing a noise in the garden, looked out the window, and presently found that there were Christians in it; 1978, 1.41.502; 2008, 369). Throughout the tale, then, windows serve as ways to look at another's culture, whether with love and desire or dread and hatred.

We have glanced at the window that overlooks the prison, but there is yet another building that frames the narrative. At the beginning of the story Ruy Pérez de Viedma tells how he was made captive at the battle of Lepanto, "con cadenas a los pies y esposas a las manos" (with chains on my feet, and manacles on my hands; 1978, 1.39.477; 2008, 347), and how he had to serve the enemy for years hence. While the main story is one of triumph, as Zoraida and the captive reach Spanish shores, the frame is far from optimistic. Marina Brownlee affirms: "Indeed, the trajectory posited by the Captive (from Lepanto to Navarino to La Goleta) points to Spain's decline as a military power" (2005, 570). Emperor Charles V had conquered Tunis in 1535 and placed it in the hands of a pliable vassal dynasty of the Hafsid. Although Lepanto some thirty years later would help to cement European control of the Mediterranean, it would not last long. Tunis changed hands, going first to the Algerians and then to the Spanish. But in 1574 Selim II brought a large Ottoman force, with close to three hundred vessels backed by troops from Algeria and Tripoli. At the battle of La Goleta all was lost. Cervantes describes the defeat in great detail, including the following lines:

> Perdióse en fin, la Goleta; perdióse el fuerte, sobre las cuales plazas hubo de soldados turcos, pagados, setenta y cinco mil […] Fue común opinión que no se habían de encerrar los nuestro en la Goleta sino esperar en campaña […] porque si en la Goleta y en el fuerte apenas había siete mil soldados ¿cómo podía tan poco número aunque más esforzados fuesen, salir a la campaña y quedar en las fuerzas, con tanto como era el de los enemigos? (Cervantes 1978, 1.39.480)

> (In short, the Goleta was lost, and the fort also; before which places the Turks had seventy-five thousand men in pay […] It was the general opinion that our troops ought not to have shut themselves up in the Goleta, but have met the enemy in the open field […] For if there were scarce seven thousand soldiers in the Goleta and in the fort, how could so small

a number, though ever so resolute, both take the field and garrison the forts against such a multitude as that of the enemy?) (Cervantes 2008, 349)

There is no better contrastive opposition. The tale tells of seven thousand men slaughtered as they sought the security of place, of the inside, as they were faced with a dreaded danger outside. Although the captive is liberated, the Spanish soldiers are slaughtered. The story is then created with a double focus, with an elliptical shape, and, as we recall from the discussion in the introductory chapter, this geometrical figure, symbol of the baroque, has two centres, one that stands out and one that is shaded. The brief defeat of the Spanish is followed by the lengthy and delightful tale of the captive's liberation. It is as if the second, lengthier part, with its many windows, seeks to dispel the claustrophobia of the slaughter inside. Two poems follow the fall of La Goleta. Stephen Rupp explains: "The terms 'wall' and 'sword' (in Spanish 'hierro' iron) describe by metonymy the circumstances of the assault, standing respectively for the defensive works at the fort of La Goleta and the weapons of the Ottoman invaders. These lines evoke the difficult situation of soldiers trapped between their own fortification and the enemy's weapons, but they achieve this effect through a technique of displacement, attributing violence to instruments of assault and defense rather than to human agency" (2014, 131).

Through metonymy the work once again attempts to diffuse the horrors of claustrophobia, of an enclosed place. But neither windows nor rhetorical devices can fully erase the shadowing of the story and of Spanish imperial history. If anything illumines the space of dread, it is the vision of the human body as an architecture that is in itself a prison. The first quartet of the first sonnet reads: "Almas dichosas que del mortal velo / libres y esentas por el bien que obrastes, / desta la baja tierra os levantastes / a lo más alto y lo mejor del cielo." (Oh happy souls, by death at length set free / From the dark prison of mortality, / By glorious deeds, whose memory never dies / From earth's dim spot exalted to the skies!; Cervantes 1978, 1.40.483; 2008, 351) To the pessimism of a moment in history, of prisons and claustrophobic fortresses, Cervantes adds two elements of hope: the life beyond the body's impermanent architecture, and the windows as a way to look at other cultures.

Facing Windows

We will leave out a rather singular architecture that is described in the "Captive's Tale," and we will stay closer to home, turning to a tale that also takes us on an epic journey to a faraway land where the gods demand a sacrifice. At the inn, listening to the sweet songs of a muleteer, Dorotea, who is lying awake next to Clara, wakes her up. Clara confesses that the songs are addressed to her and then goes on to tell the story, which we might call the tale of facing windows. Clara, before departing with her father, Juan Pérez de Viedma, a judge who was to take an important post in America, lived with him at the court in Madrid. Of the house we know very little except for the detailed description of some windows: "y aunque mi padre tenía las ventanas de su casa los lienzos en el invierno y celosías en el verano, yo no sé lo que fue ni lo que no, que este caballero, que andaba al estudio, me vio ni sé si en la iglesia o en otra parte" (And though my father kept his windows with canvas in the winter, and lattices in summer, I know not how it happened, that this young gentleman, who then went to school, saw me; nor can I tell whether it was at church or elsewhere; Cervantes 1978, 1.43.524; 2008, 389). The reader is left to wonder where the young man saw her. Although Clara denies that he could have seen her at home due to her father's care in keeping the windows closed all year, it is possible that she is an unreliable narrator and is not telling the full truth. The home may represent safety, but it is also confinement. That she may have opened one of them is certainly a possibility, particularly because he lived across the street. Clara goes on to explain: "finalmente, él se enamoró de mí y me dio a entender desde las ventanas de su casa con tantas señas y con tantas lágrimas, que yo hube de creer, y aun querer" (but, in short, he fell in love with me, and gave me to understand his passion from the windows of his house, by so many signs, and so many tears, that I was forced to believe, and even to love him; 1978, 1.43.524; 2008, 389). No other details are narrated regarding the young man's home. Through the windows in her home she fell in love with him: "cuando estaba mi padre fuera de casa y el suyo también, alzar un poco el lienzo o la celosía y dejarme ver toda" (when his father and mine were both abroad, to liftup the canvas, or lattice window, and gave him a full view of me; 1978, 1.43.524; 2008, 389). If we follow Vitruvius, windows characterize the setting of comic plays, not tragic ones (1960, 150), thus we would expect a happy resolution. Given that through these windows the two see each other, these architectural elements also point to the eyes through which bodies perceive. This doubling of perception, albeit indicating a comic action, will later take on an ominous turn and cast this tale of airy and hopeful young love into something approaching a tale of tragedy.

The separation of the lovers intensifies when Clara's father takes her on his journey to the New World. But Luis will not stay behind as they travel from the court to the coast. He follows, disguised as a muleteer. Appearing at the inn, he sings to her of Palinurus:

> — Marinero soy de amor
> y en su piélago profundo
> navego sin esperanza
> de llegar a puerto alguno.
> Siguiendo voy a una estrella
> que desde lejos descubro,
> más bella y resplandeciente
> que cuantas vio Palinuro. (Cervantes 1978, 1.43.521).
> ('A Mariner I am of love,
> And in his seas profound,
> Toss'd betwixt doubts and fears, I rove,
> And see no port around.
> 'At distance I behold a star,
> Whose beams my senses draw,
> Brighter and more resplendent far
> Than Palinure e'er saw.') (Cervantes 2008, 386–7)

The crazed knight transforms inns into castles, Lotario transforms a woman within the house into a fortress, and here Luis describes his pursuit of Clara as that of Aeneas' helmsman who follows the stars and constellations to stay on course. And yet, Palinurus was cursed by Neptune and was not able continue his journey, falling asleep, falling from the vessel, and being killed in a foreign land. It seems as if Luis succeeded in reversing one of the elements: in spite of falling asleep in the tale, the Spanish Palinurus actually wakes up his beloved. But the poem is sufficiently hermetic as to hide its prophetic intent, and the inn is a liminal place as travellers go to and fro. Inns bring together space and place, danger and safety. His love, it seems, is not to be. Four servants sent by his father catch up with him there. Although he would die rather than return home, a solution is reached, while Clara travels on. The place promised by the double windows of desire and perception has come to naught. What Luis sees as an epic journey ends with his demise in the sense that he may never see Clara again. Treacherous fortune mocks him in the image of Don Quixote. The knight is tricked by Maritornes (pretending to be his princess) into giving her his hand through a hole or window at the inn. To do so, the knight has to stand on top of Rocinante. Binding his hand, Maritornes leaves him to spend the night in this impossible position. Clara must also leave, and Luis is left with an image of windows as dangerous and deceiving spaces.

Window as Teichoskopia

As discussed in the previous chapter, towards the end of the novel Don Quixote is taken home in an "enchanted" chariot, or so he thinks, and accompanied by the barber, the priest, the canon of Toledo, and his faithful squire, Sancho. The company, while taking a meal, witnesses a goatherd chasing a she-goat and speaking to her in curious language, as if she were able to understand him. Standing before the curious company, the goatherd asks for a "breve espacio" (*brief space*; 1978, 1.50.589; 2008, 445) to tell his tale. The space of the tale is as curious as that of *El curioso impertinente*, for it seems to interrupt for no purpose the monotony of the slow road home. Up to this point, as Don Quixote rides a chariot pulled by slow oxen, the reader has been relishing the conversations between the knight and the canon. The tale, as Raymond Immerwahr explained long ago, is the seventh and last of the interpolated stories in the 1605 novel.[37] As such, it has important thematic and structural elements that connect it with the others. Don Quixote is certainly willing to grant the goatherd such a space "[p]or ver que tiene este caso un no sé qué de sombra de aventura de caballería" (Seeing this business has somewhat the face of an adventure; 1978, 1.50.589; 2008, 445). Chapter 51 is dedicated to the tale of Eugenio,[38] the spurned lover who vents his frustrations on the goat.

Eugenio tells of the beauty of a rich and honourable villager's daughter Leandra: "La fama de su belleza se comenzó a extender por todas las circunvecinas aldeas, ¿qué digo yo por las circunvecinas no más, si se extendió a las apartadas ciudades y aun se entró en las salas de los reyes [...] que como a cosa rara o como a imagen de milagros de todas partes a verla venían?" (And now the fame of her beauty began to extend itself through all the neighbouring villages: do I say, through the neighbouring villages only? It spread itself to the remotest cities, and even made its way into the palaces of kings [...] who came to see her from all parts, as if she had been some relic, or wonder-working image; 1978, 1.51.591; 2008, 446.) Leandra's reputation, albeit of rustic origins, resembles that of many princesses of the romances, in which knights come from all over to gaze upon their beauty – as in the *Partinuplés* as well as in the play by Ana Caro based on this romance.[39] There are even princesses like Niquea, who is kept in a tower because her immense beauty can kill enamoured knights (Laspuertas Sarvisé 2000, 83). Cervantes' tale parodies such romances. Content with neither Eugenio nor Anselmo, her village suitors from a young age, nor with the foreigners who come to view her beauty, Leandra wiles away her time observing passers-by from a window in her home.

One of the many who come to town, but in this case not because of her, is Vicente de la Roca, the son of an impoverished farmer. He has served in the wars in Italy and now returns, dressed in flashy clothes. Seated in the town's main square, he regales his audience with unbelievable tales of faraway lands: "No había tierra en todo el orbe que no hubiese visto, ni batalla donde no se hubiese hallado; había muerto más moros que tiene Marruecos y Túnez" (There was no country on the whole globe he had not seen, nor battle he had not been in. He had slain more Moors than are in Morocco and Tunis; Cervantes 1978, 1.51.592; 2008, 448). Musician, poet, soldier and mostly a *miles gloriosus*, this newly arrived figure is a boasting charlatan who inflates his deeds and craves admiration.[40] Leandra gazes at him repeatedly from a window: "fue visto y mirado muchas veces de Leandra desde una ventana de su casa que tenía la vista a la plaza" (he was often seen and admired by Leandra from a window of her house which faced the market-place; 1978, 1.51.593; 2008, 448). The window is often seen as a woman's privileged site because she can gaze from the safety of her realm, that of the home, on the danger outside. In most representations the woman remains inside. Yi-Fu Tuan reminds us that looking out, we can see open space that "suggests adventure but it also entails risk" (2014). Cervantes transforms woman's role and the function of the window, having Leandra, who is desirous of adventure, fall in love and escape the home with Vicente. In many ways she becomes a quixotic figure who paints what she sees with more attractive colours. She sees none of Vicente's foibles, only his flashy dress. She is also drawn by his music and his many tales and conceives of a world akin to the romances of chivalry.

The romances of chivalry often allude to the epic, and references to Helen of Troy are plentiful.[41] Don Quixote, as reader of romances, mimics these references and early in the novel compares his Dulcinea to Helen: "píntola en mi imaginación como la deseo, así en la belleza como en la principalidad, y ni la llega Elena, ni la alcanza Lucrecia" (I represent her to my thoughts just as I wish her to be both in beauty and quality. Helen is not comparable to her, nor is she excelled by Lucretia; Cervantes 1978, 1.25.314; 2008, 203).[42] I would argue that in Leandra's tale the romances and the Homeric epics come together in the representation of a woman who is exceptionally beautiful and desired by many – in other words, a rustic Helen of Troy. Furthermore, the scene of Leandra gazing down at the plaza seeks to parody the famous moment in which Helen comes to the battlements at Troy. What Leandra sees through the window may be an idealized scene, a quixotic ekphrasis, but her very actions impel the reader to paint over her figure and her gaze and recall Helen's famous teichoskopia. The term *teichoskopia*, or "view from the wall," is, as Norman Austin asserts, "the *locus classicus* for the traditional Helen portrait" (1994, 17). It derives from the famous passage in the third book of the *Iliad* in which Helen comes to the walls of Troy to view the deadly contest between Greeks and Trojans that began with her abduction by Paris and the fury of her husband, Menelaus. Helen is sent to the city walls at a time that she is weaving "many battles of the horse-taming Trojans and the brazen-coated Achaeans" (Homer 1988, bk. 3.125–7). Thus, ekphrasis (the tapestry) and teichoskopia are closely allied. Here, Cervantes, who had already used teichoskopia and ekphrasis in the tale of Marcela, conjoins them again, while parodying the literary devices and those that are portrayed therein (De Armas 2008, 83–102). In other words, the first and last tales of the novel present a woman standing above, gazing at the men below.

Like Helen, Leandra is famed for her beauty; like Helen, Leandra looks down from above; like Helen, Leandra sees a handsome warrior. Helen sees the two men in her life, her husband and her abductor, at war with each other, and Leandra sees in Vicente de la Roca a future husband, one whom she encourages to abduct her. Different versions of the Helen story praise or blame her, telling that she was abducted by force or that she willingly departed with Paris, but here Leandra wants to escape with Vicente. Of course, Leandra is no Helen of Troy but a rustic of some beauty, which the narrative hyperbolically links to the princesses of the epic and romances. And as we have seen, Vicente is no great warrior but a boastful and arrogant soldier. These characters and their actions are raised by epic echoes and chivalric memories, only to be brought down by parody and their own folly.

Five key windows in the first part of Cervantes' *Don Quixote* have exhibited scenes of treachery and mendacity, of faithlessness and deception, of young love and tragic futures. These windows seem to have little to do with a knight who fails to imagine the wondrous architectures of an empire he would revive. And yet, as we see through these architectural devices echoes of chivalric and epic genres, we wonder how they affect the knight's world. While windows are liminal spaces that often separate place and space, the inside and the outside, in the interpolated tales of Cervantes' novel windows seem to announce danger, whether the character stands inside or outside. Cervantes composes a daring ekphrasis as Cardenio and Fernando look into Luscinda's room, which he adorns with orientalist images and chivalric loves. The threatening outside, fostered by her loved one, seeps into Luscinda's home, fomenting doom. Anselmo's phantom-like home, which will be closed under lock and key at the end of the story, remaining forever empty, looms over, like an enchanted castle, like a haunted house, the amorous narratives in part one of the novel. Anselmo's abode has never shown the beauties of the outside, its evanescent windows being markers of illusion and doom. Inside, Anselmo's impertinent curiosity and his blindness at its consequences arouse feverish passions. They ricochet off the walls, trapping its inhabitants in a place of epic tension and chivalric marvel. The anxieties, passions, and shadows of Anselmo's abode seem to cascade over other interpolated tales, as its hermetic ambience spills over Zoraida's home, which overlooks a jail populated by captives; it also spills over windows and balconies of love that lead to a mournful separation.

Placid and devoted passions are evoked by two windows, one in Clara's and the other in Luis' home at court. An impending voyage to the Indies obstructs the affair, as Luis becomes an epic oarsman who follows his star. But this very metaphor suggests doom, in a tale that lacks an ending, inviting us to peer through the window into the future. A fifth window, through which a woman looks onto the outside, may seem to "normalize" the roles of this architectural device. Instead, it turns into a parodic teichoskopia in which a new Helen gazes upon a warrior whose treachery will mark her forever. These windows elevate the novel with epic and chivalric textuality, while darkening the spaces the knight must tread with ominous tales that rewrite and refuse future glory. Even in amorous domesticity the windows of empire are closing.[43]

5 Grotesque: Vying with Vitruvius; *Don Quixote*, Part 2

We now have fresco paintings of monstrosities, rather than truthful representations of definite things. For instance, reeds are put in the place of columns, fluted appendages with curly leaves and volutes, instead of pediments, candelabra supporting representations of shrines and on top of their pediments numerous tender stalks and volutes growing up from the roots and having human figures senselessly seated upon them [...] Yet when people see these frauds, they find no fault with them but on the contrary are delighted, and do not care whether any of them can exist or not. Their understanding is darkened by decadent critical principles.

Vitruvius, The Ten Books on Architecture (7.5)

In part 1 of *Don Quixote* the architectures related to the adventures of the knight are diminished, hidden, or turned anthropomorphic as in the case of the windmills; they appear surprisingly in the interpolated tales. In the second part, of 1615, such is not the case. Interpolations are transformed into conversations and anecdotes with allusions to architecture. At the same time, the text follows Don Quixote's and Sancho's adventures, exhibiting a number of structures, some of which stand against any kind of eurithmia as envisioned by Vitruvius; they appear as grotesque, composite, impossible, or devilish. They exceed the games of metamorphic superimposition found in the first part. I have chosen ten architectures for our viewing. Six will be discussed in this chapter, and the remaining four in chapter 6. This chapter begins by foregrounding the architectures of the ancients, and particularly the Pantheon. Although eurithmia will later resurface in the home of the Knight of the Green Cloak, most of the architectures discussed subvert Vitruvius through the grotesque.

We will begin with the most architecturally dense chapter in the novel. It should be thus because Don Quixote is imagining his arrival at Dulcinea's palace in chapter 8. It may be no coincidence that in each of the two parts of *Don Quixote*, chapter 8 reveals particularly astounding architectures. In part 1 the windmills hid giants, or vice versa. Here, although Dulcinea's palace is a trigger for the imagination, it is Roman buildings that are foregrounded, such as the obelisk in front of Saint Peter's Basilica, and most particularly the Pantheon, home of all the gods. Indeed, this chapter discusses the only mention of the term *architecture* in Cervantes' novel. Connected to one of the most famous ancient Roman buildings, the Pantheon, the Vitruvian architecture will be briefly transformed into a space of danger, while being preserved in its solar and circular perfection. If the windmills of part 1, also circular with their moving sails (or the arms of the giants), questioned Vitruvian proportions, the Pantheon affirms them.

Moving past Dulcinea's palace, ancient buildings, and the Pantheon, the architect leads us to the trickster, Sansón Carrasco, disguised as the Knight of the Mirrors. He will be at the centre of the third and fourth sections of this chapter. He tricks the knight, claiming to have succeeded in the four labours that his lady commanded. The first labour revolves around a tower, and its analysis will constitute the third section of this chapter, "Tower." As a student of Don Quixote's adventures, Sansón was keenly aware that giants were connected to towers in part 1 of the novel, with their great height. As a trickster, he may have been spying on the knight and be cognizant of his confrontation with a palace/church in the earlier chapters of part 2. He thus erects his first edifice as an impossible addition to and ornament of a church tower. Flaunting Vitruvius' classical principles, he fabricates a giant where one should not be. The fourth section of this chapter, "Hell-Mouth," will deal with an opposing structure, the hell-mouth, yet another of Sansón Carrasco's invented adventures. The fifth structure is not so much architectural but anatomical. While alluding to Vitruvius, it will serve to immerse us even further in the realm of the grotesque. Only when Don Quixote has managed to succeed in his own adventure that rivals the hell-mouth will he be allowed to turn away from the grotesque. The lion's gaping mouth signifies both the hell-mouth and the zodiacal sign Leo, which identifies the Cabra chasm or cave as an entrance to the underworld. Accompanied by the man in the green cloak, Don Quixote enters the sixth and last architecture of this section, perhaps the most enigmatic and the one that will lead us back to the cosmic eurithmia of the Pantheon.

On the Way to Dulcinea's Palace

As Don Quixote and Sancho travel to Dulinea's palace in Toboso, they conduct a most pleasant and amusing conversation. Don Quixote imagines the galleries and loggias of aristocratic architectures, with their gardens and iron grates. There Dulcinea must be weaving tapestries. Sancho does not agree and argues that she sieves or winnows wheat, with dust flying everywhere as it did when he delivered a letter to her (Cervantes 1978, 2.8.93; 2008, 514). Being pushed beyond his abilities to comprehend this kind of Dulcinea, the knight tells Sancho to remember some verses from Garcilaso's *Third Eclogue* in which nymphs abide in crystal mansions under the river Tagus (1978, 2.8.94; 2008, 515). If Sancho did not see her in a magnificent palace, then enchanters must have transformed his vision. The conversation briefly detours to questions of envy, to which Sancho replies that he does not care what others say of him in the book in which their adventures are recounted. At the same time, the knight's repeated mentions of this allegorical figure recall the famous abode of Envy, found in Ovid's *Metamorphoses* (2.768–82). Entering this "filthy slimy shack" and "gruesome sunless hovel," one can find her "eating viper's flesh." She is the opposite of the knight's imaginings of Dulcinea: "Her cheeks are sallow, her whole body shrunk. / Her eyes askew and squinting; black decay / Befouls her teeth, her bosom's green with bile." Reinforced with words for seeing, this passage creates an architecture and a bodily architecture that oppose Dulcinea and her palace. As Invidia, she looks into things to discover what is foul. Sancho fails to understand this second architecture and the knight's not so subtle recriminations. Since the squire expresses indifference to others' opinions, the conversation slowly turns to other buildings, this time associated with antiquity and questions of fame. Perhaps in this way Don Quixote can awaken in Sancho a recollection of Dulcinea's palace.

Stories connected to two ancient buildings come up in this discussion. Don Quixote tells the tale of how Herostratus burned the Temple of Diana in Ephesus, one of the great wonders of the world. He did so in order to be remembered, to gain fame (albeit negative). Although a *damnatio memoriae* (forbidden memory) law was enacted so that no one would remember the name of Herostratus in the future, it did become known. Turning to modern times, the knight tells the tale of Emperor Charles V's visit to the Pantheon – perhaps the architecture most carefully described in the chapter.

The knight then turns to a series of heroes of the Roman Republic praised by the Augustan historian Livy; also included is Julius Caesar.[1] The third section of Cervantes' chapter begins when the knight, in an *ubi sunt* moment, asks where Julius, Augustus, and all the famous figures from the past are today. Sancho, however, is not so interested in historical subtleties; he is more interested in material structures, asking where *these* ancient figures are today. The knight replies with three examples of sepulchers that preserve a person's memory. The fourth section of Cervantes' chapter flows out from this one, as Sancho wants to know who are best remembered – saints or knights – and points to the relics of many saints, though never specifying a specific church or chapel.

Thus, a total of six major architectures are described in Cervantes' chapter 8, and in ascending order. One appears in the first section (Dulcinea's palace); two in the second (Diana's temple at Ephesus, and the Pantheon in Rome); and three in the third (the obelisk at Saint Peter's Basilica, Hadrian's tomb, which became later the Castle of Sant'Angelo, and the Mausoleum in which Artemisia buried her husband).

Although it makes sense for Don Quixote and Sancho to become preoccupied with architecture as they near Dulcinea's "palace," the placement of different architectures remains a curious one. One way to interpret them is incrementally: the closer they get to the lady's imaginary palace, the more the knight wants to discuss famous buildings, as if to underline Dulcinea's palace in relation to the classical past. In a sense, what we have is a kind of Vitruvian or classical architecture as related to her palace. While the second group of buildings consists of temples and can thus serve to deify Don Quixote's beloved, the third group adds an element of disenchantment and gloom, being architectures that hold the ashes or bodies of the dead, from an obelisk to a mausoleum. The closer the pair gets to Toboso, the more the men worry about what they are going to find, Don Quixote becoming more imperious and Sancho cleverer because he knows he is about to be caught in a major lie: he never delivered a letter to Dulcinea.

There are, however, other ways to interpret some of the buildings that will allow us to understand why the Pantheon is foregrounded with the longest description. Sancho, when asking about the remains of the ancients, mistakes names for months, referring to Julius Caesar and Augustus Caesar as "Julios o Agostos" (those Julys and Augusts; 1978, 2.8.97; 2008, 517). The text foregrounds in this manner these two rulers and questions of time. If we turn to Julius Caesar, we find that he appears in sections two and three of the chapter. The first reference to Julius Caesar concerns his crossing of the Rubicon, thus underscoring that timing is of the essence in the attainment of fame. The second reference seems to allude simply to the prominent placement of Julius' ashes in an obelisk and to his continuing fame through time. This double allusion to Caesar also points to the differences in time before and after Julius' days of glory. In ancient Rome the inconspicuous yet continuous slippage of time destabilized sacred festivals. In 45 BCE,

Julius Caesar ordered a reform of the calendar because by this time the spring equinox was falling in midwinter. From then on, a new and more accurate calendar, the Julian calendar, emerged, with 365 days and a leap day every fourth February.[2] Not to be outdone, Augustus Caesar incorporated the Julian calendar in a new and wondrous monument. He had an obelisk placed in the Campus Martius to show Rome as the ruler of time (Borst 1993, 7). As Carole Newlands explains, "[t]he Horologium […] was a gigantic sundial […] The gnomon of the sundial was a tall obelisk transported from Hellenistic Egypt, surmounted by a bronze globe that symbolized world power" (1995, 23). At the autumn equinox, which happened to be Augustus' birthday, the shadow of the dial fell upon the Ara Pacis, or Altar of Peace (Everitt 2006, 273). The monument, then, showed Augustus as the architect of time, peace, and empire.

This Augustan command over time was disputed and appropriated by Renaissance popes. Obelisks were of concern to Julius II – particularly the one related to Julius Caesar. Ingrid D. Rowland explains: "The bronze ball on its summit was rumored to contain the ashes of Julius Caesar, a figure of great symbolic importance to Pope Julius" (1998, 172). However, Julius II rejected Bramante's plan to reorient the basilica towards the south so that it would face the obelisk. It was still south of Constantine's temple when Cervantes visited Rome. In 1586, more than a decade after Cervantes' visit, "Domenico Fontana, at the behest of Pope Sixtus V, managed the engineering feat, regarded by contemporaries as extraordinary, of transporting the obelisk […] to its present position in front of the basilica" (Stinger 1985, 186). Cervantes may have known that when Fontana removed the ball from the obelisk, no ashes were found inside and that the pope still went ahead and "exorcised the pagan spirits […] and consecrated the monolith to the Holy Cross" (Scotti 2006, 208).

The Pantheon

Ancient architecture, the Roman Empire, the movements of the sun, and the importance of time find their most developed moments in this chapter of *Don Quixote* in the discussion of the Pantheon. Following a historical event recounted by Prudencio de Sandoval, Don Quixote explains that Emperor Charles V wanted to see "aquel famoso templo de la Rotunda, que en la antigüedad se llamó el templo de todos los dioses, y ahora, con mejor vocación, se llama el templo de todos los santos" (the famous church of the Rotunda, which by the ancients was called the Pantheon, or temple of all the gods, and now, by a better name, the

Church of All the Saints; 1978, 2.8.95; 2008, 516). Following the inscription found in the temple, authors of the Renaissance, including Cervantes, believed that it was built by Marcus Agrippa. He was one of the great generals and architects during the time of Augustus Caesar, responsible for making Rome a more sumptuous and habitable place with new aqueducts and new porticos to embellish buildings. Although Agrippa did build the initial temple, it burned down twice and was completely rebuilt under Hadrian. It is quite probable that the circular structure was already present in the first building (Wilson Jones 2000, 177, 182). The name used by Cervantes is based on the circular structure of the main building, which was entered through a portico sustained by eight Corinthian columns and a rectangular portico. *Rotunda* was also part of the name given to the structure when it was turned into a church in the seventh century, and usually called Santa Maria Rotonda, although today its official name is Basilica di Santa Maria ad Martyres (Basilica of Saint Mary and the Martyrs). Cervantes also refers to the temple of all the gods, the meaning of the name Pantheon, and how in Christian times it was dedicated to all the saints (in reality to the martyrs, whose numerous bones from the catacombs it guarded). Cervantes is correct in calling it the best preserved building from antiquity, and this was due to its early transformation into a church and to its compactness. Don Quixote goes on to give Sancho a detailed lesson on the building, using an image that would be easy for his squire to understand: it has the shape of half an orange. Its interior is also clearly illuminated with natural light: "y está muy claro sin entrarle otra luz que la que le concede una ventana o por mejor decir, claraboya redonda que está en su cima" (and very lightsome, though it has but one window, or rather a round opening at the top; Cervantes 1978, 2.8.95; 2008, 516). The immense dome, the largest before Brunelleschi constructed his in Florence, was deeply admired, and the central oculus or opening at the very top of the dome continues to be one of the most salient characteristics of the Pantheon. Although Vitruvius praises the circle and devotes a chapter to circular temples, he seems to describe them more as an exception, rather than the rule (1960, 122–5). It is also an exception because it is dedicated to all the gods.

The site served both in antiquity and in the times of Cervantes to create wonder and admiration. Wilson Jones further explains: "At one level its function was simply to astound the Roman populace; at another it spoke of a universal cosmology, representing [...] the celestial home of the gods" (2000, 182). A number of specific elements are adduced by Wilson Jones to further buttress his notion of the building's relation to celestial cosmology: "The articulation of the ground plan according to a sixteen-part geometry recalls, as does Vitruvius' radial city plan, the sixteen-part Etruscan sky implicitly at the centre of a celestial scheme" (182). The twenty-eight parts of the coffering of the cupola refer to the lunar cycle, as mentioned by Vitruvius,[3] and the oculus is a dramatic representation of the sun: "As the sun moves across the sky, so the pool of sunlight strokes the cupola, the walls and the floor, acting as a magnet for the viewer's attention. Each day its course is different, and the effect changes too with the weather and the season" (Wilson Jones 2000, 183) (see figure 5.1).[4]

Don Quixote's description of the Pantheon is followed by a shocking anecdote. A Roman gentleman is explaining to the emperor the intricacies of the building as they observe from above. The Pantheon has two sets of stairs between the interior and exterior walls of the building, which allowed for repairs and for access to other spaces. Although today these stairs are closed to the public, the very top could only have been reached from the outside. When the emperor and the gentleman come to the skylight, Cervantes makes his only use of the term *architecture*. The gentleman is "declarándole los primores y sutilezas de aquella gran máquina y memorable arquitectura" (showing him the beauty and ingenious contrivance of that vast machine and memorable piece of architecture; Cervantes 1978, 2.8.95–6; 2008, 516). Yet, as they descend, he confesses to the emperor that he has thought many times of grabbing him and taking him down with him from the oculus so they would crash together on the ground. This would mean certain death, but it would have assured the Roman of eternal fame (albeit of a negative type).

The presence of Charles V at the Pantheon and the attack by the gentleman may serve to draw attention to a key moment in *translatio imperii* and its dangers. In ancient times the Pantheon served as a "celebration of imperial institutions" and, at least since the times of Hadrian, was used as a place where emperors held court (Wilson Jones 2000, 180). It was then a place in which to glorify emperors even before their death. Although Virgil, through Jupiter's prophecy in the *Aeneid*, proclaimed that Rome and the Roman Empire would have no boundaries in space or time, and that its rule would last forever, there came a time when the poet was proved wrong. The fall of Rome brought with it a Christian revival under Charlemagne, and later under Charles V who would rule not only the German lands but also Spain and all its possessions. It became a universal empire on which the sun never set. This new translation of empire, now seemingly centred in Madrid, and with a large population of Spaniards flocking to Rome, did not sit well with some Romans and the papacy, which had to balance Spain's rise with other rivals such as France. While the Julian obelisk pointed to a new calendar, and an Augustan

Figure 5.1. Giovanni Paulo Panini, *Interior of the Pantheon, Rome*, ca. 1734. National Gallery, Washington, DC. Open access, public domain

Horologium made Rome the ruler of time, the Pantheon became the symbolic centre of power. Charles' visit exhibited him as the new emperor of the Romans. The tensions in the transition were reflected by a Roman who wished to acquire eternal fame by bringing down the emperor.

Although this threat perhaps tarnishes and shadows the beauty of the temple of all the gods and its intricate and wondrous architecture, a contemporary architect has found in the passage yet another confirmation of the importance of the Pantheon in literature and has pointed not only to Cervantes but to descriptions from Stendhal, Henry James, and Marguerite Yourcenar. Late in his career, Spanish architect Alberto Campo Baeza was delighted to discover this ekphrastic moment from Cervantes, asserting: "He describes it so well in chapter VIII of the second part of *Don Quixote* that I have no doubt but that he was there" (2019).[5] Campo Baezas exclaims: "How many times have I written about the Pantheon in Rome? I wrote about Beauty in my inaugural speech at the Royal Academy of Fine Arts of San Fernando, on 'Relentlessly Seeking Beauty.' And I wrote 'On Intellectual Enjoyment,' in my recent farewell lesson from the School of Architecture on the occasion of my retirement. And in both speeches I spoke about the Pantheon, because in the Roman Pantheon both come together, Beauty and Intellectual Enjoyment" (2019).

If, on the one hand, we can read a political subtext in the Pantheon anecdote, I would argue that Campo Baezas comes closer to the central meaning of the building in the novel. The beauty and intellectual enjoyment that the observer draws from a visit to the Pantheon is linked, in the knight's mind, to Dulcinea's imagined palace. For him she is the most beautiful woman in the world and amazes, much like the Pantheon does with its beauty. Don Quixote extols it as the home of all the ancient deities and all the saints; Dulcinea is for him the highest deity. He merely wants to catch a glimpse of her in her palace: "que por ventanas, o por resquicios, o verjas de jardines que cualquier rayo de sol de su belleza que llegue a mis ojos alumbrará mi entendimiento y fortalecerá mi corazón" (be it through pales, through windows, through crannies, or through the rails of a garden, this I shall gain by it, that how small soever ray of the sun of her beauty reaches my eyes, it will enlighten my understanding and fortify my heart; Cervantes 1978, 2.8.93; 2008, 514–15). The solar beauty of Dulcinea is that of the Pantheon that forms new miracles of solar light every day. Her sight will light his intellect, much as the Pantheon provides the utmost intellectual enjoyment to Campo Baezas; it will also fortify the knight's heart, just as the Pantheon satisfies the architect's desire for beauty. And yet, the chapter shadows the Pantheon with the threat made by the Roman gentleman. Dulcinea is also obscured by Sancho as he points to dust and clouds – "el mucho polvo que sacaba se le puso como nube ante el rostro" (the great quantity of dust, that flew out of it, overcast her face like a cloud, and obscured it; 1978, 2.8.93; 2008, 515) – and by the knight who attributes to the enchanters his inability to see.

Let us recall that the perfected human body serves to construct the ideal architectures, the holiest and most harmonious of temples, partaking of eurithmia.[6] As Don Quixote approaches his beloved's palace, one erected in his imagination, the desiring yet tortured knight visualizes the perfection of the cosmos in her body as microcosm, and her palace as akin to the Pantheon, home of all the gods. She is the sun that rises miraculously every day to astonish him and lead him to reverie. Vitruvian perfection triumphs in this passage, even while the knight is besieged by enchanters. Don Quixote is once again gazing at the heavens, as he did at the inn in part 1, but this time with the certainty that Dulcinea stands at the centre of the cosmos. He will be her emperor, and she will provide him the courage to rule the world.

Tower

Sansón Carrasco can be regarded as Don Quixote's main antagonist in part 2, not only because he strives to defeat the mad gentleman in a knightly contest but more importantly because he seeks to deflate, mock, erase, and surpass the hidalgo's mental images of his knightly self. While in part 1 of the novel, the priest and the barber, whose impetus led to the burning of Don Quixote's books, can be seen as images of "cancel culture," in this second part Sansón Carrasco is even more insidious. A graduate of an elite university, he is convinced he knows the cultural modes that are acceptable. He picks on the knight as someone whose outmoded ideas must be countered, and, in so doing, he will eventually destroy not only Don Quixote's will but also his very sense of self. His tricks are meant to "cancel" Don Quixote. At the same time, they puff up the knight who feels as if he is finally recognized. He no longer "has to bear the weight of his ordinariness in an unjust world" (Burningham 2008, 87). Yet, this is precisely what Sansón is seeking, to show him an unjust world in which trickery reigns, and, while praising the knight, he seeks to return him to ordinariness, to cancel his figure, his ideals, his culture.

Although appearing to be his friend, Sansón becomes worse than any of the enchanters imagined by the knight. His strategy is to mimic legends, romances of chivalry, mythological tales, classical texts, and even biblical passages that had served to construct Don Quixote's persona – images that the knight guards in his memory, enabling him to imagine new adventures that exasperate, amaze, and even inspire those around him. Some argue that the knight's imagination is diminished in this second part because others regale him with ready-made chivalric scenarios in which he can participate, but he still can surprise the reader with careful descriptions of Vitruvian architectures, as in the case of the Pantheon, or with metamorphic elements and the superimposition of structures, as in the episode of the Cave of Montesinos.

The very name of the graduate from Salamanca foregrounds the struggle for ascendancy. Throughout the Middle Ages and beyond, two heroes were often pitted against each other in the popular imagination: the biblical Samson and the classical Hercules. Treatises were written on who had the greater strength and valour, and their images were placed next to each other in statuaries.[7] Since Don Quixote sees himself as Hercules, Sansón will try to deflate this notion and mock the knight's pretensions. Don Quixote, however, appears not to understand the *bachiller*'s wily attacks. He thus opens himself to very insidious challenges.

Don Quixote's desire to be a new Hercules is intimately tied to the land itself. Chronicles asserted that Hercules visited Spain, founding numerous cities such as Seville, Tarazona, Urgel, and Barcelona, and that he constructed a tower in Cádiz and another one in La Coruña. Spain was witness to two of his most famous labours: he not only stole cattle from King Geryon but had to kill this monstrous being with three heads and six legs; in addition, as Hercules was taking the cattle to Eurystheus, Cacus stole some of the animals. Although Cacus hid them in a cave, Hercules found the fire-breathing thief, killed him, and recovered the full herd of cattle. In a variation of the tale this encounter took place not in Italy but in Spain, where Cacus lived with a giant sister in a cave by Mount Moncayo. The *General Estoria* (Universal history) lists not twelve but twenty-eight labours for Hercules, and in 1417 Enrique de Villena wrote his well-known *Los doze trabajos de Hércules* (The twelve labours of Hercules), which was printed in 1483 and 1499. Attempting to trace the genealogy of Spanish kings to the heroes of antiquity, humanists of the sixteenth and seventeenth centuries most often connected them to either Hercules or Aeneas. With the advent of Charles V, the link between the Habsburgs and Hercules was sealed with the motto *Plus ultra*, an appeal to go beyond the Pillars of Hercules; the motto was first used in Spain in a heraldic painting by Juan de Borgoña that decorated Charles' seat in the choir at the cathedral in Barcelona where the king met the Order of the Golden Fleece in 1519.[8] This cult of Hercules culminated with Francisco de Zurbarán's paintings of ten of the labours of Hercules, which were executed for Philip IV at the palace of the Buen Retiro. Jonathan Brown and John H. Elliott assert that "Philip IV, following the path blazed by his great-grandfather the emperor, naturally identified himself with Hercules *Hispanicus*. In Philip's case, the association was exceptionally appropriate because Hercules, like the king, was also identified with the sun, itself another symbols of *Virtú*" (1980, 160).

Don Quixote, then, invites associations with both Hercules and the Habsburgs. While in part 1 the knight's Herculean status can survive his many defeats, in part 2 Don Quixote's self-perception is slowly unravelled. One of the main culprits in this process of demythologizing is, as stated, Sansón Carrasco. So, let us turn to the moment in which the wily graduate decides to steal from Don Quixote any of his aspirations to be Hercules: the moment in which Sansón, using his malicious wit, decides to disguise himself as a knight.[9] Among some "altos y sombrosos árboles" (lofty and shady trees; Cervantes 1978, 2.12.120; 2008, 537), Don Quixote and his squire find a place to sleep after their encounter with the Chariot of Death. The vigilant gentleman from La Mancha wakes to an unexpected sound. An unknown knight throws himself and his mighty weapons on the ground as if despairing and orders his own squire to dismount because the green grass surrounding this area would be useful to their mounts. The Knight of the Forest, the disguised Sansón, soon starts singing of his lady love. This counterfeit knight tells his equally fictitious squire that he has been ordered by his imperious lady, Casildea de Vandalia, to accomplish a series of feats akin to the twelve labours of Hercules: "Esta tal Casildea, pues, que voy contando, pagó mis buenos pensamientos y comedidos deseos con hacerme ocupar, como su madrina a Hércules, en muchos y diversos peligros, prometiéndome al fin de cada uno que en el fin del otro llegaría el de mi esperanza." (This same Casildea I am speaking of repaid my honourable thoughts and virtuous desires by employing me, as Hercules was by his stepmother, in many and various perils, promising me at the end of each of them that the next should crown my hopes; 1978, 2.14.134; 2008, 549).[10] Two of these deeds include false architectures.

The hope, in this invented tale, is to win the lady, but Sansón's real hope is to vanquish Don Quixote and become the true Hercules of the narrative. He will conquer him through the imagination and in actual battle. The episode, then, serves to foreshadow the knight's final defeat on the beach in Barcelona. The Knight of the Forest creates a false tale that follows Hercules' labours in a way that may seem as imaginative as any of Don Quixote's adventures. Indeed, his labours are as filled with Ovidian transformations as Don Quixote's adventures.[11] While Sansón stands for Hercules, Casildea might be taken as the goddess

Juno herself, or Eurystheus, whom she commanded to impose the labours upon the Greek hero.

The first "labour" that Casildea ordered the knight to perform consisted of defying "aquella famosa giganta de Sevilla llamada la Giralda, que es tan valiente y fuerte como hecha de bronce, y sin mudarse de un lugar, es la más movible y voltaria mujer del mundo" (the famous giantess of Seville, called Giralda, who is so stout and strong, as being made of brass, and, without strirring from the place, is the most changeable and unsteady woman in the world; 1978, 2.14.135; 2008, 549). By using the term *Giralda*, Sansón Carrasco is referring to the tallest tower in Europe at the time, which is even more famous than the leaning tower of Pisa. It was a composite building, thus echoing many of Cervantes' architectures. The bottom two-thirds were built by the Muslim Almohade dynasty as an *alminar* or minaret for the mosque in the twelfth century, a mighty structure worthy of Seville, which was at that time the capital of Al-Andalus. When Ferdinand III conquered the city, the mosque was consecrated as a church, and bells were added to the minaret. When an earthquake destroyed the top part of the tower in the fourteenth century, a small gable was placed on top. Much later, in the sixteenth century, Hernán Ruiz the Younger from Córdoba was awarded the task of adorning the top with a belfry. Luis Martínez Montiel and Alfredo J. Morales summarize the results of Ruiz's labours: "The belfry, which combines ashlar, bricks and glazed tiles, comprises five superimposed storeys of diminishing size, popularly known as the Clock, the Stars (or the Well), the Billiard Balls (or round section) and the crest. It is crowned by the monumental statue of Faith Triumphant, popularly known as El Giraldillo, which also serves as weathervane" (1999, 13–14). When Sansón Carrasco speaks of the Giralda, he is referring not to the belfry but to the new statue that tops the bell tower of the cathedral of Seville. This term would later be applied to the whole tower. *Faith Triumphant* was placed on top of the belfry in 1568 and considered the largest bronze statue of the European Renaissance. Sansón Carrasco refers to the statue as the Giralda or Giraldillo (small Giralda) because it stands on a ball and turns round and round (from the verb *girar*) with the wind, serving as a weathervane.

As noted, the new upper third of the tower, including the statue, was designed by Hernán Ruiz the Younger. We have already encountered him as the architect of the Royal Jail in Seville. It should be recalled that he translated parts of Vitruvius *Ten Books on Architecture*. It may be no coincidence that he reappears here, because he was one of the most famous architects and builders in Andalucía and one whom Cervantes could well have met. The Giralda or moving statue is an invention that derives from the reading of Vitruvius. Discussing the number of winds and how they affect buildings, the Roman architect states that Andronicus of Cyrrhus contradicted the belief that there were only four winds, building an octagonal tower in Athens: "On the several sides of the octagon he executed reliefs representing the several winds, each facing the point from which it blows; and on top of the tower he set a conical shaped pied of marble and on this a bronze Triton with rod stretched in its right hand. It was so contrived as to go round with the wind, always stopping to face the breeze and holding its rod as a pointer directly over the representation of the wind that was blowing" (Vitruvius 1960, 26). An engraving by Cesare Cesarino, in his translation into Italian of Vitruvius, shows a rather fanciful depiction of this tower, which further resembles the Giralda in its diminishing levels as it moves upwards. It is thus likely that Hernán Ruiz used this or a similar depiction in his design.

Very much like the Triton of old, the statue built for the Giralda was made of bronze and pointed in the direction of the blowing wind. The upper building was finished in 1565, and the statue was cast as a bronze figure by Bartolomé Morel and carried to its pride of place by eighteen Moriscos on 13 August 1568.[12] The statue could have been based on the pagan goddess Minerva, albeit now turned into a Christian figure. Once again, there is a doubling here, as a pagan figure is transformed into a Christian one. Thus, when Sansón Carrasco is detailing his adventure, the reader recalls several doublings, that of the tower as an Islamic and Christian architecture and that of a pagan deity and Christian figure. Even though the story of the defeat of the Giralda is invented, we may wonder at Sansón's feat: is he defeating a Christian figure? Or does his attack include the other religious identities in the tower? It is worth asking if Sansón Carrasco's attack on the Giralda is a way for the author to take revenge or poke fun at an architect who had created an impressive façade that hid a horrendous prison. Thus, the text turns the figure of *Faith Triumphant* into a grotesque giantess, and giants, as noted in chapter 3, were often evil figures in the books of chivalry – Sancho at one point, mentions the giantess Andandona, who appears in the *Amadís*. She is immensely fierce and ugly and leaps from crag to crag, wearing bear-skins and attacking knights. Here Giralda does not appear particularly ferocious and serves as contrast to the windmill as giant; perhaps one even questions why the perfectibility of humanity has to have a specific gender, the Vitruvian man. Having a giantess stand on what appears to be a not-so-solid base, the text may also be pointing to Vitruvius' rejection of the "grotesque" images that began at the time of Augustus and

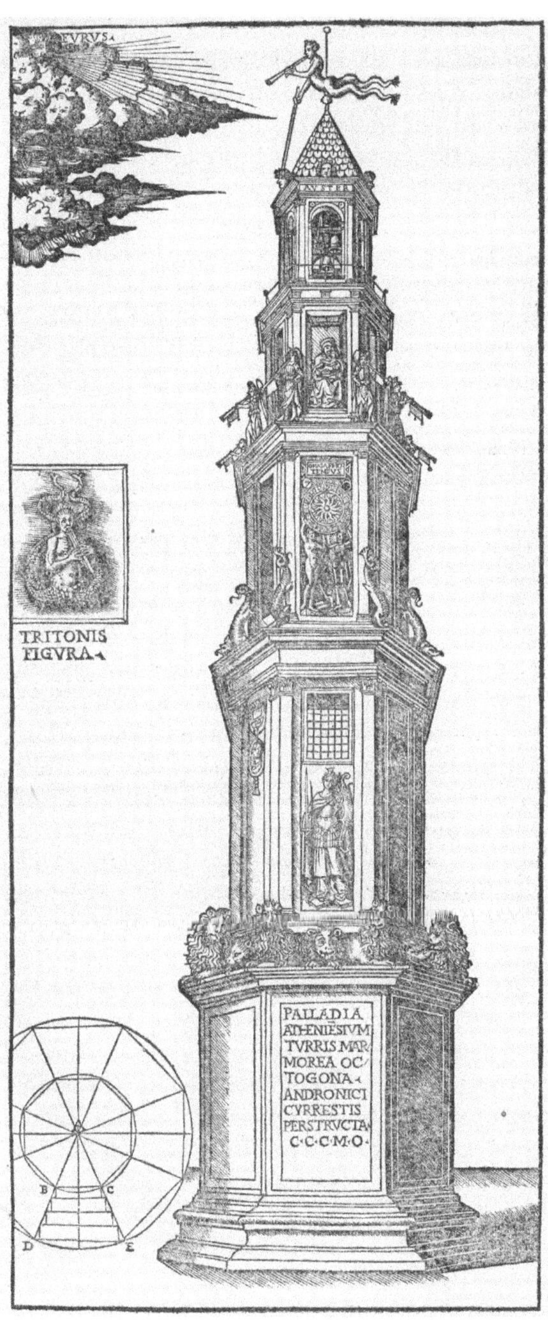

Figure 5.2. *Tower of the Winds by Andronicus of Cyrrhus in Athens*, engraving from a drawing by Cesare Cesariano, in *De Architectura libri dece traducti de latino in vulgare* [The ten books on architecture translated from Latin to Vulgar], volume 1, by Lucius Vitruvius Pollio, 1521. Photograph by Icas94. De Agostini/Getty Images

flourished with Nero. If in these "decadent" works (Vitruvius 1960, 26) people can be seated on tender stalks above pediments, a giant figure (if we are to believe Sansón) can easily stand above any slender contraption.

If there is some kind of criticism against the architect Hernán Ruiz in this passage, it is quite subtle and can be simply ascribed to Sansón Carrasco's wily deceptions or to the narrative's continuing satire against the romances of chivalry. But if we place it in context, we discover that Cervantes was not the first to criticize Hernán Ruiz's many labours, and, if there is indeed satire, it is quite gentle. Francisco Pacheco (1540–1599) was one of the leading figures in the culture of Seville; the teacher of the most important painter of seventeenth-century Spain, Diego Velázquez; a painter himself; and author of *El arte de la pintura* (The art of painting). He lived in Seville in the years that Cervantes spent there, and he witnessed the building of the Giralda. His poem "Sátira contra la mala poesía" (Satire against bad poetry) is filled with mockery against Hernán Ruiz and his role in the Giralda. Juan Montero Delgado, who has studied this aspect of the poem in great detail, shows that the architect is portrayed as an astute rather than valiant Prometheus who ends the Golden Age of humankind through this invention. He is both a false alchemist and a charlatan. To get his revenge, Jupiter secretly tells Vulcan to "help" Hernán Ruiz and his cohorts (Luis de Vargas and Bartolomé Morel). A jar is given to them in which is hidden, as in Pandora's box, all kinds of evil. On opening it, Hernán Ruiz delivers a series of malefic gifts to Seville: "Abriólo, y al punto de aquel nido, salieron landres, pestilencias, hambres" (He opened it, and immediately from that nest emerged curses, pestilences, hunger; Rodríguez Marín 1907, vv. 388–9). Montero Delgado proves that it is "la tinaja o cúpula hemisférica de bronce sobre la cual se sustenta el coloso de la Fe victoriosa" (the jar or rounded ball of bronze upon which stood the colossus called Victorious Faith; 2000, 243). The statue then becomes the lid to the evil bowl or jar.[13] Thus, not all see the turning Giralda as a construction and invention worthy of Andronicus and Vitruvius.[14] Rather, it calls forth famine and the plague, at a time of changing weather patterns and sudden drought. By the time Cervantes wrote on the subject, the plague had already devastated Seville. Let us remember that in the period, pestilence derived from corrupt air, and *Faith Triumphant* moves with the wind. The narrative traps us among a series of paradoxes and into making a judgment on Hernán Ruiz's architectures, seeking to transform our vision of faith and the knight's vision into a disproportionate figure that attacks Seville.

In a sense, Sansón Carrasco is creating a story that seeks to surpass Don Quixote's most whimsical and grandiose imaginings. The graduate from Salamanca uses his wits to invert the episode of the windmills.

While, on seeing the *molinos*, the knight transformed an edifice into a sentient being, here Sansón Carrasco points to a useful decoration on top of a building and turns it into a giant woman. Both the windmill and the statue as weathervane move with the aid of the wind. The very fact that he will struggle against a Christian figure placed over a minaret shows that Sansón mimics Don Quixote. After all, the mad knight often confuses friends with foes, attacking priests and freeing galley slaves, He sees giants where there are only windmills. Sansón further challenges Don Quixote's strange visions of knighthood through the use of similes and puns. He claims that the giantess is strong as if made of bronze; of course, the statue is made of bronze, as was the one described by Vitruvius. As the two fake knights try to surpass one another through the imagination, the building still remains as a composite structure. A student of Vitruvius, Hernán Ruiz the Younger sought to bring symmetry, proportion, and above all eurithmia (or at least a kind of plurithmia that takes into account Arabic and Christian modes) to the cathedral tower. But if we are to listen to Pacheco or to Sansón Carrasco, the work (or, at the very least, the moving statue that was placed on top) is far from having the harmonious proportions and beauty the architect meant it to have.

In addition, by foregrounding a tower of the cathedral of Seville as his first adventure, Sansón is mimicking Don Quixote's first major adventure in the 1615 novel. Here, however, the knight has a very different motivation than he had in part 1. Now, he leaves his home in order to search of Dulcinea. In his mind, her magnificent palace must be in Toboso. He and Sancho arrive at the village in the afternoon but wait until it is quite dark to surreptitiously search for the lady's abode. Chapter 9 begins ominously: "Media noche era por filo" (Half the night; Cervantes 1978, 2.9.99; 2008, 520). Not only do they enter the village at the witching hour, but they also hear the sound of animals, which in the silence of the night only increases their concern: "rebuznaba un jumeto, gruñían puercos, mayaban gatos, cuyas voces, de diferentes sonidos, se aumentaban el silencio de la noche, todo lo cual tuvo el enamorado caballero como mal agüero" (an ass brayed, swine grunted, and cats mewed; which different sounds were augmented by the silence of the night. All of which the enamoured knight took for an ill omen; 1978, 2.9.100; 2008, 520). In spite of the eeriness of the moment and the evil omen, Don Quixote commands Sancho to take him to Dulcinea's palace. Although in part 1 Sancho had pretended to travel from Sierra Morena to deliver a letter to her from her beloved Don Quixote, he, of course, had never been to her home – much less to a palace that did not exist. As Sancho protests that this is not the time to "hallar la puerta abierta" (to find the gates open; 1978, 1.9.100; 2008, 520), the knight insists that they go on. Although this open door is but a metaphor, it is interesting to note that doors do play a role as an architectonic device in the novel. We need only remember that, when at the very beginning Sancho knocks on the door of the knight's house, the housekeeper hides so as not to answer – she detests the squire for going out on adventures with her master. Once they are inside, the door is shut so that knight and squire can lock themselves in and plot their future (1978, 2.6–7.84–5; 2009, 506–7). Is the knight, as he arrives in Toboso, imagining that he can lock himself with his beloved in her palace?

As Don Quixote guides them to the largest building in town, knight and squire eventually discover that, far from being a palace or a castle, what they had seen was the town's church and its tower, the dark shadow (see figure 5.3). Curiously, the construction of the church was started in 1525. The first section of the tower is dated 1552, and the rest (which included two other sections) was not finished, along with the main entrance, until some time in the seventeenth century.[15] Thus, what knight and squire were glimpsing in the dark was a rather new and as yet unfinished architecture. In what is perhaps an ironic moment, the novel presents us with what the travellers may think is a finished building, while in reality it was not – thus playing with the many partial architectures in the book. Furthermore, the ominous elements, including the cemetery by the church, which Sancho seeks to avoid in the middle of the night, turn the whole scene into an unsettling and devilish moment. This is, of course, a premonition of things to come.

As a result of this failed attempt, Don Quixote decides to remain in the woods around the town the next day and to send Sancho in search of his princess. This leads to Sancho's most famous lie, a true feat of the imagination that parallels those of his master. He waits until the afternoon and, on spotting three peasant women leaving Toboso, he calls Don Quixote, telling him that Dulcinea and her maidens are approaching. In what may be a dramatic ekphrasis,[16] and parody of Botticelli's *Primavera*, the three peasants are transformed by Sancho into the three Graces, and their leader is also Venus.[17] Don Quixote, who is always ready to accept chivalric imaginings, cannot see the scene, but he can see the beauty and enchantment of the picture that has been drawn by Sancho with amazing rhetorical impact. But Sancho's lie or imitation has failed to convince. The knight laments that a veil hides the truth and that he may have cataracts in his eyes. Eventually the idea that Dulcinea has been enchanted becomes one of the prime motifs of this second part, as the lover pines for a lady he may never see again – if he ever saw her. Later in the text he will lament to the Duchess that he found her transformed "de ángel en diablo, de olorosa en pestífera"

Figure 5.3. *It Was Late at Night When Don Quixote and Sancho Left Their Retreat and Entered Toboso*, illustration for *The Adventures of Don Quixote* by Miguel de Cervantes (Ward Lock, ca. 1925). © Look and Learn / Bridgeman Images

(from an angel to a devil, from fragrant to pestiferous; 1978, 2.32.289; 2008, 679). It may not be without significance that the church of Toboso was dedicated to Saint Anthony, one of whose duties was to save people from the plague. Called *peste* in Spanish for the odours produced, it is indeed *pestífera*. The ugliness of Dulcinea and her horrid smell may recall the effects of the plague and her possible death. Indeed, the evil enchanter, to whom he attributes her transformation, calls to mind the witches that were often accused of bringing about the plague. Once again, let us remember that the first great plague to ravage Spain in the seventeenth century occurred between 1597 and 1602. Cervantes would have experienced it. There may be traces here of his suffering.

Sansón Carrasco, then, utilizes in part 2 a number of elements from Don Quixote's first major adventure. First of all, he locates the event in a church, recalling the church in Toboso. Secondly, he points to a tower whose parts were erected at different times, much like the tower of Toboso's church. He also demonstrates his lady's agency and freedom, contrasting with the enchanted Dulcinea. Finally, the wind plays a significant part in both adventures. In Sansón's adventure the giantess moves with the wind. In the idealized painting drawn by Sancho of the rustic women as Dulcinea and her attendants, there is a zephyr or soft springtime wind blowing; in the rusticity of Don Quixote's lack of vision, Dulcinea and the maidens flee in their donkeys, going as fast as the wind: "todas corren como el viento" (1978, 2.10.111; 2008, 530). Their quick retreat is like unexpected gusts of wind, alien to springtime and closer to the strong winds that move Sansón's giantess.

Not only is the giantess "movible" (changeable) because she turns to show the direction from which the wind is blowing, but also Sansón calls her "movible" to underline the misogynistic attitudes of the period in which women were said to always change their minds. The wily graduate claims that he was able to defeat this giantess with the aid of the elements. The winds, blowing from the north for seven days, held her steady. This immobility allowed him to triumph. Sansón claims victory over the fickle statue, stating, "Llegué, vila y vencíla" (I came, I saw, I conquered; 1978, 2.14.135; 2008, 549). This time he mimics Julius Caesar's famous words, knowing that Don Quixote also admires the Roman warrior and writer, repeatedly referencing him in the novel.[18]

By alluding to Julius Caesar in the narrative of this adventure, the *bachiller* may be conflating two famous sites in the centre of Seville: the cathedral with its Giralda and the Alameda de Hércules, a park built in the late sixteenth century. Here, a branch of the Guadalquivir was drained to avoid future inundations. The park exhibited two ancient Roman columns that had been brought from elsewhere in the city.[19] On top of each was placed a sculpture by Diego de Pesquera, the first one a copy of the Farnese Hercules and the second a Julius Caesar.[20] Thus, the reference to Caesar together with that of the Greek hero would lead the listener of Sansón's invented labour to recall the Alameda de Hércules. The ancient hero would further bring to mind that Seville, according to legend, was founded by Hercules, who left six columns at the site. It was then up to Julius Caesar to name and fortify the city. Sansón, then, with calculated vainglory, compares himself to the two builders of Seville. As a feigned architect, he becomes the architect of Don Quixote's defeat, a failure that builds upon Sancho's most admirable and appalling lie, one that will contribute to the knight's melancholy and loss.

Hell-Mouth

We will skip the second of Sansón's "labours," that of the bulls of Guisando, because it does not fully fit our architectural theme. We will focus on the third, which in many ways contrasts with the first, moving from a high tower to an underground cave and from the element of air to that of fire. Indeed, many of the architectures in this second half of the novel have demonic connotations and can be read as echoes of Cervantes' imprisonment.

In the third labour, Sansón is ordered by his lady "que me precipitase y sumiere en la sima de la Cabra, peligro inaudito y temeroso y que le trujese particular relación de lo que en aquella escura profundidad se encierra" (to plunge headlong into Cabra's cave (an unheardof and dreadful attempt), and to bring her a particular relation of what is locked up in that obscure abyss; 1978, 2.14.135; 2008, 549).[21] The entrance to this deep chasm is to be found close to Córdoba and in a mountain range adjacent to the town of Cabra.[22] The macabre nature of the Sima de Cabra was furthered in 1683 when an expedition was sent to recover a dead body lying close to the surface of the chasm. It has also been argued that Cervantes visited this inhospitable and deserted locale or, at the very least, that he spent time in the town of Cabra.[23] Whatever the case may be, I would argue that Cervantes, in using the Sima de Cabra for one of Sansón's labours, had in mind a lengthy allegorical poem that was published by Juan de Padilla in 1521.[24] In *Los doce triunfos de los doce apóstoles* (The twelve triumphs of the twelve apostles) the Sima de Cabra is compared to one of the mouths of hell. As Robert Lima reminds us, the hell-mouth was one of the most terrifying images in medieval and Renaissance theatres, where it had "greater impact than the most imposing 'fire and brimstone' sermons" (2005, 31). Indeed, Cervantes included it in his theatre. Turning to Padilla, María Amor Martín Fernández shows how each of the twelve triumphs is divided into four sections: (1) contemplation of the heavens (which includes the zodiacal sign under which the apostle placed a description of associated constellations; the narrative of the life of the apostle; and allusions to other saints whose festivities fall in the same sign); (2) contemplation of the earth; (3) contemplation of purgatory; and (4) contemplation of hell (through a particular mouth of hell) (1988, 18). Thus, Padilla narrates the apostles' triumphs over paganism and paradoxically connects each of these figures to one of the twelve signs of the zodiac, while being guided by Saint Paul in these journeys.[25] Such an association is not new; it was encountered in Alfonso X's *Setenario* (The seven) (Martín Fernández 1988, 19–21).

As for the myths that are woven around the constellations, Padilla turns to Hyginus' *De Astronomica* (On astronomy), one of the most popular books on the constellations during the Middle Ages and the Renaissance, which was published for the first time in Venice in 1482.[26] These myths are then fused with hagiographic elements taken from Jacobus de Voragine. The work begins with Aries, the sign of spring, and ends with Pisces, the last sign of winter. In the fifth triumph the Apostle Santiago is seen to abide in Leo, the fifth sign of the zodiac. As this sign is ruled by the Sun, Santiago is linked to the Solar Christ. And in a political move Padilla also makes Leo the sign for Spain, as Santiago is shown with the Sun, the castle, and the lion. Furthermore, the apostle is praised for leading the struggle against the Moors.

The fifth triumph also shows the mouth of hell where those who infringe upon the fifth commandment are held. Centaurs carry the damned, except that these creatures are no longer half man, half horse; they are half man, half lion, as befits the sign of Leo. They have arrows of fire and with their lion claws tear apart the skin and open the hearts of the condemned. Rivers of blood literally flow into the mouth of hell into which the condemned fall forever, drowning in boiling blood. It is this place that, in the ninth stanza, is compared to the Sima de Cabra:

> La boca sangrienta continuo hervía
> Como en Adaques su cálida fuente:
> Allí la dañada misérrima gente
> Con alarido muy grande caía,
> Remedio ninguno la triste tenía,
> Como quien cae en la sima de Cabra.
> (The bloody mouth boiled continuously
> As if in Adaques and its hot springs
> With horrid sounds people fell,

No remedy for such a sad place
As if someone fell in Cabra's Cave.) (Padilla 1891, 73)[27]

Sansón Carrasco, therefore, has chosen his fictitious labour with much thought. Not only is he is sent to the most horrendous and hellish place, but, in triumphing, he could be seen as a new Santiago, the apostle who rules the fifth entrance under the sign of Leo, a new heavenly knight who rids Spain of its enemies. He, and not Don Quixote, is then to be identified with the renewal of Spain. In addition, Sansón Carrasco uses his third labour as a way to establish parallels with Hercules' twelfth labour, in which the ancient hero descended to Hades, battled with Cerberus, and struggled to bring this beast back to the world of the living. Cerberus is not mentioned at this point in the novel, but he is evoked in Grisóstomo's song of despair in part 1.[28] The mention takes place in chapter 14, thus mirroring Sansón's allusion, which is also in chapter 14 but of the second part. The infernal images found in two equally numbered chapters can hardly be a coincidence. In addition, this guardian of the underworld appears at least twice in Padilla's poem, in the first and the tenth triumph (Martín Fernández 1988, 92, 122). *Los doce triunfos* mediates between the ancient text and the modern novel, providing the reader a more concrete linkage.

Although Don Quixote does not comment on this fictitious labour by the Knight of the Mirrors, it must have had a deep impact on his being, for it displaces him as Hercules and distances him from his dreams to be the ideal knight. Thus, it is no coincidence that Don Quixote later attempts to engage in his own voyage to the underworld. Not long after Sansón Carrasco tells of his third labour at the Sima de Cabra, the knight from La Mancha decides to descend into the Cave of Montesinos. The similarities between the two adventures point to an imaginative rivalry between the two knights. Although Sansón may have been imitating Don Quixote in his fictive creation of the first labour, it is Don Quixote who will imitate Sansón in the descent into a hellish cave.[29]

Sansón Carrasco, then, has used sacred architecture and demonic "natural" architecture to provide Don Quixote with *evidentia*, placing before his eyes his feigned triumphs. He defeated the giantess by having her stand still, and he triumphed over a devilish threat by entering the mouth of hell and revealing what was hidden: "saqué a luz lo escondido de su abismo" (he brought to light the hidden secrets of that abyss; 1978, 2.14.135; 2008, 549). Although he never explains what he saw within, he leaves it to the knight's imagination. The crazed gentleman in his many readings could have come across Padilla's book and its zodiacal architecture. Indeed, a number of arts of memory relied on the twelve signs. Thus, in addition to an architecture of hell, Sansón Carrasco is providing the knight with a mnemonic chart of the underworld to torture him further. We will thus have to follow the knight, who will face a lion in order to triumph over Leo's gate and will enter the Cave of Montesinos to illuminate the mysteries of the underworld.

Grotesque Anatomy

Sansón Carrasco is not finished with Don Quixote. He claims that he has succeeded in a fourth labour, defeating the greatest knight in Spain – "haber vencido en singular batalla, a aquel tan famoso caballero don Quijote de la Mancha, y héchole confesar que es más hermosa mi Casildea que su Ducinea" (having vanquished in single combat the so renowned knight, Don Quixote de la Mancha, and made him confess that my Casildea is more beautiful than his Dulcinea; 1978, 2.14.135; 2008, 549). The scene is set for Don Quixote's furious denial that leads to the main point of the feigned labours, a contest with the knight in which Carrasco expects to defeat him and send him home. The Knight of the Mirrors has brought with him a squire who frightens Sancho: "Mas apenas dio lugar la claridad del día para ver y diferenciar las cosas, cuando la primera que se ofreció a los ojos de Sancho Panza fue la nariz del escudero del Bosque, que era tan grande que casi le hacía sombra a todo el cuerpo." (But scarcely had the clearness of the day given opportunity to see and distinguish objects, when the first thing that presented itself to Sancho's eyes was the Squire of the Wood's nose, which was so large that it almost overshadowed his whole body; 1978, 2.14. 140; 2008, 533.) For Salvador Fajardo, "the nose concentrates in its grotesque and fearsome shape all the references to the topic of lying that run through the beginning of part II" (2002, 203). This critic utilizes the Bakhtinian conception of the grotesque as a carnivalesque reversal of hierarchies in which misrule and deception are the rule. But the grotesque in this episode also reflects the artistic notions of the Renaissance.[30] The squire's nose is described in terms of a vegetable: "Cuéntase, en efecto, que era de demasiada grandeza, corva en la mitad y toda llena de verrugas, de color amoratado, como de berenjena" (In a word, it is said to have been of an excessive size, hawked in the middle, and full of warts and carbuncles, of the colour of a mulberry, *like an eggplant*; 1978, 2.14.140; 2008, 553). This grotesque link between body parts and the vegetable world flourished in Italian art through the works of Giuseppe Arcimboldo. Cervantes may have come to know his works and those of his imitators during his visits to Milan or he may have heard or seen some of them in Spain.[31] Cervantes would have been attracted not only by his overall fame but also by his service to the Habsburgs. Arcimboldo worked for successive emperors in Prague. In fact, Rudolph II sent Arcimboldo's painting *The Hunter* as a present to Philip II, and the work would have been exhibited at Spanish palaces in Cervantes' lifetime (Levisi 1968, 221).[32] We now know that Arcimboldo sent Philip II eleven paintings from two of his series, *The Elements* and *The Seasons*, most of which are deemed lost. In 2017, Bilbao's Museum of Fine Arts held an exhibit of the three paintings by Arcimboldo that can be found in today's Spain: *Spring* (1573), *Flora* (1589), and *Flora Meretrix* (1590).[33] His paintings are a natural development of what we will view in the following section as particular to Nero's Domus Aurea (Golden Palace) in which humans, nymphs, and satyrs grow arboreal extensions. In Arcimboldo's paintings the vegetable world does not extend outward from human anatomies but constitutes the physical body.[34]

The fantasies of the classical grotesque in which one shape leads to the other culminate in Arcimboldo's many portraits in which vegetables shape the features of an individual, as in the images of the allegories of *Spring* and *Summer* (see figure 5.4). In both of these paintings a vegetable nose is particularly prominent. And these nasal protuberances include the "verrugas"(warts) described by Sancho. In *The Gardener* (figure 5.5) an even more grotesque face is formed from a series of vegetables. Although the large carrot that serves as a nose has no warts, this painting can be linked to Cervantes' text through trickery. When the work is turned upside down, the face disappears and the painting shows merely a dish of vegetables. Giancarlo Maiorino asserts: "By exploiting duplicity and reversibility, the artist makes of the canvas at once a grotesque portrait and a still life" (1991, 34). In the novel the grotesque is also related to trickery. The giant nose that frightens Sancho is a mere disguise, exposing the duplicity of those who wish to bring about Don Quixote's downfall. The menacing squire is quickly transformed into a familiar sight (Sancho's neighbour Tomé Cecial) when the fake nasal adumbration comes off.

While introducing the grotesque, Cervantes may also be contrasting the nasal protuberance to the Vitruvian man, which became one of the most popular images for the Renaissance, as discussed in chapter 3. Thus, Cervantes turns again to one of the most famous images in the ancient work, one he had evoked in the episode of the windmills. Let us recall that in his third book Vitruvius discusses how to build symmetrical and perfectly proportioned temples, exuding harmony and eurithmia. He argues that the most perfect structure designed by nature is the human body. Thus, temples should follow such perfection. In order to prove his theory of the human body, he envisions it as sitting within a circle (the most perfect of forms) with outstretched hands and feet touching the circumference, and with the navel or phallus as the centre. Vitruvius details the different parts of the body and how they echo in measurement the other sections. For example: "If we take the height of the face itself, the distance from the bottom of the chin to the under side of the nostrils is one third of it; the nose from the under side of the nostrils to a line between the eyebrows is the same; from there to the roots of the hair is also a third" (1960, 77). The nose, then, is a most important element in the measuring of the human body, particularly the face, in Vitruvius – and it is the human body that is the model for perfect proportion and eurithmia in the construction of temples to the gods. Diego de Sagredo, the first to disseminate Vitruvius' ideas in Spanish, went into greater detail about the human face. In one of his images he draws a square with nine equal sections and places the three on the right on the human face to fit it perfectly. He explains: "[...] un cuadrado partido en tres tercios iguales. Del primero se forma la frente. Del segundo la nariz. Del tercero, la boca y la barba [...] En el primero consiste la sabiduría, en el segundo la hermosura, en el tercero la bondad." ([...] a square divided into three equal thirds. From the first, the forehead is created; from the second, the nose; from the third the mouth and the chin [...] The first consists of wisdom, the second of beauty, and the third of goodness; 1526, 6r.) Since the perfectly shaped nose denotes beauty, there can be no question of the dysrithmia associated with the squire's nose. All beauty and proportion are denied.

The Knight of the Mirrors has disguised his squire, providing him with a nose so large that it shadows his body. The immense nose breaks the symmetry and proportion of the human figure. Since the body is the example of perfect proportion that should be emulated in temples, it is no coincidence that the giant statue on top of the tower of the church or temple, the Giralda, is so large as to break eurithmia. It is, in a way, another huge nose that breaks symmetry, a sign of dysrithmia that extends from body to temple.

Although Don Quixote is able to win the contest against the Knight of the Mirrors, the grotesque, in its proliferations of forms and fantasies, forever confounds the knight and his squire.[35] In addition, the configuration we are following has moved from the mouth (of hell) to a protruding and immense nose, signal of lying and dysrithmia.

Figure 5.4. Giuseppe Arcimboldo, *Summer Allegory*, 1563. Kunsthistorisches Museum, Vienna, Austria. Erich Lessing/Art Resource, NY

Figure 5.5. Giuseppe Arcimboldo, *The Gardener*, ca. 1587–90. Museo Civico, Cremona, Italy. Scala/Art Resource, NY

Structures of Silence

Don Quixote wins the battle against the Knight of the Mirrors. Such are the latter's grotesque and disproportionate creations that he cannot stand even to the weakened and maddened don. This triumph will win Don Quixote some moments of harmony and self-validation in the midst of challenging adventures. After Don Quixote and Sancho depart, they soon meet on the road the Gentleman of the Green Cloak. Not at all a trickster, he is both a mirror and a contrastive figure to the knight.[36] In his fifties, like the gentleman of La Mancha, Diego de Miranda seems to be a very balanced figure, believing in *aurea mediocritas*, the notion of the golden mean, which became a literary topos through Horace's tenth ode and was invoked in Spain by writers such as Juan Boscán and Antonio de Guevara (Sánchez Robayna 2000, 139). The green knight is neither too rich nor too poor and abides in a pleasant home with his wife and children. His life is devoted to fishing and hunting. He is also a reader, but, as opposed to Don Quixote, he delves into various topics, from history to religion, and the books are a mixture of those in Latin and those in the romance language. More importantly, he is described as having an eagle-like long and narrow countenance (Cervantes 1978, 2.16.150; 2008, 563), which is also a feature of Cervantes' own portrait as he presents it in his *Novelas ejemplares*. Furthermore, the eagle-like nose and countenance, rather than a giant grotesque nose, was said to be a most auspicious trait: "According to della Porta, a man with a hooked nose was said to be magnanimous, since the eagle was considered the queen of all birds" (Cheng 2012, 206). In addition, the eagle is a bird of empire and acute vision. Thus, Cervantes is a figure akin to Diego de Miranda, a magnanimous and insightful person. Diego Miranda's look is somewhere between happy and grave. It may be that Cervantes is here contrasting his crazed hero with the kind of person Cervantes would have wished to have become: someone with sufficient means to lead a leisurely life devoted to reading; someone with sharp eyes who could see (and describe) humanity's aspirations and foibles.

This chapter allows us to ponder the hierarchy of the senses as understood in the early modern period and how they may relate to human habitation. The mouth of hell represents taste, which along with touch is the lowest of the senses. With Arcimboldo's nose we move to the middle sense, smell. Finally, with the Knight of the Green Cloak we move to the highest, sight – and we expect to see a home that is attune with the highest vision. Diego de Miranda has attracted the attention of countless critics because the green of his cloak, as well as the deadly *alfanje* (curved knife) he carries as a weapon, has yielded numerous interpretations. Some link him to the crazed knight because green is the colour of buffoons and madmen, while others go so far as to relate the green of his attire to Islam, otherworldliness, and even the Egyptian god Osiris (Fernández Morera 1987, 125–33). After all, the *alfanje* was a curved long knife associated with the Turks and the Moors and utilized for combat in close proximity.[37] For Monique Joly, it merely means that Christians were fond of adopting Moorish dress (1996, 64), a fact that has been thoroughly detailed by Javier Irigoyen-García.[38]

While the two gentlemen and Sancho journey towards Don Diego de Miranda's home, they pause as the crazed knight conceives of a new adventure, the episode of the two lions from Oran. For some, this is but a continuation of Cervantes' interest in Moorish questions. Ángela Morales links the episode to the Islamic threat: "El león cautivo traído de Orán, enclave español en la costa argelina desde principios del siglo xvi, representaría la amenaza turco-berberisca en la costa africana mediterránea [...] y que no existía el peligro musulmán inminente con el que se había justificado la necesidad de expulsar a los ciudadanos moriscos ante el riesgo de tener una 'quinta columna' dentro de España." (The captive lion, brought from Oran, a Spanish enclave on the Algerian coast since the beginnings of the sixteenth century, would represent the threat of Turks and Berbers from the Mediterranean African coast [...] and that there was no such imminent Muslim threat that served to justify the expulsion of the Morisco citizens because they threatened to form a fifth column within Spain; 2014, 502.) Robert Stone takes up this point of view, while tempering it with Spain's maurophilia: "The surprisingly tame lions of Oran, on the way to the king's palace, underscore the idea that the North African threat of Islam is no more [...] Don Quixote now adopts these former enemies when he dubs himself *El caballero de los Leones*. This could be taken as an example of *maurofilia*" (2017, n.p.). It could, however, simply be a satire of epic and chivalric moments from Yvain to the Cid, and from Samson to Amadis, pointing to the prudence of the man in green and the rashness and impetuousness of Don Quixote.

A number of critics have questioned the integrity of the man in green. Francisco Márquez-Villanueva, for example, calls him "'cuerdo de atar': "Embriagado de prudencia, zambullido en el piélago de la cordura, el Verde Gabán se juega la vida tan locamente como pueda hacerlo don Quijote con sus caballerías" (so sane as to be fit to be tied: drunk on prudence, swimming in the deep ocean of sanity, the Green Cloak plays at life as madly as Don Quixote does with his chivalric ímpetus; 1975, 214). Others vehemently disagree. Gerald L. Gingras asserts: "the ostentatious colors applied to expensive fabrics accord perfectly with the aesthetic preferences of the Spanish gentry before and during Cervantes' time" (1985, 131). Charles Presberg, although he will later question the man in green's positive characterization,[39] begins by summarizing the overall impression given by Diego de Miranda: "in these three chapters the temperate gentleman exemplifies the most important cardinal virtue of prudence or *discreción* – always and everywhere the quintessence of the golden mean" (2001, 201). It contrasts with Don Quixote's lack of prudence: "His rashness vitiates the cardinal virtue of courage or fortitude; and virtually in all his actions Don Quixote is shown to be extravagant, choleric and unrestrained" (203). His portrayal thus contrasts with that of the prologue of the first part, where the gentleman from La Mancha is described as possessing all four cardinal virtues. As previously noted, the virtue of *fortitudo* – valour, strength, and perseverance – is depicted in Raphael's fresco at the Vatican as a woman holding a pet lion. In Cervantes, the knight sets out to prove his valour. When the male lion's cage is opened, the beast, instead of rushing out, "abrió luego la boca y bostezó muy despacio, y con casi dos palmos de lengua que sacó fuera, se despolvoró los ojos y se lavó el rostro" (gaped and yawned very leisurely; then licked the dust off his eyes, and washed his face; 1978, 2.17.164; 2008, 574). In many ways, the knight may have been expecting a "mouth of hell," a lion's fierce opening that would be ready to attack him. None of this happens. My point here is that this allows Don Quixote to "triumph" over the mouth of hell, represented by the sign of Leo, and thus "surpass" the Knight of the Mirrors even though the lion finds Don Quixote not at all interesting and turns his back to him.

So much is said along the way, and so witty is the dialogue between Diego de Miranda and Don Quixote, that the text raises the expectation of viewing how the Gentleman of the Green Cloak lives and how he has constructed his home. Arriving at the village and his abode, the text regales us with small details. The house is made of rough stone, and while it is impressive, the narrator emphasizes that it resembles other homes built by rich farmers. It displays the abundance of the owner, exhibiting a *bodega* or store-room by the patio and the *cueva* or cellar, which generally houses bottled wine and perishable foods by the entrance. Numerous earthenware jars (*tinajas*) are scattered outside of the cellar, again pointing to abundance. Curiously, the jars come from Toboso and thus remind Don Quixote of his Dulcinea as he sighs and recites the first two verses of the tenth sonnet by Garcilaso de la Vega.[40] The poem is about the loss of the beloved and could be applied to the Dulcinea of the second part, who, according to the knight, has been "enchanted." Not satisfied with Garcilaso's words, the knight expresses his own suffering, pointing to the jars: "¡Oh tobosescas tinajas que me habéis traido a la memoria la dulce prenda de mi mayor amargura!" (O ye Tobosan jars, that have brought back to my remembrance the sweet pledge of my greatest bitterness!; Cervantes 1978, 2.18.169; 2008, 578.)

On hearing these verses, Diego de Miranda's son Lorenzo, who prides himself on being a poet, comes out of the house, along with his mother Cristina, to receive the new guest. An unexpected ellipsis takes place at this point: "Aquí pinta el autor todas las circunstancias de la casa de don Diego, pintándonos en ellas lo que contiene una casa de un labrador y rico; pero al traductor de esta historia le pareció pasar estas y otras semejantes menudencias en silencio, porque no venían bien con el propósito de la historia; la cual más tiene su fuerza en la verdad que en las frías digresiones." (Here the author sets down all the particulars of Don Diego's house, describing all the furniture usually contained in the mansion of a gentleman that was both a farmer and rich. But the translator of the history thought fit to pass over in silence these, and such like minute matters, as not suiting with the principal scope of the history, in which truth has more force than cold and insipid digressions; Cervantes 1978, 2.18.169; 2008, 578–9.) Here, the ellipsis points to missing elements, a gap in the description, but it may also refer to the geometrical shape that has two centres, one that is evident and a hint at an important second one that is hidden – the particulars of the house. As Cervantes paints the house with his pen, he chooses to highlight some elements and leave most others to the reader's imagination. A second ellipsis with double focus occurs when one type of item seems to overwhelm the description of the house – the many large earthenware jars scattered about in front. This second "centre" is no longer hidden and seems to vie for importance, leading the reader to wonder why these jars are so important. Taking this as his cue, Gustave Doré foregrounds the jars.[41] However, these are magnified by Apeles Mestres (1854–1936), a poet and illustrator from Barcelona. He draws a number of gigantic jars that almost overwhelm his illustration of this scene (see figure 5.6).[42] Indeed, they almost seem to barricade the house and prevent Don Quixote, Sancho, and Diego de Miranda from entering the abode. On the one hand, Sancho seems totally exhausted, his large frame lying almost horizontal on his donkey, while he exhibits his large behind to the spectator. On the other hand, Don Quixote seems very excited, sitting upright on Rocinante, his lance held up, perhaps thinking that he has indeed arrived at the kind of castle that conforms to his fantasies. Besides the gigantic jars, some even taller than the knight sitting on his horse, everything else seems to be welcoming: a small dog sniffing Rocinante, a second one coming to participate in the welcome, a number of servants coming down the stairs, Cristina waving from the first floor, and her son looking down with curiosity at the new guest.

The gigantic jars may have to do with memory and imitation. As noted earlier, since Toboso was a large producer of earthenware jars, the knight immediately thinks of Dulcinea, and her "loss" brings up Garcilaso's poem (an imitation of Virgil's *Aeneid*). The gigantic size of the jars is in tune with a previous episode. After all, Sansón Carrasco has fought a giantess named Giralda. Don Quixote can then bask in hyperbole and surround himself with jars that stand as storehouses of memory, in which all his thoughts of Dulcinea may be collected. Perhaps these jars point to abundance, to poetry, to desire (and loss). But if we accept Apeles Mestre's interpretation, they also seem to be blocking the house. Although it is a scene of welcoming, the barricade may represent the dangers outside. The fact that the translator refuses to describe the house is also suspicious. This is one of his few intrusions into the narrative.

There can be a multitude of interpretations here, thus making this architecture one of the most mysterious in the text. David Quint, though generally approving of the man in green, cautions that his example points away from literature: he "may lead a good, contented life, but not one about which anybody would want to read [...] This is the life of modern virtue, but it appears duller and more restricted than the old aristocratic culture," which Don Quixote wishes to imitate (2003, 114). And yet, the knight, from the start, turns his jars into poetry. Taking the lead from the chapter's title, he can also see the abode as a castle, and the jars that surround the "castle" may stand for the moat or the ramparts of such an edifice, thus ready to repel any attacks, any dangers outside. And, true to the customs in a castle of old, Don Quixote is given every attention as if he were a great knight. At the same time, this home has little to do with the inns that for the knight must always be castles. While castles and inns evoke adventures, Diego de Miranda's home is totally measured and devoid of action and drama. Thus, it stands apart from other architectures in that it is truly a "place" of safety and comfort. It can even be seen as the home envisioned by Bachelard.

The question remains, however: Why barricade the house with jars? In some ways the home of the man in green subtly deviates from place as it acquires the contours of other buildings that are not quite as welcoming, and thus we can see a wavering between place and space. There is no description, because the other architectures are carefully hidden. At least two other architectures may have had a very small impact on the construction of Diego de Miranda's home, and then we turn to a fourth one, which I think is much more important. First, as Vernon Chamberlin and Jack Weiner have suggested, Cervantes knew a man named Diego de Miranda who was his neighbour in Valladolid and "had been tried, reprimanded and punished for illegal cohabitation" with a widow named Doña Mariana Ramírez (1969, 344). They claim that the colour green

Figure 5.6. Apeles Mestres, *Oh dulces prendas por mi mal halladas…! Oh tobosescas tinajas*, in *El ingenioso hidalgo Don Quijote de la Mancha*, 1879. Biblioteca Valenciana Digital. Open access, public domain

that he wears symbolizes erotic desire. The humour in this scene, the authors conclude, comes from the very respectability of the man in green that contrasts with the historical Diego de Miranda. If such is the case, then, two habitations are merged, one the perfect place that abides by the golden mean, and the second a well-known site of transgressive desire.

As José Manuel Lucía Megías has explained, this whole situation had to do with Cervantes' neighbours when he moved to Valladolid in 1604. His was one of five multifamily homes built by Juan de Navas in the fields next to the Rastro Nuevo to take advantage of the number of people moving to the city because the court had moved there from Madrid (2019, 23). Cervantes and his family lived on the first floor, which also housed Luisa de Montoya (widow of the chronicler Esteban de Garibay) and her family on the right-hand side. The second floor was inhabited on the right by Juana Gaitán and her family and acquaintances, while on the left, just above the Cervantes family, lived Mariana Ramírez. A *beata* (an excessively pious woman) living in the building started all kinds of rumours and gossip after Gaspar de Ezpeleta, severely wounded in a duel, was taken to Luisa de Montoya's apartment. The investigation, instead of revealing Ezpeleta's assailant, probably a deceived husband, veered off to even more salacious petty crimes (Lucía Megías 2019, 44–5). Among the unfortunate results was that the constable, as Jean Canavaggio explains, "had the author of *Don Quixote* incarcerated, along with ten other persons, among them Andrea, Isabel, Constanza, Juana Gaitán, Mariana Ramírez and Diego de Miranda [...] Miguel found himself stranded in the same prison where his grandfather and his father had been shut up before him" (1990, 225). It appears that the Cervantes family only remained imprisoned for a couple of days, and not much was made of it. In spite of innuendos by the *beata*, the event was of little interest in terms of Cervantes and his family, as José Manuel Lucía Megías asserts (2019, 47). At the same time, any kind of confinement such as this one would shadow Cervantes' vision of Valladolid as a place of danger, as one that would remind him of his Algerian captivity and his imprisonment in Seville. If the pleasant home of Diego de Miranda can be transformed through allusion into the multifamily home where Cervantes lived in Valladolid, and all the disruptions that occurred there, then it can also be linked to the jail where he was held. The silence experienced in Diego de Miranda's home is the exact opposite of both sites, one of family disarray and the other of imprisoned cries.

As for the second superimposed and allusive architecture, José Solís de los Santos has noted the extensive laudatory remarks regarding

Lorenzo Ramírez de Prado (1583–1658) in verses 112 to 126 of the *Viaje del Parnaso* (*Voyage to Parnassus*) (Solís de los Santos 2016, 97–120), in which his stoic demeanour is unshaken, both when he is rewarded with many honours and riches and when, deprived of these later in life, he enjoys instead the inner riches (100). Given that the poem was already in press by the time Lorenzo had become embroiled in a judicial process with the Jesuits over a pamphlet in Latin, which went back to an interpretation of Martial, it is possible that Cervantes' praise for Lorenzo may have had as much to do with his father, Alonso Ramírez de Prado (1549–1608). Alonso, who had held a high position under the Duke of Lerma, was suddenly cast down, accused of corruption, and sent to jail in 1606, where he remained until his death in 1608; he had yet to be convicted (102). Such was Cervantes' sympathy for someone who like himself had been thrown in prison over financial matters that he praised the son while actually seeking to praise the father. The son, however, is given a strategic place in the episode of the Gentleman of the Green Cloak. After all, Diego de Miranda is not at all happy with Lorenzo's constant study of poetry: "Todo el día se pasa en averiguar si dijo bien o mal Homero en tal verso de la *Ilíada*; si Marcial anduvo deshonesto, o no, en tal epigrama; si se han de entender de una manera o otra tales y tales versos de Virgilio." (He passes whole days in examining whether Homer expressed himself well in such a verse of the Iliad; whether Martial in such an epigram was obscene or not; whether such a verse in Virgil is to be understood this way or that way; Cervantes 1978, 2.16.154; 2008, 566.) Solís de los Santos argues that these lines clearly point to Lorenzo Ramírez del Prado, who had participated in a polemic with the Jesuit Matthaeus Rader over the meaning of a certain passage by Martial (Solís de Santos 2016: 101), and thus to the Lorenzo in the text. Perhaps the disagreement between Diego and his son Lorenzo over the importance of poetry is simply a reflection of the accusations and polemics that raged around father and son. The abode of Diego de Miranda can thus metamorphose through its changing architectures into castle, peaceful home, conflictive multifamily home, and prison. However, I would argue that these added architectures are drawn so faintly into the text that they do not intrude on the reading. So spacious and open is the home of the Gentleman of the Green Cloak, so easy are his dealings with the knight, that these recede as a massive second architecture comes into being.

The home itself, dispossessed of all the allusions recounted previously, remains a place of peace and silence that divests itself from disruptive and dysrithmic metamorphoses. It is instead a site of such perfect eurithmia that it recalls temples and sacred sites: "pero de lo que más se contentó don Quijote fue del maravilloso silencio que en toda la casa había, que semejaba un monasterio de cartujos" (but that, which pleased Don Quixote above all, was the marvellous silence throughout the whole house, as if it had been a convent of Carthusians; Cervantes 1978, 2.18.173; 2008, 582). This silence transforms the home into a kind of holy refuge as it becomes a place for those in need. Here Don Quixote can rest for four days before continuing his adventures. This silence contrasts with the constant noise of the jail and allows the novel not only to pause its adventures but also to include moments of great power and beauty, such as Don Quixote's praise of chivalry as a science encompassing all others, and Lorenzo's poem on the myth of Pyramus and Thisbe.[43] Indeed, this poem speaks of the silences rather than the words exchanged between the lovers, since the small opening in the wall that separates them can only allow souls to come together (1978, 2.18.175; 2008, 584). Their whispered love comes to fruition as they set a time to escape, a place to meet. But a lioness with Thisbe's bloody cloak convinces Pyramus that she has been killed. He falls upon his sword. On her return, after mourning for her love, Thisbe stabs herself. None of this is mentioned directly in Lorenzo's poem, which deals more with the sepulcher as an architecture of death, memory, and resurrection. In some ways this sonnet concludes Don Quixote's adventure with the lion. Both Quixote and the lovers have achieved fame through the threats of a savage beast. While Don Quixote sought to rival the hell-mouth created by Sansón Carrasco, Lorenzo turns to a different architecture, a wall that separates the lovers. The union of their soul, achieved in the beginning, leads to their death and complete union.

It is as if silence brings out both the night of the soul and the joys of the inner self. This architecture of silence then contrasts with baroque churches whose purpose is to overwhelm the senses. It calls instead for inner prayer and meditation, the stuff of mystics. For Pierre Groult, this mystical experience reachs its culmination at the Cave of Montesinos, where Don Quixote, emerging with eyes closed and having had inner experiences, albeit grotesque and comical, akin to those of Saint Teresa or Saint John, has a difficult time expressing his experiences (1954, 231–51). The jars surrounding the house like a barricade point to dangers outside, for the inner silence may hide practices that waver from the orthodox or lead to suspicion: are there remnants in this "monastery" of the *devotio moderna*? Are there instances of quiet recollection, of meditation practices led by Teresa? Or are we closer to the quasi-mnemonic *Spiritual Exercises* of Ignatius of Loyola? I would agree that the home is akin to a sacred space, that it in fact redraws the place as a very specific Carthusian monastery, the one located in Seville, which Cervantes would know well, having lived there and having been imprisoned in that city.

Indeed, very much like Seville's tower of the Giralda, the monastery of Santa María de las Cuevas (Saint Mary of the Caves) was constructed in an area utilized in Islamic times. During the Almohad Caliphate this area next to the Guadalquivir River was rich in clay, which was used to create pots. Here we have the first indication that Cervantes' text is reconstructing Diego de Miranda's house: the many *tinajas* found there echo the uses of this island in the river by Seville. Legend has it that in one of the caves the Almohads fashioned an image of the Virgin in the thirteenth century, once the city was in Christian hands. This resulted in the building of a chapel and a hermitage. The Carthusian monks moved there around 1400, thus providing the second analogy with the home of the man in green. By the sixteenth century the monastery was noted for its abundance. It possessed vineyards, olive groves, vegetable gardens, and much more. Both wine and olive oil were often kept in large earthenware jars, the very pottery that had been produced in the area since the twelfth century. Very much like Diego de Miranda's house, the monastery had a library. At his death in 1572 the humanist Benito Arias Montano had left his library to the monastery, except for the manuscripts that he gave to Philip II to be housed at the Escorial. His polyglot Bible, his theological works, and his works on history are attuned to Diego de Miranda's volumes: "Tengo hasta seis docenas de libros, cuáles de romance y cuáles de latín, de historia algunos y de devoción otros" (I have about six dozen of books, some Spanish, some Latin, some of history, and some of devotion; Cervantes 1978, 2.16.153; 2008, 565). Indeed, his son's interest in Martial is echoed by Arias Montano's youthful epigrams, written around 1551 and influenced by this Latin writer (Pascual Barea 1998, 1017–27; 2000, 259–76). In addition, the opposition father – the son in Cervantes' text with regard to poetry and particularly with regard to Martial's "dishonest" poetry – corresponds to Arias Montano's own transformation. He borrowed from Martial in his youth, but as a professor he claimed that this poet "no es para leer en público" (is not to be read in pubic; Pascual Barea 1998, 1024).

Two more elements conclude the subtle construction of the Carthusian monastery in Seville, now superimposed on the abode of the Knight of the Greek Cloak. The first has to do with the marvellous silence that encompassed the house. Arias Montano, who spent the last year at the monastery of Santa María de las Cuevas in Seville, had before him in his cell a painting of Christ carrying the cross, a painting that had been crafted by Giulio Clovio and based on a drawing by Michelangelo. In the silence required by the order, he was able to meditate on its meaning (Sylvaine 1999, 208) While Cervantes was composing the second part of *Don Quixote*, Lope de Vega published *Four Soliloquies* (1612) dealing with his penance and suffering as he knelt before a crucifix. The prologue tells that while Saint Bruno and his companions at the University of Paris were lamenting the death of his closest friend, he sees the judgment of God, who condemns him to eternal damnation. This event leads Bruno and his companions to found the order of the Carthusians. Lope exclaims that the tongue is humanity's worse enemy, destroying people's fame. Since his friend was guilty of malicious gossip, he will impose silence as one of the rules of his order (Raynié 2004, 66).

Don Quixote has recently emerged from the tricks and malicious manipulations of Sansón Carrasco. He is yet to come to the nadir of his fortune: the palace of the Duke and the Duchess and the tricks and humiliations he will have to endure in Barcelona. At this moment, the architecture in the narrative is a place of comfort and silence in which he is accepted for who he is. The home of the Gentleman of the Green Cloak is shielded by the silence of the Carthusians and by their desire to speak, when they must, with a sweet tongue rather than slander. It is under Diego de Miranda's sphere that Don Quixote can make a most eloquent discourse on the merits of poetry; it is in the home that he can pronounce a most eloquent speech on chivalry, which is heard by attentive ears; and it is at Diego de Miranda's home that he comes to hear the tragic but inspired poem on Pyramus and Thisbe, of which silence again is a key component.

One last element completes the structure, and it is a human one. Juan de Padilla, "el Cartujano," was one of the monks who abided in the monastery of Santa María de las Cuevas. We have already met him as the author of *Los doce triunfos de los doce apóstoles*, a poem that identifies the chasm or cave at Cabra as a hell-mouth. In opposition to Sansón Carrasco's false bravura, claiming that he descended into this hellish place, we now find that the home of Diego de Miranda that harbours Don Quixote for four days is a place that takes on aspects of the monastery; here a monk is able to create a marvellous architecture based on the twelve signs of the zodiac, each of which houses one of the apostles. As if to acknowledge his debt to Juan de Padilla, Don Quixote admits that a good knight needs to know many sciences, among them theology and astrology (Cervantes 1978, 2.18.171; 2008, 580–1).

As we leave Diego de Miranda's home, we feel a sense of awe that stems from simplicity. No other edifice is quite as strikingly evoked. We appreciate place as a sign to go inwards, to turn away from the deceits of the world, to put aside the noises outside and the many conflicts that disguise the deeper function of this place, a place of safety and meditation. None of the other architectures that envelop it – be it the building in which Cervantes lived in Valladolid, the jail in which he was imprisoned, or the incarceration that threatened the Ramírez del Prado family – come close to the mysterious silence of Diego de Miranda's home, where the green cloak may stand for the hope of a better world, for the fertility of the fields, for the abundance of the silent and benefic Carthusians who offer their large jars of oil and wine to the weary traveller. There are no giants, hell-mouths, or grotesque anatomies here – not even the sounds of battle. It is a silence that leads to benevolence and to an architecture of eurithmia, one that exudes topophilia and foregrounds the harmonies of the heavens and the earth, of buildings and fields. Framed by the Pantheon and by Diego de Miranda's home, the dysrithmia of the grotesque appears to be the more monstrous and threatening. Abiding within the frame of the portent of sunlight and the miracle of silence, the grotesque seems but a veering away from Vitruvian harmony.

6 Treacherous Architectures: *Don Quixote,* Part 2

He retires to his room, declines any servant to enter, and having locked the door proceeds to undress by the light of two wax candles. He is alone, but the curtains are, as it were, not drawn upon the window of the story and we see through the window bars the gleam of the bright green stockings that he is slowly shedding and studying – just as in reading another famous story, where the grotesque and the lyrical are similarly interwoven.

Vladimir Nabokov, *Lectures on Don Quixote*

Don Quixote has been exposed to a grotesque giantess as counter to his adventure with the windmills; the tower in which she gyrates recalls the partially constructed tower of the church in Toboso, where began the knight's defining adventure, one that will transform the second part of the novel into a search for the enchanted Dulcinea. The knight has also faced his own hell-mouth, no longer a cave but the open mouth of a lion that, instead of roaring, is yawning. Having survived these adventures that allow him to compete with the trickster Sansón Carrasco, he is able to enter a place of silence, which comforts him. It is a pause in the narrative, filled with harmony and eurithmia, shrugging off the compound architectures that could have ensnared the home of the Knight of the Green Cloak into becoming part of the metamorphic structures that make us wary of the world and of the senses. The silence, safety, and harmony of the home direct Don Quixote to his next destination, perhaps the most complex architecture of all in the novel. A "humanist" guides him to the Cave of Montesinos, which may hold as frightful an adventure as Sansón's hell-mouth. As he descends, it may appear as if he is going to the underworld, into a demonic cave. Down below, seemingly in a dream, Don Quixote transforms the cave into a magnificent palace, using the double architecture that is so prevalent in many of the buildings we have encountered. This palace may at first recall the crystal cave or tomb in which Merlin was interred or perhaps the crystal palace or home beneath the Tagus River, suggested in Garcilaso's third eclogue as cited by the knight. It could even point to the House of Fortune in one of the romances of chivalry. The crystal of its structure may even bring to mind the experimentation with concave and convex glass in the period. But the cave may hide yet other secrets. Jesús Botello, in an audacious and suggestive interpretation, establishes a parallel between Don Quixote and Philip II. Both have a melancholy temperament and enjoy reclusiveness (2016, 174). For Botello, the Escorial built by the Spanish king has its double in the Cave of Montesinos. At the Escorial the king can enjoy the many artistic wonders that he collects, and at the Cave of Montesinos the knight is astonished by unheard-of wonders. Within the cave, enchanted beings and their possessions take on grotesque elements as evoked by Sansón Carrasco. The ambience recalls the famous Domus Aurea, Nero's sunken palace, which was the main source of the development of the grotesque during the Renaissance.

After transiting through this ancient and dream-like structure in the first two sections of this chapter, we will follow Don Quixote to another palace that is even more devilish. Here we will encounter the Duchess's torture chamber as she, with her band of cats, transforms the knight's room into a space of shock and conflict. While Don Quixote's trials are horrifying, Sancho's term as governor of Barataria is no less contentious. We will, however, sail around Sancho's "island" and fly over myriad adventures in order to concentrate on the knight's arrival in Barcelona. Don Quixote is surprised at the astonishing welcome he receives, not realizing that Antonio Moreno's home is as devilish in its tricks as the palace of the Duke and the Duchess. The city becomes a kind of ambush in which his belief in a talking head strays from orthodoxy, grotesque shapes envelop him and the city, and wily Sansón Carrasco plans to humiliate and defeat him one last time.

Crystal

One of the most famous episodes in the second part of *Don Quixote* is the knight's visit to the Cave of Montesinos. In this section I would like to underline that the episode, like the prologue to the first part of the novel in which we encountered the Vatican Palace superimposed on Seville's Royal Jail, shows again an instance of a metamorphic architecture, where it doubles and then doubles again in unexpected ways, creating monstrous dysrithmias. Indeed, I would argue that four or five architectures are at work here: the "natural" architecture of the cave with its yawning and ill-omened mouth; the palace encountered by the knight inside the cave; the nymph's crystal palace; Merlin's crystal prison; or even the House of Fortune from the romances of chivalry. Superimposed upon all of it we can discern elements from the holy monastery of the Escorial and the devilish and grotesque Golden House built by Nero.

The cave is described as having a wide mouth, already a rather ambiguous sign for the knight, who has heard of Sansón's hell-mouth and seen the yawning mouth of a lion. Sancho sets the scene, warning his master that he would be buried alive there, and calls the cave "peor que mazmorra" (worse than any dungeon; Cervantes 1978, 2.22.208; 2008, 611). Once again, the novel evokes Cervantes' biography and his many hardships in captivity and imprisonment. Further adding to the worrisome aspect, the dark opening is surrounded by brambles, and once don Quixote had started cutting them down, "una inmensidad de cuervos y grajos, tan espesos y con tanta priesa, que dieron con don Quijote en el suelo y si él fuera tan agorero como católico y buen Cristiano, lo tuviera a mala señal y escusara en encerrarse en lugar semejante" (an infinte number of ravens and daws flew out so thick and so fast, that they had beat Don Quixote to the ground; and had he been as superstitious as he was Catholic, he had taken it for an ill omen; 1978, 1.22.209; 2008, 612). It thus appears as if he is entering some kind of magic cave. There were numerous such openings into the earth in Iberian legends and in chivalric romances. We need only recall the famous Cave of Toledo, later called the Cave of Salamanca, in which the devil was said to reside under a Catholic university, teaching its pupils opposing arts (Waxman 1916, 1–42); or even the cave, tower, or castle of Hercules that should never be opened, and the opening of which led, according to legend, to the fall of Rodrigo, the last of the Visigoth kings of Spain (García-Diego 1974, 683–700). Disregarding the evil omens, and making sure no other creatures come out, and even mentioning that bats are among the ones that do, the knight, tied to a rope, begins his descent as the remaining rope is held by Sancho and by the humanist who accompanies them, so they can pull him out. Half an hour later they do so and find that for most of the trajectory the rope feels very light, so the knight could not have descended very deeply into the cave.

On his return from the cave Don Quixote tells a fantastic tale, one that has been the subject of multiple interpretations. Our purpose here is merely to bring out some of the cave's many hidden architectures. As he descended, Don Quixote tells his rescuers, he found a concave space where he stopped to rest but fell deeply asleep. He awoke and discovered before him a beautiful landscape. Beyond this field, in what is perhaps a dream vision, albeit Don Quixote asserts that it is real, the knight perceived an immense crystal palace rising in this space. Thus we move from the premonition of a hell-mouth or other kind of difficult adventure into Hades, to a beautiful palace. That one should enter a palace through a cave would be immediately repellent to Vitruvius. He proclaims: "for there will be no propriety in the spectacle of an elegant interior approached by a low, mean entrance" (1960, 15). Breaking from Vitruvius, Don Quixote encountered "[u]n real y suntuoso palacio o alcázar cuyos muros y paredes parecían de transparente y claro cristal fabricados" (…a royal and splendid palace or castle presented itself to view; the walls and battlements whereof seemed to be built of clear and transparent crystal; Cervantes1978, 2.23.212; 2008, 615). Perhaps this is but an illusion, as he stares at the stalactites in the cave. Could he have descended the Tagus River to find the crystal abode of Garcilaso's nymphs? More likely, most readers of chivalric fiction of the time would have associated the crystal palace with the story of Merlin, who was trapped in a hole in the forest of Brocéliande, or in a crystal palace, or in one made of air, from which he never escaped. The legend of Merlin originated in Welsh poetry, but it developed and became truly prominent in medieval France. Norris J. Lacy asserts: "If the modern Arthur is to a considerable extent the property of the English-speaking world, it is only a slight exaggeration to suggest that he was, in his literary manifestations, the invention of the French Middle Ages" (1987, 187). He would be called a French enchanter in this episode because, as Henry W. Sullivan asserts, "[f]rom Cervantes's stance at the end of the sixteenth century, who could Merlin be, if not French, considering the vast outpourings of Gallicized Arthurian chivalric romance and the progressive elaboration of the *matiere de Bretagne* as the stuff of Spanish novels of chivalry now turned into the butt of Cervantes's parody?" (1998, 227). It is quite possible that Cervantes has here in mind Robert de Boron who wrote *Merlin* and perhaps the *Suite de Merlin*, which were translated into Spanish. Another Spanish text, the *Baladro del Sabio Merín* (1498), with a second edition in 1535, is also related to these versions.In these earlier texts we hear the desperate cries of the wizard, imprisoned forever in a magic tomb by his beloved but treacherous Viviane, the Spanish Niviana. But, as stated, it is equally possible to find the wizard living in a crystal tower or palace, where he is visited by his beloved. Indeed, he is commonly depicted in the Renaissance with a crystal in his hands, which gives him the ability to foretell.[1]

A dark cave protected by nightly or infernal creatures; a crystal cave covered with shiny stalactites, a crystal palace with frolicking nymphs beneath a river; a prison of crystal, a tomb forever, akin to that of

Merlin – all these architectures are conjured up as Don Quixote first speaks. Merlin's crystal cave may yet merge with a second one. In Antonio de Torquemada's *Olivante de Laura* (1564) the main structure in the Isle of Destiny (Ventura) is the House of Fortune, in which some of the great figures from the past abide. Here Olivante succeeds in a number of trials and is proclaimed not only the great champion but also lord of the isle. (Duce García 2002, 87). The walls of the House of Fortune resemble Don Quixtote's vision of the palace: "con muros de piedra y cristal y salas con gradas sobrepuestas de forma incomprensible" (with walls of stone and crystal and with stands superimposed one upon another in an incomprehensible manner; Duce García 2008, 195). Torquemada is actually foreshadowing the formless nature of the metamorphic and composite buildings found in Cervantes. If the knight waits to be immortalized here, he is sorely disappointed.[2]

In Cervantes' novel an old and wise man opens the doors. His beard, reaching his waist, clearly denotes him as a man of wisdom. He could be a Merlin figure, but if so, the knight might fear being trapped in a crystal cave for eternity. Don Quixote is not worried. Dulcinea, unlike Merlin's beloved, would not and cannot trap him because she herself has been enchanted by an evil wizard. He would certainly prefer the site to be the House of Fortune, where he can become a great champion and lord. Yet, the full description of the old wise man shows that the knight has not entered a place of pure magnificence or a house where his valour will be tried.[3] Let us recall that in the late nineteenth century the Spanish writer Ramón del Valle-Inclán, a master of the grotesque, insisted that in a concave mirror the most beautiful images become absurd (Lima 2003, 139). Don Quixote, as we may remember, had gone to sleep in a concave opening, thus alerting us that what we are about to perceive will be deformed. Enrique García Santo-Tomás asserts that "the manipulation of concave and convex lenses beginning in the 1590's in Italy, arriving in the Low Countries around 1604, and spreading throughout all of Europe by 1610 – first as an instrument of navigation and later as an astronomical tool – radically changed the prevailing understanding of the cosmos" (2017, 30). Concave lenses for myopia had been available long before that time. Earlier in the novel Don Quixote had claimed that he suffered from cataracts. Now we encounter him in a concave opening that will lead to a glass palace. There are clear references, then, to eyesight and how it can be corrected with glasses – and perhaps how the knight's eyesight, now in the crystal palace, is even more askew than before. He has just entered a carnivalesque site, where all is seen in deformed and comical or grotesque mirrors.

Gold and Alabaster

I would argue that, although all the previous architectures can be combined within the cave, there is one that stands out. Cervantes has entered a palace akin to the Domus Aurea, the Golden Palace, source of the grotesque in the Renaissance. A number of critics, including Eduardo Urbina, Helena Percas de Ponseti, Henry Sullivan, and John Weiger, have discussed grotesque elements in *Don Quixote*,[4] but they have not done so through the development of lenses for better seeing, or through the lens of Renaissance artistic discoveries.[5] We have already seen instances of the grotesque in an enormous nose and in the statue of *Faith Triumphant* as giantess. Now the classical notion of *katabasis* (a journey to the underworld that is often undertaken to acquire knowledge)[6] is mediated through Italian Renaissance art. I would argue that what we have here is a structure in which a number of objects and people echo the rediscovery of Nero's Golden House by Renaissance artists and humanists at the end of the fifteenth century.

After a fire had destroyed parts of Rome, Nero decided to appropriate some 125 acres to build a sumptuous palace and gardens, together with a lake that, according to Suetonius, resembled the sea. It was said that all parts of the palace were covered in gold. The building became "an embarrassment to subsequent emperors" (M. Hall 1999, 1) and was abandoned or at least used sparingly after the emperor's demise.[7] Finally, the fire of 104 CE led Trajan to destroy parts of the Golden Palace and build baths in its place. Halls that were not used were filled with rubble. More than a thousand years later, in the 1480s, areas of the palace were rediscovered underground, as humanists picking through the rubble of ancient ruins came across openings that led them to amazing rooms, labelled caverns or *grotte*, with perfectly preserved decorations. As more entrances were unearthed and more underground rooms were revealed, a procession of famous writers and painters came to observe, copy, and plunder. Giorgio Vasari explains that the works they found "were called grotesques from having been discovered in the underground grottoes – executed with so much design, with fantasies so varied and so bizarre" (1996, 2.489).[8]

Indeed, this type of decoration soon became famous throughout Europe. As Michael Squire has pointed out, it attracted a vast number of artists after its discovery around 1480, and it broke with what the Renaissance understood to be classical art. Criticized in ancient times by Vitruvius and Horace (Squire2012, 454), the grotesque offered unexpected perspectives: "But all variously engaged with what they perceived as the balance between order and chaos" (460). Some even found licence here to "put together parts of a composition in whatever way they chose" (461), while there were some who even related these findings to hieroglyphic signs. In Spain, grotesques can be detected in decorations that border the paintings in the vault and between frescoes in the library at the Escorial – offering further proof to Jesús Botello's theory of locating echoes of Philip II's palace/monastery in the Cave of Montesinos.[9] The term *grotesque* soon became well known in the Iberian Peninsula, not only to students of the arts such as Antonio Palomino but also to the educated layman.[10] Sebastián de Covarrubias defines the term in his encyclopaedic dictionary (1943, 661). Indeed, in *Casa de locos de amor* (The house of mad lovers), a text that was for a long time attributed to Francisco de Quevedo, we discover the term in a description of this madhouse.[11]

Thus, while discussing Cervantes' grotesque architectures in the cave, I will veer away from modern theories on the subject from Mikhail Bakhtin to Wolfgang Kayser.[12] I will centre my analysis on the grotesque in antique and Italian art. The notion of the grotesque, as we have seen, pervades Sansón Carrasco's tricks, and Don Quixote, wishing to surpass his extravagant adventures, fully expresses the grotesque in the cave. Let us recall that what he sees is a very personal interpretation that no one can corroborate. The knight has already shown some interest in evoking this kind of architecture in part 1 of the novel. In chapter 50, Don Quixote offers a vision of the delights of chivalric reading as he evokes a scene in which the hero must descend to the depths of a lake, fighting innumerable monsters.[13] Once there, he finds himself in a beautiful sunlit meadow with the sounds of a fresh stream and birds chirping. Although this is clearly a scene taken from the romances of chivalry, the text also points to a more recondite architecture.

The Domus Aurea was said to be covered in gold, and the hero of this adventure, as he looks beyond the valley, sees a palace "cuyas murallas son de macizo oro" (whose walls are of massy gold; Cervantes 1978, 1.50.585; 2018, 441). Two fountains come into view: "acullá vee una artificiosa fuente de jaspe variado y de liso mármol compuesta; acá vee otra a lo brutesco adornada, adonde las menudas conchas de las almenas con las torcidas casas blancas y amarillas del caracol, puestas con orden desordenada, mezclados entre ellas pedazos de cristal luciente de contrahechas esmeraldas, hacen una variada labor de manera que el arte, imitando a la naturaleza, parece que allí la vence." (There he espies an artificial fountain of variegated jasper and polished marble. Here he beholds another of *grotesque* rustic work, in which the minute shells of the mussel, with the white and yellow wreathed houses of the snail placed in orderly confusion, interspersed with pieces of glittering crystal and pellucid emeralds, compose a work of such variety that art, imitating nature, seems here to surpass her; 1978, 1.50.584–5; 2008, 441.) We thus see the opposition of styles: while one fountain is simple and elegant, exuding Renaissance harmony and eurithmia, the other is decorated "a lo brutesco." By placing them side by side, the knight may be commenting on the Canon of Toledo's vision of ordered art versus the romances of chivalry, "que los componen con tantos miembros, que más parece que llevan intención a formar una quimera o un monstruo que a hacer una figura proporcionada" (that are composed of so many members that the authors seem rather to design a chimera or monster, than to intend a well-proportioned figure; 1978, 1.47.565; 2008, 425). For the canon, these romances lack symmetry and proportion. They must thus recall architectural dysrithmia.

Cervantes places the grotesque fountain in a most appropriate setting, the garden, a place where such fanciful creations were allowed to proliferate. The fountain, then, typifies Don Quixote's own artistic perceptions. The fountain's adornments clearly exemplify the grotesque. The first objects mentioned are "menudas conchas" (minute mussel shells).These marine shells are often present in both grotesque classical and Renaissance art. They can be located, for example, in the most famous instance of the grotesque in Renaissance Rome, Raphael's loggia at the Vatican. Although the frescoes here are called "Raphael's Bible" because they depict scenes from Genesis to the New Testament, they are surrounded by amazing grotesque decorations, some prepared by Raphael and others by his disciple Giovanni da Udine. In the eighth bay of Raphael's loggia, for example, shells appear underneath fantastic nude bodies. From the very bottom of one such shell emerges a winged female figure. The connection between a shell and the female body was common in antiquity because, as W.S. Heckscher asserts, "the *concha marina* was the traditional and original attribute of Aphrodite" (1987, 148); it thus became both an image of the womb and of woman's genitalia. As "a purely erotic symbol," its *locus classicus* is found in Plautus. The erotics of Venus' shell are also located in authors as disparate as Augustine and Boccaccio (Heckscher 1987, 150). It is thus not surprising that Botticelli's Venus comes to land on a shell. *The Birth of Venus* is in many ways an archaeological attempt at recapturing the lost *Aphrodite Anadyomene* of Apelles. Pliny tells us that the painting "suffered from age and rot," and thus Nero decided to discard it for a newer work by Dorotheus (1952, 35.91). It is curious, then, that Renaissance artists copied newly discovered shells from Nero's Golden House and also attempted to re-envision Venus and her shell, from a painting discarded by Nero. The sea-shell, then, forms a new architecture, one of erotic pleasures. Don Quixote will find this minute and alluring grotesque in his vision of Dulcinea in the cave.

Another element found in the fountain decorations is the "casas blancas y amarillas del caracol" (white and yellow wreathed houses of the snail; Cervantes 1978, 1.50.584; 2008, 441). The move from the *concha* to the snail-shell in Cervantes' text also indicates a repetitive symbolic pattern. The snail appears in both antique and Renaissance grotesque; it should come as no surprise that it is found throughout Raphael's loggia. Here, there is a snail-shell in the first bay, under Bacchus (Nesselrath 1993, 53). And in the ninth bay, at the base of a grotesque, there is also the shell of a snail, an image that is repeated six times. The snail is always shaped in the form of a spiral, that is, a figure that always curves around a centre, always increasing in size. Like a grotesque fantasy, the spiral keeps producing new curves into infinity. The grotesque is that infinite play of forms that transforms itself from snail to flower to tree to human torso. The chivalric, then, is this fantastic play in which reality keeps changing and metamorphosing into something else. Windmills can be giants, and inns can easily be castles in a dream of wish-fulfilment. If these figures can coexist in Nero's Golden House with heroic and lyric murals, then Don Quixote's adventures can weave their infinite web of fantasies amidst classical forms.

Don Quixote as tourist, who comes to view the wonders of the Cave of Montesinos, resembles the many who went to Rome to descend into the grottoes of the Domus Aurea. Martin van Heemskerck, a painter from Nuremberg, inscribed his name in the ancient Roman caves and painted landscapes with ancient ruins. In these palatial caves there are also graffiti from Spaniards such as Isidoro Velasquez (Dacos 1969, 160), "Francescho Amad … espan(ol)," and "Pietro espanolo" (145), some even dated in the 1570s when Cervantes was in Italy.[14] A poem written about the descent into the grottoes tells us of the many perils that a visitor such as Miguel de Cervantes would face. The anonymous poem *Antiquarie prospettiche romane* (Roman antiquities in perspective), possibly written by one of the architects of Saint Peter's Basilica in Rome,[15] Donato Bramante circa 1499, is dedicated to Leonardo da Vinci and describes many of Rome's antiquities for the benefit of tourists or pilgrims (Giontella and Fubini 2006, 325–4). Among them is what would later be known as the Domus Aurea. In order to view the beautiful art therein, one had to find a suitable entrance to the "grotte." These openings would often be covered with rocks, ruins of art objects, or vegetation. In Cervantes' novel the knight also has to "cortar de aquellas malezas que a la boca de la cueva estaban" (hew down the brambles and bushes at the mouth of the cave; 1978, 2.22.209; 2008, 612). In both texts the visitor must face winged creatures of the night. Consonant with Don Quixote's surprise encounter, the Italian text mentions owls ("barbagianni") and bats ("nottoline") (stanza 129). As Sancho and the humanist pull out Don Quixote from his descent into the Cave of Montesinos, they ask him to tell "lo que en aquel infierno había visto" (what he had seen in the hell below; 1978, 2.22.210; 2008, 613). Even though Renaissance humanists were extremely excited about the underground discoveries of Roman antiquities, certain moralists viewed the endeavour with great suspicion. The Florentine Dominican Zanobi Acciaiuoli (d. 1519), for example, claimed that these archaeologists would find not a golden world but a site for "iron war and ruthless rapine" (Singer 1985, 81). This underground world of paganism was thought to be the realm of the devil. Although Don Quixote denies that he has visited a hellish place, his description is not particularly paradisiacal either. Merlin's enchantments, together with grotesque elements described in his dreamlike adventure, cast doubts as to whether he has visited a golden place or a demonic one. Pointing to Durandarte's "two-pound" heart that has been salted for preservation, to the strange appearance of Belerma, and to Dulcinea's monetary distress, Henry Sullivan concludes that "the overall outer framework of the spelunking episode has a grotesque and incongruous air" (1996, 64).

These elements also point to the Domus Aurea and to the poem that describes the journey to Roman underground sites. The dreadful state of Belerma, after having been enchanted for centuries, does not improve her original appearance, as the text relishes a grotesque portrayal. The transference of grotesque characteristics from metamorphic monsters in the walls to humans began as early as 1500 with the appearance of the anonymous poem. Here the visitors who must crawl along the dirt and become "more bizarre than the grottesche" (stanza 127; Dacos 1969, 10; Rowland 1998, 106). The figures in Montesinos' cave also seem to have a dusty, musty, and worn look. Even before Don Quixote hears of Belerma, the knight faces Montesinos whose "gorra milanesa negra" (black Milan cap; Cervantes 1978, 2.23.212; 2008, 215) would remind the reader that the city of Milan was a centre of grotesque art during the sixteenth century. Montesinos carries a rosary with beads so large that they resemble "medianas nueces" (middling nuts) and "huevos medianos de avestruz" (ordinary ostrich eggs; 1978, 2.23.212; 2008, 215).The slow metamorphosis of one object (in this case the rosary) into elements of nature is typical of the antique grotesque. The Renaissance takes them up and includes them in portraits. Gregorio Comanini, for example, revels in descriptions of Arcimboldo's portraits with "stinging acorns" (Maiorino 1991, 81). And even though we may not find ostrich eggs in Arcimboldo, his portrait of *Air* exhibits many birds, from rooster to peacock.[16] In his edition of Cervantes' novel Diego Clemencín argues that reference to the ostrich, though, may serve to recall the presence of these exotic birds in the gardens of Aranjuez (Cervantes 1833, 2.424).

In the palace/cave, Montesinos tells the knight how he was ordered by Durandarte, one of the greatest knights in the world, to remove his heart and take it to his beloved Belerma. Unfortunately both are enchanted, and she now has become less beautiful with her lamentations, carrying around her beloved's heart and accompanied by her ladies as in a procession. The macabre scenes of the removal of the heart, although stemming from ballads of the period, have no parallels elsewhere in the novel and are absent from the more playful grotesque.[17] Nor have I discovered an enlarged heart among Renaissance grotesques, but Mercury points to another bodily organ, a phallus among vegetables, in the grotesque decorations made by Giovanni da Udine for Raphael's loggia of Cupid and Psyche at the Villa Farnesina in Rome (Jones and Penny 1983, 184–5, fig. 196). Indeed, the whole episode of the Cave of Montesinos exudes a kind of sexual aura reminiscent of many grotesque fantasies. When Don Quixote sees Dulcinea and her attendants in the cave, they are "saltando y brincando como cabras" (dancing and capering like any kids; 1978, 2.23.220; 2008, 620). For Javier Herrero, the goat "is a metaphorical vehicle for the sensual, pagan, in Christian terms, 'fallen' nature of women" (1985, 20). I would add that such creatures abound in the grotesque fantasies of classical and Renaissance art.[18] Indeed, goats and the goat-legged Pan are important decorative features of the Domus Aurea.[19] In Cervantes' novel the erotic link between the maidens and the goats is further enhanced by the use of the verb *brincar*. Javier Herrero reminds us that this verb often means sexual intercourse. Diana De Armas Wilson confirms this interpretation, pointing to "Don Quixote's dream of unaffordable sexuality – of the excessive cost, for a man with only *cuatro reales*, of redeeming Dulcinea's petticoat" (1991, 74).

This grotesque mode is sustained as Don Quixote emerges from the cave. As Henry Sullivan has argued, the grotesque purgatory of part 2 of Cervantes' novel is framed by two katabases. It begins with the Cave of Montesinos and ends with Sancho falling into a pit. In this section of the novel Don Quixote is faced with enigmatic women who grow beards and with two fountains that turn out to be open sores on the duchess's legs, replicating in grotesque fashion the classical and grotesque fountains of Don Quixote's dream in part 1, chapter 50. Indeed, these "fountains," according to Mercedes Alcalá-Galán, conceal and reveal a greater secret.[20] The main grotesque elements appear to come to an end with Sancho's fall at thirty-two chapters after the initial katabasis.

Abdicating the governorship, Sancho journeys back to Don Quixote. Searching for a place to sleep, he deviates from the path and, along with his donkey, tumbles into a dark pit: "cayeron él y el rucio en una honda y escurísima sima que entre unos edificios muy antiguos estaba" (he and Dapple fell together into a deep and very dark pit, among some ruins of old buildings; Cervantes 1978, 2.55.454–5; 2008, 823). Such an entrance into an underground domain surrounded by ancient buildings clearly recalls visits to the subterranean palaces of Titus or Nero by humanist adventurers who had stumbled upon them while exploring ancient Roman ruins.

If the grotesque objects, people, and inventions in the Cave of Montesinos are akin to the Renaissance grotesque and particularly to the Domus Aurea, so is the intricate architecture of this world of enchantments and dreams. In a lower chamber, all made of alabaster, we encounter Durandarte's marble tomb, which exhibits a living corpse, yet another parallel that confirms Jesús Botello's theory of the Escorial as a building that is inserted within the cave. After all, it ought to be remembered that in 1573 Philip II ordered the transfer of all royal bodies to the Escorial so that they could rest there along with their many successors. This chamber may be reimagined as a place in which all the "enchanted" must abide. The grand royal burial vaults were erected as a sign that these royals would be forever revered and their bodies would resemble and perhaps have the power of the saints' relics, which also pervade the Escorial. Such sepulchers are necessary according to Diego de Sagredo, the first Spaniard to bring out Vitruvius' main points. The Spanish treatise even argues that such architectures are repositories of memory and a warning of the fugacity of life, pointing to the biblical David and the pagan Mausoleus (1526, 2v, 3v).

Through the crystal walls (Cervantes 1978, 2.23.217; 2008, 618), as if they are no longer made of alabaster, the knight discovers another room with the lamenting Belerma and a procession of her attendants – a procession that, according to Montesinos, she undertakes four times a week. The conjoining of two materials (crystal and alabaster) next to the marble of the tombs calls for an understanding of this commingling. Alabaster was preferred in earlier times for the construction of tombs, given its brilliant whiteness; later fashion called for marble, particularly that imported from Italy. Alabaster was also translucent and was once used even for windows. Thus, it seems at first that these three materials are correctly used and have little meaning beyond either their funerary connotations or their relation with opulence. However, given Cervantes' penchant for composite architectures, the doubling of crystal and alabaster may conceal meaning. We have already seen that crystal points to Merlin, his prison, and his enchantments. Alabaster may point in two directions. First, it relates to the Domus Aurea. Among its many rooms there is one with a bath and a waterfall, made particularly bright by its alabaster walls. The waters of the palace recall the many metamorphoses created by Merlin, who transformed Belerma's duenna along with her daughters and nieces into lakes, while Durandarte's squire became the river Guadiana.

Second, this material points us forward in the text. The Kingdom of Aragon had one of the largest deposits of alabaster in Europe, and its sites were around the river Ebro, which Don Quixote navigates in chapter 30 in order to meet the Duke and the Duchess. In Roman times, the walls that surrounded the city of Caesaraugusta, today's Zaragoza (Don Quixote's destination), were reworked with alabaster; in Muslim times, such was the prevalence of this material in building that Zaragoza became known as the "Medina Albaida," the White City. By the time of Cervantes, many famous artists from Zaragoza had been doing their best work using alabaster. Thus, alabaster points us to the palace of the Duke and the Duchess.

Although crystal, alabaster, and marble are sumptuous materials, the actual state of people in the palace is less than ideal. They have lived more than five hundred years under Merlin's enchantment but have grown old and worn; Belerma's teeth like almonds, the bags under her eyes, and her laments over her beloved's heart are but one indication of the atmosphere of the place. The presence of an impoverished Dulcinea is another, and the existence of a living man without a heart causes us to ponder the nature of this underground space. Perhaps this palace corresponds to just that, the lack of heart. Nero's palace, though sumptuous, had no heart because its owner's cruelty was well known. Although the knight is welcomed, he sees only sadness and lack around him. Descending into the cave, Don Quixote wants to triumph, to show that he is better than the Knight of the Mirrors who has come to know the secrets of yet another cave. Here, perhaps, Don Quixote, without realizing it, comes to know himself as someone who is aging and lacks a lady-love, as someone who can no longer envision a great palace akin to the novels of chivalry as he once did in part 1 of the novel. Although he affirms that this has been a major adventure and triumph, he has entered the realm of the chthonic grotesque. Its playful erotic images must be left behind, for he will soon be welcomed in another palace, only to be used as a plaything by its owners. It is as if the cruelty of Nero will accompany the knight to his next space of suffering.

Torture Chamber

The scenes at the Duke and the Duchess's palace encompass some thirty chapters, much more than a third of the 1615 *Don Quixote*. Nabokov reminds us that the many sadistic tricks played on Don Quixote at the palace and its surroundings cannot be ignored.[21] They are based on the desire for entertainment: "She [the Duchess] read the first part of the adventures of Don Quixote and she and her husband are anxious to meet its hero and have some good tigerish sport with him" (1983, 62). When they first meet, she is wearing green for the hunt and thus becomes "a diabolical Diana" (62). But Nabokov fails to mention that in order to arrive at her palace, the knight must travel down the river Ebro and encounter what seem to be ghostly figures. While the episode recalls enchanted boats in the romances of chivalry and it echoes shipwrecks by Ulysses and Aeneas (Marasso 1959, 28), while it points to Cervantes' knowledge of cosmography (Domínguez 2009, 139–57), and while it even serves as a kind of initiation or baptism (D'Onofrio 2006, 355–63), I prefer to view it as passage to the underworld or to an alternate space in which demons, foreign deities, and other dark creatures abide. Once this crossing has been undertaken, and after this moment of death in life at the mill, Don Quixote and Sancho meet the cruel Diana, who welcomes them to her palace of torture. Even Sancho does not escape, and while thinking he is rewarded with the Isle of Barataria, he comes to suffer like Tantalus as food comes close to his mouth, only to be removed.

Even though the palace is expansive, with gardens and woods surrounding it, and with many delightful rooms and surprising inhabitants, it is still what Nabokov calls a "torture house" (1983, 70). Within this house of pain and pleasure there is a snug, closed-in place that is Don Quixote's private room. Nabokov in some ways surpasses in his description what is about to transpire, arguing not only that the window in the knight's room will be the cause of his suffering, but also that the narrative itself opens the window to the knight's inner sentiments. Alone, having lost his Dulcinea, and without Sancho, he starts to undress. "Oh disaster, the narrator sighs as he contemplates the bursting of several stitches in the left stocking which now has the appearance of lattice work. The wretched sense of poverty mingles with his general dejection" (Nabokov 1983, 69). This metaphorical window of narrative opens up to yet another window, that of the stocking turned into a "celosía" (lattice window; Cervantes 1978, 2.44.370; 2008, 749). This new window allows us to see that the suffering comes not only from the Duke and the Duchess but also from what their palace represents. The utter poverty of the would-be knight clashes with his desire for fame and fortune.

The narrative, with astounding agility, moves from the inner window to the self to the outer window: "hacía calor y no podia dormir, levantóse del lecho y abrió un poco la ventana de una reja que daba sobre un hermoso jardín" (the weather was hot, and he could not sleep: he got out of bed, and opened the casement of a grate-window, which looked into a fine garden; 1978, 2.44.372; 2008, 750). He then hears a conversation in which he is called a new Aeneas who has come to the palace, an obvious reference to the arrival of Virgil's hero at Dido's kingdom and the love that Aeneas and Dido immediately feel for each other. This new Dido will sing to him in the hopes of awakening his desire. Don Quixote immediately thinks not so much of the epic poem but of the many scenes in the books of chivalry in which maidens fall in love: "ventanas, rejas y jardines, músicas, requiebros y desvanecimientos que en los sus desvanecidos libros de caballerías había leído" (of casements, grates, and gardens, serenades, courtships, and faintings away, of which he had read in his idle books of chivalry; 1978, 2.44.372; 2008, 750). The scene is thus cleverly set so that the knight will imagine that a lady from the palace has fallen for him. In her long lament Altisidora acknowledges the knight's love for Dulcinea but hopes that he can at least let her sit beside him on the bed or even massage his feet. Frustrated, she sings: "No mires de tu Tarpeya / este incendio que me abrasa / Nerón manchego del mundo" (*Don't look from the Tarpeian rock / at this fire that burns my soul / Nero of La Mancha and of the world*; 1978, 2.44.373; 2008, 752).[22] She thus imagines Don Quixote as a new Nero, standing on top of the Tarpeian rock, watching Rome burn. The reader who has followed him through the grotesque and melancholy atmosphere of the Cave of Montesinos, which in one of its doublings reveals the Golden Palace of the emperor, will surely realize that the knight is being haunted by Nero's cruelty. In actuality, it is not the knight who is cruel, but those who impel Altisidora to mock him with laments.

The Tarpeian rock was a steep cliff at the summit of the Capitoline Hill from which murderers and traitors were flung to their death. A legend tells of Nero fiddling on the rock as Rome burned. In this case, the knight in his apartments imagines finding delight over the fire of love with which Altisidora burns. As the lady sings, then, we encounter yet another double architecture so common in Cervantes. Altisidora, surrounded by her companions, is set to sing from below: "levantaron la voz los de abajo" (*those below* raised their voices so high; 1978, 2.44.372; 2008, 750). Don Quixote listens to her from above. In the legend Nero stands above and Rome burns below. In the architecture of the narrative

Don Quixote, a carefree Nero, is above while Altisidora sings of the fires of love from below. This doubling serves to underline the mendacious and cruel architectures of the palace. Cervantes had utilized this well-known legend of Nero's fiddling in part 1 of the novel where Ambrosio accuses Marcela of being a new Nero, watching with glee Grisóstomo's amorous fire. Nero is again evoked in the second part, in which we have seen how the Cave of Montesinos is configured as Nero's palace and as a double architecture. In this new double architecture Don Quixote will not fare well. For him, the palace and his room there are indeed torture chambers.

On discovering the next day that Altisidora has fainted (she actually appears to faint) on seeing him, the knight asks for a musical instrument. That night he utilizes the open window to sing a song in praise of Dulcinea, explaining to Altisidora that she is but a passing fancy. The response is almost immediate as his "place" is violated by the use of the window. Windows may seem to be pleasurable openings that alleviate enclosure, but, as we have seen in previous chapters, they may allow outside influences; they may attract dangers from outside. A sack containing one hundred bells is repeatedly lowered and raised from above through the window of his room, creating the most dreadful noise. Then, a sack full of cats with smaller bells tied to their tails is emptied just outside: "dos o tres gatos se entraron por la reja de su estancia, y dando de una parte a otra parecía que una región de diablos andaba en ella" (two or three of the cats got in at the casement of his chambers, and scouring about from side to side, one would have thought a legion of devils was broke loose in it; 1978, 2.46.385; 2008, 762). These creatures even manage to extinguish all the candles in the room. In the dark one of the cats attacks the knight, hurling itself at his face, clinging to his nose, and using its claws and teeth against him. David F. Richter explains: "The Duchess and the Duke's cruel deeds differ from the other cruelties in *Don Quixote* since they present a sustained effort to inflict suffering and signal the culmination of all cruelties previously displayed in the text" (2010, 47). In what this critic calls a *methectic* play, one that resonates beyond the game, "Don Quixote enters a state of melancholy as a result of the cruelty that causes pleasure to the Duchess and Duke" (50). In the prologue to the first part of the novel, we learned that one of the text's purposes was to lead the melancholy to laughter. Here, a laughter based on cruel tricks leads to melancholy. The space of the book then is at odds with the events at the palace.

Steven Wagschal is one of the few critics to speak up for the cats in this episode, arguing cogently that the episode "suggests a brief but focused attention to the perspective and mental processes of felines"

(2018, 205). Aside from this insightful new approach, others consistently show the shadowy aspects of these creatures. The use of cats in the literature of the period, as J. Ignacio Díez reminds us, brings a certain dark aura to the episode. They are labelled as traitorous and ravenous like tigers. Furthermore, *gato* is often used to refer to thieves. More importantly, it is associated with sexuality and witches. Indeed, the sound made by the cats that enter his chamber is compared to that made by a legion of devils, and Don Quixote calls them malignant enchanters. On the one hand, J. Ignacio Díez rejects the notion that the cats embody Altisidora who scratches the knight. For him, their bells contrast with the pleasant music performed at the palace (2019, 91–112). On the other hand, Alicia Gallego Zarzosa sees the poem at least as part of a sexual awakening episode (2019, 128–47). There is no question that a poem of love sung by a very young woman to Don Quixote is bound to have an effect. His rejection of Altisidora is done not in prose but in song. It is as if the knight wanted to continue the amorous dalliance while saying no. At the same time, the mysterious and darkening aspects prevail. Although the response has been carefully orchestrated by the Duchess as part of the palace entertainment, it also partakes of the hermetic. Augustin Redondo reminds us that the name Altisidora is made of *Alta* (tall) and *Isidora*, and the latter means "disciple of Isis," the goddess of hermetic secrets as portrayed in Apuleius' *Golden Ass* (1998a, 54–5). I would add that Isis was associated with the cat goddess, Bast, and thus felines were often in attendance at Isis' many temples (Regula 2001, 137).[23] Indeed as a lunar goddess, she was also associated with Artemis/Diana (Witt 1971, 147). Thus, the cruel Duchess/Diana punishes the knight for rejecting the Isis-like Altisidora, utilizing her own felines for this task.

Certainly there are carnivalesque and humorous elements in this episode, but it also seems to connect the Duchess to Diana (often said to be a witch) and to the hermetic rites of Isis. The palace may seem to be a site of pleasure and relaxation, but the parodic infringement of the cult of Isis/Altisidora brings about immediate retribution. After all, she was often invoked in love affairs (Witt 1971, 147). While Don Quixote may have thought that he was safe in his hermetic room, by using the window to reject Altisidora he opens his place to lunar influences. His room becomes a space of frightful darkness, horrid sounds, and hellish creatures. Later on, the cruel Altisidora "repents" her actions as the Duke and the Duchess send her with "aceite de Aparicio" (Cervantes 1978, 2.46.385; 2008, 763) to cure his wounds. This balm was invented by a Morisco named Aparicio de Zubía sometime in the sixteenth century. It became exceedingly expensive owing to its effectiveness in curing wounds, one of its ingredients being hypericum, a flowering herb associated with the feast of Saint John and planted around homes for protective purposes. Would such flowers bloom in the gardens of the palace? We may doubt it because their many devilish pranks are quite a success as the knight continues to suffer. Given that its yellow flowers are said to bloom at the time of the solstice, this might be one more indication that the time is approaching for the fateful day: Don Quixote arrives at Barcelona on the eve of Saint John's Day and enters the city on the following day (1978, 2.61.506; 2008, 868).

Barcelona

The helpful bandit, Roque Guinart, takes Don Quixote and Sancho close to the city, where they wait out the night. Thus, Don Quixote, as a solar knight shining in splendour, enters Barcelona at dawn. Advised of his arrival, others who are celebrating Saint John's Day come to him as if the feast were all in his honour. He is carried about in triumph, but his departure inverts this situation. Aurora Egido states: "El alba luminosa de Barcelona, supondrá, sin embargo, el ocaso de don Quijote, pues partirá de ella como caballero vencido tras un forzado duelo personal y sin salir triunfante de justa alguna que mereciese el nombre de tal." (The luminous dawn in Barcelona will become the sunset of Don Quixote because he will leave as a vanquished knight after a forced personal duel, and he will leave without having won any jousting contests; 2007, 95). And thus it should be, since the sun inverts its course during this feast of the solstice that celebrates the longest day of the year. Until now it has been ascending in the heavens, but at this time it is taking a turn of descent towards less light, towards fall and winter. In reality, the architecture of the heavens is slow to catch up with the knight whose adventures have already turned towards darkness and melancholy.

Yet, at this point, Don Quixote, having befriended Roque and having arrived at his destination, feels awe and happiness. What first amazes knight and squire is the sea, which they encounter for the first time: "hasta entonces dellos no visto" (till then they had never seen [it]; 1978, 2.61.506; 2008, 868). However, much earlier in the novel, Don Quixote had come to the river Ebro and, finding a boat, thought it had been left there by enchanters as an invitation to adventure. As they sailed, Don Quixote imagined that they had crossed the equator, while Sancho just trembled with fear as he was surrounded by water and had no oars with which to navigate. The knight thought he perceived in the distance a "ciudad, castillo o fortaleza" (1978, 2.29.265; 2008, 659), which turned out to be a flour-mill. The pair would have capsized and drowned if it had not been for the mill workers. This adventure points to Barcelona.

Starting with in the Middle Ages, a legend grew in Catalonia regarding the founding of Barcelona. Although there are a number of versions, all tell of nine "barcas" (boats), one of which separated from the others, possibly due to a storm.[24] This lone ship was led by Hercules who landed on a beautiful coast and founded a new city. In a volume published in 1775, Henrique Flórez explains: "y la nona llegó al sitio donde Hércules edificó esta Ciudad, y la dió el nombre de Barcanona, esto es, Ciudad de la nona o novena Barca" (and the ninth arrived at the site on which Hercules built this city and named it Barcanona, that is, city of the *nona* or ninth boat; 1775, 1).[25] Although a number of humanists reacted against the authenticity of this story, it became one of the most popular foundational myths of Barcelona.[26] The chivalric or enchanted boat that takes Don Quixote and Sancho to unknown and undiscovered places is transformed into this legendary ninth boat that gives its name to the city, foreshadowing the knight's arrival in Barcelona. If Sansón Carrasco had wanted to become a new Hercules with his false adventures, Don Quixote succeeded in arriving at his destination. And yet, the knight may have gone too far. Like the sun, he must move away.

In order to confirm the boat as a foreshadowing of Don Quixote as the Hercules of Barcelona, there ought to be other pointers in the text that would reinforce this notion. Studying the role of Barcelona in *Las dos doncellas*, Barbara Fuchs views the city not just in terms of its laudatory description in the *novela*. She argues that this geographical space ought to be viewed in terms of "both the limits and limitations of Spain's imperial reach" (2003, 57). Thus Barcelona, for this critic, recalls the motto that Hercules placed in the columns that led to the ocean, *Non plus ultra*, as Cervantes seeks to contain Spain's imperial expansionism. Barcelona, I would argue, also stands as the sailing point to the Italian shores, and we know that Cervantes spent his life desiring Italy, a desire that is often represented in his literary texts through allusions to the art, architecture, and culture of the Italian peninsula (De Armas 2006, 4). In the same way that Cervantes cannot return to Italy, the knight cannot continue his adventures. Both character and author must return home in defeat. Fiction and biography intersect at this point. Cervantes went to Barcelona to seek patronage from the Count of Lemos. He wanted to embark on a journey to Italy. But this was denied.[27] In this sense, Don Quixote's praise of Barcelona is also a cruel reflection on Cervantes. The city known for its perfect friendships is the place in which the writer discovered that his friend Lupercio Leonardo de Argensola was not willing to help him obtain patronage, that he was not willing to argue for Cervantes, and that Lemos, in spite of all the praise Cervantes had heaped on him, would not take him on his ship.[28]

Although we have so far looked at the celestial architectures and at the terrestrial journey, we have yet to view the city's architecture and its ambience. Sometime after his defeat and departure from Barcelona, Don Quixote intones a lengthy and laudatory description of the city, a rather curious *laudatio* given his unfortunate adventures there. The *laudatio* is linked in the text to the publication of the "false" second part of the novel by Avellaneda and to Cervantes' response. The knight first saw the volume in chapter 59, and, given that the imposter had gone to Zaragoza, he determined to change course: "no pondré los pies en Zaragoza, y así sacaré a la plaza del mundo la mentira dese historiador moderno, y echarán de ver las gentes que yo no soy el don Quijote que él dice" (I will not set a foot in Saragossa, and so I will expose to the world the falsity of this modern historiographer, and all people will plainly perceive, I am not the Don Quixote he speaks of; Cervantes 1978, 2.59.490; 2008, 855). When he was told that other jousts would be held in Barcelona, he decided to journey there. After Barcelona, in chapter 70, he encounters the resurrected Altisidora who tells him that she has been to hell and back and that in those infernal spaces devils were playing ball with books. One of them was the second part of *Don Quixote*, written by an Aragonese from Tordesillas (1978, 2.70.566; 2008, 921). Almost home, in chapter 72 the knight encounters Álvaro Tarfe, a character from the false second part. He tells him how he deviated from Zaragoza and travelled towards Barcelona in order to foil Avellaneda: "en todos los días de mi vida no he estado en Zaragoza; antes, por haberme dicho que ese don Quijote fantástico se había hallado en las Justas desa ciudad, no quise yo entrarme en ella, por sacar a las barbas del mundo su mentira." (I never was in Saragossa in all the days of my life: on the contrary, having been told that this imaginary Don Quixote was at the tournaments of that city, I resolved not to go hither, that I might make him a liar in the face of all the world; 1978, 2.72.578; 2008, 931). It is at this point that Don Quixote describes Barcelona in terms that recall the *laudatio* of cities in plays and prose of the period.[29] Don Quixote calls Barcelona "archivo de la cortesía, albergue de los extranjeros, hospital de los pobres, patria de los valientes, venganza de los ofendidos y correspondencia grata de firmes amistades, y en sitio y en belleza única" (that register of courtesy, asylum of strangers, hospital of the poor, native country of the valiant, avenger of the injured, agreeable seat of firm friendship, and, for situation and beauty singular; 1978, 2.72.578; 2008, 931). Jean Canavaggio warns that we ought "apreciar con cierta prudencia semejantes declaraciones" (to accept with a bit of prudence such declarations; 2007, 50). For him this is a place of defeat rather than triumph, and thus Don Quixote's words cannot be taken at face value. The knight even admits that he found there "mucha pesa-dumbre" (much to my sorrow; 1978, 2.72.578; 2008, 931). Our view of Barcelona's architecture will then echo through inversion the knight's "praise."

According to the "archivo de la cortesía" (register of courtesy), the city ought to offer the knight all its favours. In the midst of the Saint John the Baptist celebrations, which turn the beautiful rising of the sun into a chaotic experience, full of martial moments and smoke, a gentle-man welcomes Don Quixote to the city, calling him the true knight, not the false one. Such are his praises and his high rhetoric that Don Quixote, according to Christina Lee, appears as if he were enchanted (2005, 209). He is left speechless, in a state of wonder and submission, and follows a group of horsemen as they envelop him in "un revuelto caracol" (*a disordered snail mantle / shell*; Cervantes 1978, 2.61.507).[30] This expression connotes a kind of ominous feeling, as if the knight now belonged to this group of enchanters. Indeed, there is a saying that makes it even more sinister: "Si a tu marido quieres matar, dale caracoles en el mes de San Juan" (If you want to kill your husband, feed him snails during the month of Saint John; Santiago Álvarez 2011, 35). Ever since antiquity the snail had been generally perceived in a negative light as an image of distrust, cowardliness, and opportunism, and it thus appears in sixteenth-century imagery (Heredia Moreno and López-Yarto Elizalde 2001, 128).[31] Here, although the horsemen seem to be showing deference and courtesy to Don Quixote, the opposite is the truth. They want him as a plaything for amusement and surround him in a rather ominous and commanding manner. Their grouping is like the "house," shell, or mantle that the snail carries with it, mov-ing him along in their sphere. Although we have seen how two perfect friends can create a "place" wherever they are, given their rapport and sympathy, in this instance the horsemen are fashioning the opposite of place, a space of deceit. In terms of the enchanted Dulcinea the sea-shell pointed to desire and even lust, but here the snail signals disorder, deceit, and treachery. More than that, they are images of dysrithmia. Let us recall that these creatures were often used as grotesque decora-tions and that Cervantes included them as part of the decoration on a fountain in chapter 50 of part 1. In Nero's Golden House, horses with legs made of leaves, a man with crane legs, and snails were part of the decorations, and these decorations, at times, merged with the food deli-cacies that were served. Snails were placed at the edge of trays among greenery and edible vegetables. As noted previously, the Renaissance delighted in these new discoveries and placed grotesque images even in bathrooms. Thus, Cervantes is pointing to a snail "house," a grotesque variety of treacherous riders who get hold of the knight and carry him around as one more metamorphic plaything of the grotesque. Our first impression of Don Quixote in Barcelona, then, is that he does not resonate with the site; his image is not concordant with the cityscape – there is no eurithmia.

The formation of those escorting the knight is not a sufficiently closed place/space that would prevent disruptions. Youngsters want to interfere and create their own fun, sticking "aliagas," briers or thorny bushes (Cervantes 1978, 2.61.508; 2008, 869) in Rocinante's tail as well as in the behind of Sancho's ass. Both knight and squire are flung from their conveyances. The fall from the horse is often symbolic of the inability to control one's passions and destiny. Here it refers to the latter because the knight has lost control of those poking fun at him and his horse, and those leading him to a place unknown. Eventually the leader takes Don Quixote to his well-appointed and spacious home. After helping the knight with his armour, the gentleman and his entourage take him out onto a balcony facing one of the main streets of Barcelona. The text clarifies that his presence there is to amuse, "como a mona le miraban" (as if he had been a monkey; 1978, 2.62.509; 2008, 870). Antonio Moreno's home, then, is not a place of safety, comfort, meditation, and rest such as the home of the Knight of the Green Cloak. It more closely resembles the palace of the Duke and the Duchess. At the dinner table, knight and squire are questioned, just as in the previous palace, about their notions and adventures, their whole purpose there being to amuse. The same can be said of the "sarao" or dance that is organized and in which the knight is forced to whirl around with many ladies until he is more than sore and exhausted. Curiously, he eventually utters an expression in Latin while telling them to leave him alone: "*Fugite, partes adversae*" (Begone all evil powers; 1978, 2.62.513; 2008, 874). Commenting on this phrase derived from church exorcisms, Hilaire Kallendorf remarks: "Cervantes utilizes the linguistic register of diabolical mysteries as one of multiple narrative techniques which lend verisimilitude to Don Quixote's madness. But he also allows his character to act as his own exorcist, even reciting the words of the *Rituale Romanum*" (2003, 15). In a sense, then, we can view the homes of the Duke and Duchess and of Antonio Moreno as a space of suffering, one in which devilish aristocrats play pranks on the knight for their own amusement. It is no surprise that this episode is followed by that of the enchanted head, a bronze bust that foretells the future.[32] On the first day, Antonio Moreno takes Don Quixote to a secluded and distant room. The term *apartado* (Cervantes 1978, 2.62.510; 2008, 871) is used throughout literary texts to point to a place in which secrets are kept and imparted. We thus find it repeatedly – for example, in the eleventh tale of Don Juan Manuel's *Conde Lucanor* – as a place to which a magician takes his would-be apprentice. In this episode, as in the tale, magical knowledge may be imparted, and thus the apprentice (in this case, Don Quixote) is sworn to secrecy. Other precautions are taken such as closing and locking the door. Indeed, the word *secreto* is used repeatedly (1978, 2.62.510; 2008, 871).

Don Quixote witnesses a bronze statue standing on a table made of jade, which in turn stands on a central leg made of the same material, supposedly constructed by the magical arts of a disciple of Escotillo,[33] and using astrological principles. Jasper, as Marsilio Ficino explains, belongs to the planet Saturn, the most malefic of celestial bodies, and yet the one that reveals the highest and most occult secrets (Schaffer 2016, 63). The table thus signals the occult and perhaps devilish magic of the bronze head. It will not speak on a Friday, Moreno explains, so they will return with some guests the following day. Saturday is the day of Saturn and the most propitious moment to visit the statue. In addition, Antonio Moreno explains that the bust was made according to appropriate astrological knowledge. During the early modern period, statues or idols thus created were believed to be inhabited by demons (Kallendorf 2005, 173–86). Of course, this is all but one more trick to amuse his guests as the knight comes to believe in its enchantments. In reality it is a mechanical invention. Antonio Moreno wants to regale his guests with Don Quixote's belief in enchanters. The trick borders on heterodoxy, and the knight's belief sets him outside Church doctrine. Indeed, this is the only time that Don Quixote's chivalric convictions are explicitly contrasted with orthodoxy. Cervantes carefully explains the mechanics of the statue and still claims that it must be dismantled after the adventure because it could become a matter for the Inquisition (Cervantes1978, 2.62.517; 2008, 878).

Even upon leaving the house to see the city, Don Quixote runs into difficulties as he comes upon a printing press. Barcelona was known for presses that released numerous short *relaciones* or brief news items of events taking place in the Mediterranean and throughout the world. Henry Ettinghousen shows that of the 267 known publications that contained four pages in quarto format, more than 50 per cent had to do with this kind of news items. They included engravings that had to do with the topic discussed. For example, the picture of a galley on the front would have to do with a naval battle, and of a knight would signify a battle on land. Ettinghousen exclaims: "¡Imagínense la alegría que habría tenido don Quijote en la imprenta que visitó en Barcelona, de haber podido ver como se imprimía alguna de las muchas relaciones barcelonesas de batallas en tierra que llevaban en su primera página un grabado – algunas veces idéntico a los que adornaban las portadas de los libros de caballerías – de un caballero armado!" (Imagine Don Quixote's joy, on seeing the press to which he was taken in Barcelona, to discover how some of the many chronicles from Barcelona were printed, those dealing with battles on land carrying on their front page an engraving of an armed knight, sometimes identical to those used on covers for the romances of chivalry; 2007, 166.) But perhaps Don Quixote would not have been quite as enthusiastic if he had known that in this printing press (according to the Cervantine text) Avellaneda's false second part was being produced, thus undermining the true knight's authority. Curiously, he has little to say on the subject. Perhaps the diabolical tricks and treachery are taking their toll, or perhaps he somehow intuits his coming defeat. This press is in the midst of translating a book from Italian, entitled *Le batagele*, now called *Los juguetes*. Would a knight who pays attentions to portents understand that this may signal that he has become a plaything for the inhabitants of Barcelona?

Since the Barcelona episode had commenced with a view of the sea, it cannot end without a return to the beach. Don Quixote is entertained at a galley about to leave Barcelona, while tricks are played on Sancho. The news of an Algerian corsair brigantine ends with the capture of its leader, who turns out to be a Christian woman disguised as a man; she has come to plead for the rescue of her beloved Gaspar Gregorio, held in Algiers and much coveted for his youth and good looks.[34] This unexpected interpolation will eventually reveal its meaning after the second adventure by the sea. Sansón Carrasco, disguised as the Knight of the White Moon, challenges Don Quixote. They charge each other on the beach and in the presence of the viceroy and Antonio Moreno among others. The knight's defeat results in his being sent home and forbidden from practising chivalry for a year. It takes six days for the knight to recover from his defeat, and this time Antonio Moreno takes good care of him, while chiding Sansón Carrasco for having deprived Barcelona and the world of the knight's comical antics. Talking with Sancho after his recovery, Don Quixote comments: "En verdad que estoy por decir que me holgara que hubiera sucedido todo al revés, porque me obligara a pasar en Berbería, donde con la fuerza de mi brazo diera libertad no sólo a don Gregorio, sino a cuantos cristianos cautivos hay en Berbería. Pero ¿qué digo, miserable? ¿No soy yo el vencido? ¿No soy yo el derribado? ¿No soy yo el que no puede tomar arma en un año? Pues ¿qué prometo? ¿De qué me alabo, si antes me conviene usar de la rueca que de la espada?" (In truth, I was going to say I should be glad if it had fallen out quite otherwise, that I might have been obliged to go over to Barbary, where, by force of my arm, I should have given liberty, not only to Don Gregorio, but to all the other Christian captives that are in Barbary. But what do I say? Wretch that I am! Am I not he who has been vanquished? Am I not he who is overthrown? Am I not he who has it not in his power to take arms in a twelvemonth? Why then do I promise? Why do I vaunt, if I am fitter to handle a distaff than a sword?; Cervantes 1978, 2.65.538; 2008, 896.) Before the completion of his novel Cervantes returns once again to a topic that has occupied him in different moments of the text: the fate of the Moriscos and the empire's seeming indifference towards North Africa. Lucas A. Marchante-Aragón points to the feminization of the knight as he gives up the sword for the spinning wheel. This critic adds: "Don Quixote's words certify the end of the belief in the imperial narrative as all its representatives had given up the virtues of imperial virility of *virtus* and *pietas*, a state of affairs that pushed Ana to have to fight her own battles" (2016, 14).

However comical or based on trickery it was, we have witnessed a mythical battle on the beach, one between Sansón Carrasco, Knight of the White Moon (in the guise of the biblical Samson), and Don Quixote who wanted to be a new Hercules.[35] But Hercules was forced to abide with women for a time. His feminization was part of his growth as a hero. While some emphasize "the hypermasculine icon's shocking dereliction at gender performance" (Fox 2019, 89), others such as the foremost woman artist of the period, Artemisia Gentileschi, revel in it (89).[36] Apparently, Cervantes' protagonist would turn away from any hint of perceived feminization. He refused to take up the spinning wheel as Hercules did at the court of Omphale. A more playful attitude towards the myth will be encountered in the *Persiles*.

Don Quixote could have continued his quest after his exile from chivalry; he could have bided his time. But his disillusionment with the world and with his quest takes over. At the Knight of the Greek Cloak's home he had received encouragement to go on, but his enemies' "castles" have proven too strong. The grotesque anatomy of the lying nose, the false adventures of Sansón Carrasco including a giantess and a hellmouth, the palace of the Duke and Duchess with its chambers of torture, the horsemen as snails that lead Don Quixote on the wrong path, and Antonio Moreno's home in Barcelona have shown him to be a mere plaything of an aristocracy that must find amusement to fill their lives of unproductive leisure. This is what Don Quixote hides in the deepest recesses of his soul: the belief in chivalry and in a fantastical Dulcinea, a certainty that all he wishes for has now gone from the world and been replaced by edifices of illusion and lies. On his return home, he is benevolent to all, including Sansón Carrasco. But he has made his decision. His next adventure will not include the edifices of an empire whose ideals he no longer understands; nor will it include castles in the air – the monstrous and composite buildings that metamorphose into this or that in a land whose splendour and decadence recall the infamous Domus Aurea. Like Hercules, he will wear the poisonous tunic of disillusionment as he ascends to another sphere in search of the mansions promised by his religion. Barcelona, then, has proven to be his last stand. If others can be deceitful so can he.

Don Quixote's laudatory speech on Barcelona is filled with irony, replete with dubious statements that also undermine the beauty of its location and architecture. As "archivo de la cortesía" (register of courtesy) the city ought to be welcoming. But his stay with Antonio Moreno evinces a sadistic and hypocritical bent that recalls the treatment of Don Quixote at the home of the Duke and Duchess: "Así, tanto don Antonio como el duque, para no herir su sensibilidad, disimulan su hilaridad tras una apariencia de cortesía" (Thus both Antonio and the Duke, in order not to hurt his sensibilities, hid their hilarity beneath the cloak of courtesy; Close 2007, 65). The city's architectures hide the sinister purposes of Antonio Moreno and his circle. Horsemen surround the knight as if they were housed inside a snail, only to deceive him. The snail, as a common feature in grotesque paintings and adornments, points to the city's architectures as related to Nero's Domus Aurea. The knight's own exclamation of exorcism while he is at a ball underlines the devilish nature of his surroundings. So does the enchanted head. As for "albergue de los extranjeros" (asylum of strangers), the city's openness allows for brigands to roam the countryside and even come into the city. The city also welcomes Sansón Carrasco, the wily figure who will defeat the knight. For Don Quixote the city could not represent the "patria de los valientes" (native country of the brave) because he has been defeated, and it cannot be seen as a place providing "venganza de los ofendidos" (vengeance of the injured) because he is obliged to return home in defeat. Finally, it is not a city of friendship because Antonio Moreno is not Don Quixote's friend but uses him for amusement, and it is in Barcelona that Sansón Carrasco (hidden under the disguise of the Knight of the White Moon) makes the final treasonable act that shatters any possible notion of *amicitia*. Even a balcony, an architectural feature that is often used in love scenes, is here utilized to display a ridiculous Don Quixote. The one building that he would truly welcome, the bookstore, reveals its treachery by displaying a copy of the false second part of the novel. The knight's last point in his laudation of Barcelona is that it is "en sitio y en belleza única" (for situation and beauty, singular). And yet, the placement of it by the sea allows corsairs to threaten it at will, while the beauty of its architectures is tainted with the demonic and the grotesque and thus eschews the eurithmia of classical buildings. For Vitruvius, temples and other buildings are the measure of the ideal human being. For Don Quixote, the cityscape does not measure up, given the character of those he has come to know in Barcelona.

7 A Windowless North: *Persiles y Sigismunda*, Books 1 and 2

Don't you know that I have possessed this land for many a year?
Lope de Vega, *The Discovery of the New World by Christopher Columbus*

In search of his architectures, we now arrive at Cervantes' last novel, the final element in the scaffolding of the author's Virgilian literary career that goes from eclogue (*La Galatea*) to epic. There are no *Georgics* in the middle. Instead, we have *Don Quixote* as an apprenticeship to epic, but a work so different from his posthumous novel that he must have decided to question or abandon many of the traditional elements of the chivalric and epic traditions. Cervantes warns us that his *Persiles y Sigismunda*, an epic that would bring him lasting fame, is his best work.[1] Even when announcing its future publication in the prologue to the *Novelas ejemplares*, he considered it a work "que se atreve a competir con Heliodoro" (that dares to compete with Heliodorus; Cervantes 2015a, 68). He had already used this term, *daring*, in *La Galatea* where he was announcing his Virgilian career. In this case he dares to compete with Heliodorus, a writer whose *Aethiopica* was considered the best example of an epic in prose. As he put his pen down, as if his work on this earth had been completed, Cervantes expected a visit from the Count of Lemos, his patron, who had just returned from Naples. All through the years, he had dedicated works to him without seemingly much success. Now that he had finished his epic, the Count, as a *deus ex machina*, or a phantom of desire, appeared to him. As José Manuel Lucía Megías states, this visit "[p]uede presagiar, por fin, lo que tanto ha aspirado y ansiado Cervantes a lo largo de su vida: entrar a servir en una casa nobiliaria" (this can presage, finally, what Cervantes had so much hoped for and aspired to throughout his life – to serve a noble house; 2019, 186).[2] And as he readied to put down his pen, Cervantes was writing about Rome, recalling with nostalgia the trip to Italy he had undertaken in his youth. Although he tried time and again to return, he never could, and thus his works are filled with this "desire for Italy" (De Armas 2006). While the last two books of the *Persiles* deal with the familiar, the world of the Mediterranean, of France, Italy, Spain and Portugal, it is the first two that most dazzle with their *inventio*.[3]

Cervantes was so proud of this work that, in the dedicatory to the Count of Lemos in the second part of *Don Quixote*, he describes his forthcoming book (albeit citing his friends' praises) as "ha de llegar al extremo de bondad posible" (*extreme possible goodness*; Cervantes 1978, 2.39).[4] This notion of "bondad," coupled with the division of the novel into two distinct sections, the darker north and the solar south, invites comparison with Plato, who states: "When [the soul's] gaze is fixed upon an object irradiated by truth and reality, the soul gains understanding and knowledge and is manifestly in possession of intelligence. But when it looks towards that twilight world of things that come into existence and pass away, its sight is dim and it has only opinions and beliefs which shift to and fro" (1979, 219). It is as if the darkness of the North, a darkness that seems to stem from Norway,[5] created such shifting views, equivocations, and vanishing shades. However, what I propose in this chapter veers somewhat from a Platonic view, for this is not the first time that Cervantes has taken the concept of *bondad* in order to question it, or the opposition of light and darkness in order to see beyond the dichotomy.[6] In the *Persiles* the darkness of the North also points to southern blindness as Cervantes constructs a Rome whose very architecture belies its godliness. He also transforms the geography of his model, Heliodorus' *Aethiopica*, to include a north that remains in the darkness of the unknown.[7] What Michael Armstrong-Roche calls a "boldy new kind of epic" now comes to life in areas never found in classical or romance epic.[8] Thus, the *Persiles* seeks to open new spaces of discovery, capitalizing on the maps and histories of the North as depicted by Olaus Magnus, Nicolo Zeno, Antonio Torquemada, and others.[9]

These northern lands consist of almost endless spaces, endless islands of night, where all seems lost, or lost in wonderment. Steven Hutchinson explains: "the sensation of travel is highly surreal and charged with adventure, and the kinds of experience to be had are of an equally extraordinary nature" (1992, 160). In the south we will encounter more places, more architectures of comfort and protection. Let us recall once again Yi-Fu Tuan's contrast between the two: "Place is security, space is freedom; we are attached to the one and long for the other" (1977, 3). Place is often constructed as a house, church, villa, or palace – and perhaps even city – although cities harbour their own perils. While the empty spaces that surround structures of safety are sites of freedom, in the North this freedom seems mostly constrained by its many dangers.[10]

As a space of discovery, the North can regale the reader with curious stories and objects, unusual flora and fauna, from the tasty little bird *barnaclas* (barnacles; Cervantes 2015b, 212; n.d.)[11] to the horrid *náufrago* or *Physeter*, a marine monster some fifteen or twenty feet wide that could sink ships (Cervantes 2015b, 379; De Lollis 1924, 168–9; Forcione 1972, 80).[12] The North is a kind of cabinet of curiosities or museum that displays many marvels, while at the same time breaking any kind of unity through the proliferation of episodes, becoming what Mercedes Alcalá-Galán calls a "semillero de historias" (a seedbed of stories; 2009, 205–9). Mystery, curiosity, and marvel coexist.[13] As Covarrubias defines it, a mystery is "cualquier cosa que está encerrada debajo de velo" (anything hidden under a veil; 1611, 551r). In the *Persiles* the veil is the very North and its vanishing forms. It is also a world that calls for discovery and the partaking of the anxieties created by an unstable geography and a changing sky.[14] Perhaps the very changes that astronomers were finding in the heavens are here configured by the chiaroscuro of the changing sky, from bright sunshine to deep and demonic darkness: the enchantress Cenotia affirms that she can make the light of the sun disappear in an instant.[15]

It is a space not so different from the one evoked by Johannes Kepler in his *Somnium* (1608, 1609, 1634),[16] in which Duracotus, a youth from Iceland "which the ancients called Thule" (1967, 11), is shown the geography of the moon by demons who have been summoned by his mother, a witch. The parallels between discoveries and witchcraft suggest that the new was always suspect and shrouded by the demonic. Kepler's work, which embedded a number of scientific discoveries, led to the arrest and trial of his own mother on the charge of witchcraft. Indeed, discoveries (be they geographic, celestial, or scientific) seem to go hand in hand with magic or witchcraft in a number of works of fiction of the period. While Pantaleón de Ribera's *Vejamen de la luna* (Satirical discourse on the moon, 1626, 1634) returns to the dream and the maculate moon as found in Kepler and Galileo, Luis Vélez de Guevara's *El diablo cojuelo* (*The Limping Devil*, 1641) associates Copernicus and the telescope with the devil.[17] New spaces, new discoveries, and new wonderments make the world even more mysterious, less easily decipherable, and less comfortable. Curiously, the moon, so important for these novels of anxious wonderment, is almost absent in *Persiles'* northern lands.[18] It does shines brightly in a kind of piscatorial eclogue inserted in the midst of the northern trials, its very artificiality contrasting with the rest of the rugged North.[19] Is this to remind us that the Ptolemaic moon can only exist now in clearly configured poetic spaces? This almost ephemeral site may seek to assuage the discomfort of the new. The balm is to be further enjoyed by taking us from a newly "discovered" North to the more comfortable lands known by Cervantes and his contemporary readers, lands that, as Isabel Lozano Renieblas states, are enlightened by a shared history.[20] But the discomfort does not go away, creating an anxious wonderment. The mystery of the new lands prevails deep within the *Persiles* as the dreamlike spaces with their demonic auras suffuse the text through its vanishing architectures.

The *Persiles*, I would argue, is one of a number of early modern novels of what I would call "anxious wonderment" – in which wonder is associated with destabilizing discoveries. From the start the North is described as a windowless space, one replete with darkness and danger, with a strange chiaroscuro, where bright sunlight often augurs a storm,[21] where light serves to emphasize the gloom of existence,[22] where light seldom shines on the characters as they labour in a world shrouded, and where architectures seem to dissolve in the gloom. Only the main characters, Persiles and Sigismunda, disguised as Periandro and Auristela, seem to shine with an almost celestial light in the North. As Cory Reed reminds us, two stars, the Guardians of the North, which are part of Ursa Minor (the Little Dipper) and which revolve around the North Star (Polaris), help mariners navigate in the dark. I would see Persiles and Sigismunda as these two stars that lead the pilgrims they take with them, away from the darkness of the north.[23] Let us look, then, at five spaces or architectures in the North through the light of southern places or through the lenses of other texts in order to reconstruct Cervantes' vanishing architectures in this novel of anxious wonderment.

The Prison

Critics have often debated on when Cervantes first conceived of this strange and wondrous text. Could parts of it have been written concurrently with *Don Quixote*? Just as Cervantes evokes the Royal Jail of Seville in the prologue to his canonical novel, he begins the *Persiles* with a prison far away. This new dungeon is in a barbarous northern land, and, instead of displaying an elegant façade that pretends to eurithmia, it is an immense hole or cavern in the ground that imprisons a myriad of captives with the very earth that surrounds it. The sounds that emanate from this prison, the moans and cries of the prisoners, are heard close and far. The noises are meant to astonish and even overwhelm, much like the sound heard by Philip II coming from the Royal

Jail in Seville. But here those listening are mostly "barbarians" who seem unperturbed by the sounds. Both the 1605 *Quixote* and the 1617 *Persiles* begin with cacophony, with discordant sounds. In the *Persiles* they are but a prelude to a complex narrative in which a series of voices compete to be heard in a number of different tales told by pilgrims and those with whom they come in contact. Although the prologue of *Don Quixote* explained that the textual body, the book-child that was born from these sounds, had to be, of necessity, whimsical, the first chapter of the *Persiles* brings to light, as if born from the cave or womb, a most handsome figure – which may be seen as a personification of the epic narrative that has sprung to view *in medias res*, as prescribed by the genre. The action begins as the barbarian Corsicurvo orders that a handsome young prisoner, recently taken, be brought to the surface, lifted by a "gruesa cuerda" (great hempen rope) (Cervantes 2015b, 128; n.d.). While Corsicurvo stands for the entangled and obscure languages, tales, and voyages in the North, the prisoner points to a clearer future.[24] Once his hands have been freed from cuffs, his face cleared of the dust from below, and his hair disentangled, he presents an almost unbelievable sight in this northern hell – his beauty and his golden hair are a marvel to behold. Addressing the heavens, the youth offers thanks for being allowed to die in the light instead of in the darkness of the underground prison.

From the start there is a close connection between architecture and the architecture of the human body, a trait common in Cervantes' fiction. The cavernous prison is extremely wide underneath, but its mouth is very narrow, so much so that a stone can cover it. The shape of the prison may recall the monstrous columns described by Sagredo, with a rounded or belly like bottom part. The prison also resembles the human being in that it has an "estrecha boca" (narrow mouth; Cervantes 2015b, 127; n.d.). Vitruvius had created a close link between temples and the human body, and here we find a comparison and contrast between jail and body. While the jail is monstrous, Periandro's face and body astound in contrastive opposition: "hermoso sobre todo encarecimiento" (more beautiful than could be expressed; 2015b, 128; n.d.). The personified jail sends out its horrible cries, but the youth's clear voice calls on the heavens in words the "barbarians" could not understand.[25] Periandro, then, is a kind of Vitruvian man who stands in opposition to his captors and their architectural forms. The prison is shaped like a monstrous architecture or human anatomy, totally opposed to Vitruvian proportion, symmetry, and eurithmia. The text, then, is foregrounding the monstrous that prevails outside of *oecumene* in contrast with the "civilized" Vitruvian measures.

The monstrous nature of the barbarians and their architecture is further reinforced by the fact that many of their prisoners are actually captives, taken in order to be sacrificed. Their hearts are then pulverized and included in a beverage that is to test the most courageous, the one who can drink without flinching. Here Cervantes combines his own experiences of captivity in Algiers with tales of cannibalism in the Americas. And to further point to this northern world as akin to the islands of the Caribbean, he describes a primitive raft that will take Periandro to the next isle, where he is to be sacrificed. Carlos Romero Muñoz, in his edition of the *Persiles*, warns: "Las balsas no parecen, a primera vista, el medio de transporte más adecuado, siquiera sea entre islas vecinas, para los duros mares septentrionales" (The rafts do not seem, at first sight, the most appropriate type of transport between neighboring islands in these rough northern seas; Cervantes 2015b, 129n9; n.d.). In addition, the term *bejuco,* a type of vine, is of Caribbean origin (129n9). To further underline the barbarian nature of the inhabitants and their propensity for violence, the narrative tells that once Periandro is seated in the raft, he again fears for his life: "y luego uno de los bárbaros asió de un grandísimo arco que en la balsa estaba, y poniendo en él una desmesurada flecha, cuya punta era de pedernal, con mucha presteza le flechó, y encarando al mancebo, le señaló por su blanco, dando señales y muestras de que ya le quería pasar el pecho." (One of them took a bow lying upon the raft, which he quickly bent, and therein set an arrow whose head was of flint, placing himself over against the young man, at whom he aimed as his white [*target*], and was ready to pierce his heart; 2015b, 129; n.d.)

Although it is true that, as Michael Armstrong-Roche asserts, some of the shocking events in the barbarous North have a unifying function because their actions are reflected in the south (2004, 1130), it is still a question of emphasis. The North's lack of measure and proportion as well as its chiaroscuro and its dark and phantom-like structures are never equalled or surpassed in the south. There seems to be no distinction between place and space in these northern lands. Its excesses transform most places into spaces. Whether inside the prison or outside on land or sea, dangers are always confronting Persiles, disguised as Periandro, the pilgrim of the tale. Indeed the extreme size of the arrow, the fact that it is "desmesurada," shows its lack of measure. What takes place in the North thus echoes, through this adjective, the disproportionate size of the giants as described in *Don Quixote*. Let us remember that the adjective is used in the second part of the novel to describe both Goliath's size (1978, 2.1.50; 2018, 477) and Malambruno's weapon. As we know from Sagredo and Vitruvius, all construction should be of precise measure. Christian Andrés asserts: "Lo que importa más destacar en el caso presente es la voluntad de extrañamiento de parte de Cervantes, su deseo de asombrar inmediatamente al lector" (What must be pointed out in this case is Cervantes' will to evoke the strange, his desire to amaze the reader; 2004, 183). A sudden storm surprises Periandro and his captors, recalling in miniature the many such tempests that caused the shipwreck of galleons from the Indies or brought about the defeat of the Armada by the English at the time of the Little Ice Age. Turning to the north, the novel is reflecting the surprising and unexpected changes in weather that take place in the south. Geoffrey Parker points to the words of a botanist who wrote in 1614: "unfortunately, on account of our sins, for some time now the years have shown themselves to be more rigorous and severe in the recent past, and we have seen deterioration amongst living things, not only among mankind and the animal world" (2013, 3).

The sudden tempest breaks up the raft, and while the barbarians drown, Periandro is able to hold on to one of the logs. Christian Andrés points to the tragic reversibility of the story, to the providential nature of Periandro's survival (2004, 184). I would add that the severity of the storm points both to climatic conditions in the seventeenth century and to the lack of measure that prevails around these isles, one that goes against a narrative that is to end up in Rome, the very place in which Vitruvius wrote his book on measures and architecture.

At the same time, the barbarian narrative is not without its ironies. The term *barbarian* derives from the Greek and was used as an antonym to *citizens*. The Romans preserved this appellation because it referred to the tribes at the edges of empire that they sought to ward off. Some they even sought to conquer in order to further expand their empire. Cervantes is quite cognizant that the northern tribes may at first have been subdued, but they eventually conquered Rome and became one of the major myths of origins for Spain through the Goths. Indeed, as Adrián J. Sáez asserts, "Cervantes es ejemplo de todos los sentidos y las variantes del mito neogótico, desde el simbólico valor nacional de los godos [...] hasta la dimensión didáctica de la historia visigótica y la cómica degradación del tópico de la nobleza" (Cervantes exemplifies all the senses and variants of the neo-Gothic myth, from the symbolic national value of the Goths [...] to the didactic dimension of the Visigothic history and the comic degradation of the topic of Gothic nobility; 2019b, 152). Although Cervantes describes here what would appear backwards to Romans or Europeans, the northern barbarians constitute a force that cannot be ignored. At the same time, the passage, although exalting the shining Christian vision of Periandro, ironizes the moment by pointing to a barbarian prophecy that they would become masters of the world – echoing the idea of Charles V as a world emperor. If the great architectures exalted by Vitruvius could come to ruin, so could those of future empires.

A Moment's Place

It would seem that place, a site of safety and comfort, is not to be found in the North. And yet we will catch glimpses of it, not so much in its dark and phantom-like buildings but in the most unlikely moments. We have already caught a glimpse of one of them. Periandro, on being brought out of his dark prison, enjoys a moment in the light. Although surrounded by "barbarians," Periandro "con ojos al parecer alegres alzó el rostro y miró al cielo por todas partes y con voz clara y no turbada lengua dijo" (with face lifted up, looking upon heaven, and with eyes in outward appearance full of cheerfulness, thus spake with a clear voice; Cervantes 2015b, 128; n.d.). Periandro has been moved from the terrors of the inside of the prison to the paradoxically harmonious outside, where the heavenly architecture and the light of the sun give him hope that his death will take place under the light of the heavens. For this very reason he thanks the heavens, almost desiring a death that will liberate him. Although he is surrounded by danger, it is a kind of eurithmia, a kind of topophilia, a love for the beauty created by the heavens, that gives him a sense of safety.

Not long after Periandro escapes from the isle, his beloved (who he claims to be his sister) is trapped by the barbarians and dresses as a man, worrying that they are seeking a beautiful woman to give as wife to the future ruler of the world. Little does she know that these barbarians are also looking for a man to follow the prophecy that will make him such a lord. This man, as we remember, will be the one who can eat a potion containing the ashes of a sacrificed foreigner. Being advised of the situation, Periandro asks Arnaldo, the captain of the ship that had rescued him, to let him return to the isle dressed as a woman. Arnaldo tells the barbarians that he is a corsair from Denmark and has a beautiful maiden to sell. When the cross-dressed Periandro is asked to raise the veil that covers his face, the result is astonishing: "descubrió el rostro; alzó los ojos al cielo; mostró dolerse de su ventura; estendió los rayos de sus dos soles a una y otra parte, que encontrándose con los del bárbaro capitán, dieron con él en tierra (a lo menos así lo dio a entender el hincarse de rodillas, como se hincó, adorando a su modo en la hermosa imagen que pensaba ser mujer)." (*He uncovered* his face, lifted his eyes to heaven, showed sorrow for his hard fortune, and darted the beams of his two suns here and there; which meeting with those of the barbarous captain, bore him to the earth: at the least he gave him to conceive so much, by adoring upon his knees this fair image whom he believed to be a woman; Cervantes 2015b, 148; n.d.)

This is the second time in the work that Periandro has amazed his captors, first as a man and this time dressed as a woman. The first had created for him a moment of eurithmia as he contemplated the heavenly architecture, providing him with a momentary "place" at a time of great danger. In this second moment he uses his immensely handsome visage, a kind of microcosm, to amaze the barbarian captain. By "bending the knee," the captain acknowledges that he has been transported, by what appears to be a superhuman beauty, to the realm of the gods. He is momentarily in a "place" well beyond his own, as he renders homage to the captive. Whereas in the first moment of "place," Periandro felt the architecture of the heavens and delighted in an eternal moment, in this second he manipulates his beauty through the act of unveiling (as if he were unveiling a sacred mystery) to astonish his captors, particularly the captain. He succeeds to such an extent that the captain believes this to be a moment of theophany, in which time stops and he reaches an almost ineffable place. This, however, soon turns out to be a false "place," one in which the captain pays an enormous amount for the captive, whom he believes to be a woman. The narrative underlines this lack of harmony when, to celebrate the event, Arnaldo's ship shoots its artillery in triumph, while the barbarians play their music: "y en un instante atronó el cielo la artillería, y la música de los bárbaros llenaron los aires de confusos y diferentes sones" (and in one instant the cannons thundered on the one side, the music of the barbarians filled the air with many confused and different sounds on the other; 2015b, 148; n.d.). Cacophony supersedes eurithmia.

The third such moment is perhaps the most astounding, as we are set to witness the reunion between Periandro and Auristela. The latter is saved from the sacrificial rites when Cloelia tells that Auristela is in reality a woman. Their encounter and embrace is narrated as follows:

¿Qué lengua podrá decir o qué pluma escribir lo que sintió Periandro cuando conoció ser Auristela la condenada y la libre? Quitóse la vista de los ojos, cubriósele el corazón, y con pasos torcidos y flojos fue a abrazarse con Auristela, a quien dijo, teniéndola estrechamente entre sus brazos: – Oh querida mitad de mi alma, o firme coluna de mis esperanzas, oh prenda, de que no se diga por mi bien o por mi mal hallada, aunque no será sino por bien, pues de tu vista no puede proceder mal alguno! Ves aquí a tu hermano Periandro. (Cervantes 2015b, 153–4)

(What tongue might express, or pen set down, the motions which Periander felt when he knew that she who was judged to die, and after freed, was
Auristela? His sight and breath failed which, as soon as he had recovered,
with a weak and staggering pace he ran to embrace that fair one, whom he
held in his arms, and said unto her, "O dear half of my soul, pillar of my
hopes, and a pledge which I cannot say I have found by my good or bad
fortune; albeit it cannot but be for my good, because no evil can proceed
from thy sight: see here thy brother Periander.") (Cervantes n.d.)

This, in many ways, is the third "place" elaborated from the notion of
an eternal moment in the first chapters of the novel. Medardo Rosario
explains that the impossibility of language to describe such a meeting
points to the mystics of the period and particularly to John of the Cross
(2015, 346).

I would go further and contend that these three moments, together
with the previous architecture of the prison, have much to do with
Dante's *Divine Comedy*, a work that, as we have already seen, Cervantes
knew well. First of all, the dark and underground space of the prison
could well recall the *Inferno*. The narrow mouth that opens and closes
(with a stone) may not derive directly from Dante, but it does recall the
many mouths of hell or entrances to the underworld. We have already
discussed the cavern of Cabra in the second part of *Don Quixote*. There
is a distant echo of the entrance to Dante's *Inferno* in the *Persiles*, as the
stone that closes the mouth of the jail recalls the moment the character
Dante stands before the opening to the Tower of Dis and is threatened
by the Furies who call on Medusa to turn Dante into stone. Virgil turns
him around and covers his eyes as protection. The stone in the *Persiles* is then a reminder of the difficulty in entering or leaving such a
doomed architecture. As Periandro is taken out from this infernal place,
he glances at the heavens in gratitude. This recalls the moment in the
first canto of *Purgatorio* in which pilgrim and guide witness the blue
sky, its hue of oriental sapphire (Dante Alighieri 1982, 1.13). The second
moment is the most complex because it seems paradisiacal, through
the beauty of Periandro dressed as a woman, but it is in reality one of
error because the barbarian captain worships beauty as if it were an
idol. Indeed, he pays for the captive with "infinitos pedazos de oro y
con luengas sartas de finísimas perlas" (with an infinite number of gold
pieces and long strings of fine pearls; Cervantes 2015b, 148; n.d.). In
canto 19 of the *Inferno*, Dante accuses some of the popes of worship-
ping wealth as if it were the golden calf of *Exodus* (1980, 19.112–14).
The worship of idols and gold pervade these pages of the *Persiles*, and
error is found in the covetousness of the corsairs and the idolatry of the

barbarian. The result is a cacophony of sound as the two sides celebrate the sale of Periandro. Kristina Aste, who has studied the 146 references to music in the *Divine Comedy*, locates fifty-nine of them in the *Inferno*. Since Hell is "the farthest from its spiritual center," it "is the realm of disharmony" (2008, 67). Here, there is a "shuddering din" of different tongues (68), much as in the island. And yet, in the midst of it all, Periandro reveals a beauty that seeks to transcend the world, while he is pretending to be a woman. In a sense, his beauty is that of sacrifice. He is unveiling his virtuous nature to the captain, through the captain's two "suns" or eyes. Let us recall that the sun is "silent" in the *Inferno* (Aste 2008, 72), and thus Periandro's captor cannot partake of it and is overwhelmed by the physical beauty that he worships.

We now come to the third and most intricate of the three allusions to the architecture of the sites in which humans may abide beyond this world. We have already seen that, as Periandro and Auristela are about to embrace, the author claims he cannot possibly describe the scene. As Paul Michael Johnson suggests, "certain tropes of ineffability have undergone a peregrination as long and roving as that of the novel's protagonists. From the Neoplatonists to Petrarchan poets, medieval monastic thinkers to the troubadours, the ineffable has historically proven to be a vexing yet fertile concept for a host of philosophical and cultural spheres" (2016, 300). He echoes Medardo Rosario's views, stressing that Periandro's emotions are indescribable: "Here the rhetorical use of adynaton allows the narrator to openly ponder his own limitations in portraying Periandro's feelings, thus underscoring their intensity" (307). Both Johnson and Rosario point to the language of mysticism. I would again argue that this instance may stem from the *Divine Comedy*. From the very beginning of the *Paradiso*, the Dante figure warns the reader that it is difficult to put into words what is above;[26] Beatrice warns him that the full sight of her could have him burst into celestial fire as was the case with Semele (Dante Alighieri 1975, 21.4–12).[27] As Kevin Brownlee asserts, "Dante's two senses of sight (*viso*) and hearing (*udir*) have been singled out as exemplifying his Semele-like incapacity to bear unmediated celestial experience" (1986, 150). In the case of Periandro, it is as if he cannot see, while his heart is covered, shadowed. Like Dante, he cannot see the full light of Auristela/Beatrice, not being fully attuned to the divine. His loving heart has not reached the capacity of divine love. Dante will eventually comprehend Beatrice's and God's light, being ordered to speak of his experiences even though they are beyond expression. Cervantes' text shows the embrace of Auristela and Periandro as he tells her that she is his other half. Cervantes thus evokes the platonic myth of human beings as circular, cut in half by

Jupiter's thunderbolt due to their power. They are destined to look for the other half of their souls in this world. Like Dante, Cervantes turns to a classical myth and one in which Jupiter seems to be extremely cruel to human beings. And, like Dante, he transforms the myth, emphasizing providence and the possibility of a benefic and loving deity that will spare them this danger and provide them with a happy conclusion, one that is most of all a union of souls. Place has been achieved, albeit tenuously, in the midst of outside dangers, as Dante's architecture shelters the lovers.

Inns and Ships

In Cervantes' north, architectures often stand in opposition to those in the south. They partake of elements that contrast with Vitruvian classicism. They are monstrous, primitive, phantom-like, and even impossible. In a number of Cervantes' works, and particularly in *Don Quixote*, the inn is a key location, a composite site conjoining both space and place. It looks towards the spaces of freedom and danger, calling on weary travellers to share meals and find shelter, and thus becoming a simulacrum of place. In chapter 3 we alluded to William Hogarth, who did a number of illustrations of *Don Quixote*. Turning to Henry Fielding, an imitator of Cervantes, Hogarth depicts a country inn yard, where much of the goings-on in Cervantes' inns are replicated, with greetings and farewells, and with unexpected company either joyous (reinforcing place) or dangerous and part of space. Here "new identities are revealed" (Paulson 1984, 200) as there are amorous trysts and sad farewells. The wheel in Hogarth's print is certainly no coincidence – being Fortuna's device. Inns also make their appearance in the southern adventures of the *Persiles*, such as the outsized one in Lucca that shelters what appears to be an *endemoniada*, a woman possessed by the devil (Cervantes 2015b, 611), but in the north they seem to be replaced most of the time by ships.[28] Although a place of safety, the ship is as hybrid as is the inn, for it gives shelter to diverse groups, and as some join the ship and others depart, the dangers of space threaten these vessels. The ship actually conflates inn and stagecoach because it is not stationary but leads its passengers from site to site. While the wheel in Hogarth's drawing represented Fortuna and its constant turning, the ship itself is an emblem of Fortuna. The many storms that lead ships away from their planned course or cause them to capsize, as survivors escape in lifeboats or come to land in distant shores, add an epic dimension to the *Persiles* and are constant reminders of Fortuna, whose winds of fortune lashed humans even more during the Little Ice Age.[29]

Indeed, the ship in a storm is an iconographic commonplace, as in Geffrey Whitney's *A Choice of Emblems* (1586). Emblem 11 exhibits an image of the ship in a storm and includes a poem that counsels the fortunate: "Which warneth all, on Fortunes wheel that clime / to beare in mind that they do have but a time" (1866, 11).

This repeated reversal of fortune, as voyages on the seas move from fortune to misfortune and vice versa, fosters an oppressive feeling, a lack of control and agency, in a world ruled by Fortuna and shrouded in the texture of storms.[30] As noted earlier, in the very first chapter Periandro escapes imminent death. When he is about to be sacrificed by *bárbaros*, a storm hits the crude barge in which he is being taken from one island to the neighbouring one.[31] Once Periandro has been saved and brought on board Arnaldo's ship, the reader can experience the very materiality of the vessel, with compartments down below whose walls are so thin that Periandro can hear the laments of another. Indeed, if there is an architecture that fully acquires materiality in the north, it is that of the ship, a floating building that Cervantes knew well from joining Spanish fleets in the Mediterranean. [32]

Although the ship may be a place of safety, it can become a space for treachery. In chapter 19, two sailors, driven by lust, plot to disable Arnaldo's ship, only to have it fall apart. Some are saved in a small barge, others in a skiff or flat-bottomed boat, but as they seek to stay together, darkness and a storm separate them and lead them to different sites and fortunes: "la noche se cubría de oscuridad y los vientos comenzaron a soplar por partes diferentes" (the night was all covered with darkness and the winds began to blow from divers places; Cervantes 2015b, 252; n.d.). The winds of fortune not only take the travellers to different sites but also break the narrative as it follows the skiff in which Auristela and others seek land and are thus led to the Isla Nevada (Snowy Isle). As if to underline the images of fortune, the narrator exclaims: "Miserables son y temerosas las fortunas del mar" (Miserable and full of terror are the fortunes of the sea; 253; n.d.). But perhaps the most impacting reversal of fortune with the ship as both image and place is found at the beginning of the second part. Here a storm so violent, the likes of which no mariner can even understand (280), leads the captain to faint and the ship to turn upside down, serving as monument to and mausoleum for the living dead who must float in darkness (281). The upside-down ship, of course, is an image for a most extreme reversal of fortune. And yet another reversal is at hand.

Led to Policarpo's kingdom, where the ship becomes a site of marvel, an old gentleman remembers that a Spanish galleon was seen upside down off the coast of Genoa. The remedy is to open a hole in the keel and let in some light. The frightful spectacle is attenuated when they find some bodies with life still in them. Thus Auristela is again rescued (Cervantes 2015b, 286). Cervantes is once again pointing to seafaring stories in the south to compose detailed dealings with ships in the north. Perhaps the light in Genoa may have been brighter, but, nevertheless, good fortune comes about from certain death. Indeed, this opening in the keel is perhaps the only semblance to a window that can be discovered in the northern spaces. Contrary to the many openings to the outside found at inns and villas in both *Don Quixote* and the last books of the *Persiles*, the north covers its own darkness with a deeper darkness still, that of the ship as tomb. In contrast, once in Rome, the women pilgrims must show themselves at the window at the request of the populace that wishes to admire their beauty.[33] A Genoese anecdote, Mediterranean seafaring, and southern windows shape fortune's northern ships in the light of southern light and the materiality of the known and familiar. In the windowless north, a window, an opening in the ship's keel, becomes a marvel, a space of discovery.

A Spectral Palace

Once in sight of Rome, after all their trials, Periandro and Auristela may feel safe with the city's seven churches but a walk away. Rome is certainly not the north. Amazing gardens lead to the famous gates, and the city itself beckons the wayfarers, showing off its antique and Renaissance architectures. Amidst these buildings we encounter the villa of Hipólita. Accepting her invitation, Periandro marvels at the many paintings found in her *camerino*, from those of the Greek Apelles to the Renaissance's Raphael. But Hipólita's *camerino* turns out to be a false place, one that shows, in the darkness of a closed loggia, works of art that are nothing but replicas or illusions. Paintings from classical antiquity, for example, no longer existed during the Renaissance. If, as Mercedes Alcalá-Galán suggests, the figure of Hipólita hides that of the courtesan Imperia, then she may have possessed significant works of art but certainly not originals by the great masters of the period (Alcalá-Galán 2016). Hipólita may wish to have paintings by Michelangelo and Raphael, but like her own figure, these works are deceitful. The architecture inverts Yi-Fu Tuan's notion of place, in this case showing that a home or villa is not safe. The paintings are but a cover for the courtesan's artful designs. Periandro tries to flee but is stopped. Wanting revenge as a woman scorned, Hipólita uses the window to announce that Periandro has come to rob her. She seeks to turn the outside into a space as dangerous as her own treacherous self and site. The civilizing window reveals the treachery of unfettered passion.

In many ways, the lusts of Rome are but a reconstruction of the dangerous desires that ricochet in the many rooms at Policarpo's palace in the north. Yet, while there is a rich architecture and ornamentation in the south, and the city and the villa are carefully materialized through description, such is not the case in Rome's northern twin. As the pilgrims are welcomed by Policarpo, they seem to pass into a spectral site: "Llegaron a la ciudad y el liberal Policarpo honró a sus huéspedes real y magníficamente, y a todos los mandó alojar en su palacio" (They came to the city, where Policarpus caused his guests to be lodged magnificently in his royal palace; Cervantes 2015b, 289; n.d.). If *specere* is to see and *spectrum* is an intangible vision, then Cervantes asks the reader to see what can be barely glimpsed. Nothing is said of the city, and very little is said of the palace even though numerous and portentous events will take place within its walls.We read in chapter 8 of book 2:

> Sucedió en este tiempo que, estando Antonio el mozo solo en su aposento, *entró* a deshora una mujer en él [...] *Levantose* Antonio a recebirla cortésmente, porque no era tan bárbaro que no fuese bien criado. *Sentáronse* [...] Y diciendo esto, [Cenotia] *se levantó* para ir a abrazarle. Antonio viendo lo cual, lleno de confusión, [...] *levantándose*, fue a tomar su arco [...] y, poniendo en él una flecha, hasta *veinte pasos* desviado de la Cenotia, le encaró la flecha. [...] a este y por huir el golpe, *desvió* el cuerpo y pasó la fecha volando por junto a la garganta [...] que a este instante, *entraba por la puerta* de la *estancia* el maldiciente Clodio. (Cervantes 2015b, 329, 334)

> (At this time it happened that, the young Anthony being alone in his chamber, there *came* in a woman [...] He courteously *rose up* to receive her, not being so barbarous as he was well brought up; and then, both of them *sitting down* one by another [...] And with these words she *rose* up to embrace him, which, Anthony perceiving [...] *running* to his bow, which was always near him, if it hung not at his back, he put therein an arrow, and shot against the magician *about the distance of twenty paces*. The amorous Zenocia, fearing the threatening demeanour of this young barbarian, *turned* her body, and let the shaft pass by: whereunto the unhappy Clodio, *coming into* the chamber at the same instant, served as a mark.) (Cervantes, n.d.)

Notice the many verbs of motion and action and the lack of description of the chamber.

At its most visible, the text exhibits verbs that imply that there are walls, structures, and furnishings, but these remain intangible.

Policarpo's northern palace feels empty, shadowy, without windows, and with implied walls. There are no paintings or other adornments here, only those that are etched in the heart. Policarpo's daughter develops an irresistible passion for Periandro and confesses it to Auristela, not knowing that she is much more than his sister: "Esta pintura me la grabó en el alma, y yo, inadvertida, dejé que me la grabase, sin hacerle resistencia alguna y, así poco a poco, vine a quererle, a amarle y aun a adorarle" (This painting was engraved in my mind and I, not well advised, willingly suffered it there to be graven, without making resistance; and so by degrees I came to love and adore him; Cervantes 2015b, 294; n.d.). If there is to be art, it can only be envisioned in the south. Clodio, the gossip, imagines one of the pilgrims, Antonio, painting all the perils of the north once he reaches his home.[34]

The palace seems constructed of deceits and desires, of unfulfilled passions and jealousy: "Estas revoluciones, trazas y máquinas amorosas andaban en el palacio de Policarpo y en los pechos de los confusos amantes [...] Todos deseaban, pero a ninguno se le cumplían sus deseos." (Such revolutions and amorous inventions walked up and down in the palace of Policarpus and in the hearts of those confused lovers [...] All had endless desires, but accomplished nothing; Cervantes 2015b, 299–300; n.d.). It is as if a shadowy chaos of passion enveloped the characters. Like the evanescent walls, these desires never materialize. We may move from room to room, but all seems the same, and nothing is said of their location or their furnishings. Instead, impossible desires echo in the chambers of the palace as even King Policarpo falls prey to lust, ignoring his old age: "no tomaba pulso a su edad" (he never felt the pulses of his age; 322; n.d.). He allowed his passions to take over, desiring Auristela and conniving with his own daughter so that they can both attain their desires. And if this were not enough, the palace houses a Moorish witch, Cenotia, who attempts to place amorous spells on young Antonio to no avail. Antonio is not impressed and shoots her, but she is clever enough to turn away from the arrow, which then hits Clodio in the mouth: "le pasó la boca y la lengua y le dejó la vida en perpetuo silencio" (It pierced his mouth and tongue, and made him leave his railing and life in a perpetual silence; 335; n.d.). Steven Hutchinson finds here the coming together of recurring elements: "three phenomena so often associated in Cervantes' novels: silence (the mouth closes), immobility (the tongue stops moving), and death (the soul departs)" (1992, 51). This immobility allows for the emergence of a painting or emblem. Georg Pencz, for example, imagines the punishment of a slanderer: a lock placed on his lips and tongue (Cacho Casal 2006, 316). The *Persiles* may eschew spatial representations, but it allows for characters to possess in their hearts engravings of love or desire or, in this case, to point to an emblem that reveals and punishes the slanderer.[35]

In a desperate attempt to possess those whom they desire, Policarpo and the witch Cenotia plot to set fire to the palace and, in the confusion they have crafted, to have their soldiers kidnap Auristela and Antonio and take them by ship to another part of the island. Even in this night of confusion, all the reader can perceive is darkness and flames, as the pilgrims escape and take over a ship at the dock. Not even a single line of description is to be found of either the burning palace or the city that lies next to it. One detail, a tower, as a kind of synecdoche, stands for all. This is where the two daughters of Policarpo seek refuge and where their father comes in the morning hours to see if any hope remains of possessing the escaped Auristela. This small architectural detail is given, not to describe the palace but to link the moment to Virgil's *Aeneid*, thus enlivening epic echoes in the novel and invading the north with "civilized" cultures. Muñoz Sánchez has noted how heroes are often detained in palaces in antique epics. He also points to the moment in which the hero has to flee. Indeed, in our text Sinforosa is equated with Dido who suffers as she watches her beloved Aeneas escape Carthage (Muñoz Sánchez 2008, 210). The tower itself recalls the one in the epic poem, from which Dido sees the fleet depart at dawn. In Cervantes, Sinforosa observes in despair Periandro's ship now sailing far from land.[36] These moments may also evoke the burning of Troy as Aeneas and his family escape. Cervantes would have known a number of paintings on the subject and particularly Raphael's *The Fire in the Borgo*, in which he folded the burning of Troy into the burning of Rome, thus giving it an epic feel (De Armas 1998, 54). Here Cervantes may be folding the burning of Rome into the fire at Policarpo's palace. In what has been called "one of the most famous incidents Raphael ever painted" (Hersey 1993,155), the artist follows in great detail the second book of the *Aeneid*. We see a young man (Aeneas) carrying on his shoulders his father, Anchises. Behind him is his wife, Creusa, and next to him, his son. The pilgrims fleeing in the *Persiles* are a more amorphous mass, although, like in Virgil, Periandro and the men are in front.

Although the fire may seem to light up the scene, the narrative presents it as a dark night of confusion. The light that comes through Hipólita's Roman window contrasts with the shadowy north, and the many paintings in the courtesan's *camerino*, including those of Raphael, must be gleaned in Policarpo's palace through scenes that echo Virgil's epic or through emblems etched in the bodies of those who wander the night. It may be that the materiality of the south can better contain the passions unleashed.

A Witching Space

So far we have connected the darkness and spectral architectures of the north with sunnier and more material episodes in the south. There are, however, a number of characters in the north that originate in southern lands. Four of them tell their stories at length: Cenotia and Antonio (from Spain), Rutilio (from Italy), and Manuel de Sosa (from Portugal). All four can be associated with the demonic or heterodox: Cenotia is a witch; Antonio visits an island of wolves and hears one of them speaking to him (lycanthropy); Rutilio partakes of or witnesses witchcraft, transvection, and lycanthropy; and Manuel lets himself die of love melancholy (an affliction associated with the devil).[37] Of these, Rutilio is the one who most clearly connects north and south and who is most prone to the demonic. He is hired to teach a young lady how to dance, and they both fall for each other and, to satisfy their desire, flee towards Rome. What we have is a counter-pilgrimage in the sense that the central movement in the novel is from the north to the south, from spectral darkness to the light and tangibility of Rome, where Periandro and Auristela will end their religious, amorous, and secular pilgrimage. Rutilio never even thinks of Rome as a sacred place but as a large city where he can hide his misdeeds. This counter-pilgrimage both points to the ambiguities of the image of Rome and brings about his immediate downfall. While his beloved is given back to her father, he is imprisoned and condemned to death. The prison erects itself as one of the most sinister architectures in the *Persiles*. After all, the novel begins with a cavern that goes deep underground and is covered by a huge stone that muffles the horrid sounds of the incarcerated; it serves as a tomb for the living, "antes sepultura que prisión de muchos cuerpos vivos que en ella estaban sepultados" (resembling [more] a grave where many bodies had been buried alive than a prison; Cervantes 2015b, 127; n.d.). This initial episode, as described previously, shadows the north in its own gloom and may even point to one of the gates of hell. Not only does Rutilio's jail share in the darkness of this *mazmorra*, but also he is seen as trapped by it, being there and pretending to be one of the barbarians who guard the prison.

Turning back to Italy, the description of how Rutilio is miraculously released from his Italian prison recalls the deliverance of Saint

Peter while he was imprisoned by Herod. This event, derived from Acts, chapter 12, is depicted in a number of Renaissance paintings, from Jacopo de Cione to Antonio de Belli. Years after Cervantes' posthumous novel, Bartolomé Antonio Murillo fashioned a spectacular liberation scene with dramatic chiaroscuro. The most important Renaissance painting on the subject is Raphael's fresco at the Vatican (where Cervantes would have seen it while serving Cardinal Acquaviva) (see figure 7.1).[38]

The centre of the fresco exhibits an angel, shining with celestial light, who wakes Peter, while the two guards who watch over him are miraculously sleeping. A faux stairwell on the left and on the right of this central scene conveys the presence of other guards. On the right, the angel escorts Peter, now unchained, out of the prison, while on the left, guards seem to awaken. Rutilio's scene replicates but inverts the sense of this miracle. He is visited by a witch, but when he hears that she will free him, she becomes an angel in his eyes: "Túvela […] por angel que enviaba el cielo" (I esteemed her, not as a sorceress, but an angel sent from heaven to deliver me; Cervantes 2015b, 186; n.d.). This "angel," like the one who visits Peter, causes him to be unchained: "moví los pies para seguilla y hallélos sin grillos y sin cadenas" (I stood on my feet, finding myself without fetters; 187; n.d.). In the fresco the angel also causes the jail to open, while the guards are asleep. In Cervantes we read: "las puertas de toda la prisión de par en par abiertas" (all the prison doors open and as well the prisoners as the keepers buried in a dead sleep; 187; n.d.). Peter, now free, returns to Mary's house, but here the witch requires that Rutilio marry her. It is as if Rutilio enacted this miracle *in malo*. Such a reversal is of itself a demonic trait. Although based on a hagiographic tale and, most probably, on a fresco by Raphael, the episode is a kind of wish-fulfilment for a writer who was imprisoned at least thrice. Utilizing the fresco, Cervantes adds vividness to the scene and imagines two means of release, angelic in the fresco and demonic in the case of Rutilio.

In her flying carpet or *manto* the sorceress transports Rutilio to the land of darkness, Norway.[39] Rutilio closes his eyes during a journey that takes some four hours. Thus, Cervantes' work transformed and partially reversed an important trend in the novelistic tradition that was about to become popular. With the discovery of the telescope, numerous works used magical glasses to look down on the earth rather that up to the heavens. As Enrique García Santo-Tomás has argued (2017), many Spanish texts turned to this view from above, such as Fernández de

Figure 7.1. Raphael, *The Liberation of St. Peter from Prison*, 1514. Stanze di Raffaello, Vatican Palace. Scala/Art Resource, NY

Ribera´s *Los anteojos de mejor vista* (Eyeglasses for better viewing, 1625) and Vélez de Guevara´s *El diablo cojuelo* (*The Limping Devil*, 1641). In this case the flying carpet is not used as a point from which to look down, thus reversing the novelistic trend; furthermore, it serves as a means of "discovery," the finding of other habitable lands mostly unknown to Europeans. These discoveries are tied not only to anxious wonderment but also to the lands' demonic aura and its monstrous dangers. Once in the northern lands, Rutilio perceives the sorceress in the shape of a wolf and thus plunges a knife into her.

This episode, as the most opposed to verisimilitude and everyday reality, has elicited a number of responses that include statements close to rejection. William Childers, for example, points out that "we have only Rutilio's word as evidence" (2014, 58). Michael Armstrong-Roche comes up with a tantalizing model: "In Book I of his history of Rome, Livy narrates the well-known Roman foundation story of the she-wolf ('lupa') who suckled the exposed infants Remus and Romulus (Liv.

6–7). Nevertheless, he also reports the view of skeptics who believe that *lupa* refers not to a fabulous she-wolf, but to the meretricious wife of Faustulus, the shepherd who discovered the boys –lupine in the more scurrilous sense of prostitute or courtesan (hence the name *lupanar* for brothel) (Liv. 7–8)" (Armstrong-Roche 2009, 81). Recently, Hilaire Kallendorf, taking as a point of departure Armstrong-Roche's revelation, and delving into the *Malleus maleficarum* (*Hammer of Witches*), the most important treatise on witchcraft and a bestseller during the Renaissance, has come up with some new arguments that give impetus to the argument of illusoriness rather than a real moment of lycanthropy. She explains that Rutilio did indeed escape with the witch but was not able to detect her figure behind the illusory one of the wolf because his sense of sight was far from saintly and thus could not see beyond the devil's illusions.[40] The lupine figure, she suggests, is nothing but a prostitute or courtesan (2019, 4–5).

Yet, Rutilio's is not the first instance of lycanthropy in the novel. Antonio, on being set adrift in the north comes to an island full of wolves and is approached by one that, speaking in human tongue and even in Spanish, warns him away.[41] Antonio seems to have come across one of the very rare "licántropos bondadososos" (benevolent werewolves), a type that Lozano Renieblas locates in the legend of San Antonio Abad (2016, 355). One could also add the legend of Saint Francis and the wolf of Gubbio. This beast terrorized the countryside, waiting outside the town for those foolish enough to come out so that he could feast on their flesh; Saint Francis turns him from cruel to kind. Whatever the model, Antonio's encounter is typical of the demonic darkness of the north: "me pareció, por entre la dudosa luz de la noche, que la peña que me servía de puerto se coronaba de los mismos lobos que en la marina había visto, y que uno de ellos [...] me dijo en voz clara y distinta en mi propia lengua" (Then methought, by the uncertain brightness of the night, that the rock which served me instead of a haven was all covered with wolves, as indeed the truth was, and that one of them spake unto me with an human and intelligible voice; Cervantes 2015b, 169; n.d.).

As with the vanishing architectures, the lupine shapes are hardly distinct from the night. If the text hints at shadows of the imagination, at dreamlike apparitions in Antonio's tale, it actually foregrounds demonic illusion in Rutilio's tale. He is told that he is in Norway, a land in which sorceresses abound. His tale is a common one but utterly false in that "todas estas transformaciones son ilusiones del demonio" (these transformations are nothing else but the devil's illusions; Cervantes 2015b, 189; n.d.). Darkness, then, triggers the imagination as the landscape becomes replete with spectral pseudo-forms. Furthermore, darkness is associated with the melancholy humour, particularly when it becomes acute and is labelled *balneum diabolic* (bath of the devil), and it is even associated with lycanthropy (Boase 2017, 2.575n138).

Rutilio's story does not end here. Kallendorf asserts: "When Rutilio stabs the witch, he performs an act of exorcism of demonic forces which then subsequently allows him an opportunity for moral growth" (2019, 5). She argues that this is not a full exorcism. Indeed, his deliverance is still problematic because he goes to work as a smith, a profession often tied to the infernal. He does so in one of the cities in Norway, and we would thus expect to view the textual architectures of the north in this urban setting. And yet, all we are told is that people go about their business in the darkness of the day with lit torches (Cervantes 2015b, 191). Darkness engulfs the cityscape, as neither buildings nor any objects in the city can be properly perceived. Perhaps Cervantes refrains from architectural description because he does not know these lands, or perhaps he relishes in the telling of gloom and night, of wolves, barbarians, and other wonders that can be treasured and stored in the memory.

There is yet another possible explanation, however, which will serve as conclusion. Rutilio has undergone two rather impossible experiences: transvection and lycanthropy. Although it is admissible to represent the marvellous far from known lands, it is quite another thing to partake of practices that are denied by the Catholic Church. While in the first telling of Rutilio's story in the *Persiles* there are no objections to its veracity, later, characters who listen to Rutilio's tale affirm more than once that lycanthropy is an illusion. First, his Italian host denies its existence, asserting that as a Catholic he cannot believe that such a metamorphosis can take place. They are illusions brought about by the devil as punishment (Cervantes 2015b, 189). Much later, when Mauricio hears the tale, we would expect some semblance of acceptance from a man who practises astrology. But this is not the case: "quede desde aquí asentado que no hay gente alguna que mude en otra su primera naturaleza" (not that there are any kind of people who can change their nature; 246; n.d.). Curiously, Mauricio turns to the sunny south for his example. In Sicily there are those who suffer from *mania lupina*, but it is just an illness that makes them believe they are wolves (244). Antonio Cruz Casado, studying the bewitching of Auristela, quotes from a discourse on magic in Matías de los Reyes' *Para todos* (For everyone): "no se ha de entender que estas transformaciones hechas por el demonio son reales y naturales, sino prestigiosas, porque lo contrario es error herético, que el transformar una cosa substancial y realmente es lo mismo que criarla o resucitarla. Cuya potestad es solamente de Dios y con consecuencia es negada a los demonios y a sus magos, como afirman los doctors." (One should not accept that these transformations made by the devil are real and natural, but illusory, because the opposite would be a heretical error, because transforming a thing in its very substance and in reality is the same as creating or resuscitating it. This power belongs to God and in consequence it is denied to the devils and their magicians, as the doctors affirm; Cruz Casado 1992, 94; Reyes 1640, fol. 36v.)

Studying Rodríguez de Monforte, John Slater shows that this writer divides transformations into four types: "false (i.e. that only appears to happen); natural (such as the birth of satyrs [...]); supernatural (as when men appear to be changed into beasts); and true mutation of the substance and essence of things wrought by divinity" (2014, 227). In Rodríguez de Monforte's book, lycanthropy is among the false transformations. The *Malleus maleficarum* confirms it as "the Devil's ability to deceive a man's fantasy so that a real person is seen as an animal" (Institoris and Sprenger 2006, 2.155).[42] However, Martín del Río believes that the flight to the Sabbath or the reunion of witches does happen, as the devil himself takes them, adopting different forms (1991, 328–54). This is one of the few exceptions, and one that can validate transvection, or Rutilo's flight with the witch to the northern lands. From the *Malleus maleficarum* to Matías de los Reyes' *Para algunos* (1640) to Pedro Rodríguez de Monforte's *Sueños mysteriosos de la escritura* (Mysterious dreams of writing, 1687), authorities confirm that lycanthropy is nothing but an illness or an illusion. Although the case is not as clear with transvection, the notion that witches can fly through the air, with or without carpets or other contraptions, was still questioned by most authorities.

The north, then, is a space of dark magic and demonic illusions. After all, its spectral darkness makes it possible to see shapes that are not there. Is Rutilio an unreliable narrator who is influenced by devilish illusions?[43] Is he the poet of the new novel of anxious wonderment who represents the challenges of discovery through demonic images? Is his story but a dream of the north?[44] The reader herself is caught among the spectral architectures, seeking to construct castles from airy darkness. One logical conclusion would be to assert that perhaps many of these northern lands do not fully exist but are half-formed spaces in which the devil rules. Some kingdoms may well take form in speculative maps and fictive annals, like the Frislanda home to Auristela;[45] others may evoke Virgil, such as the Tile home to Persiles;[46] and yet others may be well established, such as the Dinamarca home to Arnaldo. But many have not yet unchained themselves from the dark abyss that has as its origins the *mazmorra*, perhaps a mouth of hell in the barbarians' island, the central locus from which darkness and devilish practices seem to emerge and cover many of these lands; perhaps a prison that we may imagine as connected to Rutilio's own jail and that filters south to the Royal Jail of Seville and the places of captivity in Algiers. It even makes it to Rome, whence Rutilio would have fled to disguise his escape among the city's corruptions and pagan practices. The darkness of the north represents both the failure to create a truly "enlightened" European society and the inability of France, Italy, Spain, and Portugal to fully see the "discovered" Other, to bring to light what has not been seen by them. Eyeglasses thus become a symbol for viewing what has remained covered.

In Lope de Vega's *El nuevo mundo descubierto por Cristóbal Colón* (The discovery of the new world by Christopher Columbus) the devil demands to be heard by Providence. When the divinity asks him who he is, he responds "el rey de occidente" (the king of the East; 2001, 116). He then asks, "¿No sabes que ha muchos años / que tengo allí posesión?" (Don't you know that I have possessed this land for many a year?; 116). This early play could have led Cervantes to conceive the north as yet another space in which the devil rules. As a demonic site, it partakes of illusion, and any architecture that seeks to rise out of darkness is bound to vanish. Thus, Policarpo's palace is a site for lust and contention paradoxically contained within illusory walls. The cities of Norway can only be seen through dim lights. Only the ship, a floating edifice that connects all parts of the world, can materialize. It can be described in full because it is not part of the northern lands. Still, the ship must sail the waters of fortune. In the north such waters, echoing the great weather changes across the world, are frequently tempestuous. Indeed, the ship was often cursed as the vehicle that brought down the first golden age of humankind: new worlds, new lands, and new gods may be dangerous.[47] Thus, Cervantes crafts a world of darkness and illusion in which civilization is tenuous, and its culture menacing. It lacks fully formed churches, hermitages, palaces, or even inns. In this anxious vision of the Other, lands, cities, and marvels fade as if only seen through a devilish eyeglass – they come into being once the European pen maps them into "place." And yet, the north is also a Christian and Neoplatonic metaphor for this world as illusion. Whatever seems to materialize will quickly vanish, for in this tempestuous land the "cloud-cappedd towers, the gorgeous palaces […] shall dissolve" (Shakespeare 2016, 4.1, vv. 152, 154). They will surely melt into thin air and leave behind naught but the darkness of desire, the urge for possession, and the gloom of unearthly illusion, one that seeps south and infects with anxious heterodoxy even the Rome of Christendom – a devilish heterodoxy that may always be present at the heart of civilization. The she-wolf that suckled and first raised Romulus and Remus howls and shows its illusory and forbidden form in the faraway lands, in its caves and unmapped spaces.

8 Structures of Flight: *Persiles y Sigismunda,* Book 3

They looked up towards heaven, and saw a shape fall, which was upon the ground hard by Periander's feet before they could discern what it might be. It was a very fair woman thrown down from the top of the tower, which fell to the ground upon her feet without any harm, being upholded by her clothes in the air, as it were by miracle.

Cervantes, Persiles y Sigismunda

Having gazed at the windowless north in books 1 and 2, we find the pilgrims wandering through Portugal, Spain and France, where new and more solid architectures take shape, in the third book. Yet, this solidity is a kind of mirage because the Spanish reader of the period, with mere hints from the narrative, can easily fill in the many cityscapes and structures in a known space. At the same time, these urban sites point to new ways of looking. Many descriptions of urban environments are left out, turned into ellipses, while our gaze is directed elsewhere. Ellipses in these moments recall the elliptical shape in geometry and the elliptical planetary orbits proposed by Kepler in 1609. Instead of the circle and its centre, keys to Ptolemaic astronomy and Platonic perfection, we move to a figure with a double focus. As one is hidden, the other is foregrounded. If cityscapes are hidden, something else appears. But the hidden may be just as important. The first section of this chapter discusses the cityscape mainly in Lisbon and Toledo, and the second section turns to the description of *lienzos* (canvases). We will inspect them in search of buildings and ponder their relations to the art of memory. Although they are apparently devoid of architectures, we will pinpoint at least one that inverts a forging ekphrasis.[1]

The third section turns to sacred places, as we follow Feliciana de la Voz to the monastery of Guadalupe. At first, ekphrastic description is erased in order to turn to feelings of devotion, to an aura of the sacred.

In the end, the power of architecture surfaces through Feliciana's song and the miraculous results through the power of its flight. The divine architecture evoked in Feliciana's song contrasts with contentious human architecture. This infusion of the sacred and the miracle in the third section is complemented by a very human miracle in the fourth, where technology arouses admiration and awe. Whereas the pilgrims had experienced a vision of what has been called a "grotesque" miracle of flight at Guadalupe, now a flying woman is the subject of admiration. The "Varenze woman," as I would call her, in many ways surpasses the Vitruvian man. The fifth section of this chapter enters the edifice from whence she fell, in order to question why Hercules' tower is located in France rather than in Spain.

Cityscape as Ellipse and Ellipsis

The third book of the *Persiles* begins with a virtual definition of the pilgrimage of the soul in this world: "Como están nuestras almas siempre en continuo movimiento, y no pueden parar ni sosegar sino en su centro, que es Dios, para quien fueron criadas" (Like as our souls are ever in continual motion, and cannot stay nor rest but in their centre, which is God for whom they were created; Cervantes 2015b, 429; n.d.). Halfway through the novel, and now sailing to the European mainland, the pilgrims are still changing and moving, but they are much closer to the divine, since their ostensible purpose is to go to Rome, the centre of Catholicism. It appears as if we are in the presence of a well-ordered universe, with the circle as the perfect geometrical form, its centre being not the earth but the divinity to which it aspires. Since ancient times and through sayings by Hermes Trismegistus and Nicholas of Cusa, it has been thought that God is constituted by a sphere, whose centre is everywhere and whose circumference is nowhere. Rome is merely the earthly centre, a most propitious place to worship the Christian God. And yet, as we enter lands buttressed by the Catholic faith in this novel of anxious wonderment, the circle, the perfect geometrical form that connotes divinity, will be displaced by the elliptical and the consequent uses of the ellipsis, of a glaring omission.

In the north, sailing is often difficult, and the pilgrims seem lost in the storms of fortune. Cory Reed reminds us that "[n]avigation within the parameters of Cervantes's *Septentrión* is at times an almost Sisyphean challenge, a futile attempt to reach unreachable destinations that results in frustration and confusion " (2016, 452). These voyages are often east–west, and no instruments can aid the sailor. Going north–south, however, was made easy using "instruments that could measure the declination of the sun or the North Star" (452). Thus, the pilgrims swiftly and easily sail to Lisbon. In seventeen days they come in sight of land. Antonio, proud of his native soil, describes it to his daughter Constanza. After telling her that she will find here the richest of temples and the most Catholic of rituals, he goes on to explain: "La ciudad es la mayor de Europa y la de mayores tratos; en ella se descargan las riquezas del Oriente y desde ella se reparten por el universo; su puerto es capaz no sólo de naves que se puedan reducir a número, sino de selvas movibles de árboles que los de las naves forman." (The city is one of the greatest, and best frequented for traffic, of any that is in Europe. Therein are unshipped the riches of the East, and from thence dispersed throughout the world. The haven is able to receive, not only so many ships as may be reckoned, but moving forests of innumerable trees; Cervantes 2015b, 432–3; n.d.). In contrast to the dark forests and lands of the north, here the port is described as a jungle of moving trees, pointing to the myriad masts of the ships at the port. Lisbon, then, is the greatest centre of trade coming from the Orient. More than the churches or other buildings, what is to be admired are the riches of commerce.

The pilgrims' first stop is the gate or fortress of San Gián at the entrance to the estuary of the river Tagus, a location also mentioned in the laudation of Lisbon in one of the Golden Age's most famous plays, *El burlador de Sevilla* (*The Trickster of Seville*).[2] The name is all that is given, without description, creating an initial ellipsis. As if this were one of the many examples of allusive ekphrasis found in Cervantes,[3] the narrative simply states: "el castellano del castillo y los que con él entraron en la nave se admiraron de la hermosura de Auristela, de la gallardía de Periandro, del traje bárbaro de los dos Antonios, del buen aspect de Ricla y de la agradable belleza de Constanza" (the captain of the castle, and such as came aboard with him, wondered at the perfection of Auristela, the gallantness of Periander, the barbarous apparel of the two Anthonys, the sweet looks of Ricla, and the pleasing beauty of Constance; 433–4; n.d.). Readers knowing the fort could picture it in their minds as part of the art of memory; those having heard of it could "place" it in the memory as one of the main buildings in Lisbon. Absence or ellipsis foregrounds its importance. In this sense, we need only recall again Severo Sarduy's striking theories of the baroque. Discussing Góngora's poetry, he suggests that the ellipsis evokes its geometric double, the elliptical curve (1973, 23). In 1609, Kepler published his first two findings (later to become two of his three "laws" of planetary motion), in which he broke with the sacredness of the circle to propose that the planets revolved in an elliptical orbit, with one of its focuses being the sun. Turning to the rhetoric of the baroque, Sarduy claims that there is always a double centre, one that is suppressed in favour of another (23–4). In this case, the lack of description of an architecture triggers the memory and takes us from its absence to a series of hidden possibilities that remain obscure.

The ellipsis also allows for a view of the unexpected. Rather than describing the fort, the novel turns to the characters in the novel. It is as if Lisbon looked at the pilgrims rather than vice versa; it is as if Europe looked to the lands beyond as sites of anxious wonderment.[4] Given licence to proceed, the pilgrims go up river and disembark at Belén (Belem). Again, we encounter an allusive ekphrasis and an ellipsis that can trigger the memory. This sixteenth-century fort served as site embarkation and disembarkation. Designed by architect Francisco de Arruda, this four-storey tower or fort was completed in 1519. The tower is also important because in 1580 the Duke of Alba defeated the Portuguese here as Spain annexed the Kingdom of Portugal. This leads us to a third and most important ellipsis. None of the pilgrims mentions the new status of the city and the kingdom. The brilliance of the Spanish empire obscures the second focal point, Portugal, whose own empire was subsumed within the first from 1580 to 1640. While imperial aspirations and the anxieties of new lands are foregrounded, the very act of imperial land seizure is hidden.

The narrative is very careful not to completely erase this imperial "triumph." however. Periandro visits a chapel that is not described, creating an ellipsis that calls for the hidden focus. He is taken there because it is the place in which the Portuguese Manuel de Sosa is buried. Part of the epitaph reads: "No murió a las manos de ningún castellano, sino a las del amor" (He died not by the hands of any Castilian, but by those of Love which can do all; Cervantes 2015b, 437; n.d.). The narrative seems to set aside any conflict between nations. It obscures and sets aside the human cost of conquest in order to focus on love as a dangerous passion.

The entrance into Lisbon, then, although somewhat detailed, uses allusive ekphrasis as a kind of ellipsis. Instead of focusing on the architecture or its history, the narrative recalls the pilgrims' journeys as to render them mnemonic in the European lands. Focusing on the pilgrims, describing how their arrival amazed and even frightened the citizens of Lisbon, it denies the perfect circle in its rhetoric, establishing the double focus of the elliptical. In a marvellous and unexpected reversal or shift in focus, Cervantes' narrative seeks to replicate the many arrivals from Brazil, Goa, and other faraway colonial sites, and the city's anxious awe at the proliferation of marvels beyond the sea.

As the pilgrims move throughout the European countryside on their way to Rome, the text praises a number of cities. The further we move into Spain the more sparse or problematic the ekphrasis of the cityscape becomes. When the pilgrims arrive in the vicinity of Toledo, something similar to what happened in Lisbon takes place, though in a minor tone. Just as in the description of Lisbon, we must first turn to the ocean through which the pilgrims approach it; here the narrative first turns to the river Tagus that frames the city (Cervantes 2015b, 503–4). More to the point, if the Tagus flows into the ocean by the city of Lisbon, as the longest river in Hispania, it also cradles Toledo almost at the centre of the peninsula. In a sense, we return to circle and centre, an ancient view of the universe: Lisbon is at the edges of this circle, while Toledo, the imperial city, is the centre. And yet, the two cities and their contrastive powers are decentred by the river. In addition, if Toledo is a symbolic centre, Lisbon is a centre for international trade – again, a double focus, creating an elliptical figure.

The eighth chapter of the third book begins as we are told that Periandro is well versed in the Latin classics and thus knows of the greatness of the river. Through a northerner (one who may be considered at the edges of *ecumene*), this site thus becomes even more important because its fame has reached the edges of the "civilized" world. Not only that, but the pilgrim also knows the praises of the city found in Spain's canonical poet, Garcilaso de la Vega, as he cites from the first eclogue. For Elias Rivers, Cervantes' use of Garcilaso reflects "una cierta nostalgia muy particular, la que añoraba la autoridad perdida de una literatura clásica" (a very particular kind of nostalgia that longs for the lost authority of a classical literature; 1983, 570). He recalls how the poet's praise of the golden sands of the Tagus passes from land to land, from language to language. Thus, Garcilaso, albeit not the latest fashion, has "conquered" many lands. This praise once again has a double and elliptical focus, the power of cultural capital and the power of imperial conquest.

Curiously, Cervantes, in this one instance, seems to turn away from the visual, arguing that the written is superior to the seen. The narrator claims that Periandro is best able to see the wonders of the river Tagus and of the city of Toledo because he had first read about it. The ones who just see the landscape are not as affected as those who have read before seeing, because they have placed their attention on all the details and wonders. Thus it is through Garcilaso that Periandro and others see the Tagus, and it is through the Tagus that the pilgrims look upon the city of Toledo. Precisely because the narrative rejects the visual, the reader might think of a new double focus, the hidden work of art (the visual) that is obscured by poetry (or by Cervantes' praises of Toledo). This unexpected rejection of ekphrasis (a technique that is present throughout the works of Garcilaso) invites us to look at Toledo through the visual. It would certainly be possible to study this moment through El Greco's two famous paintings depicting the city. We will pause briefly to look at the best known in order to compare it to the representation of Toledo in Cervantes.

Most critics are astonished at the darkness and lugubriousness of *View of Toledo* (figure 8.1), which depicts the city in daylight but hides it in darkness, revealing its phantasmagoric unreality (Brown and Kagan 1982, 23). Periandro begins his description of Toledo with an apostrophe and exclamation: "Oh peñascosa pesadumbre" (Cervantes 2015b, 504). The pilgrim's words suggest what appears in the painting, where the city recedes in order to foreground the hills, the *peñascos* that uphold it. Although *pesadumbre* may refer to the weight of the city (Cervantes 2015b, 505n5), it can also weigh in on the melancholy air and greyish architecture of Toledo. Perhaps the reasons for this can be found in the historical moment: El Greco sought to present a city that was in decline because Madrid had become the capital, starting in 1566. Seeking to assert itself, Toledo then attempted to remain relevant through its myths and through the power of the Church. But as such, it is a fading light. While for some it highlights a kind of mysticism, for others it is clearly a representation of decadence, even in its affirmations (Brown and Kagan 1982, 25). Cervantes, as if having this painting in mind, attempts to bring light to the city, while accepting that its fame rests in the past: "luz de tus ciudades, en cuyo seno han estado guardadas por infinitos siglos las reliquias de los valientes godos, para volver a resucitar su muerta gloria y a ser claro espejo y depósito de católicas ceremonias" (the light of her cities in whose bosom, during infinite ages, have been kept the relics of the valiant Goths *in order to resuscitate its dead glory and become a clear mirror and repository of Catholic ceremonies*; Cervantes 2015b, 505; n.d.). The relics here are related to the gothic myth, to a legendary past, which in modern times has turned to Catholic ceremonies. Again, we are in the presence a double focus, an elliptical formation of past and present. The city in a sense is resuscitated, but given El Greco's painting, we could even say that what we have is a necromantic return, one over which the phantasmagoric reigns. Cervantes deliberately turns away from the city as if he did not wish to dwell on past glories. Elsewhere, he uses Toledo as the city in which one of his *Novelas ejemplares* takes place. In the first scene of "La fuerza de la sangre" (The

Figure 8.1. El Greco (Dominikos Theotokopoulos), *View from Toledo*, ca. 1599–1600. The Metropolitan Museum of Art, New York. Open access, public domain

power of blood), we encounter violence, brutality, and abduction, which take place as a family returns to Toledo. The story exhibits the clash between decadence and religious architecture as Leocadia, after being raped by Rodolfo, asks to be left "junto a la iglesia mayor" (next to the main church; Cervantes 2015a, 351). In the *Persiles*, in order to preserve the brilliance of Garcilaso's vision, the pilgrims must literally turn away from Toledo. They do so in order to listen and view the happiness of song and dance in the countryside. In this sense, the description also recalls the greenery in the foreground of El Greco's painting. The beauties of the approaching damsels as bright as the sun are not in El Greco and serve to attenuate the view of the ancient light of Toledo.

We could continue with cityscapes in the third book, noting that the pilgrims by-pass Valencia, albeit praising it as the most beautiful city in Europe.[5] When they are in Barcelona, almost nothing is said of the urban space, the action focusing on its beach and port. In part, this distrust of the city may stem from its dysrithmia, the impossibility of locating Vitruvian harmony in haphazard constructions, where streets go every which way and houses are built haphazardly. As stated, the harmonious music of the peasants dancing outside of Toledo serves as contrast to the city itself. To recapitulate, Toledo is a guiding light from the past that has become a greyish phantasm, suggesting a "plurythmia" of light and shadow, a chiaroscuro that is just as much about time (past and present) as about space (foreground and background). Certainly, the Vitruvian city, carefully built so that the winds will not hurt the inhabitants, is nowhere to be found, be it Toledo or Barcelona. Not only did Cervantes' view of cities echo the ancients, but it also calls to the future, to architects like Frank Lloyd Wright for whom "the urban environment was regarded as a fallen world, as an alienating 'occidental' nowhere beyond redemption" (Lipman 1986, xi). But let us abide by Cervantes' ellipsis and turn to the second view of Toledo by El Greco and the canvases of the pilgrims' adventures.

Lienzos

While still in Lisbon, Periandro goes to the home of a famous painter. There he orders him "en un lienzo grande le pintase todos los más principales casos de su historia" (to trace with his pencil in a great table [canvas] the principal matters of his history; Cervantes 2015b, 437; n.d.). It clearly contrasts with the second painting of Toledo by El Greco. As Antonio Sánchez Jiménez and Julián Olivares remind us, *View and Plan of Toledo*, somewhat warmer with its earth colours and brighter sky, includes flying figures, in particular the Virgin descending, thus adding to the religious impact. For our purposes, what is most important is that it also shows a young man with a plan of the city, in which the main edifices are numbered to make them easy to locate – although at least one is "dislocated" (Sánchez Jiménez and Julián Olivares 2011, 28–30). Whatever distortions, the plan of the city seeks to simplify our view. Indeed, the young man portrayed is said to be El Greco's son Jorge Manuel, who, besides being a painter, was also an architect. He was working on Toledo's Casa Consistorial (City Hall) while Cervantes was writing the *Persiles*. Begun by Juan de Herrera, the work was continued by Herrera's son and then by Jorge Manuel, who made the plans for the slate spires and the stairs.

Returning to Cervantes, we can locate his plan or picture of the northern adventures very close to the middle of the novel. It can be related to the many mnemonic devices of the period, perhaps even recalling the precepts of Della Porta. Cervantes and the Neapolitan humanist were part of the same network of artists and patrons. Cervantes dedicated to the Count of Lemos a number of works such as the *Persiles* and the second part of his *Don Quixote* (1615), and Della Porta dedicated to Lemos his 1610 Italian translation of *De humana physiognomia*. In addition, Cervantes' *Retablo de las maravillas* (A theater of wonders) is a satiric re-creation of the architectonic art of memory as explained by Della Porta in his *Arte del ricordare* (*The Art of Remembering*) (De Armas 2005, 633–48). The canvas from the Portuguese painter will be carried in the pilgrims' journey so that they do not have to tell the full story. A person or an audience needed only to point to one of the adventures depicted, and they would hear the narrative. In this strange and curious canvas the adventures are not depicted chronologically, and we could even get lost among the many depictions – totally the opposite of what El Greco sought.

Elizabeth Bearden rightly points out that, although painted by a Portuguese artist, the work's "program" belongs to Periandro, whose subjective view of events at times leads to self-glorification, as when he shows himself the winner of the contest at Policarpo's palace: "Periandro includes his most glorious chivalric moments; but the events are not depicted chronologically, nor is there any differentiation between real and dreamed – or potentially false – episodes, such as Periandro's dream island" (2006, 741). A search for a description of buildings within this extended ekphrasis (an ekphrasis within an ekphrasis) would leave the reader disappointed. While both the fire on Policarpo's island and the pilgrims' arrival in Lisbon are depicted, nothing is said of the buildings themselves. I would argue that the closest the canvas comes to a description is a kind of reverse forging ekphrasis dealing with the overturned ship that trapped so many: "acá estaban serrando por la quilla la nave que había servido de sepultura a Auristela y a los que con ella venían" (here, the ship was cut at the keel, which had served as a tomb to the fair Auristela, and all her company; Cervantes 2015b, 438; n.d.). It is the moment in which the bottom of the ship is opened up rather than the moment in which it was built. The inversion of the ship's construction points to the reversal of the forging ekphrasis. Again we have an elliptical image, one with a double focus.

As the pilgrims move through the third part of the novel, they open their canvas to show who they are and what has happened to them. Elizabeth Bearden points out that it falls to the young Antonio, a "barbarian," to describe the work. She likens his voice to those of Native Americans, or more precisely to a "hybrid mestizo gaze" (2006, 741), given that he is the offspring of a Spaniard and a barbarian. At one point, when the pilgrims are threatened, "Antonio's ekphrastic evidence resembles Native American testimonials in New World courts, in which indigenous peoples presented traditional *lienzos* as evidence in their cases, demonstrating their adaptability in using their iconic languages in a colonial context" (2006, 741). But we can also look at the canvas as a way of "discovering," removing the cover of darkness from the north through a mnemonic document that validates the northern lands now that they are viewed by Europeans. It is a kind of cartographical canvas for future intrusion into this world, as the light of European civilization is sent to the north. It is no coincidence that the pilgrims arrive in Lisbon, the centre for colonization and conquest of the world. I would argue that the voice of the young Antonio simply serves to validate the discovery and to point to the conversion of the north to the Catholic faith. This impetus is seldom presented without irony, for, as stated, Rome will be seen as infected by paganism and corrupt practices. While it is the case that the cannibalism from the north will turn into the sacrament of communion in the south, it is also the case that violence and hypocrisy mark a number of the southern scenes. The narrative is not intent as a move to cancel culture; it has a more complex and thoughtful purpose, to ironize some of European civilization's practices and to present the north as a mirror so that readers can consider some of the actions, customs, and foibles of their time. It is not a cancel outburst but a learning experience.

In some ways, the criticism is more Erasmian than essential. While affirming miracle (and the advances of science and culture), the text calls for a reformation of the Church. The uses of religion for deceit and personal gain are depicted in the second of the *lienzos* that adorn the third part of the novel. The pilgrims arrive at a town that suspiciously sounds like the home of Don Quixote: "El hermoso escuadrón de los peregrinos, prosiguiendo su viaje, llegó a un lugar, no muy pequeño ni muy grande, de cuyo nombre no me acuerdo" (I say that our pilgrims, following their journey, came into a place neither too big, nor too little, whose name I remember not; Cervantes 2015b, 527; n.d.). At the centre of the main plaza two youths, in the garb of recently rescued captives with the appropriate accoutrements (chains), narrate their captivity through a canvas set on the ground. One of them begins by saying: "Esta, señores, que aquí veis pintada, es la ciudad de Argel, gomia y tarasca de todas las riberas del mar Mediterráneo, puesto universal de cosarios y amparo y refugio de ladrones, que, deste pequeñuelo puerto que aquí va pintado, salen con sus bajeles a inquietar el mundo, pues se atreven a pasar el *plus ultra* de las colunas de Hércules." (Gentlemen, this city whose portrait you see, is the town of Algiers, the fear and terror of all the coasts of the Mediterranean sea, the general haven of pirates and the common refuge of thieves, who from this little port, which there you see painted, issue with their ships to rob all nations, adventuring to pass beyond Hercules' pillars; 528–9; n.d.) As with the first canvas, the architecture here is never described. Although the captives portray themselves as bloodied by the enemy, one of the town officers decides to question them to make sure they are not making false claims. After a somewhat lengthy interrogation this second canvas proves to be false because the impostors cannot answer the questions as to how many gates surround the city of Algiers and how many fountains and wells does it have. Indeed, these are the only architectural details invoked.[6] The false pilgrims turn out to be students from Salamanca, searching for ways to pay for their education. On the one hand, for Alban K. Forcione, this canvas reflects the tension between artistic freedom and Aristotelian rules and theories (1970, 172). On the other hand, Jeremy Robbins prefers to study it as delineating the tension between history and fiction (2004, 627–39). Although Stephen Harrison has compared the false captives to the two main picaresque characters of Cervantes' *Rinconete y Cortadillo*, thus creating somewhat sympathetic characters with picaresque traits (1993, 98), I would emphasize that their use of wit and art are not just entertaining. The use of false knowledge by students from a prestigious university may serve to question what they are actually learning. Learning and the Church, the pillars of culture, suffer from misuse.

One of the more gruesome images in this *lienzo* has to do with the way in which a Turkish captain beats a Christian captive: "con un brazo en la mano, que cortó a aquel Cristiano que allí veis […] Aquel cautivo primero del primer banco, cuyo rostro le desfigura la sangre que se le ha pegado de los golpes del brazo muerto, soy yo" (that first captive from the first bench, whose visage is covered by the blood which emerged from the blows he received from the dead arm, is me" (Cervantes 2015b, 529; n.d.). The blood recalls the blood of martyrdom, giving a holy aura to the canvas. At the same time, the image serves to confirm the "truth" of the *lienzo* because the false captive claims that the one who is being beaten is himself.[7] This kind of "signature" in blood recalls Caravaggio's famous *Beheading of St. John the Baptist* (1608): the artist signed the painting using the (painted) red blood that spills from the body's cut throat.Following the Council of Trent, the Church had underlined the appropriate uses of images, but here these are subverted.

The captives' mention of the Pillars of Hercules is but a reminder that the pilgrims are now in the known lands surrounding the Mediterranean. At the same time, one of the columns, as it stood on the Spanish side of the Straits of Gibraltar, was associated with the infamous cave or tower whose desecration by King Rodrigo had brought about, according to the gothic legend, the fall of Christian Spain to Islam. The allusion to this legend may have been used by the fake captives to arouse further the fear of the Turks and Moors and thus make their story more persuasive. Later Hercules' feats in Spain will reappear as the pilgrims enter France. Even there, so close to Italy, the marvellous shimmers as if it were an illusion. Armstrong-Roche emphasizes that "la enajenación de lo familiar que resalta la percepción de lo extraño en lo conocido" (the alienation of the familiar underlines the perception of the strange in the known; 2019, 25). The everyday is conjoined to elements that separate the reader from it, much like this Quixotic town, whose name the narrator cannot remember, leads us to question the limits of representation, the ability of the historical to appear fictive and vice versa. While the plan of Toledo seeks to clarify a cityscape and foreground the salient architectures, the pilgrims' plan is also mnemonic in the sense that it makes it easier to remember episodes. However, it is a plan that moves away from architectural design because it places adventures in a haphazard manner. Taking this to an extreme, the plan of the fake captives is not just haphazard but hides its own mendacity. At a time when the architect was becoming a most important figure in the liberal arts, Cervantes warns of the uses of his inventions or *trazas*. Weary of the cacophony and dysrithmia of cityscapes, he compares cities to chaotic northern adventure and further warns of fake architects who falsify their knowledge, not just of captivity but perhaps even of Vitruvian principles.

Sacred Architectures

Although Toledo, in Cervantes' novel, does not succeed in representing the sacred, there are other moments that point to Catholic devotion. As the pilgrims continue their journey, it becomes clear that, even though buildings acquire solidity, they are seldom drawn with words. One example, perhaps the most memorable, will suffice. The pilgrims arrive in the valley that houses the monastery of Guadalupe and immediately feel a sense of *admiratio*. By the mid-seventeenth century, René

Descartes will have placed this emotion as the primordial one, to be followed by the other five – love, hatred, desire, joy, and sadness. *Admiratio* was already a key to the composition of literary works, as Antonio Minturno in his *De poeta* (1559) demonstrated. For him and many other theorists of the time, its uses are to delight, teach, and move the reader. Francesco Patrizi went further, claiming that it should not be limited to the verisimilar but should even emphasize the incredible (Platt 1992, 390). Patrizi states: "something new and sudden and unexpected which appears before us, creates a movement in our soul, almost contradictory in itself of believing and not believing. Of believing because the thing is seen to exist; not believing because it is sudden, new, and not before either known or dreamt of" (Platt 1992, 391). This feeling, which pervades the first two books of the *Persiles*, reappears as the northerners arrive in Portugal; it is also the anxious wonderment felt by the Europeans at the sight of strangers from far away. This is precisely the sensation felt by the pilgrims when the monastery of Guadalupe comes into view, but the feeling is now enveloped in a Catholic discourse: "con cada paso que daban nacían en sus corazones nuevas ocasiones de admirarse, pero allí llegó la admiración a su punto, cuando vieron el grande y suntuoso monasterio, cuyas murallas encierran la santísima imagen de la emperadora de los Cielos" (but at every step they made new subjects of admiration arose in their minds, which then came to their height when they saw the great and sumptuous monastery whose walls enclosed the holy image of the empress of heaven; Cervantes 2015b, 471; n.d.). The narrator is here inviting the reader to join in the admiration felt by the pilgrims at the sight of the building. For the many Spanish readers who had been there, this became an exercise in memory, recalling its majesty; for those who had not, it became a challenge to their imagination, a way to construct an image they would admire.

J.R. Muñoz Sánchez argues that the description of the building is an extended ekphrasis (2015a, 178). And yet, when we turn to the description, we see that it begins with negation: "Entraron en su templo y, donde pensaron hallar por su paredes, pendientes por adorno, las púrpuras de Tiro, los damascos de Siria, los brocados de Milán, hallaron en lugar suyo muletas que dejaron los cojos, ojos de cera que dejaron los ciegos, brazos que colgaron los manco." (They entered into her temple and, instead of Tyrian purple, Syrian damask or satin embroidered with gold of Milan, which they thought to find hanging on her walls, they found crutches, which such as halted had left there; eyes and arms of wax, which the blind and lame had hung up; Cervantes 2015b, 471; n.d.). As with cityscapes, there is a sense of ellipsis and the elliptical. Instead of its architectural exterior and interior beauty, we come to see the temple through the *ex-votos*, objects left to ask for a favour, but in this case mainly to show gratitude for a miracle. These signs of faith and gratitude are so plentiful that the pilgrims "volvieron los ojos a todas las partes del templo, y les parecía ver venir por el aire volando los cautivos envueltos en sus cadenas a colgarlas de las santas murallas, y a los enfermos arrastrar las muletas, y a los muertos mortajas, buscando lugar donde ponerlas, porque ya en el sacro templo no cabían." (Turning their eyes to every side of the temple, they thought they saw captives come flying in the air, wrapped in their chains to hang them upon the holy walls; the diseased there to hang their stilts, and the dead their winding-sheets, seeking new places where to put them because there was no more room left in the temple; 472; n.d..) It is as if the pilgrims experienced for themselves a series of past miracles in a new miracle or vision in which the sick, the maimed, and even the dead flew through the air. Américo Castro, pointing to a similar moment in *El licenciado Vidriera* (The Glass graduate), seeks to make these descriptions ironic (1925, 259). Like the editor of the *Persiles*, Romero Muñoz (Cervantes 2015b, 472n4), I take them at face value. For Mercedes Blanco the scene, instead of a moment of Counter-Reformation piety, turns into a "visión de pesadilla grotesca" (version of a grotesque nightmare; 1995, 632–3). Such a switch is not at all uncommon in Cervantes, as we have seen prisons turned into palaces, and Vitruvian towers turned into grotesque images. Are we looking at something akin to El Greco's *Vision of Toledo*? I would problematize a phantasmagoric or grotesque reading here for four reasons: relic, chains, poem, and miracle.

The dead, the ailing, and the captives flying through the air, looking for a place to leave their shrouds, their crutches, and their chains in a church already filled with objects, brings to mind the importance of relics, along with *ex-votos*, as powerful signs of the sacred. Scott Dudley explains that numerous Catholic tracts of the period "privilege the corpse not only for its ability to contain the sacred, but also for its capacity to underwrite cultural and institutional certainty" (1999, 279). In other words, the corpse of a saintly person becomes a site for miracles, as every part, finger, or ear can have the power to bring about a miracle. The more *ex-voto* objects and the more relics found in a church, the more its miraculous power is confirmed, one that strengthens the authority of the Catholic Church. Presided over by the Virgin of Guadalupe, the agglomeration of objects sustains her power as intercessor and furthers the role of miracles in the monastery. Rather than a grotesque moment, the pilgrims' vision authorizes the link between objects, corpses, and miracles, creating a vision of celestial outpourings in the midst of the frailties of living and the decay of the dead. Since corpses of the saintly were once "temples" of the Holy Spirit as Thomas Aquinas argued, we can now see temples within temples, shrouds within architectures (S. Dudley 1999, 181). It assures the pilgrims that even corpses can partake of the divine: the grotesque here embodies the sacred.

At the same time, this visionary moment refers to the chains that constrict those in captivity. Rather than a grotesque moment, it partakes of biographical allusion. Rachel Schmidt reminds us that "Cervantes held the Virgin of Guadalupe and her sanctuary in special esteem, for she was famed for working miracles in favor of Christians held captive by the Ottoman Turks" (2016, 480). The chains would remind Cervantes of his captivity in Algiers and even of imprisonment in Seville. This moment recalls, for example, Pero López de Ayala, who was imprisoned for years by the Portuguese. He included a series of verses in praise of the Virgin in his otherwise satirical *Rimado de palacio* (Palace rhymes). These Marian verses, as Ryan D. Giles remind us, "include repeated vows to go on pilgrimage to Santa Maria la Blanca ('prometí'), the shrines of Guadalupe and Montserrat" (2015, 29). He adds: "In keeping with countless other freed prisoners and pilgrims during the Middle Ages and beyond, it is likely that López de Ayala physically brought his real chains and irons to Mary as votive offerings, in addition to memorializing his vows together with the objects themselves in the *Rimado de Palacio*" (32). Although Cervantes could not bring his actual chains from Algiers, these brief lines, along with other instances in his work, may memorialize vows that he made. Indeed, numerous pilgrims in the period carried chains as symbolic of their sins. Leaving them at the site of pilgrimage meant for them freedom from the weight of their errors, a kind of purification. This moment, then, is far from grotesque but points to liberation. The notion of imprisonment and liberation can also point to the metaphorical prison of this earth, and liberation in death, key to *desengaño*, a central concept of the baroque. The next moment within this architecture will further open up the heavens to the pilgrims.

Once the vision is over, the narrative turns to Feliciana de la Voz's ecstasy: "sin mover los labios ni hacer otra demostración ni movimiento que diese señal de ser viva criatura, soltó la voz a los vientos" (her lips closed, and the rest of her body without motion or token that she was a living creature, gave passage to her voice; Cervantes 2015b, 473; n.d.). She becomes a kind of statue that can sing in a manner that moves all those present. It is as if she were re-enacting the legend of Guadalupe, be it to fully affirm it or to modify it, as William Childers argues.[8] Her ecstasy leaves no doubt that she is in communion with the heavens, that her song is a new flight that again affirms the importance of air as a medium to encounter the sacred. Her song is in praise of God's creation and particularly of the Virgin's benevolence. It fills the air of the church, overcoming any feeling of death and decay. Thus, two statues resonate with each other, the Virgin of Guadalupe and Feliciana de la Voz. Aurora Egido points to this resonance, reminding us that we are dealing with two mothers and that each has a child: "Feliciana madre canta ante una Virgen María que sostiene al Niño en sus brazos, loando los triunfos de tan gran mediadora" (Feliciana as a mother sings in front of the Virgin Mary who holds in her arms the Child, as she praises the triumphs of the mediator; 1998, 19). The song also points to the monastery as an architecture that seeks to rise to meet the heavenly architectures. Indeed, her voice brings about a miracle in which this persecuted woman, whose one "error" has been to choose the man she loves over the one she is supposed to marry, and to have a child with Rosanio, finally finds happiness. The "miracle" is not presented as a direct intervention from the heavens. Feliciana must face her father and brother, the latter holding a knife and seeking to avenge the honour of the family with her blood, before all can be solved outside the walls of the temple. Rosanio arrives with two friends and asks that marriage be allowed to substitute for her death.[9] Each of the two friends pleads for Feliciana to be spared. Armstrong-Roche explains that they use as rhetorical strategy "the language understood by the disputants [...] the code of honour [...] the religion of honour" (2009, 158). I would add that this is done through metaphors of building. Turning to the father, Pedro Tenorio, the first asks, "¿Cómo y es posible que vos mismo queráis fabricar vuestra ofensa?" (How is it possible that you should contrive [*construct*] your own harm?; Cervantes 2015b, 476; n.d.) Feliciana's death will further the fabric of her dishonour. The second companion, facing Feliciana's brother, asserts: "Tomar venganza de que no se guardaron las debidas ceremonias y respetos no será bien hecho, porque os pondréis a peligro de derribar y echar por tierra todo el edificio de vuestro sosiego" (And for you to take revenge for this, that they have not observed such respect as they ought you, it were to put in hazard to overthrow the foundation of your quiet; 476; n.d.). He suggests that taking vengeance is not a satisfactory outcome, because it would bring down the edifice of his well-being.

These metaphorical constructions stand in contrast to the architecture of the monastery, where the Virgin stands for attenuating the sufferings of humankind. In the end, the inner miracle prevails. The metaphorical architectures have served to underline the importance of the physical and celestial architecture. When all is forgiven, Feliciana gives

Auristela the full poem that she started to sing at the church of Guadalupe. Although she sang four stanzas at the church, all twelve are given to Auristela, who, as will be discussed later in this chapter, also embodies many of the attributes of the Virgin, being a personification of chastity and a golden star. Cervantes' fifth chapter comes to a close with these verses and with images of peace and harmony among all. The initial verses, as Rachel Schmidt explains, clarify that "[t]he Virgin's genesis precedes time and cosmic order, for she will become the house of God, her flesh having been made adequate to the divine substance of her Son: 'fabricó para sí Dios una casa / de santísima y limpia y pura masa' [God built for himself a house / of pure and sanctified material]" (Schmidt 2016, 483; Cervantes 2015b, 477; n.d.; translation mine). Schmidt, making an argument for the poem in support of the immaculate conception, shows her above all four elements, atop the crescent moon, an image common in painting and recalling "Murillo's multiple paintings of the *Virgin of the Immaculate Conception* and Velázquez's *Virgin of the Immaculate Conception* (about 1619)" (2016, 483).

Following on the image of the building of the house, which lauds God as builder (*Deus artifex*), the tower and the fortress continue the architectural elements of the song; their pillars are constructed of faith and hope, while the walls are fashioned by charity and other virtues. Within this mansion are many gardens and fountains, thus containing "huertos cerrados" (*enclosed gardens*).[10] Of course, the tradition of the Virgin as a closed garden or *hortus conclusus* goes back to the *Song of Songs* and came to mean that the Virgin conceived in a miraculous manner, without disrupting her virginity. The walled monastery containing the image of the Virgin of Guadalupe thus resonates with the walled-in home in the heavens and with the walled-in gardens. Feliciana's poem in praise of the Virgin, her ecstasy in her presence, is a sign of a future miracle. Feliciana comes to the walled-in monastery of Gaudalupe for a miracle, for redemption, and it is here that she finds it. It is also a miracle in terms of the patriarchal order because here woman's voice can be heard, and the role of the father as arbiter in marriage loses its potency.[11] The fifth chapter of the *Persiles*, then, presents us three architectures: the divine one, fashioned by the creator; the sacred one (the sanctuary itself), forged by human hands to aspire to the divine; and the architectures of contention, presented metaphorically and physically, outside the wall.

The Veranzio Woman

Somewhere in France, at midday, the pilgrims decide to rest from the sun and take their meal and siesta. The shade provided by one of the noble villas or pleasure homes seems an ideal "place." After all, it is sufficiently apart from the Royal Road that its tranquility is inviting. As they sit in a circle to eat, to enjoy "place" and communion, as they raise their hands to enjoy their first taste, Bartolomé raised his eyes upwards. At this very moment of eurithmia, tranquility, and the place created by the pilgrims, one that is foregrounded by the circle of perfection, some-thing wondrous seems to break the peace, something that will recall the wonders of miracle. Bartolomé warns the group to look up, that some-one is falling down: "y vieron bajar por el aire una figura, que, antes que distinguiesen lo que era, ya estaba en el suelo junto casi a los pies de Periandro. La cual figura era de una mujer hermosísima, que, habi-endo sido arrojada desde lo alto de la torre, sirviéndole de campana y de alas sus mismos vestidos." (They looked up towards heaven, and saw a shape fall, which was upon the ground hard by Periander's feet before they could discern what it might be. It was a very fair woman thrown down from the top of the tower, who fell to the ground upon her feet without any harm, being upholded by her clothes in the air, as it were by miracle; Cervantes 2015b, 573; n.d.) The pleasure palace has suddenly turned into a strange tower as marvellous and as dangerous as those in the romances of chivalry.[12] In *Don Quixote*, menacing giants are like towers, and the Giralda tower becomes a giantess, a structure based on Andronicus Cyrrhus' Tower of the Winds. In this new itera-tion a woman falls from the tower, but her dress opens like a bell and allows her to float down to safety. Although it may appear that Cer-vantes is stretching our imagination and taking us to the romances of chivalry in which dragon ships can fly, as in *Las sergas de Esplandián* (The adventures of Esplandián), in reality he is reflecting the latest sci-entific experiments.

We may surmise that Francesco di Giorgio Martini, the well-known Vitruvius enthusiast, may have been the first in Europe to design a para-chute (Boric 2016, 64n31). Some years later, Leonardo da Vinci sketched such a contraption in his *Codice Atlantico*. Others also attempted to find ways that would slow the motion of a falling object by creating a drag in the air, culminating in the famous invention of the contraption and sketch of an *homo volans* (flying man) by Fausto Veranzio (Faustus Verantius). Marijana Boric does not believe that Veranzio knew or was copying predecessors such as Leonardo. At any rate this critic shows the importance of his sketch: "Vrančić's design was the first printed project for a parachute in the history of techn(olog)ical literature. In the description of the parachute, Vrančić stressed the importance of the size of the linen and the weight of the man" (65–6). At any rate, recent tests have shown that Veranzio's parachute is much safer than Leonardo's and allows the person to jump from greater heights (66). Cervantes, in this case, focuses on one section of the pleasure palace, a tower, in order to point to the sketch and description found in a new book by Fausto Veranzio entitled *Machinae novae* (New machines). According to Boric, Veranzio "was precisely an example of the successful Renaissance type of man, the so-called *homo universalis*. Vrančić (Šibenik 1551–Venice 1617) was one of the most influential persons in the Hungarian Kingdom of that period, a secretary to the emperor Rudolf II, bishop, engineer, designer, lexicographer, while he also wrote historical, philosophical, theological and literary texts" (46). His contacts, from Kepler to Emperor Rudolph II, made him a most influential figure at the time, even though few today study him. These contacts increase the possibility that Cervantes may have known his work; after all, the Spanish writer was well acquainted with the work of Arcimboldo, who was at Rudolf's court for many years.

Although a number of scholars, including Boric, assert that *Machinae novae* was published in Venice in 1615–16 (Boric 2016, 48), the New York Public Library claims to have a copy from a 1595 edition with its many illustrations (Triplett 2012), and so does the University of Chicago in its special collections.[13] Even if he did not read the full book, Cervantes could have easily glanced at the forty-nine large illustrations contained in the book that depicted some fifty-six inventions. The book was very rare, published by its own author in four languages (Italian, French, German, and Spanish). The rarity of the book would have made it difficult for Cervantes to have or view a copy, although we know that he seemed quite interested in mechanical inventions, a topic that critics have failed to investigate in detail. For example, the windmills episode in the 1605 *Don Quixote* may be indebted to Juanelo Turriano, an inventor from Cremona, Italy, who built a famous astronomical clock for Charles V and was appointed chief mathematician by Philip II.[14] Cervantes also mentions the famous device created by Juanelo to bring up water from the river Tagus to the city of Toledo, in *La ilustre fregona* (The illustrious kitchen maid).

Illustration 38 in Veranzio's book shows a man "floating" down from a tower in what is not very different from a modern parachute (figure 8.2). This particular tower, the campanile of Saint Mark's Basilica in Venice, was the tallest structure in the city. Constructed as a watchtower, it was built up with a belfry and a spire starting in the twelfth century and concluding in 1513. Very much like the Giralda tower, it is thus a composite building, one that combined different builders and purposes over the centuries. It includes a weathervane, much like the Giralda, but in this case of the copper-plated archangel

Figure 8.2. Fausto Veranzio, *Homo volans* [Flying man] from *Machinae novae* [New machines], illustration 38, ca. 1615–16. Alamy Stock Photo

Gabriel. Like the one at the Giralda, the weathervane at Saint Mark's was inspired by Vitruvius' description of the Tower of the Winds. In the illustration the man seems halfway down, and the top part of the tower with its campanile is not shown. It is said that when he was sixty-five years of age, Veranzio actually tried out his invention and successfully floated down from Saint Mark's campanile. Some claim this was done in 1617, the year of Veranzio's death and the year of the posthumous publication of Cervantes' novel (Miller 1930, 101–6). Others prefer to set the event in 1595, the year of the proposed first edition of his *Machinae novae*. After all, Paolo Giodotti, around 1590, had attempted a jump, using Leonardo's contraption – not very successfully. The story may be just a legend. However, Veranzio could have attempted this jump much earlier, and thus the anecdote may have reached Cervantes. Whatever the case, it seems as if Cervantes transformed the villa or pleasure palace in France, or simply focused on its tower in order to replicate a very famous jump in the late Renaissance. He transforms the man falling into a woman who uses, instead of the wooden contraption with a large linen cloth to slow the fall, her own dress opened in the shape of a bell. In so doing, Cervantes contrasts a dangerous giantess above a tower with a woman who, in a way, experiments with flying. If in some of Cervantes' works we can detect a Vitruvian man, here we discover a Veranzio woman, who goes even further than the former in extolling the perfections of humankind. If the Vitruvian man is perfect because he fits into the most ideal geometrical form, that of the circle, which points to the heavens, the Veranzio woman in Cervantes' novel discovers how to fly. Her proportions are so perfect and the sartorial customs of the country so ideal that she can float down from a tower rather than plunge to her death. At a time when Kepler was crafting his laws of planetary motion, which would later blend into Isaac Newton's law of universal gravitation, a female character in Cervantes echoes the scientific concerns of the times, turning a dreadful fall almost into what could become a moment of delight, turning space into place.

Hercules'/Domitian's Tower

The tower episode is far from over at this point. The Veranzio woman, recovering from the fright at having been tossed out of the tower, asks the pilgrims to help save her children and others who are on top. Periandro rushes up with his knife, battles the madman who had thrown her from the tower, but both fall from the top, the madman below the pilgrim and now cut by Periandro's knife. Since Periandro is bleeding profusely from the eyes, ears, and mouth, Auristela thinks that her beloved is dead. She tries to kiss him, an impossible task given that his teeth are clenched. In the next chapter we will return to the curious description given here, but for now, let us move ahead, not even commenting on the sudden irruption of a troop in pursuit of three French ladies, Deleasir, Belarminia, and Feliz Flora. While at the tower Auristela laments and hopes that Periandro will recover,

Claricia, the Veranzio woman, tells how her husband, Domicio, had succumbed to the jealousy and envy of Lorena. Lorena gave him some beautiful shirts that were apparently poisoned, and on wearing one of them, he went mad: "no de loco manso, sino de cruel, furioso y desatinado: tanto, que era necesario tenerle en cadenas" (but with his wits so troubled, that he performed no action but like a fool, yea, as a cruel, furious and enraged fool, so that it was necessary to chain him up; Cervantes 2015b, 579; n.d.). Having freed himself, he tossed his own wife from the tower. Claricia compares the poisoned gift to the poison tunic given by Nessus to Deianira and then by Deianira to her husband, Hercules. Both Hercules and Domicio go mad and die as a consequence of wearing a poisoned garment given to them by a jealous woman.

Given the many towers said to have been built by Hercules in Hispania, and given the labours of Hercules that also took place in the peninsula, it is curious that Cervantes moves the episode to France. I would argue that Cervantes is intending here to satirize or, at the least, problematize the Gallic Hercules. This version of Hercules originates in the writings of Lucian, as here he holds club and bow in his hands. With chains of gold and amber originating in his tongue, he drags along his followers to whose ears the chains are entwined (Hallowell 1962, 242). Not only is this French Hercules set to replace Mercury as the god of eloquence, but also he is said in the chronicles of pseudo-Berosus (as invented by Johannes Annius of Viterbo) to have married Galatea, daughter of a Celtic king. Legends were suddenly altered to show that French kings were the descendants of not just Francus, the son of the Trojan Hector, but also Hercules and Galatea. Having written a whole pastoral novel entitled *Galatea*, consciously relating it to the myth of Polyphemus, Acis, and Galatea, Cervantes must have found this tale rather incredible, although he does allude to it in the second book of *Persiles* to praise the eloquence of Periandro.[15] Here Cervantes sets out to subvert the French legend found in Alciati, Vincenzo Cartari, Jean Le Blond, Joachim du Bellay, and Pierre Ronsard through his tale of the tower. First and foremost, he turns the old and venerable Gallic Hercules, famed for his eloquence, into a madman. Second, the golden chains by which this French demigod holds his listeners in thrall are transformed into the shackles that hold the madman as a prisoner in the tower. Third, Cervantes names his character Domicio, thus recalling Emperor Domitian, a cruel tyrant according to Suetonius, and one who particularly enjoyed being depicted as a new Hercules. A statue of Hercules is said to replicate Domitian, and a bust of the emperor points to Hercules. Writers of his time often made the connection between emperor and hero, particularly Martial, as well as Statius in his *Silvae* and his epic, *Thebaid*. As Olivier J. Hekster asserts, the laudatory remarks were so extreme as to declare that "more than Hercules, Domitian deserved deification" (2005, 204). Fourth, among the few great works accomplished by Domitian was a series of watchtowers to keep enemies from entering the empire. Unfortunately some had to be moved back due to the enemies' pressure. Thus, as opposed to Hercules who built a series of towers in Spain, Domicio/Domitian, a new Hercules, cannot even have his troops defend the watchtowers they constructed.

If Domicio, in spite of his wife's assertion, is no Hercules, is there someone who approximates the stature of the hero in this episode? To answer this question we must recall the interpolated tale of the three French ladies. As they are pursued, one of the aggressors takes Feliz Flora, holding her captive on his horse, and gives the order to depart. The Spaniard Antonio "puso una flecha en el arco [...] y, tomando por blanco el robador de Feliz Flora, disparó tan derechamente la flecha que, sin tocar a Feliz Flora sino en una parte del velo con que se cubría la cabeza, pasó al salteador el pecho de parte a parte" (set an arrow in his bow [...] and taking the ravisher of Feliflore for his white, he shot so right, that without touching the gentlewoman, save only a piece of the veil that covered her head, he pierced the body of him that carried her away, through and through; Cervantes 2015b, 575; n.d.). Hercules was known for his prowess with bow and arrow, and he accomplished a similar feat when the centaur Nessus stole his wife, Deianira. Thus, it is a Spaniard who becomes a figure akin to Hercules, restoring the myth to its "proper" origin through this narrative. The French tower is therefore a false architecture, one that belongs not to Hercules but to a madman whose name recalls that of a tyrannical emperor who in his thoughts of grandeur claimed to be better than Hercules. While Cervantes seems to despise the Gallic Hercules, he appears to have great respect for the floating woman, one whose eurithmia and power of flight allow her to surpass the Vitruvian man.

The third book of the *Persiles*, then, is replete with geometrical figures, visions of the heavens, and visions of flight. Here ellipsis and the elliptical come together as a double focus, one hidden and one foregrounded. We envision them in a kind of contest that recalls Kepler's new theories of planetary motion. While the monastery of Guadalupe stands for the sacred and a miracle of flight, the French tower calls for very human miracles of new technologies and places the human being at the centre of things. Here the Veranzio woman vies for supremacy with the Vitruvian man. A pagan tower points to the battle for cultural appropriation between Spain and France as the pilgrims make their way to the "centre" that is Rome, an eternal city that has been decentred through continuous evocations of a different geometrical and celestial figure.

9 Roman Architectures: *Persiles y Sigismunda*, Book 4

My last chapter follows the pilgrims into Italy and describes their arrival and stay in Rome. The "eternal city" is the focus of this chapter, but a few words must be said about their route down the Italian peninsula. Milan is the first city described in book 4. While the text pictures it in general terms as were the Spanish cities before, it emphasizes the grandeur of her temples and the fame of the city as crafter of weapons, as if Vulcan abided there (Cervantes 2015b, 608–9), thus recalling the opposition letters (the Church) and arms, as well as the double focus of the elliptical shape in geometry and astronomy (myth and craft). Furthermore, the pilgrims delay their journey for a few days to see the sights and learn of a literary academy that is in session. The narrative refers to it as the "Academia de los Entronados," but the term does not mean "enthroned." It is instead the Academy of the Dazed Ones (609). Not only is it mistranslated but it is also misplaced because the academy first gathered in Sienna in 1525 and became the centre of cultural life in that city in the mid- and late-sixteenth century. Adrienne Martin argues that Cervantes introduces it here in order to contrast it with the frivolous Spanish academies:

The *Intronati* were an elite and erudite organization similar to the more famous Accademia della Crusca. Both were founded during the heart of the Italian Renaissance and dedicated wholly to humanistic pursuits. The *Intronati* especially favored the cultivation of Greek, Latin, and Tuscan poetry [...] In all probability this is the type of academy that Cervantes wanted for Spain – one based on the search for knowledge and the perfection of the poetic art [...] Its members would be cultivated intellectuals capable of stemming the vulgarization of poetry represented by the phenomenon of the *comedia* . Instead, he saw infantile, frivolous *tertulias* dedicated to pure, antiacademic entertainment (1991, 153).

The question for discussion while the pilgrims are in Milan/Sienna revolves around love and whether it could exist without jealousy. Although commonplace at the time, the subject was crucial to Periandro because he wanted to show Auristela that his love for her was so high minded that it could exist without jealousy (but never without fear). Indeed, throughout the novel, acting as Auristela's brother rather than as her betrothed, he had been showing her the value of his unwavering devotion. She, however, is beginning to have doubts about earthly love. The ongoing conversations between the two also echo the important role of women in the Intronati. Alexandra Coller asserts: "women were awarded much more than a merely ornamental presence within the context of the academy, whether as sources of inspiration, correspondents in educationally-oriented literary exchanges, or as discussants in female-centered dialogues" (2006, 223). Once again, the elliptical shape comes into being, as men and women vie for the shining centre of the elliptical, and as love shines, but other feelings begin to emerge, although shadowed. At the same time, the architecture of the academy remains veiled, its name obscured and its location dislocated. All these artifices point to a space that the narrative and its author wish to elide so that others can ponder on them.

The pilgrims' next stop is Lucca, a rather odd route since the route to Rome should have been through Sienna. The narrative obscures the more important city (hidden within the geometrical shape of the ellipse through the Academy of the Intronati) and focuses on Lucca. Nor is Florence mentioned as another obvious stopping place. One of the reasons may be that the narrative wants to foreground Lucca as a city that is under Spanish tutelage, one that around 1613 had to resort to an armed conflict to preserve its independence (Cervantes 2015b, 742). However, the narrative once again surprises us and turns away from politics and architecture. Furthermore, instead of making a pilgrimage to the *Volto santo* or Holy Face, they encounter at an inn a woman supposedly possessed by the devil. Indeed, the Holy Face was one of the great miraculous artworks of the world, a sculpture said to be by Nicodemus, who had helped Joseph of Arimathea to place Christ in his tomb. The wooden carving had been in Lucca since the eighth century. Ironically the pilgrims stand in admiration, not before the body of Christ but before a woman who is tied to the bed and acting as if she were possessed by the devil. In reality, she is waiting at the inn for her beloved to come for her. The pace is so rapid, and so many are the tales told, that the inn is not described, but the story of Isabela Castrucha is narrated in detail. The "false" miracle here contrasts with the sacred carving in Lucca, the celestial intervention in the tale of Feliciana, and the natural "magic" of the flying woman. In Lucca, substitution once again bedevils the text. After a lengthy episode on the possessed woman, the reader comes to the fourth book and the town of Aquapendente on the road between Sienna and their destination. The pilgrims, moved by desire, gravitate towards Rome.

Rome is the eternal city, the city of empire, the site for pilgrimage, and the centre of all relics. It will conjoin the "relics" feared and desired by Auristela with the view of the city and the intonation of a sonnet. The first four sections on Rome in this chapter will point to ellipsis, as we imagine the three dots that connote the dearth of architectural descriptions. This contrasts with the last two sections, which take place within and without the city. Here some structures become much more visible, arising from the last and hurriedly written pages by Cervantes. This may seem a paradoxical transformation because we would expect that the shortest and last book, one that swiftly moves to a resolution, would leave aside architectures. This is not the case, because here Cervantes provides the reader with a much more tangible view of the eternal. We discover an astonishing vision of the city's pagan riches and Renaissance art as well as a somewhat conflictive view of the city as the centre of Christendom. Throughout the perilous journey to Rome, Persiles tended to care more for Auristela as a human being than for her as a way to the sacred. While discarding the pomp of the popes, Cervantes, through Periandro's brother, opens a door to the author's celestial ascension.

Chapter 9 will look at six sites: two pagan (two villas), one Jewish (one home), two Christian (curiously, both are outside the city – the poetic view of relics and the church outside), and in their midst an almost invisible but clearly threatening tower. First, we will turn to the view of Rome from above, emphasizing the city's relation to Christian relics and to the eternal city. Strangely, the view shows nothing because the city is not described. Second, we will seek to view the invisible Villa Madama, first commissioned by Pope Leo X to his painter and architect Raphael. We will recount how the pilgrims fail to view the villa and its pagan art and how they pass through its gardens to arrive at the Porta del Popolo. Thus, these first two sections will serve as contrasts between the Christian and the pagan, where the narrative avoids the visible and uses allusive ekphrasis to point to a cityscape and a villa. The third section discusses the paradoxical presence of a Jewish home in Rome, which adds a third culture to the panorama. Here windows make the outside visible and point to the danger outside. This will be followed by a look at the Roman jail, as if the book were returning to the claustrophobic architectures at the beginning of the first part of *Don*

Quixote, or to Vulcan's world, a myth that was already in play with the arrival in Milan. Bartolomé's imprisonment in this jail may point to the famed Roman monster and to images that threaten the pope and his city. We will turn, in the fifth section, to Hipólita's pagan and erotic loggia, which will serve as contrast to our sixth and last section, "The Church Outside." Thus, the city of Rome, a place that evokes topophilia from the pilgrims, will be presented as disjointed and contrastive, much like the trip down the peninsula meets dislocated sites (Milan and Sienna) and an elliptical frame that shadows Christ, and now his minister on earth.

A City of Relics

The closer we come to Rome, the more the pagan myths are activated and the more the Christian sacred comes into play. In order to understand better the pilgrims' first view of Rome, still from a distance, we must return to a moment we omitted in the tower episode in the third book. After the flying lady had landed and told her story, Periandro climbed Domitian's/Hercules' tower to fight the mad husband. In the ensuing battle both fell from the tower. As Auristela watched her fallen brother/lover, in a moment of deep sadness, she did something unexpected: "creyendo indubitablemente que estaba muerto, se arrojó sobre él y, sin respeto alguno, puesta la boca con la suya, esperaba a recoger en sí alguna reliquia, si del alma le hubiese quedado" (believing undoubtedly that he was slain, she cast herself upon him with her mouth close joined to his, to gather into herself some remainder [*relic*] of his soul, if any were yet left; Cervantes 2015b, 574; n.d.). Auristela seeks to capture his last breath, his very soul. Benedicta Ward asks how in our time we would react "[i]f someone today claimed to have in a bottle the last breath of St Joseph" (2010, 274). Auristela is going beyond the act of keeping a bottle of breath and seeks to become herself the vessel that will keep Periandro's last breath. Breath, after all, means spirit, and the last breath is the distillation of a saintly soul. Like the pilgrims at the monastery of Guadalupe, here Auristela is seeking to commune with relics. The one she aspires to imbibe is the most precious of all relics because it goes beyond the flesh of the saintly individual and seems to contain an element of soul – an almost sacrilegious desire. Her attempt to capture this relic is three-fold: to have a sanctifying relic within her, to live with the very soul of her beloved, and to show her faith in his saintly devotion. In this sense her desire is one of extreme topophilia. She wishes to be the place in which a small portion of his spirit is held, a receptacle that although holding but a small portion of his breath is holding infinity because the soul is immortal and infinite. She would be not just the holder of a relic but the holder of soul.

But Periandro is not dead, and they continue their journey towards Rome, where once again there will be a conflict between Periandro's desire to marry her and Auristela's seemingly more lofty love. She sees Rome's revelations about Christianity to be as important as her wedding to her beloved, and her communion with its sacredness to be even more important. It is as if the last kiss would have been her preferred outcome, even over the living Periandro.

From the beginning of the novel, Rome has been seen as the goal. Attempting to assuage Arnaldo's suspicion and jealousy, Periandro tells him that all mysteries and suspicions will vanish once they arrive at the city of relics: "Si el cielo nos llevare a pisar la santísima tierra y adorar sus reliquias santas, quedaremos en disposición de disponer de nuestras hasta agora impedidas voluntades, y entonces será la mía toda empleada en servirte" (If heaven afford us the favour to tread upon that land, and adore the holy relics that are there, we may dispose of our wills, which are hindered at this present; and mine shall thenceforth be wholly employed in your service; Cervantes 2015b, 233; n.d.). Luis F. Avilés has underlined this passage in his study on trust in the novel (2019, 58). While Periandro is asking for trust and suggesting that all will turn in Arnaldo's favor once they reach Rome, he knows very well that at that time they will have fulfilled their vows and can reveal who they truly are – Persiles, prince of Tile (Thule), and Sigismunda, heir to Frislandia. She has been engaged to Persiles' brother. As a Nordic princess and one whose marriage has been pre-arranged, she cannot wed Arnaldo. Thus, Periandro is asking to be trusted, while he is hiding an impediment to Arnaldo's happiness. He is also hiding some of his own difficulties when it comes to marrying Sigismunda. Thus, Rome is the goal, but there are other goals within this goal that are hidden. Auristela's name, as Clark Colahan rightly states, means golden star and is thus related to the stars with which the Virgin is depicted. She is the perfect gold of the goal, a Neoplatonic reflection of the heavens, which Periandro follows (1994, 20–2). Indeed, the Virgin Mary is often associated with the City of God (34). Thus, Auristela serves as both guide and goal to Periandro. However, this goal, for him, has as its basis an earthly marriage. He wants to form one space out of two through this sacrament. While their goals are similar – a union and the end of a pilgrimage – his love, though partaking of the divine, is earthier, and hers seems to be more attuned to the spiritual. They both would find "place" in each other but with a different emphasis. And this place is to come about by fulfilment of the pilgrimage to Rome, which is yet another spiritual and earthly place.

When, in chapter 4 of the fourth part of the novel, the pilgrims are rewarded with a first view of the city (albeit invisible to the reader), they react to its sacredness: "llegando a la vista della, desde un alto montecillo la descubrieron, y, hincados de rodillas, como a cosa sacra, la adoraron" (having gotten up on a small hillock, from whence at their ease they might behold the holy city, they saluted the same, kneeling on the ground; Cervantes 2015b, 664; n.d.). The sacredness of Rome seems supreme, beyond Guadalupe and Montserrat, for it is a holy city, with its seven churches set up for pilgrims, and the abode of the pope. It is the centre of the European world and of Catholicism. As they kneel, they hear an unknown pilgrim recite a sonnet about Rome. While our pilgrims view the sacred site, they are aware that numerous travellers, artists, and poets from all over Europe also come to the city to admire its ancient monuments, the remnants of imperial Rome. The city itself was in constant tension between the Christian sacred and the pagan ruins, thus creating a space that may be seen as conflictive by some. Raphael, for example, was set to draft all the main ancient buildings of Rome, with their measurements and many adornments. As he did so in order to preserve them, he was also utilizing stones from these same buildings to build Christian churches. Cammy Brothers points to this paradox: "how could the same architects and patrons who celebrated ancient Roman culture permit and even endorse the willful and systematic destruction of its monuments?" (2001, 135).

As poets thronged to the city, sonnets dealing with Rome became immensely popular. Contemporary architect Juhani Pallasmaa asserts: "Ruins seem to have a healing mental impact, as they invite us to reflect, dream and imagine" (quoted in Amudsen 2018). And thus Rome acquired a peculiar "atmosphere" (Amudsen 2018), one that wavered between awe, devotion, disillusionment, and melancholy at the ravages of time. Perhaps the most famous sonnet of the period was "Superbi Colli" (Lofty hills), written by Baldassare Castiglione, the author of *The Courtier*. It was read throughout Europe, translated and adapted by Joachim du Bellay, who included it as sonnet 7, and it also influenced his sonnet 27 in his *Antiquitez de Rome* (Roman antiquities) Even Paul Scarron used it to deflate its laudatory and grandiose overview. Edmund Spenser rendered the French translation into English, and several Spanish poets also imitated the original (Gutierre de Cetina, Lope de Vega, Rey de Artieda) (H.G. Hall 1974, 159–81). As the most salient example of the "poetry of ruins," it sought to ponder on the opposition of greatness and ruins, echoing Pallasmaa's contention that ruins "often turn arrogant or authoritarian architectural structures into humble and humane ones" (Amudsen 2018). Castiglioni's sonnet begins with *superbi* or haughty, both because these are ruined architectures and because remnants of a glorious past have remained. It also evokes the notion that pride precedes the fall. Here admiration is triggered by a magnificent past and by the ravages of time. And yet, in most versions of the sonnet, the term *relic* is found, eliding the distinction between pagans and Christians and thus softening the pagan fall with Christian notions of resurrection. Out of this long tradition that confuses the remnants of ancient monuments as relics with the bones and body parts of Christian martyrs, Cervantes fashions his text. As the pilgrims look down on Rome from the hill, there is once again an ellipsis and an elliptical design. Although admiration is proclaimed as in many of the sonnets in this tradition, there is not a single mention of ancient monuments in the sonnet here declaimed. Instead, the unknown pilgrim who composed the sonnet elides all enumeration of ancient buildings. As the pilgrim looks down, it is not the architecture of Rome that brings about admiration but the ground on which it rests: "La tierra de tu suelo, que contemplo / con la sangre de mártires mezclada, / es la reliquia universal del suelo" (*The soil from the earth that I contemplate / is mixed with the blood of its martyrs / it is the universal relic of the land*; Cervantes 2015b, 645; n.d.).[1] Readers would immediately notice the effaced focus, that of ancient monuments, and the foregrounding of Christian relics, thus creating once again an elliptical shape with a double focus, one of which is intentionally hidden. There is also an ellipsis here because nothing of what they see is described to the reader. Curiously, once the pilgrims have descended to the city, the earth mixed with the blood of martyrs vanishes, as Jewish and pagan architectures compete with Christian ones. What we do find on the way down is the spilled blood of quarrelling lovers, who are far from being religious martyrs.

The last line of the sonnet reads: "de la ciudad de Dios al gran modelo" (*modelled after the city of God*). Clearly referring to Augustine's *City of God*, the pilgrim accepts the divisions between the earthly city and the City of God – the Rome of the ancient empire that was once destroyed and is again thriving and the spiritual city of the righteous. In the constant battle between good and evil many Christian martyrs have shed their lives, thus sanctifying pagan Rome with their sacrifice. Their many corpses, in this poem, have transformed Rome into a universal relic, the centre point for this battle between good and evil. To repeat, as the pilgrims gaze upon the city, not a word is said about its earthly architectures or even its earthly ruins, since the sonnet foregrounds the City of God, an intangible idea, over the actual panorama below. Like the monastery of Guadalupe, what is described is not an actual place but a vision. The absence of ekphrasis contrasts with the phantom buildings of the north. There we have a world in the making, still away from salvific Rome. Here, particularly in the sonnet, the city is invisible, made up of the goodness of those who accept the Catholic faith. The beginnings of book 4, then, set up a series of elliptical shapes with obscured centres. Periandro wishes to marry Auristela, her beauty reminding him of the Virgin, and Auristela, indulging in extreme topophilia, wishes to capture Periandro's last breath, thus becoming the bodily container of the essence of his immortal soul. As travellers look down at the city, they expect sonnets describing the ancient ruins and a pagan past but are instead treated to Christian relics. Which centre of the geometrical ellipsis or the astronomical elliptical is the visible and which the invisible?

An Invisible Villa

We cannot stop to glance at the dangers outside at the very beginning of the fourth book of the *Persiles*, in which, although hidden perils are described (blood detected on an arboreal setting), violent events are linked to those who are inside. We must continue, instead, with the descent of the pilgrims to Rome's northern gate. Curiously, this takes only one sentence in the text: "bajaron del recuesto, pasaron por los prados de Madama, entraron en Roma por la puerta del Pópulo, besando primero una y muchas veces los umbrales y márgenes de la ciudad santa" (they came down by the side of the hill, passed through Our Lady's meadows, and came into Rome by Del Popole gate, first kissing the threshold of the entry; Cervantes 2015b, 646; n.d.). The "prados de Madama" (Our Lady's meadows) is not a sacred site but refers to one of the great gardens of the time, constructed around the villa of the same name.[2] Once the vineyards of Pope Leo X, they were quickly reimagined by Raphael because the pontiff wished to possess structures and gardens that recalled the ancient villas of Rome.[3] As for the decorations, particularly after Raphael's untimely death, Giulio Romano "created the paintings, and Giovanni da Udine [...] made the stuccoes and grotesques [...] creating a seamless bond between the interior decoration and the trees and plants of the luxuriant gardens" (Napoleone 2008, 39).

Just the mention of Madama with her villa and gardens establishes that the Rome of the pilgrims is deeply implicated in Habsburg political and imperial influence. The name Madama as used in Cervantes is the one that still identifies the place today and refers to Margaret of

Austria, illegitimate daughter of Charles V, who considered it as one of her homes when she married Alessandro de Medici; he was assassinated in 1537.[4] Indeed, she soon married again, this time to Ottavio Farnese, the grandson of Pope Paul III. Thomas James Randell affirms: "Although this turned out to be less than a blissful marriage, it established a bond that linked the Farnese family to the Spanish crown for decades to come" (2001, 48). Although over time the villa fell into ruin, the edifice of trust between the Spanish crown and a key Italian family that influenced the papacy continued to grow. Indeed, the villa was still an imposing sight during the times of Cervantes, a reminder of the close links between Spain and Rome.

Yet, there is a double ellipsis, in the sense of absence, in the text. First, the pilgrims, who cross the gardens, say nothing of them, and second, although the fields or gardens are at least mentioned, nothing is said of one of the most important architectures of Renaissance Rome. The locus has been deflected, and its architect, Raphael, has been elided, only to reappear much later in book 4 in a most unlikely place. Very much like the poem, the earthly and pagan elements of the city are obscured in order to focus on the Christian sacred. Invisibility also has to do with the rejection of the villa as home. A home or place "is a pause in movement" (Tuan 1977, 138). The pilgrims must keep moving and must not be diverted from their route. In addition, the home becomes a "center of felt value" (138), and the pilgrims have already expressed that their sense of value lies ahead in the (sacred) city of Rome.

In the gardens Giovanni da Udine had constructed a fountain so famous that many came from all over Europe to admire it. It shows the head of Hanno, the pet elephant of Pope Leo X. A gift from the Portuguese, Hanno was a massive and endearing beast from India that first entered Rome by the Porta del Popolo.[5] It would be tempting to consider the many parallels between the pilgrims and the elephant – arrival from far-away lands, the people's worship, the awe of the exotic, and the many sketches and paintings that would circulate.[6] But none of this is in the text. It may be the case, as Isabel Lozano Renieblas has argued, that Cervantes' style, in most instances, rejects excessive rhetoric, and thus the complex texture of ekphrasis (1998b, 507).[7] This is why, perhaps, we often seem to discover images hidden deep within the text, through allusive ekphrasis, or we may encounter what Steven Wagschal calls veiled ekphrasis (2005, 104). In this case I think that the rejection of ekphrasis for descriptions of the gardens, the fountain, or the villa has to do with the quickness of allusion and the concealed referent. It may reflect the disapproval of the pilgrims as they are overwhelmed with piety: the Villa Madama was filled with images of pagan pleasures, from a drunken and love-struck Polyphemus to Daedalus constructing the likeness of a cow for Pasiphae's enjoyment (Listri 2008, 77–85).[8] At this point in the narrative, with their end in sight, the pilgrims would reject imperial Rome and even more its lustful art; they would turn away from modern reconstructions of the pagan past and seek the seven churches of Rome. Renaissance art and pagan architectures are places that fail to comfort the pilgrims. Although they traverse the gardens of Madama, either they or their narrator prefers to treat the marvellous architectures as if they were invisible. The elephant in the room is ignored.

Much different is their arrival at the Porta del Popolo. Properly displaying the fact that it was rebuilt under Pope Pius IV during the sixteenth century, it beckons the faithful.[9] Here the pilgrims worship and kiss the very boundary of the city, as Hermes, god of boundaries, shows them the entrance.[10] Always a trickster, the god fails to reveal that the new gate was crafted in imitation of the Arch of Titus, which commemorates his siege of Jerusalem and destruction of the Second Temple. Titus was also famed for completing the Coliseum, hosting inaugural games that lasted one hundred days.

A Home in Jewish Rome

It would seem that once the pilgrims passed through the gates, they would be struck by the sacred. They could well have marvelled at the church of Santa Maria del Popolo. This would have been an ideal place to exhibit the sacred and to denounce the pagan because according to legend the church was built on a haunted site. It was said that when this was empty land, the crows that gathered around a tree were ghosts or phantoms of Nero. A chapel was built in order to transform the dangers outside into a comforting place. It eventually became a church as Pope Sixtus IV fully transformed it with new images: "the evil nut tree of Nero had been replaced by the health oak of the della Rovere" (Bauman 2007, 42). Over time, many famous artists left their imprint: Raphael was commissioned to decorate the Chigi chapel, and much later (some thirty years after Cervantes' visit) Caravaggio did two paintings for the Cerasi chapel. But instead of being amazed at sacred adornments and architectures, the pilgrims stay outside and are met by two Jewish men, Zabulón and Abiud, who ask them if they are in need of lodging (Cervantes 2015b, 646).

Before turning to habitation and architectures, it is important to point out that such a passage may have shocked the Spaniards who read Cervantes' *Persiles*. Jews had been expelled from Spain in 1492, and only those who converted to Christianity (*conversos*) were allowed to stay. The fear of being linked to Jewish ancestry was prevalent in Spanish society and is clearly reflected in the literature of the period. We need only remember Cervantes' interlude *El retablo de las maravillas* in which the swindlers, Chirinos and Chanfalla, go from village to village in order to put on a "magical" puppet show that, they claim, would be invisible to bastards and New Christians (those of Moorish or Jewish ancestry). In a play within the play, the interlude is performed in one village in celebration of a wedding. Bruce Wardropper explains: "The villagers, ashamed at seeing nothing and fearful of betraying themselves to be New Christians, at first pretend that they see the various acts; it is evident that they soon come to delude themselves into believing that they do see them" (1984, 27). The tricksters claim that the author of this magical piece is Tontonelo (meaning "the foolish one"), thus poking fun at Spanish society. As many would fear to be linked to Jewish ancestry and since Jews were not allowed to live in Spain, it would be shocking to a reader to find Jews in Rome, a city considered the centre of Christendom.

Zabulón and his companion, Abiud, explain to the newcomers that their job is to furnish homes with all that visitors may require, and that the furnishings would depend on what they can pay (Cervantes 2015b, 646). The passage in Cervantes is doubly disturbing to Spanish readers of the period because the pilgrims have actually sought habitation, a place to stay in Rome, from yet a different Jewish man, Manasés. Thus, two Jews advertise housing while a third has already found them a place to stay, which seems to be his own very well appointed home: "la posada que los judíos habían pintado era la rica de Manasés, y, así, alegres y contentos guiaron a nuestros peregrinos, que estaba junto al arco de Portugal" (the house which they had furnished belonged to Manasses, and was over against the Portugal Arch: wherefore they guided our pilgrims thither, full of contentment and joy (647; n.d.). The exalted position of Jews in Rome recalls the situation during the Middle Ages, when Benjamin of Tudela, a Jewish traveller from Navarra, visited the city: "Rome is the head of the kingdoms of Christendom, and contains about 200 Jews, who occupy an honourable position and pay no tribute, and amongst them are officials of the Pope Alexander, the spiritual head of all Christendom" (1907, 5). Michael Gordon has summarized the future of the Jews in Spain and how they were welcomed by Pope Alexander VI as they were expelled from Spain by the Catholic kings (2011, 70). By the middle of the sixteenth century the situation had changed drastically, and what Cervantes recounts would not have been possible. A 1555 Bull by Pope Paul IV had restricted

Jews to only a small and very undesirable section of Rome (next to the Tiber and subject to flooding), which was then enclosed by a wall. Its gates were locked in the evenings and not opened until the following morning (Pietrangeli 1976, 44). Furthermore, Jews were forbidden to own property (Christians owned the houses in the ghetto and rented them to the Jews) and were allowed very few occupations, such as pawnbroker and fishmonger. When leaving the ghetto, these Roman Jews had to wear yellow: men a yellow hat or bonnet, and women yellow veils (Noel 2006, 314).[11] In the *Persiles*, Cervantes presents a rather positive view of the way in which Jews were treated in Rome. Rather than being confined in a ghetto, singled out by their clothing, or living in poverty, these Jews are presented as greeting Christians who come to the city, therefore being people of means and engaging in renting properties.

Michael Gordon argues that the action of the fourth book of the *Persiles* takes place in 1559, when Paul IV was dying (2011, 70–1). He adds that Cervantes "da voz al judío Zabulón, quien se presenta como un portavoz respetable para su comunidad, desafiando las bulas antijudías de la autoridad pontificia en su propia ciudad" (gives voice to the Jewish Zaulón, who is represented as a respectable spokesman for his community, defying the anti-Jewish Bulls derived from the papal authorities in his city; 74).

There seems to be, then, a double architecture in this scene. On the one hand, we have a Jewish home that is decorated as if it were a palace and readied for the pilgrims; on the other hand, we have the concealed Jewish ghetto that houses impoverished inhabitants. In the previous scene Cervantes had hidden a Renaissance villa, and now he conceals a ghetto. Ellipsis and the elliptical shape again prevail, with one focus made manifest and a second being hidden.

The villa may have been rendered invisible because of a paganism that seemed to oppose a Rome that stood for the centre of Christianity, but the same cannot be said of the ghetto because it is rendered invisible in order to foreground the Jews of Rome as rich and enterprising, owning homes coveted by the pilgrims. We must then ask, Why give a false picture of Jews in Rome? Why this sudden deviation from actual history? And why are the pilgrims staying in a Jewish home?

A glance at Pope Paul IV, architect of the Bull against the Jews, may allow us to solve some of these puzzling questions. As Gerard Noel reminds us, Paul IV, the "architect" of the ghetto, was deeply opposed to Spanish influence in Italy. He led his nephew Carlo Carafa "to ally himself with France and make war on Spain. The papal forces were defeated by Fernando Álvarez de Toledo (duke of Alba, viceroy of

Naples); and the papal state was overrun. Paul was forced to accept the, fortunately generous, treaty of Cave on 12 September 1577" (2006, 310). Although the conflict continued, it was finally over with the treaty of Cateau-Cambrésis of 1559. It confirmed Habsburg dominion. Two very different historical moments are at work as Cervantes draws the invisible villa and the invisible ghetto. The first points to Spain's influence as Madama helped to strengthen ties with the Medici and the Farnese. In the second moment a Carafa pope seeks unsuccessfully to do away with Spanish dominion. Thus, Cervantes uses invisible architectures to point to two popes and their differing attitudes towards Spanish influence in Italy.

Although never able to quell Spanish influence, Paul IV succeeded in subjecting others to his power and that of the Inquisition. In addition to issuing laws against the Jews, he pushed Inquisitors to sentence to death "fornicators, sodomites, actors, buffoons, lay folk who failed to maintain the Lenten fast and even, in one case, a sculptor who had carved a crucifix judged to be unworthy of Christ" (Noel 2006, 315). His death was welcomed by many Romans, who rioted and smashed his statue, crowning its severed head with a yellow hat as Jewish attire (318).

It could be argued that Cervantes, by exhibiting the wealthy Jews in the *Persiles*, was seeking to undo Paul IV's architectures of hatred, a hatred that ranged from despising the Spanish, to punishing many of his subjects, to relegating and incarcerating the Jew. If indeed this was the case, the text, by blaming the anti-Spanish pope, also showcases Rome as a city that is more open – Christians can abide in Jewish homes. This openness is reflected in the open spaces of the house Manasés rents to the pilgrims and to the three French ladies who accompany them. Windows, often absent in Cervantes' fiction, are here displayed as the populace calls out to the women to show their beauty: "Llegó esto a tanto estremo, que desde la calle pedían a voces se asomasen a las ventanas las damas y las peregrinas" (and this desire brought them to that extremity that they cried out in the streets that the ladies and pilgrims should come to the windows; Cervantes 2015b, 648; n.d.). While Manasés represents an aspect of *convivencia*, Zabulón will be shown to side with the lustful courtesan and her vengeful lover. Thus, Cervantes presents a double portrait of the Jew, one that is tied to the architectures he erects in his writing. Manasés points to a more open Rome and the ability of Christians and Jews to abide together, as in the Jew's house that he rented to the pilgrims and which depicts windows and thus an open architecture. Zabulón is tied to yet another opulent dwelling but one that is closed and treacherous – Hipólita's palace. It may be no coincidence that Pope Paul IV's anti-Semitism was such that he "stressed that Jews, as Christ-killers, were by nature slaves and should be treated as such" (Noel 2006, 314). In contrast to this, the name Manasses means "causing to forget,"[12] thus allowing a new rapprochement between two cultures by turning to their shared customs and possessions and thus leaving behind the contentious matter of Christ's crucifixion. The glamorous Jewish abode that the pilgrims share is a sign and a place of openness, comfort, and security that conceals the restrictive and dangerous space of the ghetto.

The Threatening Tower

Open windows, once again in Cervantes, allow for the danger outside to seep into a home. As the pilgrims wish to take their rest in their Jewish home, voices outside call out for them to come to the windows and show themselves. For these are no ordinary pilgrims. Some have come from unknown lands, while others (particularly Auristela) not only have come from afar but are already famed for their beauty. Windows are also liminal spaces that mediate between inside and outside. From the safety of the inside Periandro is able to peer out the window and discover danger. Although a future king, he is not, like the monarchs in the books of chivalry and in Cervantes, looking out to discern a famous knight. It is true, however, that the gentlemen outside are well known. Two of Auristela's rival suitors, the most violent in their passions, are at the door, it being another liminal space that either permits or forbids entrance to safe places. The pilgrims manage this threat as Periandro goes out to speak to Arnaldo, while Croriano exits the house to assuage the passions of the Duke of Nemurs.

Yet another possible threat comes about as the two rivals are pacified and made to await Auristela's decision. A man hands Periandro a letter. As he inquires of its content, he learns that it is from Bartolomé Manchego who is now imprisoned at the Torre de Nona (Tor di Nona). Although a minor character, Bartolomé keeps reappearing in the last two books of the novel. At first he is a naive figure, and his unfortunate passion for Luisa la Talaverana makes him one of several characters struck by her beauty. Ortel Banedre, for example, actually "buys" her with his gold, preventing her marriage to Alonso (Puig 2011, 216). She repays her new husband by stealing his money and running off with her lover, Alonso (Cervantes 2015b, 499). She is labelled a new Venus (498) and indeed reflects the myth: being married to Banedre (the figure of Vulcan in mythology), she commits adultery with Alonso/Mars (De Armas 1993, 407; Muñoz Sánchez 2007, 140). While the Vulcan that was mentioned in Milan is a great craftsman, the one now evoked is a cuckolded husband in the figure of Ortel Banedre.

Stephen Hessel summarizes Luisa's role in the *Persiles*: "One notable encounter […] is the ill-fated marriage of Luisa 'la talaverana' to Ortel Banedre. Shortly after their wedding, Luisa runs off with her lover Alonso. Ortel is in hot pursuit when he encounters the pilgrims who appear to convince him to cease his search for revenge. The pilgrims later encounter Luisa without Alonso who had died in prison. Subsequently, she had married an abusive Spanish soldier upon leaving prison. After receiving some aid from the pilgrims, she runs off with their servant Bartolomé. The pilgrims later find the pair in jail in Rome for murdering both the Spanish soldier and Ortel Banedre" (2020, 228–9).[13] Most critics point to Luisa's noxious and ill-fated influence on Bartolomé Manchego. William Childers, for example, asserts: "Under the corrupting influence of the *mujer liviana*, Luisa la Talaverana, Bartolomé has moved from innocent country rustic to full-fledged urban *pícaro* in the space of a few chapters" (1999, 199). Indeed, right before arriving in Italy, the pilgrims are surprised by the repentant Bartolomé, who returns the baggage he has stolen from them. They plead with him to say, but he must go after Luisa la Talaverana.

As stated, this does not end well. Bartolomé writes a letter to one of the pilgrims, Antonio, explaining that he and Luisa la Talaverana have now been condemned to death and incarcerated in the medieval Torre de Nona awaiting execution. In his exquisitely written letter to the pilgrims Bartolomé asks for help in deliverance or at least a delay so that their sentence can be carried out in Spain. After all, he claims, what great judge or authority could deny anything on seeing Auristela's beauty? (Cervantes 2015b, 654). Childers points out that Bartolomé seems to be a quick study. Not knowing how to write, he suddenly develops his own style (1999, 199). Are we faced with the recurrent topic of love as a great teacher, one that Lope de Vega puts to good use in *La dama boba* (The witless lady)? If anything, I would argue, Cervantes is inverting the topic. Although Bartolomé learns from love to write, his is an inordinate passion that teaches him to be a *pícaro* or rogue. Nevertheless, Auristela and the pilgrims will attempt such a pardon.

The generous and commensurate nature of the pilgrims contrasts with the impulsive passions of Luisa who even uses her own knife to murder her husband, Ortel Banedre. And yet, Stephen Hessel asks the reader to place both women on the same level: "Luisa is portrayed as the antithesis of Auristela, but her story contains some striking parallels: unwanted arranged marriage, escape from it, captivity at the hands of others, and a violent and tumultuous journey to Rome. I would argue that if we sympathize with Auristela, we must do the same with Luisa, but this is not the picture the authorial voice paints" (2020, 247n29). These provoking parallels should trigger much discussion in years to come; one way to answer them would be through the figure of Venus, as both Auristela and Luisa are compared to the pagan goddess.

As we approach the moment in which Luisa and Bartolomé are imprisoned in Rome, I prefer to view her character in terms of myth and space, which are intertwined in many ways. First and foremost, Luisa as a lascivious Venus who commits adultery and takes on many lovers is far from an Auristela who comes to Rome to learn the dogmas of the Catholic religion. The educaton of Auristela contrasts with that of Luisa who never seems to learn from her many misfortunes and continued imprisonment. We are told more than once that she spent a difficult time in jail in Madrid, arrested as an adulterer (Cervantes 2015b, 585). Auristela is able to meet with the pope, and Luisa finds herself in the most horrendous jail in the papal estates; she is eventually freed by the intercession of the pilgrims. Freed and now without a husband (she has killed Ortel Banedre), she marries Bartolomé, accepting the "shackles" of marriage (679). But not even this can satisfy her. As we are told enigmatically at the end of the novel, the couple, having moved to Naples, ends up in misfortune, given the "free" life in which they engage (713).

This new Venus, in many ways, refuses the "shackles" of morality, marriage, and the mores of her times and is always wilful and intent on doing as she wishes. Venus had rejected the home, an infernal smithy, and her husband, whose rough appearance and disabilities made her yearn for strong warriors and young men. Although Vulcan tolerated her escapades, he would, at least once, ensnare her by fashioning a net in which to expose Mars and Venus in flagrante. If we stretch the myth, we can imagine that killing her husband is not liberation, but the defunct Ortel, now a Vulcan figure, sets a trap, the tower, a space much more abhorrent than Vulcan's smithy. Indeed, this tower is not far from Saint Peter's and the Vatican. It is a hell in the midst of a supposedly heavenly city. While Auristela kisses the pope's feet, our new Venus, a figure of paganism, flees the city with her new husband. There is indeed a series of events and actions that allow us to see Auristela and Luisa together, but they serve as contrastive oppositions, much as the tower contrasts with the seven churches and the home of the papacy. As the sage Soldino had predicted, hers was to be a terrestrial life, far from any celestial aspirations (Muñoz Sánchez 2007, 146).

Returning to the architecture of the tower, it is not just a kind of infernal smithy ruled by a Vulcan, god of the underworld. It is an invisible and terrifying spectre that rises in the middle of the eternal city. All the reader knows about it comes from the letter written by Bartolomé in which he complains of the many bedbugs in the jail. He is most circumspect in telling of the terrors of the tower. Lawrence Buck (2014) asserts that this tower was infamous for its torture room and dungeons. Indeed, it was often in a state of disrepair.[14] During the 1495 inundations, while "Romans had to row through their city in boats" and tombs spilled remains into the muddy waters (Meserve 2018, 119–20), many prisoners drowned in their cells, and the damp walls and musty air never depart this medieval crenellated fortress. Tour guides today emphasize some of its horrors: "Before being taken to the dungeons of Tor di Nona, prisoners would have faced the grisly sight of the impaled heads of their predecessors lining the river. The heads were a warning to heretics and other law-breakers, but for the prisoners it was too late […] The prison was infamous for its dank, windowless cells, which were given names such as 'Heaven,' 'Purgatory' and 'Hell.' The most appropriate name was undoubtedly 'Hell,' considering the suffering of the prisoners. Torture was commonplace, and prisoners were often deprived of sleep and subjected to the thumbscrew" (Turney 2016).

Cervantes' narrative could have easily created an ekphrastic moment, a description of the tower, its architecture, and its horrors. But all we have is a letter that uses the bedbugs as an image for the torments of this horrifying space. Perhaps these tiny creatures stand for the famed monster that washed up on the shores of the Tiber in 1496 soon after the flood. As a combination of human and animal parts (Bartolomé and the bedbugs), it was described in lurid detail: head of an ass, body of a woman, right foot of an eagle with claws, left foot of a cow, left hand elephantine. The tail made of a serpent put the finishing touches on this terrifying creature (Meserve 2018, 118, 123). Descriptions by Giacomo Zorzi and an image by Wenzel von Olmutz created consternation among the faithful and impelled those who considered the papacy to be corrupt to use it as a presage of corruption and disaster. Lucas Cranach made a woodcut of the "Pope-Ass" while Philip Melanchthon, a Lutheran theologian, explained the monster as image of papal corruption.

Although the appearance of the monster, the arrival of the flood, and the sight of drowning prisoners at the dreaded tower in Rome took place more than a hundred years before Cervantes was writing his novel, the events did not vanish from the European imagination. When the emperor's troops invaded and sacked Rome in 1527 (against his express will), many attributed the desecration to the corruption of the papacy. Others thought of it as an apocalyptic event. The coming of the plague, killing some five thousand soldiers, was considered divine retribution for this desecration (Chastel 1983, 91). Reacting to "pagan" and corrupt Rome, the Council of Trent, decades later, brought about many stringent laws that fostered the Counter-Reformation. Still, for many, Rome remained suspect, and the jail continued to be a space for injustice. Here, legend has it, Beatrice Cenci was imprisoned among other relatives for murdering her father, Francesco, who had repeatedly raped her. In spite of a public outcry against her death sentence, Pope Clement VIII refused to show any clemency, and she was beheaded with an axe at a scaffold built nearby, at Sant'Angelo Bridge, in 1599. A portrait attributed by Guido Reni shows her dressed in white, some say, drawn the day before her execution. The tower remained a place of misery until it was rebuilt as a theatre in 1667 by Carlo Fontana. Performances were attended by many illustrious figures such as Queen Christina of Sweden.[15] Indeed, the tower, for centuries, was a theatre of cruelty and punishment. While many inside were justly accused, many others saw the tower as a centre of inhumane torture and injustice.

It is no wonder, then, that the narrative wishes to keep the tower with its monster, now the naive Bartolomé covered with bedbugs, invisible to the eyes. It is a sore spot, pointing to hell in the midst of heaven, to corruption in the midst of relics and sanctity, to criminals in the midst of martyrs, and to torture in the midst of Christian suffering. It is no wonder that Bartolomé, with the body of a woman (Luisa) etched in his mind and "chained" to him, and with repellent creatures eating at his flesh, will be allowed to flee Rome. He and Luisa are reminders of the corruption that seeps out from the tower, one that the papacy wants to banish, even as attacks on it from Lutherans and other reformers seek to destroy its image of sanctity. The tower is as invisible as the Villa Madama – the latter for its paganism and the former for what it might say of the centre of Catholicism.

Hipólita's Enclosed Loggia

Rome, rather than reconciling opposites, makes them even more pugnacious, for the earthly city must somehow come to terms with a divine architecture it is to represent. While the pilgrims seek to Christianize, many of the inhabitants try to paganize. As they view Auristela and the French ladies, a would-be poet exclaims, "Yo apostaré que la diosa Venus, como en los tiempos pasados, vuelve a esta ciudad a ver las reliquias de su querido Eneas" (I will wager that the goddess Venus now returneth hither as in times past, to see the relics of her dear Aeneas; Cervantes 2015b, 647; n.d.). It is this double movement that reveals the conjoining of two cultures. In using the term *reliquias* (relics), the sentence easily wavers between sacrilege and syncretism, recalling the many Renaissance poems in which relics could have a double meaning: the ruins of the ancient city and the remnants of the Christian martyrs. The pagan deity to which the poet refers could well be a celestial Venus, a figure that, emerging from the sea, echoes the Virgin Mary as Stella Maris. She is Maria/Maris and a celestial star (Venus).[16] Indeed, Auristela's name, as Clark Colahan has convincingly argued, derives from Horace: "tu pudica, tu proba / perambulabis astra sidus aureum" (Chaste and righteous, thou shalt be made to walk amid the stars, a golden constellation; Horace 1968, 416, 17.40–1; 1968, 417). As Periandro's golden star, she is Mary and Venus, a *stella maris* that guides him in his pilgrimage.[17] This new Venus stands in opposition to the earthly or perhaps beastly Venus as represented by Luisa.

Furthermore, this whole fourth book puts into motion what Laura Bass has called "the drama of the portrait" in which portraiture as a "quintessential courtly genre" becomes a "distinguishing mark of urban life and elite status" (2008, 15). The changing fates of portraits in plays of the period, she argues, are intimately tied to the characters, thus imitating the circulation of these portraits in urban elite society. In Cervantes' posthumous novel, the portrait of Auristela, this new Venus, is essential to the action. Mercedes Alcalá-Galán reminds us: "Los retratos de Auristela se multiplican en el texto, aparecen, desaparecen, causan duelos, pasiones, sobornos y compiten con la misma protagonista" (Auristela's portraits multiply themselves in the text; they appear, disappear, cause duels, passions, bribery and compete with the protagonist; 2016b, 4). Although a number of critics have dealt with this recurring ekphrasis, from Ignacio López Alemany (2005) to Alcalá-Galán (2009, 97–106), my only point here is that there is a battle of images. Although Auristela represents Christian devotion, many are taken with her physical beauty, as she is made into a kind of idol, a new Venus that distracts from the sacred. She may stand at the centre of the circle of pilgrims, of the circle of perfection, but her portraits transform this centre into an ellipsis, with a double focus – a double focus that also has to do with the city of Rome.

It is in this city of paradox where Christians abide in Jewish places, where a Christian is viewed as a pagan goddess, that Hipólita's palace entices Periandro. She invites him to visit "una lonja y un camerín mío" (Cervantes 2015b, 66). Vicente Pérez de León considers this the last great moment in Cervantes' narrative trajectory: "El viaje artesanamente metartístico cervantino, que parte de la admiración a Lope de Rueda y culmina en la lonja de Hipólita, se asemeja a una catedral del saber técnico-artístico de su época, en la que hacer alarde de las técnicas literarias más sofisticadas y poder juntar en su espacio cultura popular y elevada" (The journey is crafted as a meta-artistic one by Cervantes. It originates in his admiration for Lope de Rueda and culminates in Hipólita's loggia, resembling a cathedral of the technical and artistic knowledge of the times where one can foreground the most sophisticated literary techiques of the times; and one can bring together in this space high and popular culture; 2010, 710). But in evoking a cathedral, Cervantes may well be recalling and alluding to the final spaces of the *Persiles*, which are as enticing as this false loggia.

Although the loggia suggests an outside space often decorated with paintings, a *camerino* can be either a "lugar donde las mujeres guardan sus adornos" (a place where women keep their adornments; Cervantes 2015b, 669n7; n.d.) or, in the Italian sense, a place apart where precious objects and paintings are kept. While the term *lonja* traps the reader and the pilgrim into believing in an open structure, the reality is that Hipólita's hall is well enclosed and far from safe.

In Hipólita's abode this hall claims to exhibit precious paintings, from those of the Greek Apelles to the Renaissance Michelangelo and Raphael. Is the narrative recalling that Michelangelo was asked to build the northern façade of the Porta del Popolo while Raphael was the architect of the Villa Madama? In the midst of a palace of lust we have images of Raphael, known for his Madonnas; in this hidden place of pleasures we have the Michelangelo of the Sistine Chapel. Nothing is said of Titian, who would be the ideal painter for representing the desires of the flesh, from his desiring *Danae* to the paradoxical joy in *The Rape of Europa*. Alban Forcione comments: "What is particularly interesting here is the association of the noblest forms of art and the Renaissance faith in art as a conqueror of time with the false values of the paradise and its demonic forces. Cervantes momentarily approaches an ascetic tonality which is uncharacteristic of both the *Persiles* and his other writings" (1972, 102). I would argue that this is not at all a unique space. We have seen throughout the book how edifices hide other structures, and this one is no exception. Hipólita's *camerino* is a false place, one that shows, in the darkness of a closed loggia, works of art that are nothing but replicas or illusions. She may wish to have paintings by Michelangelo and Raphael, but, like her own figure, these works are deceitful. The architecture inverts Yi-Fu Tuan's notion of place, in this case showing that a home or villa is not safe, thereby becoming a hermetic and dangerous space. Periandro has been brought here not to decipher the designs of art but to acquiesce to the courtesan's artful designs. There is no need for ekphrasis here because all that matters is the figure of the painted courtesan.

Although Hipólita appears at home in her surroundings, she is as much in danger as Periandro. After all, she needs to hide her falsity. Worse still, these hermetic spaces present an imminent danger to Periandro. They evoke the banquet of the senses, in which each sense serves to draw one away from the spiritual, reconfiguring in one space what had taken many episodes to present in the third book (De Armas 1993, 403–14). Taste, one of the lowest, is represented by the abundance at her table; smell is evoked by the foodstuff and the comparison of the loggia to the Garden of the Hesperides, with its golden apples or oranges that would exude a delightful scent. Hearing is presented through the singing of many types of birds in their cages; the lure of sight is everywhere, from paintings to the courtesan herself. All that is missing is the lowest of senses in its Platonic hierarchy – touch. Recognizing the place as a trap, the pilgrim seeks to leave. As Hipólita places her hand on Periandro to detain him, she touches his cross of encrusted diamonds. Touch now embraces not only erotic desire but a craving for material wealth. The narrative does not clarify how it is that Periandro seems to be wearing Auristela's cross.[18] The ellipsis points once again to the new structures discovered in the cosmos, the new anxieties in which the unknown becomes known and vice versa, confusing sight. As we look at Periandro's cross, we must divert our sight and look backwards, much as Cervantes has taught us when looking at the cityscape and denying its ekphrasis. We, as the persons seeing, must look back, in this case, at Hipólita. Alcalá-Galán, in an astounding discovery, asserts that we are looking at the mythic power held by the courtesan in Venice, Rome, and ancient Rome. And she is not just one of many but the most famous of all, Imperia Cognati (1486–1512) (2016b, 12). Serving as a model for some of Raphael's works, she transforms herself into a work of art: "porque con la hermosura encantaba, con la riqueza se hacía estimar y, con la cortesía, si así se puede decir, se hacía adorar" (she enchanted with her beauty, made herself esteemed for her riches and adored for her courtesy; 2015b, 667; n.d.). Although Imperia owned her own palace in Rome and a villa outside the city, she often visited the Villa Farnesina built by Agostino Chigi, the richest banker of the times. Indeed, Lauren Golden has argued that Chigi's villa is a kind of fantasy created to recall all the alluring traits of Imperia (2007, 319). Here the banker entertained some of the most prominent figures of Roman society and regaled them with images of the courtesan, which appear throughout a series of works of art, in particular, Raphael's *Galatea*, which Cervantes used to compose his pastoral novel. The presence of Imperia here, then, becomes a place marker for his literary career. If Cervantes started with eclogue, he ends with epic in the *Persiles*. And each includes an image of Imperia, the first in the guise of a shepherd-ess, and the second as she was in Rome, a courtesan. This is a most curious situation because Cervantes seems to be arguing that his art, his writings, must have all the characteristics of a courtesan. His fiction must show beauty, a richness of images, and a courtesy that prevents clear satirical attacks. These qualities would then translate into patronage, as prominent figures would pay for his services. Whatever elements of irony may be found here, it is clear that Cervantes creates a very novel view of the artist as courtesan.

As we slowly turn our gaze back to Periandro, we should recall that Imperia's name is "a pun on *Empyrean* – the highest heaven, indicating the goddess-like qualities of her nature" (Golden 2007, 319). In classical texts it refers to the highest heaven, a realm occupied by fire, and in Christian times it was used to refer to God's abode. Hipólita / Imperia is then a woman who gives the highest pleasures, arousing the most fiery passions. Her abode, when Christianized, becomes the realms above. The double focus, that of her beauty and her touch, creates once again a double architecture, one that points to this earth, and another to the heavens. As she seeks to touch his chest, where the crucifix is placed, the object's mysterious reappearance reinforces the symbolic charge of the moment. Hipólita fully discovers it by opening Periandro's doublet. The cross over his heart means that his affections belong to another, that Auristela controls the inside spaces of Periandro, and that together they form one bounded place that Hipólita cannot transgress. Yi-Fu Tuan has argued that "objects define space, giving it a geometric personality," and thus they can create a sense of place (1977, 17). The cross worn by Periandro carries with it a geometric personality that exudes place, as well as a place that is configured into an apotropaic symbol, an object of protection. Thus it is a place in three senses: familiar object, apotropaic symbol, and a way to show that Periandro and Auristela are one, thus creating a sense of place from a bond of love. Tuan recalls that Augustine's birth city of Thagaste is transformed by the death of his best friend and argues that "the value of place was borrowed from the intimacy of a particular human relationship" (140).

While the cross reflects a boundary that Hipólita cannot cross, it also triggers her basest instincts. Not knowing the full import of the object, she must possess it. In a moment of pure covetousness she opens the window and yells out for the law to come, for a man has stolen her cross: "Púsose ella asimismo a la ventana y, a grandes voces comenzó a apellidar la gente de la calle, diciendo: 'Ténganme a este ladrón.'" (She went to the window, and with great cries began to call to the people, saying: "Stop, my friends! Stop this thief"; Cervantes 2015b, 672–3; n.d.)

There are very few windows mentioned in the *Persiles*, but we have already encountered such openings in the Jewish home in which the pilgrims abide. In the earlier place, people in the street had asked for Auristela and the other female pilgrims to show themselves and exhibit their beauty (648). Here, the opposite is the case, Hipólita shows herself at the window in a show of inner wickedness. In this scene Cervantes forges a hermetic abode of malevolence, something he had done previously in other works such as the interpolated tale in the first part of *Don Quixote, El curioso impertinente*, in which only one window is mentioned, one that allows an intruder to escape. There seems to be no escape from Hipólita's palace, as the window is but a site of transgression. In calling Periandro a thief, she empowers him, placing him under Hermes, lord of thieves and of wisdom and eloquence, messenger of the divine. Although she is debased by her actions, her legend remains. She is a courtesan who, seeking to conquer this world and the beyond, exhibits her beauty and her covetousness. Still, she calls herself Imperia and is called an empyrean. If the tower hides Rome's cruelty and corruption, the courtesan's home exposes the city's double image – her beauty and her falseness; her architectural and artistic exquisiteness and her covetousness; her heavenly aspirations and her concupiscence; her sacred language and her mendacity.

The Church Outside

After a number of further obstacles and confusions the narrative moves rapidly towards a conclusion that takes place in an open space, adjacent to a church: "Llegó en esto el día y hallóse Periandro junto a la iglesia y templo, magnífico y casi el mayor de la Europa, de San Pablo" (Periander saw himself over against Saint Paul's Church, which is one of the most stately temples and, in a manner, the greatest of all Europe; Cervantes 2015b, 707; n.d.), a site that is very different now because it was reconstructed after the fire of 1823. It, of course, is not the first time he and the pilgrims have visited this church. After all, it is one of the seven pilgrimage churches of Rome. Anton M. Rothbauer, Alban K. Forcione, and Michael Armstrong-Roche have come up with important insights as to this displacement, this move away from the Vatican to Saint Paul. [19]

My point here fits in with theirs, although I am not as keen to make it such a singular site. After all, as far back as the year 1300, the Basilicas of Saint Peter and Saint Paul, which housed the tombs of these apostles, were set aside as churches that had to be visited by pilgrims according to Boniface VIII. As time went on, the two became four and then seven.

In the mid-sixteenth century Filippo Neri, who ministered to impoverished pilgrims, actually prepared an itinerary of such a visit, and his route of the seven churches became the accepted one over time.[20] While finishing the *Persiles*, Cervantes may have heard of Neri's beatification in 1615 and may have thought of this route.[21] Periandro undertook this pilgrimage twice.[22] Furthermore, the Apostles Peter and Paul must be seen in tandem. Jerónimo Gracián, in his *Treatise on the Jubilee of the Holy Year* (1599), claims that Rome "possessed two resplendent eyes, the bodies of Saint Peter and Saint Paul" (Randell 2001, 99). Although these relics may be immensely important, what is of even greater import is that these apostles will rise from their Roman graves at the Last Judgment: "What roses will Rome send to Christ at that hour" (100). Let us not forget that in the last paragraphs of the novel, as Cervantes is rapidly tying the knots of his plot, Auristela goes to the Vatican – although this is mentioned through somewhat of an ellipsis and certainly a circumlocution: "habiendo besado los pies al Pontífice, sosegó su espiritu y cumplió su voto" (And having kissed the Sovereign Bishop's feet, accomplished her vow; Cervantes 2015b, 713; n.d.). The narrative circles around the exact architecture. This may even be seen as an ellipsis: we are not told that this event took place at the Vatican or at Saint Peter's, but it probably did. The narrative thus establishes a secondary focus in an elliptical geometry, of which the most visible is Saint Paul's. Thus, both Saint Peter's and Saint Paul's Outside the Wall are keys to Rome and to the novel. If Maximino and Periandro are linked to Paul, Auristela turns to the Vatican for spiritual solace.

At the same time, for the reader of the *Persiles*, Saint Paul is the last locus in the architectural mnemonics of the text, the last image to be placed in the memory. At that time Saint Paul was found next to "a beautiful field" one mile outside of Rome (Palladio 1991, 128). This delightful space seeks to comfort because it is presided over by the façade of a church, a place that will tower over all those who come near; the church is a place of safety, silence, and mystery, a place that, in the words of Yi-Fu Tuan, "reveals and instructs," exhibiting the "weight of stone and of authority" (1977, 114). And yet the field outside is not yet commanded by the structure of the church; instead, it is in flux as four different groups come together and exchange words, experiences, and emotions. The first, a single individual, is Periandro, who exhibits his vulnerability (his lack of place) after having overheard Serafido say that his disguise is now exposed, that he will be acknowledged as brother to Maximino, prince to Tile (Thule), and that his very brother has come to claim his bride, Auristela (Sigismunda): "Partiose el príncipe Maximino en dos gruesísimas naves y, entrando por el estrecho herculeo, con diferentes tiempos y diversas borrascas, llegó a la isla de Tinacria y desde allí, a la gran ciudad de Parténope, y agora queda no lejos de aquí, en un lugar llamado Terrachina, último de los de Nápoles y primero de los de Roma" (Prince Maximino went thence in two great ships; and entering the Straits of Gibraltar, after many storms he arrived in the Isle of Tinacria and from thence at the city of Parthenope. He is now sick here, hard by, in a place called Terrachina; Cervantes 2015b, 704). His brother's weighty ships, his ability to traverse the columns of Hercules, and his imminent arrival point to great force being exerted by the rightful heir and groom. This is a force that may be a detriment to Periandro's desire to marry Auristela.

The second group is an amorphous combination including Antonio, Feliz Flora, Constanza, and Antonio. It seems as if Hipólita follows them and that Pirro is not far behind. It is a very unstructured composition pointing to the dangers of space and the perils of chaotic emotions. The third group is composed of Serafido who comes with news from the north, and Rutilio who accompanies him, thus ready to transform and unveil much in this space. As three groups converge, the result is violence. The jealous Pirro stabs Periandro, who faints in Auristela's arms as life seems to ebb from his body. The fourth group includes Prince Maximino, Periandro's older brother, who, ill and near death, arrives in a carriage with great accompaniment. The text is clear as to the type of illness: "esto que llaman mutación" (*what they call seasonal illness*; Cervantes 2015b, 704; n.d.). Numerous Spanish authors discuss this kind of illness, including Diego Duque de Estrada, Diego Saavedra Fajardo, and Cristóbal Suárez de Figueroa (Saavedra Fajardo 1986, 2). Cervantes had previously referred to this moment in *El licenciado Vidriera* (The Glass graduate) (2015a, 317) Such fevers often ended in death. As the four groups meet, death appears: "En efeto, frontero del templo de San Pablo, en mitad de la campana rasa, la fea muerta salió al encuentro al gallardo Persiles y le derribó en tierra y enterró a Maximino. El cual, viéndose a punto de la muerte, con la mano derecha asió la izquierda de su hermano y se la llegó a los ojos, y con su izquierda le asió de la derecha y se la juntó con la de Sigismunda." (Observe, then, how before the Church of Saint Paul, in the midst of the plain field, horrible death grappled with Persiles and buried Maximino, who, seeing himself at the last gasp, with his right hand took his brother's left and put it to his eyes; and taking his right hand with the left, joined the same to Sigismunda's; Cervantes 2015b, 711; n.d.) In his last breath Maximino asks Periandro to marry Auristela, as he joins their hands.[23]

As the novel reaches its conclusion, these events are not without significance. Let us recall that Maximino's illness has to do with feverish mutations that were said to take place during a specific time of year, called the *caniculares*, or dog days, named after the star Sirius, which represented Orion's hound in the heavens. One of the brightest celestial stars, it was considered fiery since classical antiquity, and it ruled the heavens during late July and August, the most noxious time of the year, causing thunder, thunderstorms, and illnesses, mainly fevers. Such was its fiery power that in the *Iliad*, Achilles is described as shining with the malignity of Sirius as he faces the enemy, Priam, king of Troy. Today we know that in the swampy areas around Rome the illness was malaria, from local mosquitoes. At the time, as explained in a previous chapter, it was thought to rise from the noxious vapours of the swamp – a trait it shared in common with the plague, which Cervantes recalls in a number of his texts.

Place and time are conjoined as in a chronotope, bringing together the threads of the narrative and materializing time through allusion. Cervantes writes an epic in the manner of Heliodorus, thus making Persiles y Sigismunda into a new version of Theagenes and Chariclea. At the same time, he holds back in introducing us to Persiles' brother, Maximino. After thundering through the straits of Gibraltar, symbol of Herculean prowess, Maximino approaches Rome under the ill-starred Sirius and becomes the epic hero that is not sung in this text. He is the Achilles who shines like Sirius, and, unseen and unremarked by the reader, is the one "quien encarna eminentemente los valores bélicos en esta novela" (who embodies the warlike qualities in this novel; Nevoux 2011, 245). The novel, then, once again affirms the elliptical shape, focusing on the protagonists of the Greek novel as heroes and hiding the second focus of the ellipse, the traditional epic hero. As Maximino arrives in Rome, he loses his powers precisely because of Sirius. Achilles no longer rules Cervantes' new fiction. Sickened with the affliction caused by Sirius, Maximino passes the mantle to his brother, who will be the new king of Thule. Thus, he will be able to marry Sigismunda/Auristela. With the passing of the mantle, it is as if the ancient epic has passed its authority to a new form, the Greek novel, and Achilles' wrath has led to Persiles' love. In the *Aethiopica* the couple marries in the capital of Ethiopia, Meroe, as Theagenes becomes priest of the Sun and Chariclea priestess of the Moon. In Cervantes, Persiles inherits his kingdom during the time of the Dog Star, the hottest time of the year, when the sun shines brightest. He now shines with new power, as he is wedded to Sigismunda, the Moon. This is not only a cosmic but an elemental resolution as the four elements, represented by the four groups outside of Rome, come together. As Tuan asserts, we have "a cosmos ordered by the four cardinal points" (1977, 96) – and these are the four points of the diamond cross that Persiles and Sigismunda have carried throughout their travails; it is also the cross that saved Persiles/ Periandro from the temptations of Hipólita.

As we come to the end, the cosmic and the elemental come together; the two forms of epic, old and new, embrace; and the pilgrims marry as the now Catholic ideals of the Sun and the Moon. But I would argue that in death, Maximino not only allows all these literary and symbolic values to shine. The author of the *Persiles* could well have also conceived Maximino in his own image, the writer who with his last breath is open-handedly presenting the two lovers, as a gift to his reader, as a way to remember the harmony of the opus and the spirit of the work – not one of war but one of love. As stated before, Maximino hardly appears in the work. He is there as trigger for the action, for the *Trabajos de Persiles y Sigismunda*. It is Maximino, a new Hermes, god of eloquence and writing, that sets them in motion.[24] It is he who embraces his characters as he and Cervantes fade away.

With Maximino dead, there is one more exchange: "Recogieron el cuerpo muerto de Maximino y lleváronle a San Pablo, y el medio vivo de Persiles en el coche del muerto, le volvieron a curar a Roma" (Maximin, being dead, was carried into S. Paul's Church, and Persiles was conducted to Rome in his coach, that his hurt might be cured; Cervantes 2015b, 712; n.d.). Again, Cervantes visualizes how his own corpse is being taken to a sacred place for burial. Although Cervantes would have entered the Basilica of Saint Paul when he visited Italy, the reader is only allowed to view its façade while the body of Maximino/Cervantes is taken to its final resting place.[25] The hermetic church points to the other world. Its bronze doors crafted in Constantinople (Cervantes may have remembered this) were given by Pantaleone of Amalfi to the church with an inscription that "asks the patron saint to open the doors of eternal life" (Hourihane 2012, 319), one that he can now take to heart.[26] The body of Maximino disappears in the light and shadow of the church, and that of Periandro, still weak from the wound, is taken to Rome for healing. If Maximino is a representation of the author's last moments when he is guided by Hermes as a psychopomp and passes into the hermetic church, then Periandro is the book, still weak, still in manuscript, waiting for the healing hand of Auristela, to see the light of day. If Cervantes' volume contains something new and astounding, a new kind of epic, his body is old and tired, ready to be taken to the heavens. Throughout, the figure of the elliptical reigns supreme, always creating an architecture with a double centre: Persiles (Saint Paul) and Sigismunda (Saint Peter and the Vatican); the Sun and the Moon; Achilles and Theagenes; Rome and Meroe; and Sirius as shining shield of light and as cause of malevolent illness. The elliptical stands for Kepler, for a new way of seeing the cosmos, for a world where the circular spheres can be questioned, and a literary text that teeters towards disorder.

The fourth book of the *Persiles*, then, is a site replete with the marvellous architectures of Rome, as the peripatetic pilgrims move from one to the other, often not noticing their undecipherable meanings. Indeed, many of these architectures are not the ones that most pilgrims would view upon reaching Renaissance Rome. In his very last writings Cervantes presents us with alternate architectures for the Christian city: from an invisible villa to a vanishing ghetto; from an unseen city made up of Christian relics to a menacing tower at the very centre of the city that evokes monstrosity and corruption; and from a Jewish home that welcomes Christian pilgrims to a church that may well exist textually to welcome the dying writer. Places and spaces clash with one another as Jewish, Classical, and Christian constructions counter old ways of writing epic. Through the different constructions of a site that is both space and place, dangerous and comforting, open and restrictive, but always revelling in conflictive and ambiguous cultures and forms, Cervantes reveals to us his last vision of Italy, a place that brings comfort to his mind only when he is outside its walls, on the other side of space and time.

Epilogue

Because the individual life is cosmic, everything about individual life should be in full harmony with Cosmic Life. Maharishi Vedic™ architecture gives dimensions, formulas, and orientations to the buildings that will provide cosmic harmony and support to the individual for his peace, prosperity, and good health.
Maharishi Mahesh Yogi

Long before Vitruvius compiled principles of architecture in the times of Augustus Caesar, earlier civilizations had considered notions akin to those of the Roman architect. Even before the well-known feng shui system evolved in China, India had developed the ancient science of Sthapatya Veda. Tracing its origins to Vedic civilization, this knowledge produced a massive amount of treatises over the centuries. They reveal that India had envisioned how to build temples and houses to reflect the harmonies of the cosmos. Sthapatya Veda, revived in modern times by Maharishi Mahesh Yogi, includes as some of its principles both symmetry and right proportion. More importantly, this Vedic science relates architecture to the human being: "When a house is designed, the dimensions of the building are calculated using the ancient mathematical formulas of Vastu Vidya of Maharishi Sthapatya Veda architecture. These Vedic formulas take into consideration, among other factors, the relationship of the house owner with the sun, moon, planets, and stars to ensure a perfect resonance between the cosmic structures and all components of the house."[1] This brings about a felicitous outcome for the dwellers, enhancing harmony, health, good fortune, and prosperity. To me, some of the more fascinating aspects of the study of architecture in Cervantes are indeed the relationship between the cosmos, the natural world we inhabit (our home as Earth), and our smaller abode, the microcosm, our body. From Vedic literature to architecture at the time of Augustus Caesar, to the Vitruvian principles applied in the

Renaissance, the human body becomes central to the architect because the edifices that are drawn and built must "exhibit the proportions, strength and beauty of the body of a man" (Vitruvius 1960, 103).

It is clear from his work of prose fiction that Cervantes was acquainted with Vitruvius and some of his Renaissance followers, as well as his Spanish disciples including Diego de Sagredo and Hernán Ruiz the Younger. Even when Cervantes' work is shadowed by his captivity and imprisonment, there is always the remembrance that the new façade of the Royal Jail in Seville was built by Hernán Ruiz who attempted to imbue it with symmetry and eurithmia. Although prisons and many buildings ruled by evil enchanters in the romances of chivalry were meant to exert power and control, Cervantes' narratives at times turn to less threatening architectures, placing the danger outside. His long works of prose fiction also tend to avoid cities, perhaps because they are so crowded, lack coherent structures, and have streets and houses without appropriate orientation or direction.[2] Perhaps Cervantes knew of Seneca's objection to cities. In the ninetieth letter of his *Epistulae moralis* (*Moral Epistles*) Seneca disagrees with Poseidonius: "But I, for my part, do not hold that philosophy devised these shrewdly-contrived dwellings of ours which rise story upon story, where city crowds against city [...] What! Was it philosophy that taught the use of keys and bolts? Nay, what was that except giving a hint to avarice?" (2014, 90.7–8). Thus, cities lack the eurithmia necessary for harmonious well-being and for the pursuit of the good. Toledo, Valencia, and Zaragoza are some of the cities that seem to be praised but are by-passed in Cervantes; Barcelona betrays Don Quixote; Rome does not appear as saintly as the pilgrims expect in the *Persiles*. Florence is never described even though a lengthy tale takes place there – only Anselmo's claustrophobic home takes up space. Here the house, much more than the home of the gentleman from La Mancha, becomes a prison to be escaped.

Throughout his fiction Cervantes built a thousand or more edifices with the pen. Their variety is astounding. While architects draw plans for buildings, the narrators and characters in these novels tell of edifices – castles, fortifications, inns, mills, prisons, palaces, towers, villas, and even the Roman Pantheon – which appear on their routes or in their conversations, and which welcome them, amaze them, or entrap them. These are places in which they can find solace and rest from the dangers outside, with feelings of topophilia, or they can be spaces of contention, claustrophobia, and topophobia. They deeply affect the characters who feel "enclosed, liberated or suspended" or look upon such structures with dread, relief, or admiration (Pericoli 2013). As these peripatetic characters wander through dangerous spaces, different kingdoms, and just the Iberian countryside, they encounter an immense variety of edifices, as if the architect of the text had built new spaces for them. In conclusion, I would simply like to look back, albeit very briefly, at some of Cervantes' Vitruvian sites, places that may have had a Vedic ancestry in the way they resonate with the inhabitants. I would ask, then, what attitudes are depicted towards the relationship of the human and the cosmos in terms of habitation? Does Cervantes' perception of Vitruvius waver and metamorphose? Does it resemble the many compound buildings in the text in that the structures, or even the notions they concretize, lack fixity? Six places/spaces will stand for the whole of what has been viewed in this volume and will be divided into pairs: the windmills and the Giralda tower; the Veranzio woman and Domitian's tower; and the monastery of Guadalupe and the Pantheon. After all, six is the perfect number for mathematicians, or so Vitruvius says (1960, 74).

The windmills episode in part 1 of *Don Quixote* is one of the few in which the knight transforms buildings into living beings. As such, it partakes of the ancient notion that human proportions are perfect because the circle and the square can be drawn, taking the navel as the centre, when the limbs are spread (Vitruvius 1960, 73). Since these two geometrical forms represent the perfection of the heavens and of the earth, then the ideal human being is the Vitruvian man, drawn repeatedly during the Renaissance, with Leonardo da Vinci's sketch as the most famous.[3] In addition, each section is designed so that its measurement stems from a part of the body (such as the finger, the palm, the foot, or the face). This led the ancients to see the body's symmetry as key to architecture: "Therefore, since nature had designed the human body so that its members are duly proportioned to the frame as a whole, it appears that the ancients had good reason for their rule, that in perfect buildings the different members must be in exact symmetrical position to the whole general scheme" (73).

In the windmills episode, however, Cervantes does not present us with a Vitruvian man but with a Vitruvian giant. And this creature was far from the ideal human being as imagined by Pico della Mirandola in the Renaissance because it was deformed by vice. Francisco Acero Yus explains that the giants in the romances of chivalry, and particularly in Cervantes' main model, the *Amadís*, "coinciden en su perverso comportamiento: rapto de doncellas, captura de prisioneros, traición, usurpación de reinos, amores incestuosos" (coincide in their perverse behaviour: rape of damsels, capture of prisoners, treason, usurpation of kingdoms, incestuous affairs; 2006, n.p.) Cervantes' narrative also reverses the Vitruvian analogy because here the building with its proportions becomes a man/giant, rather than being analogous to him. For Don Quixote, there is no architecture here, just a giant with moving arms, and Sancho explains that they are the sails of the mill. Is the passage, then, a parody of the Vitruvian man whose circle of perfection is now made up of the circle of the sails of the mill, and whose perfectibility turns into a litany of evil deeds?

When looking for the quixotic ideal, we should not ignore Sancho's words. After all, this is the first adventure in which the pair stands together. Sancho is the one who warns his master that he is not looking at giants, but at windmills that, as the sails turn, make the millstones go. Given Sancho's keen interest in food, he would imagine how the mill thus transforms grain into flour. Although the mill and the millstone are basic images that derive from an ancient past, they are very much present in Sancho's mind. While gazing in awe at Don Quixote's creation, at the giants, we may forget some of the main connotations of the mill. It refers to the human body. Again in letter 90 in the *Epistulae moralis* Seneca derides Poseidonius' notion that the philosopher invented everything (in this case, the mill):

> Furthermore, not confining his attention to these arts, he even degrades the wise man by sending him to the mill. For he tells us how the sage, by imitating the processes of nature, began to make bread. 'The grain,' he says, 'once taken into the mouth, is crushed by the flinty teeth, which meet in hostile encounter, and whatever grain slips out the tongue turns back to the selfsame teeth [...] 'Following this pattern,' he goes on, 'someone placed two rough stones, the one above the other, in imitation of the teeth, one set of which is stationary and awaits the motion of the other set. Then, by the rubbing of the one stone against the other, the grain is crushed and brought back again and again, until by frequent rubbing it is reduced to powder' (Seneca 2014, 90.22–3)

With the description of the functioning of the mill, Sancho's gluttony could well be leading him to think of this famous image in which body and mill (architecture) are analogous. But the mill is also cosmic. It stands for the precession of the equinoxes, which would be a step too far in this case; more importantly, it recalls the pivots of the heavens, discussed by Vitruvius (1960, 257), from whence a number of stars around the Pole Star appear to circle due to the rotation of the earth's axis. From ancient times, the Pole Star in Ursa Minor was used for navigation, and its movement, along with that of the stars around it, was linked to the mill. Susan Watts reminds us that "Arab astronomer, al-Farghani likewise described the revolving of the sky around the

Pole Star as 'like the turning of a mill'" (2014, 62).[4] Sancho's own astronomical knowledge, which he claims to have acquired when he was a shepherd, leads him to point precisely to Ursa Minor in a later chapter (Cervantes 1978, 1.20.240; 2008, 143). Thus, while Don Quixote looks up and sees giants whose whirling arms could be conceived as the circle formed by the Vitruvian man, Sancho, in describing the functioning of the mill, may be pointing to the relationship between buildings and humans (how they eat), and to the relationship between human and cosmic architectures. It is as if both Don Quixote and Sancho, from their own perspective, emphasized, albeit in a comic manner, the relationship between earthly architecture, cosmic architecture, and the human being, a person who could be either a giant or a glutton who is constantly devouring grain as a mill does.

While Don Quixote attacks a windmill as if it were an enemy, Sancho only observes its power and importance. A wind rises, the knight's lance is caught, and he and his horse are taken up only to fall to the ground defeated. A visit to windmills in La Mancha still shows how the top part consists of a dome that allows the user to move the sails in the direction from which the wind is blowing. This can be ascertained from twelve small windows located at the very top of the mill. Vitruvius had warned that winds, depending on their direction, could bring disease; and in Sthapatya Veda, direction or orientation is also crucial. It struck me that one of the twelve winds in La Mancha was labelled as "matacabras" (killer of goats). Perhaps it was this or another evil wind that defeated the knight.

Sansón Carrasco, in the second part of *Don Quixote,* disguises himself as the Knight of the Mirrors and boasts of the many labours he has accomplished as prescribed by his (fictional) lady. One of them is the defeat of a giantess. Sansón surely modelled his adventure after that of the windmills. Here he must defeat a giantess perched on top of a tower. The Giralda tower, the tallest in Europe at the time, was one of those composite buildings that are constantly present in the novel. In this case Cervantes did not have to imagine new metamorphoses because the existing building, a Moorish minaret turned into a bell tower, accompanied the Cathedral of Seville, which had once been a mosque. Afterwards, it was reconstructed by Hernán Ruiz, a famed architect who was well versed in Vitruvius and his Renaissance followers. The giantess in Sansón's tale is actually a huge sculpture on top of the tower that serves as a weathervane, pointing to the direction of the winds. Hernán Ruiz's invention derives directly from Vitruvius, who tells how Andronicus of Cyrrhus constructed the Tower of the Winds in Athens to prove that there were eight winds. On top of his tower he placed the sculpture of a Triton that served as a weathervane pointing to the prevailing winds. Perhaps the Triton was placed there because in myth he carries a conch shell and, blowing it like a trumpet, he either calms the seas or raises waves using the wind. Hernán Ruiz transforms the Triton into the figure of *Faith Triumphant*. Here Sansón triumphs by having the statue stand still rather than move. It is as if he were controlling the winds, whereas Don Quixote was defeated by them. Once again we are faced with Vitruvian architecture. It is cosmic in the sense that the realms of the Catholic faith stand above human endeavours; the statue of *Faith Triumphant* points the way and shows the direction of the winds (orientation according to nature). There is also the analogy between the construction of a temple or church and the proportions of the human being because the episode resonates with the adventure of the windmills as giants. In the first, Don Quixote is defeated by some evil winds, but in this one Sansón triumphs. Is success related to the fact that *Faith Triumphant* must stand still and thus point only in one direction? And is the statue of Faith as a woman an important shift that evinces that gender is not an element to be taken into account in the creation of the perfect human form? Yet, it is all a false tale concocted by the trickster Sansón Carrasco. Cervantes' composite building points to the many aspects of an argument. As noted in the first chapter, "we must guard against taking reality to be one way without pausing to question its alternative identifications" (Cascardi 1986, 15). In terms of architecture, it leads us to ask if composite buildings can attain Vitruvian eurithmia, if a giant can attain to symmetry and proportion, or, more extreme still, if a giantess perched on top of a building can be part of a building's perfect harmony.

The second pair of opposites that we will be reviewing is found together in the third book of Cervantes' *Persiles*: Domitian's tower and the Veranzio woman. As the pilgrims rest in the shade of a tower at a summer villa or palace in the French countryside, they see a woman falling from above, but she actually floats down safely when her dress becomes a kind of parachute. Cervantes is here alluding to a series of inventors who sought to make possible human flight, the most famous being Fausto Veranzio (Faustus Verantius) who drew a sketch of an *homo volans* (flying man). If Cervantes is indeed pointing to this illustration, in which a man with a parachute-like contraption floats down from the campanile of Saint Mark's cathedral in Venice, he may have wished that the reader recall Sansón Carrasco's fake adventure in which the statue of a woman stood above another campanile, this time at the cathedral in Seville. As with all the scenes thus far described, wind is of the essence, for it is able to open the dress in the form of a bell. The text may be inviting the reader to compare what I call the Veranzio woman with the Vitruvian man. If the latter represents a cosmic man and a cosmic architecture through the use of the circle, the most perfect geometrical form according to the Renaissance, the Veranzio woman may go further and show her as superior because she can actually fly and reign over the winds and the cosmos. In many ways her flight in relation to the tower echoes notions from our modern world, as in the works of Frank Lloyd Wright who developed "the organic thinking which focuses on the experience of humans and nature being united" (Kim 2002, 298). Thus, the "roof plane is like 'a shelter such as the big wide open wings of a mother bird protecting little birds'" (2002, 299). Indeed, the curves in the ceiling of the Meeting House of the Unitarian Church in Madison, Wisconsin (built in 1947), recall birds in flight.[5] We are thus led to believe, at first, that the tower is a Vitruvian building that reflects the cosmos and nature and that it enables or renders possible flight in which human beings are in perfect harmony with the elements (particularly, the wind).

The Veranzio woman then tells her story. Her husband, having worn a poisoned shirt akin to Hercules' tunic, had gone mad, and she had had to imprison him in the tower. Breaking lose, he had thrown her off the tower. The tower then loses its power as a Vitruvian building because it can house a madman, one whose name recalls the evils of Emperor Domitian. It can also be associated with the watchtowers built by the emperor, many of which were unable to hold back those who would attack his empire. It would indeed be interesting to compare these watchtowers to those described by Vitruvius (1960, 22–4). The pilgrims below watch and confirm the cosmic qualities of the Veranzio woman as the orientation of the winds prove to be benefic and her proportions and her dress harmonize with the environment. Is the tower indeed a structure of dysrithmia ruled by Domitian, or has it made possible, by its orientation and harmonious qualities, the flight of its most perfect human occupant?

The last two episodes I would like to recall here come from two different works, the *Persiles* and the second part of *Don Quixote*. If we are to re-envision questions of flight, we must look back at the monastery of Guadalupe. Here the pilgrims have a sacred vision of flying corpses, ailing bodies, and captives, thus confirming the monastery as a sacred site, one in which hierophanies can take place as the "revelation of an absolute reality" (Eliade 1963, 21). Cervantes seems to connect the sacred to Marian places of worship, and here the vision of flight is linked to Feliciana de la Voz: "sin mover los labios ni hacer otra demostración ni movimiento que diese señal de ser viva criatura, soltó la voz a los vientos y levantó el corazón al cielo" (without moving her lips nor making any other movement that would signal that she was a living creature, she released her voice to the winds and she raised her heart to the heavens; Cervantes 2015b, 472). As a "statue" that imitates the Virgin's image at the monastery, Feliciana, motionless, without even moving her lips, is able to release her sacred song. This is yet a second hierophany, in which the sacred and the profane meet. Her voice is "released" while she does not move her lips, she does not speak. Such a paradox is at the heart of the sacred.[6] It is also related to that marvellous silence of which Cervantes speaks with awe throughout his works; let us only recall the "maravilloso silencio" felt at the home of the Knight of the Green Cloak (Cervantes 1978, 1.18.173; 2008, 582). Such silence is also at the heart of Vedic knowledge.[7] Released to the winds, Feliciana's song fills the monastery with perfect harmony. The sacred edifice, saturated with eurithmia, triggers a sacred song from Feliciana, and her song further imbues the monastery with a harmonious and felicitous aura, activating the infinite possibilities of sacred architecture and endowing its dwellers with the urge to rise above. A human being and a building merge, thus advancing the Vitruvian notion of cosmic architecture, the notion of the human as perfectible, and the belief that his edifications are based on human proportions but attend to the cosmic.[8] The song in silence even influences the outside where Feliciana de la Voz is later reconciled with her family.

The Pantheon, our last architecture, is also imbued with eurithmia and the sacred. Don Quixote ponders on it as he journeys to Dulcinea's palace, a non-existent place in this world but one that shines supreme in the architectural mnemonics of the knight's mind. Thinking of perfection, he must reimagine one of the most perfect of earthly buildings, one that once stood as a temple to all the gods. In his flight of the imagination he echoes Henry James. In *The Last of the Valerii* the narrator observes the Count in ecstasy in this temple. He is entranced by the sun and the clouds that are seen through the oculus, and he enjoys the light rain as if it were water from a fountain. The Count explains: "'Now, only the wind and the rain, the sun and the cold, come down; but of old – of old' – and he touched my arm and gave me a strange smile – 'the pagan gods and goddesses used to come sailing through it and take their places at their altars. What a procession, when the eyes of faith could see it!'" (James 1875, 159–60). In some ways the Count recalls the knight's somewhat pagan vision of a Dulcinea who exists more as a sculpture in his mind than as a human Aldonza.[9] Evoking the Pantheon, Don Quixote would place her here as one of the ancient deities, but much more than that, as a solar figure. Let us recall that he wants to approach her palace to view "cualquier rayo de sol de su belleza" (how small soever ray of the sun of her beauty; Cervantes 1978, 2.8.93; 2008, 514). The Count and Don Quixote both worship the impossible through a building that seems impossible in its beauty and in its complex architecture, where Vitruvian eurithmia calls upon the human to rise above and to commune with nature and the gods.

The episode of a Roman gentleman wishing to embrace Charles V and have both of them plunge to their death through the oculus of the Pantheon may well shadow the eurithmia of the building through unexpected violence. In some ways the event prophesies the impossibility of Don Quixote's love, the impossibility of reaching Dulcinea's palace outside of his mind. And yet the event does not happen. It is as if the oculus prevented its own desecration. In Sthapatya Veda the very centre of the house is left unoccupied as the place of silence and the connection between the individual, the architecture, and the cosmos. It actually favours a device above it to let in sunlight, which an oculus accomplishes.

The many buildings in Cervantes' novels point to his continued interest in architecture, and he goes well beyond the architecture or structure of a work to point to the resonances between the human being, the building, and the cosmos. While some are shadowed, filled with noise, passion, and confusion, others metamorphose into different kinds of edifices, which are difficult to view and comprehend, blending as they do with the many perspectives of the narrators and inhabitants. Some spaces are even phantom-like, at times, with a double focus that points to the ellipsis and the elliptical, to the anxious wonderment of new discoveries, and to Kepler's new vision of the universe, which replaces the perfect circle of the heavens with more complex structures. This anxious and elliptical architecture clashes with what, for me, are the most amazing architectures in Cervantes – those that in some way recall the ancient principles of Vitruvius, revived in the Renaissance, principles that led to the image of the Vitruvian man, the perfectible human being that aspires to cosmic life. Cervantes counters the perfect man with the ideal woman. While he recalls the circle, she flies above, becoming the Veranzio woman and Feliciana of the silent song.

Notes

Preface

1 In a letter to incoming students John (Jay) Ellison, Dean of Students, wrote
  to the 2020 class: "Our commitment to academic freedom means that we do
  not support so-called 'trigger warnings,' we do not cancel invited speakers
  because their topics might prove controversial, and we do not condone
  the creation of intellectual 'safe spaces' where individuals can retreat from
  ideas and perspectives at odds with their own." ews.uchicago.edu.
2 Even before we had to deal with social distancing, there developed in
  the last decade a sense of separation, as any kind of touching became
  suspicious in a world racked by revelations of gender violence. Although
  we have gained in safety, we have lost some of our ability to care. Touch,
  it is said, is one of the most comforting gestures in human behaviour.
  We know, for example that "researchers have been discovering how
  emphasizing skin-to-skin contact between baby and parent can be a
  boon to both and how consistent emotional engagement with infants
  can speed their development and recognition of self" (Harmon 2010). In
  addition, touch isolation among men has been a common rule in America,
  paralleling early modern Iberia: "This lack which seems even more
  pronounced today than in early modern times, derives from restrictive
  norms that may well stem from homophobia (the rejection of sodomy as
  sin) or the fear of effeminacy (a reaction against courtly excesses by *lindos*
  at a time when there was a crisis of masculinity)" (De Armas 2019).

1 Breaking Eurithmia

1 Terence Cave states that enargeia "may be initially described as the
  evocation of a visual scene, in all its details and colours, as if the reader
  were present as spectator" (1976, 6).

2 When dealing with *Don Quixote*, I first give the part and chapter of
the book and then the page number of that edition. This is followed
by a semicolon, after which I include the page number of the English
translation.

3 In addition to Stefano Neri's beautifully illustrated anthology (2007), see
the study by Aguilar Perdomo (2007).

4 Duce García points out, among others, the Castle of Fortune in *Olivante
de Laura* by Antonio de Torquemada, "donde se reúnen figuras reales y
ficticias del pasado más remoto, mezcladas con personajes del propio
libro, además de los entes alegóricos más retumbantes y significativos: la
Fortuna, la Fama, la Muerte, y el Tiempo, dueño supremo de la existencia
(Duce García 2008, 195; where real and fictitious figures from the most
remote past meet, mixed with characters from the book itself, in addition
to the most resounding and significant allegorical entities: Fortune, Fame,
Death, and Time, the supreme owner of existence).

5 "[L]os libros de caballerías se inclinan por las descripciones detalladas –
y fastuosas – de edificaciones, particularmente aquellas de carácter
maravilloso" (chivalry books tend towards detailed – and lavish –
descriptions of buildings, particularly those of marvellous nature; Aguilar
Perdomo 2007, 129).

6 As an example let us remember Auristela's reply to Periandro: "Nuestras
almas, como tú bien sabes y como aquí me han enseñado, siempre están en
continuo movimiento y no pueden parar sino en Dios, como en su centro.
En esta vida, los deseos son infinitos, y unos se encadenan de otros." (Our
souls, as you well know and as I have been taught, are always in constant
movement and cannot halt except in God, as if their center. In this life,
desires are infinite, and some are chained by others; Cervantes 2015b, 690.)

7 Many, from Mateo Alemán to Teresa de Jesús, called it an infernal place
(Falcón Márquez 1996, 158). Excrement from the prisoners, for example,
was kept in a kind of lagoon, creating an unbearable stench, and was only
removed every two months (Falcón Márquez 1996, 162).

8 "[E]ach city implemented its own plague restrictions designed to prevent
contact with infected people or tainted goods" (Clouse 2011, 169). In general,
restrictions were placed on areas of the city or on cities themselves. Patients
were often carted, in fear, to hospitals commonly built outside the walls.
While Ruth McKay states that "locking the sick in their homes seems to
have been an exception" (2019, 233), she admits that in Madrid there were
"special quarantine houses on specific streets reserved for the sick, except
for 'people of quality,' who should not be sent there" (233).

9 In Great Britain and the Netherlands, one of its results was the freezing
of the rivers, including the Thames, which led to the creation of winter
festivals (Cowie 2007, 164).

10 Pointing to *El Buscón* and *El diablo cojuelo*, Enrique García Santo Tomás explains that the growth of Madrid as permanent capital evokes anxieties akin to those of modern cities: "el crecimiento demográfico (con una gran población flotante), la velocidad de los cambios y los continuos reajustes que provoca un fenómeno de semejante magnitud resultan en una serie de conflictos (fragmentaciones, choques, saturaciones, violencias, etc.) cuyo diagnosis guarda no pocas similitudes con ciertos síntomas de nuestras ciudades modernas." (Demographic growth (with a large floating population), rapid changes and continuous readjustments caused by a phenomenon of such scale result in a series of conflicts (fragmentation, clashes, saturations, violence, etc.), this diagnosis does not differ greatly from certain symptoms of modern cities; 2000, 119.)

11 Bachelard, in a truly lyric text, points to the importance of the emotional response to buildings – dreams of our childhood home take us to a material paradise – but the ideal home should always be under construction (1994, 7). In *The Production of Space*, Lefebvre seeks to bridge theoretical and practical space, and mental and social space (1991, 4). He argues that space is socially constructed and that urban spaces are culturally produced as centres where through capitalism different strata negotiate with the hegemonic class (1991, 375). Zumthor prefers to see the medieval space as far from abstract but almost having its own personality (1993, 35–6).

12 There are several references to *huésped* (guest) and *hospedaje* (lodging) in *El burlador de Sevilla*. As Rosa Navarro has pointed out, they derive from the way Aeneas repaid Dido's hospitality in Virgil (2002, 263–77). Harald Weinrich, turning to this play, stresses the concept of hospitality that should be applied in our modern world even though "there is too much motion and unrest" (2005, 119).

13 In 1471 Marsilio Ficino, the most important of the Renaissance Platonists, stopped his work on Plato and, at the request of his patron Cosimo de' Medici, turned to translate the *Corpus Hermeticum*, the works of Hermes Trismegistus, an Egyptian priest whose insights into the cosmos were said to be older than Plato's. This text became immensely popular and was reprinted time and again for more than a century. Susan Byrne (2007) has studied the impact of Hermetic thought in three poets of the Golden Age, Francisco de Aldana, Fray Luis de León, and San Juan de la Cruz. This ground-breaking analysis should lead others to search for the Hermetic in other works of Renaissance and early modern Spain. While invoking the hermetic, I do not necessarily concur with all of Michael Nerlich's fascinating theories, which Isabel Lozano Renieblas summarizes: "El *Persiles*, construido según fórmulas numérico-simbólicas similares a las de la obra de Dante, se articula sobre un triple viaje romano, visigótico

y estelar" (The *Persiles*, built according to numerical-symbolic formulas similar to those of Dante's work, is articulated on a triple Roman, Visigothic, and stellar journey; 2008, 277).

14 Branko Mitrovic, in his explanation of the importance of Barbaro's translation and commentary of Vitruvius, explains the difficulties: "the original text needed to be reconstructed from manuscripts in which scribes' errors abounded; illustrations that were crucial to the understanding of important sections of the text were missing and had to be reconstructed; Greek terminology that Vitruvius used needed to be interpreted [...] Vitruvius's presentation of many topics relied on knowledge of both science and ancient Roman technology that required a polymath of massive knowledge and competence in order to cover the wide range of topics discussed in the treatise" (2019, xi).

15 Baldassare Peruzzi was critical, while Antonio da Sangallo the younger called him clumsy (Cellauro 2004, 302–3).

16 Giocondo left Venice in 1514 and moved to Rome. At the death of Bramante, he, along with Raphael and Sangallo, became part of a triad of artists who worked on Saint Peter's Basilica.

17 Several translations into Italian appeared in the following century, from Cesare Cesarino (1521) and Giovanni Battista Caporali (1536) to Giovanni Battista Bertani (1558) and Giovan Antonio Rusconi. The latter completed a translation in 1552, but it was not accepted by the publisher because there were so many others. However, a few years after his death, in 1590 his illustrations were published "whilst the text was put together by the publisher in the form of an Italian paraphrase of Vitruvius" (Kruft 1994, 72). Such was the enthusiasm for the Roman architect that a Vitruvian academy was established in Rome in 1542, centred around Cardinal Bernardino Maffei. However, little came of their grandiose plans (69).

18 In this essay I will use *eurithmia* as utilized in Italian and Spanish treatises, rather than the English *eurythmy* because its sound more clearly conveys notions of harmony and grace.

19 Di Giorgio Martini (1439–1501) was an architect, engineer, painter, and sculptor from Sienna who built about seventy fortifications, many of them star-shaped. His architectural treatise, finished ca. 1482, remained in manuscript. Elizabeth Mays Merrill asserts that, "as the first Italian, fully illustrated tract to provide a prescriptive approach to architecture, it was revolutionary. Francesco conceived of the treatise as a manual for the aspiring architect, and because there was no adequate model for this type, he had to create a new format. His project for the *Trattato*, which he drafted, wrote, and re-wrote between 1475 and 1495, became a career-long endeavor" (2013, 1).

20 On the impact of Alberti on Sagredo see Vaughan Hart and Peter Hicks
   (1988, 130–5).
21 "Pero liberales se llaman los que trabajan con el espíritu y con el ingenio:
   como son los Gramáticos, Lógicos, Retóricos, Aritméticos, Músicos,
   Geométricos, Astrólogos, con los cuales son numerados los Pintores y
   Escultores cuyas artes son tan estimadas por los antiguos […] arquitecto
   es vocablo griego; quiere decir primer fabricador; así los ordenadores
   de edificios se dice propiamente arquitectos; los cuales según parece
   por nuestro Vitruvio son obligados a ser ejercitados en las ciencias de
   filosofía y artes liberales […] cuyas herramientas son las manos de los
   oficiales mecánicos." (But liberals are those who work with the spirit and
   with invention: Grammarians, Logicians, Rhetoricians, Arithmethicians,
   Musicians, Geometrists, Astrologers, along with Painters and Sculptors,
   whose arts are so highly revered by the ancient ones […] architect is
   a Greek word; it means principal maker; thus, building designers are
   properly called architects; which according to our Vitruvius, must exercise
   sciences of philosophy and liberal arts […] whose tools are the hands of
   the mechanical officers; Sagredo 1526, 7v.)
22 "En cambio, el tema de la columna monstruosa es original. Este tipo de
   columnas aparece en los retablos platerescos anteriores y posteriores
   a Sagredo, que no hace otra cosa que recoger el tema de la práctica de
   los talleres." (On the other hand, the notion of the monster column is
   original. This type of column appears in the plateresque altarpieces
   before and after Sagredo, which does nothing other than pick up the
   theme of the practice of workshops; Bassegoda i Hugas 1985, 123). For
   Manuel González Galván, this type of column, so popular in American
   viceroyalties, was already drawn by Friar Giocondo, based on Vitruvius
   (2006, 154).
23 Turning to José de Siguenza, Carmen González Urdáñez argues that the
   term was not set, as others believe, but was still in the process of emerging:
   "El autorizado redactor de la *Fundación del monasterio de El Escorial*,
   avezado en la gestión del proceso de ejecución de la gran obra real, se
   refiere a Juan Bautista de Toledo como 'maestro en arquitectura.' También,
   redundantemente, lo llama 'arquitecto principal' –architetto' 'quiere
   dezir principal fabricador' había escrito Sagredo –. Nombrando a Juan de
   Herrera o a Francisco de Mora forma Sigüenza otra mezcla, al calificar a
   ambos en sendas ocasiones de 'arquitecto mayor." (The authorized author
   of the *Foundation of El Escorial Monastery*, seasoned in the management
   of executing the great royal work, refers to Juan Bautista de Toledo as
   "master of architecture." Also, redundantly, he calls him "main architect" –
   "architetto" "meaning main maker" – according to Sagredo. Naming
   Juan de Herrera or Francisco de Mora, Sigüenza forms another mixture,

by labelling both of them, in each occasion, as senior architect; González Urdáñez 2010, 261).

24 "Cuando cada parte importante del edificio está, además convenientemente proporcionada en razón al acorde entre lo alto y lo ancho, entre lo ancho y lo profundo, y cuando todas estas partes tiene también su lugar en la simetría total del edificio, obtenemos la euritmia." (When each important part of the building is conveniently proportioned in height and width, in width and depth, and when all these parts also have their place in the total symmetry of the building, we obtain eurythmy; Caramuel y Lobkowitz 1984, 18).

25 Utilizing Américo Castro's insight, John G. Weiger prefers to see the "real" object within any interpretation of the text: "In short, the metaphysical significance attached to an episode like that of Clavileño ultimately rests on the physical apprehension of reality [...] Stated quite simply, in the present instance any comical, ethical, social or psychological aspects of Sancho's description have their basis in *what he did in fact see*" (1985, 103). My point is that the objects that emerge from the words of the text are illusory. Thus, Cervantes seeks to reinforce the illusion by making edifices unstable and metamorphic, for the illusion of the text is a reflection of the illusion of the world, and vice versa.

26 Discussing ekphrasis, the bringing before one's eyes an object in a text, Murray Krieger explains that it will first bring exhilaration, then end in exasperation: "The first asks for language to freeze itself into a spatial form. Yet, it retains an awareness of the incapacity of words to come together at an instant [...] as if in an unmediated impact [...] to realize the nostalgic dream of an original, pre-fallen language of corporeal presence" (Krieger 1992, 10).

2 Temples and Tombs

1 "But just as Virgil wished to destroy his unrevised *Aeneid*, so Petrarch expresses dissatisfaction with his *Africa*, a poem sketched in broad design that would remain unfinished in detail" (Kennedy 2002, 149).

2 "Writing like David is profoundly different from writing like Virgil or even Ovid [...] There is no 'rota Davidica.' If David can indeed outdo Homer, Hesiod, Pindar and the others, then a pious poet – or an ambitious one – would be wise to venture out past pagan hymnody into divine poetry" (Prescott 2002, 210).

3 For a detailed study of Cervantes' literary career see De Armas (2002b, 268–86).

4 Although the author is equated with Cervantes, we should keep in mind that this is a kind of self-fashioning in which he shows the aspects he wishes to underline, thus fictionalizing his biography.

5 I am using Francisco López Estrada and María Teresa López García-Berdoy's edition (1995), which I have on hand, and have consulted Juan Montero's edition (2014). The English translation is a late edition, by Gordon Willoughby and James Gyll (1892).

6 "[L]os elementos constitutivos se reducen en forma drástica hasta quedar simbolizados en un sustantivo mínimo. Un prado, un arroyo, unas fuentes, unos árboles, tal es el escenario usual en la *Diana*." (The constitutive elements are drastically reduced until they end up symbolized in a minimal noun. A meadow, a stream, some fountains, some trees, such is the usual scenery in *Diana*; Avalle-Arce 1974, 77.)

7 "… the harmony of the stars and musical concords" (Vitruvius 1960, 12).

8 Indeed, as early as 1972, Margarita Levisi foregrounded the importance of painting in *La Galatea* (1972, 293–325).

9 The four main stories are the story of Lisandro and Leónida; the tale of the twins Teolinda and Leonarda and their potential lovers, Artidoro and Galercia; the story of the two ideal friends, Timbrio and Silerio, whose misfortune lies in loving the same woman, Nísida; and the loves of the rich shepherds Rosaura and Grisaldo, whose parents forbid the marriage, thus making it possible for Artandro to kidnap Rosaura and take her away from the region to León.

10 "[L]os cánones poéticos que tan bien conocía Cervantes, se desmoronan ante el asesinato […] La historia no tiene nada de pastoril: ocurre en un pueblo de Andalucía entre hidalgos, y el ambiente se hace irrespirable por el vendaval de odios y crímenes que azotan. El realismo exagerado de estas venganzas de sangre penetra, sin embargo hasta el proscenio del mundo poético de los pastores." (The poetic canons so well known by Cervantes, crumble in the face of the murder […] The story is far from pastoral: it is set in an Andalusian town among nobles, and the air becomes unbreathable due to the lashing storm of hates and crimes. The exaggerated realism of these blood vendettas penetrates, however, up to the proscenium of the shepherds' poetic world; Avalle-Arce 1974, 232.)

11 According to López Estrada, "Bien de Bandello o de Luigi da Porto pudo haber recordado la novela que le inspiraría el relato de Lisandro y de Leónida. Las diferencias son, sin embargo, muchas […] La tragedia no es doble como en Bandello, pues de los dos enamorados sólo muere ella, y Lisandro queda con el alma en pena vagando por los campos." (Either from Bandello or Luigi da Porto, he could have remembered the novel that would inspire the tale of Lisandro and of Leónida. The differences are, however, many […] The tragedy is not double as it is in Bandello, because, of the two lovers, only she dies, and Lisandro is left with a mourning soul wandering through the fields; 1952, 168.)

12 Dora Issacharoff, discussing this "cruda y violenta muerte" (raw and violent death; 1995, 180), this shocking act in the midst of a pastoral scenario, asserts that it recalls mannerist paintings of the period such as Titian's *Cain Slaying Abel* or *David's Triumph over Goliath* where violence clashes with the bucolic background (1981, 331).

13 The fragments in books 2 and 3 are narrated by Silerio, the fourth tells of the anagnorisis between Timbrio and Nísida, and in the fifth book Timbrio takes up the telling of the tale.

14 On the tale of the two friends in Cervantes see Gil-Oslé (2009). At times, the "intimacy" between the two friends approached homoerotic behaviour in Golden Age literature, as in Lope de Vega's play *La boda entre dos maridos*. On this subject see Julio González Ruiz (2009, 49–78).

15 "Both the age-old tradition connected with friendship and the words La Boétie uses in the *Discourse* contribute to Montaigne's reiteration in his own essay of the idea that friendship is 'sacred and divine,' a 'sacred bond.'" (Atkinson 2012, liii).

16 In a book manuscript, Juan Pablo Gil-Oslé discusses the great changes in weather and the plague as major elements to be considered in the literature of Iberia during the late sixteenth and seventeenth centuries.

17 Juan Jiménez Savariego points to poisonous animals as a possible cause of the plague (1602, 14r). Lope de Vega utilizes the serpent to point to a cause of the plague in his play *El ganso de oro*.

18 In Terrazas' poem Spain is no longer a mother but a "madrastra" (stepmother). We learn from Reyes-Mazzoni: "Otra de las actitudes críticas de Terrazas es que, aun cuando había obtenido un mecenazgo para su obra de alabanza a Cortés, *Nuevo Mundo y Conquista*, no pudo contenerse y evitar criticarlo por su trato a quienes lo acompañaron en su empresa." (Another of Terraza's critical attitudes is that, even when he obtained patronage for his work in praise of Cortés, *New World and Conquest*, he could not resist criticizing his treatment to his companions during this enterprise; 1991, 35).

19 For example, Aurora Egido states, "Los tres primeros libros desembocan en la fiesta de las bodas, el epitalamio y la comedia. Los tres últimos en la elegía." (The first three books flow into the wedding party, the epithalamium and the comedy. The last three into the elegy; 1994, 59.) Lopez Estrada and López García-Berdoy, in their introduction to the edition of *La Galatea* that we are using, also state: "Si se establece una consideración general del movimiento de acción de *La Galatea*, encontramos que los pastores (y los que con ellos se juntan), acaban por confluir en los episodios que actúan como núcleos de reunión. Uno de ellos es el de las bodas de Daranio y Silveria, y el otro el de las exequias de

Meliso. Están situados en lugares equidistantes del libro: el primero en el libro III; y el segundo en el libro VI. Ambos episodios cumplen su función y resultan compatibles con la maraña de las novelas entretejidas; ambos son de ocasión sobre todo para que se reúnan pastores y pastoras de toda clase." (If we can establish a general patter for the movement of the action in *La Galatea*, we find that shepherds (and those that are with them) end up by converging in the episodes that act as meeting points. One such nucleus is the wedding of Daranio and Silveria, and the other is Meliso's funeral. They are located in equidistant places of the book: the first one in book III; and the second in book VI. Both episodes fulfil their purpose and are compatible with the tangle of interwoven novels; both create a meeting place for shepherds and shepherdesses of all kinds; 1995, 45.) Juan Ramón Muñoz Sánchez prefers to divide the text differently: a first part comprising the first five books that take place in six days, and the last book, which encompasses five days (2003, 98).

20 Mexía asserts that this tale is found in authors such as Seneca and Pliny. It also appears in Servius' commentaries on Virgil (Mexía 1989, 1.729–30).

21 Lopez Estrada and López García-Berdoy in the introduction to their edition of *La Galatea* explain: "Meliso es, en el caso de las honras fúnebres del libro VI, Don Diego Hurtado de Mendoza. Pocas son, sin embargo, las alusiones históricas del canto de los pastores: referencia a la estancia en Venecia como embajador; el trance de fortuna y el retiro, fructífero a las letras." (Meliso is, in the case of the funeral honors in Book VI, Don Diego Hurtado de Mendoza. Few are, however, the historical allusions in the shepherds' song: reference to the stay in Venice as an ambassador; the trance of fortune and the retirement, fruitful in the literature; 1995, 165.) On this subject see also Adrián J. Sáez's article of epitaphs in Cervantes (2019a, 179–82)

22 I cite from a speech given by Juan Varo Zafra and published by the Academia de Buenas Letras de Granada, some years before the appearance of his 2012 book: "Frente al modelo de historia triunfante que indaga en el mito fundacional o en el momento decisivo que gesta el carácter de un pueblo o frente al relato histórico centrado en las hazañas de un personaje determinado, *Guerra* ofrece el cuadro – más que el proceso – de la disolución de un mundo. La elegía, por tanto, se configura como un mecanismo de recuperación de un pasado perdido en cuanto que perdido. La ironía, por su parte, es un instrumento de corrosión del presente; degrada la realidad, socava sus fundamentos y la hace si no más real, más verdadera." (Next to the model of triumphant history that searches for the founding myth or the decisive moment that gestates a nation's character or next to the historical tale focused on the feats of a determined character, *Guerra* offers a picture – more than the process – of a world dissolving. The

elegy, therefore, is configured as a mechanism for the recovery of a lost past. The irony, then, is a tool for corroding the present; it degrades reality, undermines its foundations and makes it, if not more real, truer; 2009, 19.)

3 Unstable Architectures

1 I will be citing from Andrés Murillo's 1978 edition of *Don Quixote*. I have also consulted Francisco Rico's edition (2007). I have used Charles Jarvis' translation in the Oxford World Classics (2008). In references I first give the part and chapter of the book and then the page number of that edition. This is followed by a semicolon, after which I include the page of the English translation.

2 Imprisonment apparently ran in the family. As Javier Irigoyen-García explains, "in 1552 Rodrigo Cervantes (father of Miguel de Cervantes) claimed that he had been unlawfully imprisoned because of debts, since he was an hidalgo" (2017, 40).

3 In a review Ruth Pike corrects a passage from Mary Elizabeth Perry's *Crime and Society in Early Modern Seville* to read in this manner (Pike 1981, 406; Perry 1980, 85).

4 María Veláquez de Castro, "Pedro de León," *Real Academia de la Historia*, http://dbe.rah.es/biografias/20525/pedro-de-leon.

5 A manuscript collecting all Hernán Ruiz's writings is today located at the library of the Universidad Politécnica de Madrid (Navascués Palacios 1971, 295–331).

6 The need for men at the galleys was such that "[l]os adúlteros, los alcahuetes, y los homosexuales que no llegaban a merecer tanta pena como la hoguera, acabaron recibiendo sistemáticamente el correctivo del remo a lo largo del siglo XVI" (adulterers, pimps, and homosexuals who did not come to deserve a penalty such as the stake, ended up systematically receiving the corrective of the oar, throughout the sixteenth century; Rodríguez Ramos 1990, 129).

7 Sánchez Jiménez writes: "se impone realizar un análisis detallado del funcionamiento de esta auto-representación [...] como los casos en los que algunos personajes que aparecen en el texto pudieran ser indudablemente reconocidos en el siglo XVII como máscaras o *personae* de Lope de Vega" (it is imperative to carry out a detailed analysis of the role of self-representation [...] since some characters who appear in the texts could surely be recognized during the seventeenth-century as Lope de Vega's masks or *personae*; 2006, 16).

8 Augustin Redondo asserts that Don Quixote "ha subvertido el orden social al atacar la potestad del amo, es decir una de las bases de la organización jerárquica de la sociedad" (has subverted the social order by attacking

the master's power, that is, one of the bases of society's hierarchical organization; 1998b, 317).

9 L. Rodríguez Ramos explains: "Algunos años antes de la Batalla de Lepanto, en 1566, Felipe II promulgó una pragmática, por medio de la cual se incrementó la duración de las condenas a galeras, y se introdujeron en el catálogo de delitos sancionables con ellas, varios punidos anteriormente con penas corporales muy graves […] Tras la promulgación de la citada pragmática de 1566, el primer hurto cometido por un ladrón se penó ya con seis años de galeras." (Some years before the Battle of Lepanto, in 1566, Philip II issued a pragmatic sanction, through which the duration of the galley sentences was increased, and added to the catalogue of crimes punishable by the galleys were several that had been previously punished by severe bodily penalties […] After the issue of the cited pragmatic sanction in 1556, the first robbery committed by a thief was penalized with six years of the galleys; 1990, 128.)

10 Quevedo's *El Parnaso español* (The Spanish Parnassus, 1648) brings together hundreds of his poems under the tutelage of the Muses. His *Las tres Musas últimas castellanas* (The final three Muses, 1670) was published long after his death and refers to the three remaining Muses: Euterpe, Muse of amorous poetry; Caliope, of satiric poetry; and Urania, of religious verse.

11 For Don Quixote and the virtues see Pérez Martínez (2012).

12 Javier Portús prefers to take this image of the melancholy artist (and poet) back to the fifteenth century: "A partir del siglo XV se produjo un intenso proceso de […] reivindicación de la aportación específica del individuo en los procesos culturales. Como consecuencia de todo ello, se enriqueció notablemente la casuística relacionada con la caracterología del poeta, el pintor, etc., a los que se asignaban una serie de características relacionadas con sus temperamentos, humores, o con los rasgos de su personalidad." (From the fifteenth century onwards there was an intense process of […] vindication of the specific input of the individual in cultural processes. As a consequence, casuistry was notably enriched when it pertained to the characterology of the poet, the painter, etc., who were assigned a series of characteristics related to their temperaments, humours, or personality traits; 2008, 136.)

13 Francisco de Holanda, in his *Roman Dialogues* (1548), has Michelangelo speak of talented artists who "are unsociable not from pride but because they deem only very few spirits worthy of their art; […] and in order not to debase the elevated imagination that keeps their mind in perpetual ecstasy" (Van den Doel 2010, 108).

14 Robert Burton affirms "that the Devil, being a slender and incomprehensible spirit, can easily insinuate and wind himself into human

bodies, and cunningly couched in our bowels, vitiate our healths, terrify our souls with fearful dreams" (1938, 174).

15 Clydesdale quotes here from the *Three Books of Life* (Ficino 1989, 213).

16 "'Mi manto' engloba así las estrategias narrativas que podrán eludir y superar la censura" ('My cloak' thus encompasses the narrative strategies that could evade and overcome censorship; Rodríguez Valles 2007, 507).

17 Gómez is citing here the work of Joost Van Baak (2009, 60)

18 "Miguel de Cervantes Saavedra, un hombre que toda su vida luchó por labrarse una identidad única y escapar los prejuicios a base de perseguir una mayor autonomía personal, ofrece en su ópera máxima una visión alternativa a los límites de las estrictas convenciones sociales padecidas por los españoles de su época." (Miguel de Cervantes Saavedra, a man who fought throughout his life to shape a unique identity and escape prejudice by pursuing a greater personal autonomy, offers in his magnum opus an alternative vision to the limitations of strict social conventions suffered by the Spanish people of his time; Gómez 2016, 120.) Other reasons have been proposed for this departure, from Carroll Johnson's notion of a mid-life crisis to the possibility that Cervantes seeks to compensate for some inadequacy in lineage (De Armas 2011).

19 Founded in 1476, Siguenza acquired some renown, which it held until the early sixteenth century, boasting Pedro Ciruelo as a professor. By Cervantes' time it had declined and decayed. It was finally closed in 1837.

20 All the activity that takes place seems to conform to Pythagorean norms, the novel constructing a cosmos from which the knight will deviate. Following Pythagoras, the first chapter is divided into at least four quaternities: (1) four basic possessions; (2) four names and occupations; (3) consensus as to who might be the four best knights; (4) onomastics of departure.

21 Claustrophobia was first discovered by a physician in Paris in the 1870s, and some attribute the inception of this phobia to the rise of the city.

22 Julia Domínguez has spoken of Don Quixote as Janus but in a very different context: "Don Quixote embodies the characteristics of the Janus face, a visual representation of one who looks at the past and the future simultaneously, thereby intertwining seemingly dissimilar timeframes into a continuum," *Cognitive Approaches to Early Modern Spanish Literature* (2016, 75).

23 These include the two friends (barber and priest) as well as Don Quixote's niece and the housekeeper.

24 These poems are not included in the English translation.

25 The main characters, as William Worden has pointed out, undergo witty transformations, starting with an hidalgo who becomes a knight, a labourer who assumes the role of a squire, and a peasant woman who is

somehow transformed into the knight's beloved and incorporeal Princess Dulcinea (2010, 118).

26 Margaret Greer points out that Calderón names the gracioso in his play *Casa con dos puertas* (House with two doors) Calabazas as a reminder of this court jester (2002, 161–2).

27 Augustin Redondo equates the pinwheel with the windmill, stating, "[E]l molinillo es efectivamente uno de los emblemas de la locura, como lo demuestra el caso del 'loco' (bufón) de Felipe IV, Calabacillas, pintado por Velázquez con un molinete en la mano izquierda" (the pinwheel is indeed an emblem of madness, as demonstrated in the case of the 'crazy' (jester) of Felipe IV, Calabacillas, painted by Velázquez with a pinwheel in his left hand; 1998b, 333).

28 The episode could have alternately made use of the giant Cacus, whom Cervantes had identified in the prologue as a thief and had included in the episode with the innkeeper: "no menos ladrón que Caco" (as arrant a thief as Cacus; 1978, 1.2.84; 2008, 29).

29 On Dante as model for the windmills episode see Avery (1961–2, 1–28) and De Armas (2006, 147–51).

30 Edy Legrand, alongside Picasso, Matisse, and Derain, represented France. He was the only one to receive an honourable mention. http://cervantes. dh.tamu.edu. His illustrations of Cervantes' novel are available at http:// book-graphics.blogspot.com/2013/10/don-quixote-illustrations-by-edy-legrand.html.

31 Some have questioned the title of the drawing, arguing that it merges together a number of traditions (Lugli 2019, 69–91).

32 Cesare Cesarino included two separate images: "The posture of the man in the square is Apollonian: every portion of the body becomes part of the stable order. Even the hairstyle contributes to the figure's dignified carriage. However, the man in the circle is Dionysiac to the extent that his arms and feet seem oversized, and his hair resembles vine leaves. In fact there seems to be a reference to his erect penis in the commentary" (Sgarbi 1993, 44).

33 These illustrations can be viewed together at https://leonardodavinci. stanford.edu.

34 On Dante as model for the windmills episode see Avery (1961–2, 1–28) and De Armas (2006, 147–51).

35 In the Bible Nimrod is merely a mighty hunter. In other texts he becomes a king, the builder of the tower of Babel, and even a giant (the latter mainly in the medieval period).

36 Ephialtes, a giant whose name means "nightmare," wanted to storm Olympus with his brother so that they could capture Hera and Artemis.

37 It being Friday, he is offered "truchuela" or cod, but he takes this to mean
   troutlings and he is willing to eat several (Cervantes 1978, 1.2.86; 2008, 20).
   Carolyn Nadeau emphasizes the importance of Friday as abstinence day in
   Spain, because cookbooks included recipes for a number of different fish
   (2016, 154). For the difficulty of translating this passage into English, see
   Thomas Lathrop (2006, 241–2).

38 Don Quixote labels Thebes as the city of one hundred gates. Once again,
   there is confusion because it was the Egyptian Thebes that was thus
   described; the Greek city had seven gates.

39 Key literary texts on the subject are Statius' epic poem the *Thebaid* and
   Aeschylus' tragedy *Seven against Thebes*.

40 "The poet's adage, All the world's a stage,
   Has stood the test of each revolving age;
   Another simile perhaps will bear,
   'Tis a Stage Coach, where all must pay the fare;
   Where each his entrance and his exit makes,
   And o'er life's rugged road his journey takes."
   "Times of the Day," in *The Works of William Hogarth in a Series of
   Engravings: With Descriptions, and a Comment on their Moral Tendency by
   the Rev. John Trusler*, 83. See the Gutenberg Project, www.gutenberg.org/
   files/22500/22500-h/22500-h.htm.

41 *The Rape of Lucretia* is documented at the Alcázar de Madrid starting in
   1616. Juan de Piña describes the painting in detail in *Caso prodigioso y cueva
   encantada* (Prodigious cases and enchanted cave, 1628); Pacheco mentions
   it in *Los diálogos de la pintura* (Dialogues on painting, 1633); and Vicencio
   Juan de Lastanosa has a copy of it in his collection (Vosters 1990, 154, 266,
   309).

42 Each planetary deity often has two or more possible animals to pull their
   chariot. Luna is said to have a dark and a white horse – "quando parece
   de día denota el cavallo blanco, y quando de noche, el negro" (when she
   appears during the day the white horse is seen, and during the night,
   the black one; Pérez de Moya 2002, 638). Others claim that the Moon's
   chariot was led by a mule, while others yet visualize it with two deer (638).
   Pérez de Moya lists two horses for Mars, called "Terror y Pavor" (Terror
   and Dread; 549). In many images and paintings Mars rides a chariot
   lead by a horse or two horses and is accompanied by a wolf. At times,
   two wolves lead the chariot (Seznec 1972, 190–2). Many of these images,
   according to Seznec, are derived from Albricus, an English twelfth-century
   mythographer.

43 The Collegio del Cambio was the money changer's guild. Roettgen
   states: "The chief responsibility of the Arte del Cambio was to guarantee
   the value of the coinage in circulation" (1997, 254). The Sala di Udienzia

exhibits paintings of the virtues as well as of Greek and Roman men who exhibited these qualities. There are also Old Testament prophets and classical Sibyls. But there is also a planetary cycle in the vault that many think is unrelated to the main paintings. Each of the gods "stands or sits enthroned on a car drawn by his or her attendant animals. The wheels of the cars are ornamented with the appropriate constellations" (Roettgen 1997, 260). Saturn has dragons, Jupiter is led by eagles, Mars has two horses, Venus two doves, Mercury two sparrows, and Luna two nymphs. See also Joseph Antenucci Becherer (1997, 283 and 238, fig. 106).

44 A passing reference to the seven fays can be found in the Spanish ballad of the *Infantina encantada* (Enchanted infantine) where a knight finds a beautiful young woman sitting in a tree, combing her hair. She claims that she was enchanted by the seven fays and had to remain there for seven years. The time is up, and she offers to go with the knight. His indecision dooms him (Rogers, 1974 164).

4 Windows

1 "… andar buscando estas aventuras que vuestra merced busca por estos desiertos y encrucijadas de caminos, donde, ya que se venzan y acaben las más peligrosas, no hay quien las vea ni sepa, y así, se han de quedar en perpetuo silencio" (wandering up and down in quest of those adventures your worship is seeking through these deserts and cross-ways, where, though you overcome and achieve the most perilous, there is nobody to see or know anything of them; Cervantes 1978, 1.21.258; 2008, 157).

2 "Tirante conoce a Carmesina después de haber errado a lo largo de dos enteros libros y poco menos que toda Europa. Palmerín ocupa un lugar en la corte y el corazón de Polinarda (cap. 30) tras haber combatido con un dragón, algunos caballeros, un gigante." (Tirante meets Carmesina after wandering through two whole books and a little less than all of Europe. Palmerín takes a place in court and in Polinarda's heart (chap. 30) after battling a dragon, several knights, a giant; Martín Moran 1991, 282.)

3 In part 2 the knight corrects Sancho's description of Dulcinea's abode: "¿Bardas de corral se te antojaron aquéllas […]? No debían de ser sino galerías, o corredores, o lonjas o como las llaman, de ricos y reales palacios." (Pales did you fancy them to be […]? You must mean galleries, arcades, or cloisters of some rich and royal palace; Cervantes 1978, 2.8.93; 2008, 514.)

4 Let us recall that the first window appears during the inquisition of the knight's books (Cervantes 1978, 1.6.112; 2008, 48). The second instance is found in chapter 48 when Maritornes plays a trick on Don Quixote. Pretending to be a great princess, she asks for his hand through a hole

since there are no windows at the inn that look to the outside: "Es pues, el caso, que en toda la venta no había ventana que saliese al campo, sino un agujero de un pajar, por donde echaban la paja por defuera. A este agujero se pusieron las dos semidoncellas." (Now you must know, that the inn had no window towards the field, only a kind of spike-hole to the straw-loft, by which they took in or threw out their straw. At this hole, then, this pair of demi-lasses planted themselves; 1978, 1.43.525–26; 2008, 390.) This paucity of windows will change in part 2 of the novel where we need only recall the knight's room in the palace of the duke and the duchess. The window serves as a triple conduit from inside to outside and vice versa. This episode of the "torture chamber" will be discussed in chapter 6.

5 Curiously, no mention is made of glass windows in Cervantes. His glass licentiate, in one of the *Novelas ejemplares*, is an extended meditation on this material, albeit not related to windows.

6 Mulvey states: "In Hitchcock, by contrast, the male hero does see precisely what the audience sees […] he takes fascination with an image through scopophilic eroticism as the subject of the film" (1997, 445). Turning to the figure of Jeff in *Rear Window*, she states that "his enforced inactivity, binding him to his seat as a spectator, puts him squarely in the phantasy position of a cinema audience" (446).

7 The unreal aspects of "old-fashioned romance" metamorphose into the modern in the tales by the uses of money (Quint 2003, 16).

8 In the notes to his edition of *Don Quijote*, Diego Clemencín points to *Belianís de Grecia* where the Emperor of Constantinople and the King of Hungary are at the window: "parándose a una finiestra del castillo, vieron venir de hácia la ciudad tanto número de caballeros, que pasaban de tréinta mil" (standing next to a window of the castle, they saw coming from the city such a number of knights, surpassing thirty thousand; Cervantes 1833, 1.167). Clemencín adds: "En la história de *Florisel de Niquea* y otras, hay ejemplos de Reyes, Príncipes y Princesas, asomados á las finiestras de los palácios para recibir á caballeros andantes y otros personages principales" (in the story of *Florisel de Niquea* and others, there are examples of Kings, Princes and Princesses, leaning out of the palace windows to receive errant-knights and other main characters; Cervantes 1833, 1.167).

9 "Helisena cassi desnuda como en su lecho estaba solamente la camisa y cubierta de un manto, y salieron ambas a la huerta, y el lunar hacía muy claro" (Rodríguez de Montalvo 1987, 1.287).

10 Valentín Nuñez Rivera argues that the main violation has to do with that of the secrecy the lover must preserve: "le conduce a incurrir en uno de los más graves impedimentos para el amor en la norma sentimental; es decir, la contravención del secreto amoroso, punto de partida para todo el

desarrollo posterior de la trama" (it leads him to incur one of the gravest impediments to love in the sentimental norm; that is, the contravention of secret love, the starting point for all the plot's future development; 2015, 215). This critic points to the sentimental novel as model and refers to Dorothy Severin who had proposed Diego de San Pedro's *Arnalte y Lucenda* as model (Severin 1997, 145–51).

11 Although the relationship between Cardenio and Luscinda appears doomed due to his actions, later in the novel Cervantes forges a providential meeting at the inn where numerous plots come to a happy conclusion. As Timothy McCallister states, the events at the inn show that "[h]ow a half dozen plot lines intersect at a single point, how uniform gloom gives way to ubiquitous sunshine is the stuff of marvel" (2011, 109). McCallister accuses Cardenio of narcissism and cowardliness but points out that these traits are at first hidden from the reader: "readers may be inclined at first to respond sympathetically to this mysterious tormented soul. Cervantes is able to cultivate our sympathy then gradually upend it with evidence that the narrator is unreliable" (112).

12 "As seen in the exclusion of *Sensualidad*'s image from the Lisbon canvas, the authorities tried to restrict the public from accessing materials they thought could lead to lust" (López Alemany 2008, 114).

13 One of the versions of Titian's *Danae* was composed in 1544 for Alessandro Farnese. Titian finished it in Rome between 1545 and 1546 (Pedrocco 2001, 192). Using a letter by Giovanni della Casa and other evidence, Cathy Santore asserts that the painting was done to win the favour of the grandson of the pope and that, to do so, Titian used the head of the elderly cardinal's mistress (Santore 1991, 415). The cardinal appreciated Titian's daring, and this painting hung at his palazzo for many years.

14 "Without the 'cloak of mythology,' the nude image with the features of a recognizable courtesan would have been more than unseemly in a prelate's residence" (Talvacchi 1999, 46).

15 The Ovidian tale (1986, 4.55–165) shows how the lovers were able to speak through an opening in the wall between their houses. This foments their love, but it also brings about their undoing. On the three references to this myth in *Don Quixote* see Alberto Sánchez (1998, 9–22). He finds this single reference in part 1 to be the least applicable. On Cervantes and Ovid see William Worden (2010, 116–35); and on Cervantes' use of the term *Ovidio español* see José Montero Reguera (1996, 327–34).

16 In *Tirant lo Blanch* we discover a chamber replete with mythical tapestries depicting the loves of Pyramus and Thisbe, Aeneas and Dido, and Tristan and Isolde. In *Palmerín de Inglaterra* we encounter the Casa de la Tristeza (House of Sadness), its walls covered with the stories of unhappy loves such as Hero and Leander, Pyramus and Thisbe, Aeneas and Dido,

Philomena, Medea, Progne, Ariadne, Phaedra, and Pasiphae (Sales Dasí 2009–20, 47–8).

17 Georges Guntert has pointed to this possibility in an essay on *El curioso impertinente* (*The Curious Impertinent*): "Es indudable que el recuerdo de la leyenda de Candaules ha inspirado esta escena, compuesta de dos amigos observadores, uno poderoso, el otro algo más humilde, y de la novia de este último, contemplada 'a la luz de una vela'. Cervantes ha imaginado un magnífico 'nocturno', como los de la pintura contemporánea, desde Caravaggio hasta Georges de la Tour, por no hablar del flamenco Jacob Jordaens, a quien se debe no solo una 'Adoración del niño' iluminada con una vela, sino también un famoso desnudo que representa a la esposa de Candaules." (Undoubtedly the memory of the legend of Candaules has inspired this scene, composed of two watching friends, one powerful, the other more humble, and the latter's girlfriend, contemplated 'by candlelight.' Cervantes has imagined a magnificent 'nocturne' similar to those in contemporary painting, from Caravaggio to Georges de la Tour, not to mention the Flemish Jacob Jordaens, to whom not only an 'Adoration of the Child [Jesus]' lighted with a candle is owed but also a famous nude that represents Candaules' wife; 2015, 186.) Herodotus was not translated into Spanish during the Golden Age.

18 Dorotea is by far a stronger figure than Luscinda. Anne J. Cruz explains: "for the purpose of realist narrative, marriage to Fernando is also the means by which she achieves a degree of social success [...] By virtue of her virtue, she is his equal when nobility is measured by conduct and not by birthright" (2005, 630).

19 Aeschylus' and Cervantes' tragic views may be quite similar: "Their view of the enemy's hamartia, though, was not necessarily an indictment of the Other but a warning to their own people not to exceed their humanity. *Koros* should not lead to boastfulness and indifference toward the Other" (De Armas 1998, 96).

20 Cardenio is part of the dangerous outside that threatens Luscinda. At the same time, the moment of voyeurism deep in a nocturnal landscape foregrounds the erotic through chiaroscuro. As if to emphasize the textuality of this gendered representation, the visual is tied to what I would call a written voyeurism: "Procuraba siempre don Fernando leer los papeles que yo a Luscinda enviaba, y los que ella me respondía" (Don Fernando procured a sight of the letters I wrote to Lucinda, and her answers; Cervantes 1978, 1.24.296; 2008, 189). Cardenio, in many ways, is a new Lope de Vega who allows his superior, the Duque de Sessa, now named Fernando, to read his love letters.

21 Wanting to ascertain that she will be faithful, that is, that she will kill herself, Cardenio watches the ceremony, hidden between two tapestries

and a window: "tuve lugar de ponerme en el hueco que hacía una ventana de la mesma sala que con las puntas y remates de dos tapices se cubría por entre las cuales podía yo ver, sin ser visto, todo cuanto en la sala se hacía" (I had leisure to place myself in the hollow of a bow-window of the hall, behind the hangings, where two pieces of tapestry met; whence, without being seen myself, I could see all that was done in the hall; Cervantes 1978, 1.27.337–8; 2008, 225). This is a very curious use of the window. Although Cardenio is not outside, it is as if he were looking in through the window. He thus partakes of the danger outside and of the fraught situation inside. From that space he hears her say yes before she faints at her wedding. Cardenio thus has proof that she is unfaithful to him. But this proof is suspect. If she had been "faithful" as he would have wanted, she would have killed herself.

22 All these instances of voyeurism are replicated in the scenes before Dorotea's tale, when the priest, the barber, and Cardenio himself observe her. Fajardo asserts: "The voyeur's interest depends as much on what he sees as on what he anticipates seeing" (1984, 93). In other words, although Lucinda may be dressed as a man, she reveals enough of her body that the voyeurs may expect to view her as a beautiful woman.

23 The gothic often uses the enclosed house as a place for eerie happenings, as in Poe's *The Fall of the House of Usher* and James' *Turn of the Screw*. In both, windows are prominent, opening and closing on their own in the first, and used as frames for apparitions in the second.

24 This illustration appears in several editions such as Paris (1836–7), London-Bohn (1842), and London-Willoughby (1852). See the "Textual Iconography of Don Quixote," at Texas A&M University, a project directed by Eduardo Urbina. http://cervantes.dh.tamu.edu.

25 Valbuena Briones used the term *espacios reducidos* in his 1958 book. Francisco Díaz de Revega states of Valbuena's book: "Contiene cuatro capítulos, podemos imaginar que correspondientes a las cuatro lecciones que debió de tener el curso impartido: La palabra, El último estilo de Calderón, Calderón, el demonio y las estrellas y Los espacios reducidos. Se propone, según sus propias palabras, en estos estudios examinar varias facetas del dramaturgo." (It contains four chapters, we can imagine each corresponds to the four lessons he taught in the course he gave: The Word; The Last Calderonian Style; Calderón, the Devil and the Stars; and The Confined Spaces. These studies propose, in his own words, to examine several facets of the playwright; 2014.) Valbuena again used the term in his 1965 book on Calderón and continued to use it repeatedly, often to refer to the confined spaces of *La dama duende* (*The Phantom Lady*).

26 See, for example, Francisco Ayala (1965, 287–306), Diana de Armas Wilson (1987, 22), and Frederick De Armas (2006, 201–4).

27 On their bond see the Paris (1836–7) edition, in which the illustrator
Tony Johannot shows Anselmo talking intimately to Lotario, on the right.
Lotario, fond of hunting, holds a falcon.

28 "[S]e pasaron muchos días que, sin decir Lotario palabra a Camila,
respondía a Anselmo que la hablaba" (now many days passed, and
Lothario, though he spoke not a word to Camilla on the subject, told
Anselmo that he had; Cervantes 1978, 1.33.414; 2008, 292).

29 "[L]e viese salir al romper el alba; el cual sin conocer quién era, pensó
primero que debía de ser alguna fantasma, mas cuando le vio caminar,
embozarse y encubrirse con cuidado y recato, cayó de su simple
pensamiento" (seeing him once go out of the house at break of day; who,
not knowing who he was, thought, at first, it must be some apparition.
But when he saw him steal off, muffling himself up, and concealing
himself with care and caution, he changed one foolish opinion for another;
Cervantes 1978, 1.34.426; 2008, 303).

30 See the many balconies and windows of Anselmo's home as depicted by
René Pauw in the Paris edition (1947). http://cervantes.dh.tamu.edu/.

31 "[V]io que un hombre saltaba por la ventana a la calle" (he saw a man leap
down from the window into the street; Cervantes 1978, 1.35.442; 2008, 317).

32 There is only one more reference to a window in the interpolated tale, and
it is also linked to Leonela. Camila asks her to call Lotario to come into the
house so that they can put on a "play" for the hidden Anselmo that would
prove Camila's innocence.

33 There is only one hint: Lotario's house is located in the neighborhood of
San Juan.

34 Marina Brownlee asserts: "The gesturing hand, along with the symbols
of religion and wealth that it wears, present the reader with a strikingly
hybrid mystery" (2005, 572).

35 The letters are actually translated by a renegade from Murcia. In this way
the tale replicates the very story of Don Quixote, written in Arabic and
translated.

36 A parallel that has often been invoked is the "white hand" of the Moorish
lady, which recalls Dorotea's alluring and delicate white feet.

37 The first and seventh tales, he argues, are complementary: both deal with a
"pastoral" setting (Immerwahr 1958, 121–35).

38 Robert L. Hathaway divides the tale into three parts: "(1) a personal
declaration which whets curiosity and begs explanation; (2) a narrative
of a past event; and (3) an ending which brings one back to 'the present'"
(1995, 60). He also explains the relation between goat-chasing and the
themes of the tale: "the goat and Leandra are one and the same, the animal
in imitation of the woman, each fleeing the fold (flock / family protection)
for no good reason but the impulse to seek contentment" (62). He adds:

"The adjective *manchada* may literally refer to a multicolour-spotted animal, but the association with *mancha* in its definition of an affront to one's honour cannot be overlooked" (67).

39 On the relationship between the French romance and Ana Caro's play, see Elizabeth Ordoñez (1985, 3–15) and Judith Whitenack (1990)

40 "Vicente de la Rosa representa, con no menos transparencia, un ejemplar del topos – el 'miles gloriosus' fanfarrón y jactancioso – que casi invariablemente se utiliza en la literatura para la reducción burlesca de esa profesión" (Vincent de la Rosa represents, with no less transparency, an exemplar of the topos – the braggart and boastful 'miles gloriosus' – that is used in literature almost invariably to mockingly reduce that career; Rodríguez, Tisinger, and Utley 1995, 86–7).

41 A number of the tapestries in the romances, as noted, include Helen of Troy. In addition, Sales Dasí has pointed to a tapestry from the Church of Zamora entitled *La tienda de Aquiles* (Achilles' tent), that includes her. The five-fold structure reflects that of the *Roman de Troie* by Benoit de Sainte-Maure. At the very centre Helen of Troy, accompanied by two other ladies, observes a battle from the battlements of Troy (Sales Dasí 2009–10, 60).

42 In the second part of the novel the knight proclaims that Toboso will become known due to Dulcinea, "por quien su lugar será famoso y nombrado en los venideros siglos, como lo ha sido Troya por Elena, y España por la Cava, aunque con mejor título y fama" (for whom her town will be famous and renowned in the ages to come, as Troy was of Helen, and Spain has been for (La) Cava, though upon better grounds and a juster title; 1978, 2.32.293; 2008, 682).

43 The novel plays with differing visions of empire. Although Don Quixote's desire to restore a Golden Age echoes the image of Charles V as seen in Andronica's prophecy in the *Orlando furioso*, the knight's frailties and impotence cast doubt on his ability to bring about an imperial *renovatio* (De Armas 2006, 113–33). More recently, Jesús Botello (2016) sees in Don Quixote and the novel as a whole not a parody of Charles V but elements critical of Philip II, such as excessive writing and bureaucracy, criticism of the judicial system, and an inability to reform the cavalry.

5 Grotesque

1 Mucius Scaevola, having failed to kill King Porsinna, placed his arm in the fire (Livy, 1.255–63); Mettius Curtius either fell from a horse in a marsh while fighting Romulus or, obeying an oracle, threw himself into a chasm by the Forum (Livy 3.373–7).

2 Before the Julian calendar, the year began in March "at the Kalends of the third month following the winter solstice" (Dupont 1993, 192).

3 "The moon makes her circuit of the heaven in twenty-eight days plus about an hour, and with her return to the sign from which she set forth, completes a lunar month" (Vitruvius 1960, 258).

4 In addition to the sun and the moon, the Pantheon includes the other Ptolemaic planets as the five rows of coffering in the cupola.

5 These pages from Alberto Campo Baeza's *Sharpening the Scalpel* (2019) can be found at https://www.campobaeza.com.

6 Not all artists and architects of the Renaissance believed in the perfection of the Pantheon. Wilson Jones explains: "Architects as distinguished as Antonio da Sangallo, Michelangelo, Palladio and Desgodets judged the building a flawed masterpiece. Apart from the portico […] dissatisfaction focused on the apparent lack of unity between the constituents of the interior elevation: the main order, the attic and the dome […] the attic pilasters fail to align with either the columns below or the coffers above (2000, 189). This, they argued, went against Vitruvian precepts. Indeed, eurithmia was a key to a dispute between Gianlorenzo Bernini and Pope Alexander VII during the second half of the seventeenth century. When the pope wished Bernini to redecorate the inside of the Pantheon, he apparently refused three times, offering only to paint the pilasters in the attic. The refusal, according to a letter from 1762, had to do with Bernini's belief in the perfection of the building, recognizing that "the units of four Corinthian pilasters of the attic conformed to the proportional scheme of the four-part Corinthian pilaster-and-column groups standing on the pavement. In this fundamental insight, the correspondence between upper and lower orders in the Pantheon was thus recognized as one of rhythm and proportion rather than of superimposed ordinances that align vertically" (Marder 1989, 640).

7 Ana Ávila explains: "Es curiosa la comparación que Alonso Madrigal realiza en el *Comento de Eusebio* (1506) entre Sansón y Hércules: aunque llevaron a cabo el mismo esfuerzo, el primero de ellos debe ser tenido por más fuerte. Además obra en detrimento del héroe el hecho de que sus proezas son fabulosas, inciertas, mientras que las de Sansón están avaladas por la verdad de las Sagradas Escrituras." (The comparison made between Samson and Hercules by Alonso de Madrigal in his *Commentary on Eusebius* is rather curious. Even though they put in the same effort, the first should be considered the stronger. Also, the fact that the hero's deeds are fabulous, works against him, while those of Samson are elevated by the truth of the Sacred Scriptures; Ávila 1993, 179.)

8 "The fire, steel and flint stone between the columns are symbols of that order and thus the meaning may be read figuratively as 'I promise to lead the order to glory beyond any heretofore known' that is to say, beyond the confines of Europe" (Rosenthal 1971, 218).

9 From the start, the text makes it clear that Sansón Carrasco has a malicious
  wit. Using physiognomy, the text shows how this is so: "Carirredondo, de
  nariz chata y de boca grande, señales todas de ser de condición maliciosa
  y amigo de donaires y de burlas" (round-faced, flatnosed, and wide-
  mouthed; all signs of his being of a waggish disposition and a lover of wit
  and humour; 1978, 2.3.59; 2008, 484).

10 Michel Moner describes this moment: "Il s'agit d'un *curriculum* burlesque
  donc le caractère parodique est suffisamment transparent pour qu'il ne
  soit pas besoin d'insister [...] De fait, tout se passe comme si le pseudo-
  chevalier s'était approprié, en quelque sorte, les exploits passés et à venir
  de Don Quichotte." (It is a burlesque curriculum in which the parodic
  character is sufficiently transparent that we need not insist on it [...]
  Actually all transpires as if the pseudo-knight had appropriated, in some
  ways, the past and future exploits of Don Quixote; 1989, 229).

11 *Don Quixote* is a work that imitates Ovid's *Metamorphosis*. In order to signal
  that Sansón Carrasco's intention is to mock Don Quixote's aspirations,
  Cervantes, as Michel Moner has noted (1989, 231), will again refer to two
  of these transformations, when a student tells the knight later on that he
  will write a book entitled *Metamorfoseos*, and, "imitando a Ovidio en lo
  burlesco, pinto quién fue la Giralda de Sevilla [...] quiénes los toros de
  Guisando" (imitating Ovid in the burlesque way, I show who the Giralda
  of Sevilla was [...], what the bulls of Guisando are; Cervantes 1978,
  2.22.206; 2008, 610).

12 For a study of its construction see the collection edited by Francisco Molina
  (1981).

13 Using a rather complex argument, Montero Delgado compares Pandora
  with Astraea. Perhaps as the goddess of Truth and Justice moves upwards,
  she leaves behind Pandora's many evils (2000, 245–6).

14 In the fifth dialogue in his book on painting, Pacheco foregrounds the
  conjoining of three arts – painting, sculpture, and architecture – calling
  them a creature with three heads, like Geryon. He even cites Vitruvius
  to define the inner design that must be formed. At the same time, he
  separates architecture from the other two arts, because the architect does
  not perform the work that he envisions, while those who practise the other
  two arts do their own work.

15 "La sacristía se levantó en 1610 y la portada principal en 1618 [...] Los
  dos últimos cuerpos de la torre debieron de construirse por estas mismas
  fechas." (The sacristy was built in 1610 and the main facade in 1618 [...]
  The last two sections of the tower would have been built around this time;
  Marías 1986, 222–3.)

16 Paradoxically, ekphrasis can also be dramatic, using the art object to
  construct a developing action (De Armas 2006, 10).

17 "In this double vision where narrative recalls and redraws a painting upon
a rustic landscape, Sancho appears as Mercury the messenger, Dulcinea as
Primavera/Venus herself, the three peasant women as the three Graces,
the west wind as Zephyr seeking Chloris and the flowers of springtime as
Flora" (De Armas 2002a, 52).

18 There are numerous allusions to Julius Caesar throughout the novel. See
for example Cervantes (1978, 1.56.567 and 578; and 2.57.96, 97, 228, and
361).

19 The columns came from a Roman temple in Calle Mármoles. Other
columns remained in place.

20 The Farnese Hercules was an ancient statue discovered in 1546; it was
moved to the Palazzo Farnese in Rome and surrounded by frescoes of the
twelve labours of Hercules by Annibale Carracci, executed in the 1590s. In
the statue, Hercules carries his club and the lion skin; he holds the apples
of the Hesperides in his hand, which is placed behind his back, to signal
this particular labour. Cardinal Alessandro Farnese was one of the great
collectors of the Renaissance.

21 Cervantes also refers to the Sima de Cabra in the *Celoso extremeño* and the
Viaje del Parnaso. The location is cited in Vélez de Guevara's *Diablo cojuelo*
(1641).

22 I would like to thank Alvaro Molina, who, at my quixotic insistence,
accompanied me on the search for this *sima*. First we drove down the
expressway from Córdoba to Malaga, exiting some thirty miles south,
and then followed a four-lane road to Lucena and on to the small town
of Cabra. After many twists and turns on a narrow path, we came upon
a dirt road that signalled the way to the Sima de Cabra. We followed this
winding and treacherous lane up the mountain, through partially washed-
out bridges. When it ended, we went up on foot along very narrow trails
in search of the cave. I am convinced that we did catch a glimpse of it in
the rocky and arid heights.

23 It is quite possible that Cervantes spent time in Cabra, because Andrés de
Cervantes was mayor of Cabra. See Krysztof Sliwa (2005, 97–126). In 1588,
Miguel de Cervantes gave power of attorney to his cousin Rodrigo, who
resided in Cabra, to deal with the thorny matter of wheat collection and
the incarceration of a sacristan (Lacarta 2005, 119; Sliwa 2005, 429).

24 There were several well-known figures by this name in the sixteenth
century. We are concerned with Juan de Padilla, "el Cartujano." He was a
fifteenth- and early sixteenth-century poet from Seville who is known for
his two lengthy allegorical poems.

25 Lasso de la Vega describes *Los doce triunfos de los doce apóstoles* in the
following manner: "El objeto de Padilla, fue, según sus palabras,
describirlos hechos maravillosos de los Apóstoles, divididos por los doce

signos del zodiaco" (Padilla's purpose was, according to his own words,
to describe the marvellous deeds of the Apostles, divided according to
the signs of the zodiac; 1871, 14). Indeed, the poem was singled out by
Menéndez Pelayo, who labelled Padilla as one of the major poets under
the reign of the Catholic kings. This critic finds reminiscences of Virgil and
Petrarch in Padilla's work, and considers that *Los doce triunfos* is closer
to Dante's *Divine Comedy* than to Juan de Mena's *Laberinto de Fortuna*
(*Fortune's Labyrinth*) (Menéndez Pelayo 1944, 77–99). This assessment is
seconded by Werner Paul Friederich (1950, 44). More recently, José Luis
Vicente García turns to the uses of astrology in the poem in order to
discover the author's original thinking. He shows how Padilla merges
Christianity and astrology by ascribing to each apostle the sign of the
zodiac in which his feast is celebrated. However, in this scheme, three
apostles would overlap with others in a particular sign, so he places
them in a different constellation, giving Aries for example to Santiago el
Menor, who is actually born under Taurus (Martín Fernández 1988, 32–3;
Vicente García 1992, 60). The constellation opposing a particular apostle
shows the hellish descent. Thus, the opposite of Cancer, the sign for San
Pedro, is Capricorn (the goat) representing Saturn (the least bright of
the planets), winter, and the devil as goat or *cabra* (Vicente García 1992,
61). Even though astrology is one of the main structural elements of the
poem, Padilla rejects its superstitious uses. The stars stand as ornament
for God's greatness but are not to be worshipped or deciphered. Thus,
the first mouth of hell includes the idolaters and the astrologers. Each
mouth is related to one of the Ten Commandments, but since there are Ten
Commandments and twelve mouths, the last two are given new meanings.
The eleventh is for those who do not love their neighbours, and the twelfth
is for those who do not love God above all things (Vicente García 1992, 57).

26 Hyginus' work has as its model Eratosthenes' *Catasterisms*. The *Poeticon
astronomicon*, as we have it today, may be a later abridgment, with many
errors, of Hyginus' original text. The text, for example, was used as model
for Alessandro Farnese's frieze in the Salla della Cosmografia at his palace
in Caprarola. For the out-of-place constellations and their meaning and the
importance of Capricorn and Libra in the cardinal's horoscope, see Mary
Quinlan-McGrath (1997, 1067–81).

27 I have been unable to consult the second volume of Enzo Norte Gualdini's
edition of *Los doce triunfos*; thus I am citing from the nineteenth-century
edition of the poem.

28 "Y el portero infernal de los tres rostros" (And let the triple porter of the
shades; 1978, 1.14.184; 2008, 98).

29 Moner (1989, 229) and Martín Morán (2008, 152) have mentioned in
passing a possible link between these two adventures. Helena Percas

de Ponseti has pointed to specific parallels between the Cabra and Montesinos (1975, 2.531–2).

30 Bakhtin actually points to fantastic noses in his discussion of the grotesque. Citing Schneegans, he gives as example caricatures of Napoleon III "that lend the emperor's nose extraordinary dimensions, transforming it either into a pig's snout or a crow's beak" (1984, 306).

31 Cervantes seems to have visited Milan. In his *Novelas ejemplares* he tells of the Licenciado Vidriera's impressions of the city, and in the *Persiles y Sigismunda* he states that the pilgrims spent four days in Milan, only seeing some of its wonders. Although Arcimboldo painted his most famous pictures in Prague while he was at the service of the emperors, there seem to have been copies in Milan (Levisi 1968, 222).

32 Margarita Levisi explains: "No hay noticias de este trabajo en los museos españoles, y esta obra, o una copia de la misma, volvió a aparecer más tarde en los depósitos imperiales en el Belvedere de Viena. En 1872 Francisco José donó el cuadro al Museo de Graz." (There are no notices of this work in Spanish museums, and this work, or a copy of it, appeared later in the imperial storage in the Belvedere in Vienna; 1968, 221.) Actually, Arcimboldo's painting *Spring* is found at the Real Academia de Bellas Artes de San Fernando in Madrid.

33 On this exhibit see "Las floridas obras de Arcimboldo existentes en España, en el Bellas Artes de Bilbao," EFE (8 November 2017), https://www.efe.com.

34 This is very much in tune with Bakhtin's vision of the grotesque, in which "the limits between the body and the world are weakened" (1984, 313).

35 Even from the beginnings of the novel, the knight may have had a certain affinity with the grotesque. Carlos Brito Díaz has compared Arcimboldo's portrait of *The Librarian* with the portrait of our knight (1999, 45–6).

36 Augustin Redondo asserts that there is "una oposición entre dos personajes caracterizados el uno por su locura cómica y el otro por su discreción o sea por su buen seso" (an opposition between two characters, one for his comic madness and the second for his discretion, that is, for his sanity; 1998a, 266).

37 For Augustin Redondo, although the *alfanje* is Moorish in nature, it has to do with a practical element and has no special meaning (1998a, 271).

38 Javier Irigoyen-García has pointed out that the Christian nobility dressed as Moors to take part in the *juegos de caña* (game of canes) throughout the sixteenth and seventeenth centuries. The uses of silk in these attires, otherwise prohibited in sumptuary laws, had become a sign of high status (2017, 43).

39 Presberg accuses Don Diego of never telling the full truth, first speaking of his children, and later admitting that he has only one son. More importantly, he is guilty of cowardice (2001, 205).

40 As José Manuel Blecua has pointed out, these lines recur in a number of works by Cervantes (1948, 141–50). B.B. Aschom notes that the first line is a clear echo of Virgil's *Aeneid* (4.651) (1951, 61–3). Jorge Aladro-Font and Ricardo Ramos Tremolada have produced a catalogue of all the references to Garcilaso in *Don Quixote* (1996, 89–106).

41 For Doré's image from 1863 see the "Textual Iconography of Don Quixote," collected under the direction of Eduardo Urbina at Texas A&M University, http://cervantes.dh.tamu.edu.

42 For details on this image and the biography of the author see "Textual Iconography of Don Quixote" housed at Texas A&M University, http://cervantes.dh.tamu.edu.

43 On the uses of Ovid's myth by Cervantes see Barnés Vázquez (2018, 177–90), and on the myth of Pyramus and Thisbe, discussed briefly in chapter 4, see Alberto Sánchez (1998, 9–22).

6 Treacherous Architectures

1 On the crystal as prophetic instrument see Goodrich (2003, 54).

2 Surely this is a playful moment of satire and imitation because Cervantes had criticized this particular book of chivalry in the inquisition of the knight's library in the first part. Calling it a mendacious work, Cervantes may also be hinting that the Montesinos' episode is a fabrication.

3 Cervantes pokes fun at the idea of the wise man as one who of necessity has a long beard, in his interlude *El retablo de las maravillas*, in which Chirinos and Chanfalla go from town to town presenting a play of magical powers; they claim that the play is invisible to those who are not pure of blood and of legitimate descent. They assert that it was created by the wise Tontonelo (Foolish One), who has a long beard.

4 Comparing Ovid's tale of Pyramus and Thisbe to descriptions in the Cave of Montesinos, John Weiger concludes: "What in the poem is metaphor becomes in the Cave grotesque literal enactment" (1979, 60). He also notes the "grotesque description of Montesinos' rosary" as well as other aspects of the adventure (96). Percas de Ponseti calls the appearance of Dulcinea "grotesque" (1968, 379), and Sullivan makes the grotesque a key element in his book on *Don Quixote*, part 2 (1996).

5 Sullivan points to Renaissance grotesque: "Grotesques were discovered in modern times during the Renaissance in Italy, in the course of excavations of the *Domus Aurea*, or vast palace ordered built by Nero" (1996, 61). However, he does not connect Nero's palace to Cervantes' aesthetics.

6 Henry Sullivan clearly delineates the seven main points of contact between Aeneas' katabasis in the *Aeneid* and Cervantes' *Don Quixote*, as pinpointed by Percas de Ponseti (Sullivan 1996, 32–3). See also McGaha (1980, 34–50).

7 Vespasian decided to build the Colosseum where the lake had been, and
   his son Titus used some of the structures to construct his baths.

8 Bakhtin argues that Vasari pronounces a negative judgment on the
   grotesque, using Vitruvius (Bakhtin 1984, 33). This is not always the case
   in Vasari's *Lives*, in which he often praises artists such as Giovanni da
   Udine and Raphael for their use of the grotesque. Benvenuto Cellini offers
   an explanation of the grotesque that is similar to the one found in Vasari:
   "This name has been given them in modern times from their having been
   found by students in certain underground caves in Rome, which in ancient
   times were used as dwelling-rooms, bath-houses, studies, halls, and so
   forth" (1956, 63).

9 According to Barbara von Barghahn, these grotesques may have been
   designed by Bartolomeo Carducho. Numerous critics also claim that he
   was responsible for the paintings in the library "below the cornice which
   correspond to the Liberal Arts represented in the vault" (Von Barghahn
   1985, 1:364n4). The paintings of the Liberal Arts were probably executed
   by Pellegrino Tibaldi.

10 The term *brutesco* can be found in Cristóbal Suárez de Figueroa's *Plaza
    universal de ciencias y artes* (Universal plaza of the sciences and arts) and in
    Francisco de Cascales' *Discursos de Murcia y su reino* (Discourses on Murcia
    and its kingdom. Lope de Rueda, in his *Comedia Medora*, has Gargullo
    imagine all the things he will obtain with the treasures he thinks he has
    stolen from a gypsy: "Lo primero que haré sera hazer unas casas en lo
    major d'esta ciudad; hazellas he pintar por de fuera y por de dentro al
    brutesco y al romano" (The first thing I will do is to build some houses in
    the best part of the city and have designs in Roman and grotesque styles
    both inside and outside; 1992, 252).

11 "Mas a esta sazón vi en medio del prado un maravilloso edificio, con una
    gran portada de fábrica dórica y de excelente artífice labrada [...] Estaban
    mil triunfos de amor imaginados, de medio relieve, que juntamente
    con muy graciosos brutescos hacían historia y ornato, y representaban
    misterio" (Quevedo 1997, 156).

12 Bakhtin asserts: "The initial meaning of the term [*grotesque*] was in the
    beginning extremely narrow, describing the rediscovered form of Roman
    ornament. But in reality this form was but a fragment of the immense
    world of grotesque imagery which existed throughout all the stages of
    antiquity and continued to exist in the Middle Ages and the Renaissance"
    (1984, 32). This section attempts to retain the term in its Renaissance
    meaning.

13 Edward Dudley explains: "In fact this conflict of hermeneutic horizons
    creates the 'unreadableness' that becomes a notable genre feature
    of Romance and contributes to the mixture of mystery and pleasure

purveyed to the reader. It is just this kind of pleasure that Don Quixote invokes in his discussion with the canon of Toledo as the basis for his valorization of the *libros de caballería[s]*" (1997, 130).

14 In the list of signatures from these caves collected by Weege in the nineteenth century and later by Nicole Dacos, a name that they read as Michiel appears at least twice. One such graffito is dated 1574, at a time that Cervantes was in Italy (Dacos 1969, 144). Is it at all possible that we have here a graffito by Miguel de Cervantes?

15 Michelangelo adapted his plans in the construction Saint Peter's Basilica.

16 In his portrait symbolizing Air, for example, Arcimboldo includes geese, roosters, turkeys, a pheasant, a peacock, an eagle, and a duck's beak that forms the lower eyelid (Kriegeskorte 1993, 16).

17 These images can recall the uses of dissection by artists of the Renaissance in order for them to be able to draw a more true-to-life body. John Donne, in his poem "The Legacy," begins with the executor trying to find and remove the heart and take it to his beloved.

18 Giulio Romano foregrounds the sexual nature of the goat in a fresco at the Palazzo del Te. The lubricous air of the painting is scrutinized by Bette Talvacchia: "The horns of a leering satyr who takes the form of a herm sculpture are grabbed by a bacchante whose left leg straddles the goat as she twists around to grab similarly the horn of the second creature under her domination" (1996, 34).

19 Jorge Tomás García has argued that: "In Cardinal Bibbiena's Loggia, G. Udine added naturalistic elements (goats, fish, birds […]) to the Neronian repertoire" (2019, 22). However, there are images of the goat-legged god as well as goats in the decorations of Nero's Golden Palace.

20 Mercedes Alcalá-Galán has discovered the hidden purpose of these open sores or "fuentes" (fountains) in a series of medical treatises. Infertile women in early modern Spain were subjected to painful wounding of their bodies in order to extract putrid or diseased "humours." The humours were considered a cause of infertility, and this expensive treatment was used by the upper classes. The duchess is thus concealing her anxiety, hiding from society's pressure to bear children (2013, 11–44). I would surmise from Alcalá-Galán's article that the duchess's "inhumanity" towards the knight may well be a reflection of the inhumanity of the treatment of women during this period.

21 Vladimir Nabokov's initial description of the inhabitants of this palace is as follows: "We now come to the main pair of villainous enchanters in the book, the Duchess and her Duke. The cruelty of the book reaches here atrocious heights" (1983, 62).

22 The English translation omits these verses and changes others.

23 During the Renaissance the Bembine Tablet of Isis was used to try to decipher hieroglyphs. It was acquired by Cardinal Bembo in 1527 after the sack of Rome. Almost at the centre we can see a drawing of Isis with a cat under her chair.

24 This story is told from the time of Rodrigo Jiménez de Rada in the thirteenth century to Bishop Joan Margarit in the fifteenth. On Rada see Candelaria (2005, 18).

25 Pujades gives a number of reasons why this legend must be true (1829, 77).

26 "Writing to a colleague in the Vatican, Paolo Pompilio, he avoided giving credence to the well-known myth of the city's supposed foundation by Hercules, who was said to have stepped onto the shore from the ninth ship in his fleet, thus giving the new settlement the name barca nona" (Tate 2002, 151). In the eighteenth century Flórez also objects to Pujades (1775, 4).

27 For a description of the glittering court at Naples, led by the Count of Lemos, and its many impromptu plays, academies, and distinguished visitors such as Villamediana, see Green (1933, 290–308).

28 While Lemos named the poet Lupercio Leonardo de Argensola as his secretary and also called on a number of literary figures to go with him to Naples, Cervantes was not chosen. Cervantes never gave up on his patron.

29 A most famous *laudatio* is, of course, the praise of Lisbon in the *Burlador de Sevilla*. For the prose fiction of the period, see Nieves Romero Díaz who has discussed the praise of Córdoba, Sevilla, and Madrid in Céspedes y Meneses´ *Historias peregrinas y ejemplares* (Unique and exemplary histories; 2002, 75–84).

30 For Cándido Santiago Álvarez this means: "dar vueltas a una parte y a otra, torciendo el camino" (turn round one way or another, zigzagging on the road; 2017, 62). The translator gives it a similar meaning without mentioning the metaphor: "to career and curve it around" (Cervantes 2008, 869).

31 As with most images, there can be a proliferation of meanings, even very positive ones. While the snail can stand for loneliness and poverty, it can also signify introspection and self-knowledge (Martínez Sobrino 2013, 91–9). Indeed, for both Juan de Horozco and Juan de Borja it can stand for stoic *ataraxia*, the tranquil life of the philosopher who seeks treasures within. This is the opposite of Don Quixote's search for outward fame. Thus, the snail that surrounds him is a negative one.

32 Much has been written on this episode. See, for example, Monique Joly (1991, 71–81), and Cory Reed, who argues: "Don Antonio's parlor game thus has a whiff of the demonic about it. Prohibited from creating an illusion of diabolical influence, he is sworn to advise his patrons so that they might not be fooled into believing that a demonic force is at work.

Nevertheless, he does not inform Don Quixote, Sancho, or the other *ignorantes*, who remain deceived, and happily so" (Reed 2004, 203).

33 Some believe that this name refers to the Irish Neoplatonist Johannes Scotus, the Scottish Michael Scot, or even the sixteenth-century necromancer Scoto from Parma.

34 For a discussion of the questions of masculinity and empire in this episode see Marchante-Aragón: "Ana's performance reveals the effects of actions by the crown that betrayed the duty to defend and protect the members of the Christian community of which she, as a sincerely Christian Morisca, and many like her, are a part. It is Ana, rather than the monarch, who embodies in the story the masculinity and self-sacrifice expected of imperial *virtus* and *pietas*" (2016, 14).

35 For a detailed analysis of the antagonism between Sansón as Samson and Don Quixote as Hercules, see De Armas (2009, 107–29).

36 Artemisia's painting of *Hercules and Omphale* hung at the Alcazar in Madrid but was lost sometime after 1636. Did this disappearance have to do with the demeaning imagery? After all, Hercules was a legendary ancestor of the kings of Spain. Let us remember the story: To atone for a murder, Hercules was ordered by the Delphic Oracle to serve Omphale, Queen of Lydia, as a slave and even to wear women's clothes. We know that much earlier Lucas Cranach had painted *Hercules at the Court of Omphale* (1537).

7 A Windowless North

1 For some, Cervantes' own judgment in light of *Don Quixote* has condemned the *Persiles*. As Carlos Romero Muñoz has stated, we must consider: "hasta qué punto el hecho de ser una 'obra maestra intencional' ha pesado sobre ella, a lo largo de los siglos, como una especie de condena" (up to what point the fact that throughout the centuries it is considered an international masterpiece becomes a kind of condemnation; Cervantes 2015b, 14).

2 Lucía Megías wonders about Lemos' real relationship with Cervantes over the years: "¿Fue realmente el VII Conde de Lemos mecenas de Cervantes? ¿Recibió y apoyó la publicación de sus obras, como lo había hecho con otros autores? ¿O hemos de pensar en una relación no tanto con el propio Conde de Lemos como con su red de mecenazgo o algún miembro de su casa?" (Was the Count of Lemos truly Cervantes' patron? Did he receive and support the publication of his works as he had done with other authors? Or should we think of it as a kind of relationship in which it was not so much the Count of Lemos but his network of patronage that helped, or perhaps some member of his household?; 2019, 187.)

3 "Así, desde la Isla Bárbara, irreal, pasamos a los países nórdicos, reales
pero inexactos, hasta los países del sur de Europa, en los que Cervantes
puede ser más preciso" (In this manner, from the Barbarous Island we
move to the nordic counries, real but inexact, and on to the countries in
the south of Europe where Cervantes can be more precise; Severa Baños
1990, 295).

4 The dedicatory is not included in the English translation that I am using.

5 As early as 1919 Américo Castro pointed out that Norway in the literature
of the Spanish Golden Age was associated with darkness, cold, and the
devil. Davenport and Cabanillas Cárdenas point out: "La función literaria
principal de Noruega se basaba en el rasgo hiperbólico de frialdad y
oscuridad que dicha región representaba por antonomasia" (The main
literary function of Norway is based on the hyperbolic traits of coldness
and darkness that the region represents as if by antonomasia; 2017, 15).

6 Discussing the Marcela/Grisóstomo episode in the first part of *Don Quijote*,
Emilia Macaya states: "La madre de Marcela, descrita como suma belleza
y bondad, constituye entonces desde esta perspectiva platónica lo amable
por excelencia. Su hija, por el contrario, se situará dentro de un discurso
cargado de platonismo [...] para subvertirlo desde dentro [...] ruptura de
la asociación belleza-bondad." (Marcela's mother, described as the sum of
beauty and goodness, constitutes from a platonic perspective that which
is most lovable. Her daughter, in contrast, is placed in a discourse filled
with Platonism [...] so as to subvert it from the inside [...] rupturing the
association of beauty and goodness; 1992, 54.)

7 For someone living in the early seventeenth century, the ability to compete
and surpass one of the great classics of the Graeco-Roman world would
be a crowning achievement. Countless epic poems, praised in their time,
are today read only by specialists. But Cervantes knew that he should
imitate the ancient Greek novel, more than the epic. After all, Heliodorus'
Aethiopica, the best of its kind, was first translated into Spanish in 1554
but became well known in Iberia when Fernando de Mena published his
version in 1587. And yet, as Alban K. Forcione asserts, "[t]he fact is that
the vision Cervantes embodies in the *Persiles* had a coherence of its own
[...] which compelled him to develop or 'abuse' the Heliodoran techniques
of disposition which he had studied in the *Aethiopica* and in the poetic
treatises of his time" (1972, 30).

8 "Cervantes' summa, as a boldly new kind of prose epic that casts an
original light on major political, religious, social and literary debates of the
era [...]" (Armstrong-Roche 2009, 4). Alban K. Forcione had once asserted:
"In its in-medias-res beginning and delayed exposition it even surpasses
Virgil's and Homer's epics, for the reader's interest in discovering the
events preceding the beginning is kept alive until the exact midpoint of the

work" (1972, 9). In addition, the work fulfils Cervantes' Virgilian literary career. "Cervantes consciously describes his literary career in terms of the Virgilian *cursus*. He begins with the *Galatea*, a Virgilian eclogue; he continues with *Don Quijote*, an apprenticeship for epic; and he ends with the *Persiles*, the epic of closure for life and work, an Augustan amorous epic of political dynasties and Christian fulfillment" (De Armas 2002b, 282).

9 Olaus Magnus' *Historia de Gentibus septentrionalibus* (*History of the Northern Peoples*) was printed in Rome in 1555 and was translated into Italian (1565), German (1567), English (1658), and Dutch (1665). See also Nicolo Zeno, *Dei comentari dell viaggio in Persia … e dello scoprimel1to del!' iso le Frislanda, Eslanda, Engronelanda*, and Antonio Torquemada, *Jardín de flores curiosas*. On Olaus Magnus and Torquemada see Sletsjöe (1959–60).

10 Although *Don Quixote* destabilizes space, as Alcalá Galán has shown, the first two books of the *Persiles*, I would argue, show the emergence of space out of a kind of primordial chaos or perhaps a demonic darkness. Analysing the second part of *Don Quixote*, Alcalá Galán asserts: "El mapa pasa del dominio del papel a habitar la imaginación cambiando nuestra percepción de nosotros mismos habitando el mundo" (The map shifts from its home on paper to inhabit our perception of ourselves inhabiting the world; 2016a, 16).

11 For the English, I am using the electronic text of the *Persiles* edited and translated by T.L. Darby and B.W. Ife (Cervantes, n.d.). It lacks pagination.

12 "En los dos primeros libros del *Persiles* el espacio desconocido deja la puerta abierta a la admiración ante el exotismo zoológico (el náufrago), humano (prácticas que resultaban curiosas para el mundo mediterráneo como el patinaje) o prodigios de la naturaleza (los géiseres)." (In the two first books of the *Persiles*, the unknown space opens the door for admiration through the zoological exoticism (the *náufrago*), the human (practices that appeared strange to the Mediterranean world such as skating) or natural phenomena (the geisers); Lozano Renieblas 2016, 352.)

13 These mysteries combine, as Luis Avilés has pointed out, the rare occurrence and the visual obstacle (2016, 51).

14 The first two books of the *Persiles* foreground the mysteries of discovery. Diana De Armas Wilson has shown that the first six chapters establish a contact zone in which "disparate cultures meet, clash and grapple with each other" (2003, 201). Here Cervantes subverts the civilization-barbary opposition: "The Barbaric Isle narrative neither aligns itself with facile condemnations of the European conquest nor celebrates that conquest as providential" (205).

15 "¿Ves este sol que nos alumbra? Pues sí, para señal de lo que puedo, quieres que le quite los rayos y le asombre con nubes, pídemelo, que hare

que a esta claridad suceda en un punto escura noche." (Behold this sun which now shines upon us: if in trial of my cunning you will have me take away his beams and cover him with clouds, do but command me, and I will make the dark night immediately follow this brightness; Cervantes 2015b, 330.)

16 The scientific part of the study was written in 1593 as a student dissertation at the University of Tubingen in which Kepler asked, "How would the phenomena occurring in the heavens appear to an observer standing on the moon?" (1967, xvii). Here, Kepler defends Copernicus and suggests how one can view the planets from the moon. He also discusses the size of the moon and how eclipses would look from it. He was not allowed to present this at the university, so he kept it and decided to add the dream frame to it while he was in Prague. The frame uses the dream sequence because Kepler fell asleep reading a magician's text and dreamed of the Icelandic youth Duracotus. This second version, written in 1608/9 (in Latin), seems to have been circulated. One manuscript of 1611 fell in the wrong hands, leading to the accusation of his mother being a witch. Between 1622 and 1630 Kepler added copious new scientific notes. It was published by his son in 1638 (Kepler 1967, 20).

17 Very much like Kepler's *Somnium*, the *Vexamen de la luna* uses a dream as a frame, the sleeper travelling to "Selenopolis, Corte Imperial de la Luna, situada en el centra de aquella Esphera" (K. Brown 1980, 285). There, he meets a series of poets who seem to satirize the well-ordered cosmos. Jacinto de Aguilar, for example, "is a celestial tailor charged by the gods to mend ruptures in the heavens [...] He thus implies that the spheres above the moon are not immutable" (De Armas 1999, 66).

18 There may be much to decipher in the moon's many mysteries in the novel. The *maldiciente* (backbiting) Clodio says to Rutilio that Periandro and Auristela could claim to be "hijos del sol y de la luna" (children of the Sun and of the Moon; Cervantes 2015b, 308); the magician Cenotia disparages minor sorcery and sorceresses who use "cabellos cortados en creciente o menguante luna" (hair cut off in the new or wane of the moon; 332).

19 "[Y] así, ordenaron que en aquella isla del rio se renovasen las fiestas y se continuasen por tres días. La sazón del tiempo, que era la del verano; la comodidad del sitio, el resplandor de la luna, el susurro de las fuentes, la fruta de los árboles, el olor de las flores." (Wherefore, they ordained that the feast should be renewed and solemnised three days more in the same isle. It was now spring-time at our being there. The beauty of the place, the brightness of the moon, the still noise of the waters, the fruits of the trees, and the sweet smell of flowers; Cervantes 2015b, 357).

20 "[S]e tiende hacia una fusión indisoluble entre el espacio y la historia"
   (there is a tendency towards an unalterable fusion between space and
   history; Lozano Renieblas, 1998b, 171).
21 "Tres días duró la apacibilidad del mar y tres días sopló próspero el
   viento, hasta que, al cuarto, a poner del sol, comenzó a turbar el viento y
   a desasosegarse el mar y el recelo de alguna" (This fair weather endured
   three days, and this wind blew favourably until the fourth, which then
   began about sun-setting to be tempestuous, and grow angry with the sea;
   Cervantes 2015b, 395–6).
22 Periandro, Auristela, and Cloelia for example, disembark from a ship,
   go on a small boat up a river, and come across a fishing town that is
   celebrating the wedding of two couples. Their boats are cleverly adorned,
   and their virtues sparkle as gold and pearls (Cervantes 2015b, 343).
   However, even here, the town's architecture seems veiled.
23 Cory Reed specifies that Spanish cosmographers came up with a
   "*horologium nocturnum*, an instrument for telling time at sea during the
   night by measuring the relative distance between Polaris and the *guardas*"
   (2016, 445).
24 Cory Reed explains: "Even the name of Corsicurbo, the first proper noun
   to appear in the story, homophonically recalls a curved course (*curso
   curvo*) or a route that deviates from a direct path or switches back on
   itself, characteristic of the digressions and circular movement that recur
   throughout the northern voyages of the protagonists" (2016, 449).
25 Bradley J. Nelson takes this scene further into the realm of the emblems
   (2005, 44).
26 There are a number of examples of ineffability. In canto 17 of the *Paradiso*,
   Cacciaguida tells Dante that he must report on all he sees. As Claire
   Honess explains, "[t]he poet goes on to emphasize the difficulty of this
   task, given the extraordinary and ineffable nature of his experience"
   (1994, 43).
27 Kevin Brownlee asserts that "Beatrice's evocation is very explicitly a
   negative one. Unlike Semele, Dante has not made the request that Beatrice
   reveal her divine nature. Unlike Jove, Beatrice will not engage in an act of
   self-revelation that would be fatal to her charge. She 'tempers' her beauty
   in order to spare Dante" (1986, 148).
28 Searching for a place to bury Manuel de Sosa, the pilgrims come to
   Golandia, which as its only architecture "no ocupaba más de una casa
   que servía de meson a la gente que llegaba a un puerto detrás" (had but
   one house, which served for lodging to a number of people that came to a
   harbour; Cervantes 2015b, 207; n.d.). It is not described.
29 On the storm as a Homeric and Virgilian epic motif found in the literature
   of the Golden Age, see Fernández Mosquera (2006).

30 John T. Cull was one of the first to point to the emblematic models for the sea as the perils of life and as Fortuna (1992, 200–8). Ignacio Arellano asserts: "En esa arriesgada navegación que es la vida nada de extraño tiene la frecuente presencia de los motivos que representan la variabilidad y fragilidad de las seguridades humanas" (In the dangers of navigation that represent life, it should not surprise us to find elements that show the changeability and fragility of human security; 2004, 579–80).

31 "En esto estaban cuando los maderos llegaron a la mitad del estrecho que las dos islas formaban, en el cual, de improviso, se levantó una borrasca que, sin poder remediallo los inexpertos marineros, los leños de la balsa se desligaron y dividieron en partes" (Being upon these terms, the raft came into the midst of the strait enclosing the two isles, when such a flaw unlooked-for arose that, whatsoever help these trim sailors could afford, the beams of their raft were untied and severed into parts; Cervantes 2015b, 131; n.d.).

32 Indeed, as Periandro is taken to lie on two small beds, the term used is *traspontines* (Cervantes 2015b, 133), an Italian word that became well known in Spain to mean mariners' cushions or beds (133n16), pointing to Cervantes' knowledge of seafaring terminology and recalling that he first embarked in Naples, on his way to a naval battle.

33 "Llegó esto a tanto estremo, que desde la calle pedían a voces se asomasen a las ventanas las damas y las peregrinas" (and this desire brought them to that extremity that they cried out in the streets that the ladies and pilgrims should come to the windows; Cervantes 2015b, 648).

34 "Y este bárbaro español […] ha de hacer corrillos de gente, mostrando a su mujer y a sus hijos envueltos en sus pellejos, pintando la isla bárbara en un lienzo y señalando con una vara el lugar donde estuvo encerrado quince años, la mazmorra de los prisioneros" (And our Spanish barbarian […] he will assemble all the world to show them his wife and children wrapped all in skins, and make the barbarian island to be painted in a cloth, and show unto them with a wand the place where he was fifteen years enclosed; Cervantes 2015b, 309).

35 The tongue and the sword are emblematic of a sharp tongue and slander, and John T. Cull points to Covarrubias' *Emblemas morales* of 1610 (1992, 203). Ignacio Arellano refers to Cull but points specifically to Clodio's punishment as a result of his gossip (2004, 581). On the figure of Clodio as gossip and satirist see Cacho Casal (2006, 299–321). Michael Gerli speaks of other emblematic moments in which mouth and tongue are halted, as when the governor of the barbarian isle shoots an arrow that hits Bradamiro in the mouth and tongue, thereby killing him (2012, 352).

36 "Volvió, en fin; tendió la vista por el mar, vio volar la saetía donde iba la mitad de su alma, o la mayor parte della, y como si fuera otra engañada

y nueva Dido que de otro fugitiva Eneas quedaba" (And like a new Dido that complained of her fugitive Aeneas, sending sighs to heaven, tears to the earth, and her voice to the air, she uttered such like words; Cervantes 2015b, 394).

37 A fifth and last, the French knight Renato, stands as a faithful Christian, perhaps signalling the pilgrims' departure from the north. Forcione asserts: "Unlike Antonio and Rutilio the French knight commits no sin" (1972, 116). After he is defeated by a calumniator, he goes north "and arrives at the Island of the Hermits where his spiritual rebirth occurs amid the trees, flowers, and springs of the paradisiacal region" (117). Unlike the others, he does not have to experience the harshness and darkness of the north. Forcione states: "It is significant that the first half of the *Persiles* concludes with this adventure, for it prefigures the pilgrims' attainment of the ultimate goal of their quest" (73).

38 See paintings by Filippo Lippi, Bartolomé Murillo, Jusepe de Ribera, Sebastiano Ricci, and many others.

39 Norway's association with darkness was a common motif in the period and is found in the works of Belmonte Bermúdez, Ledesma, Rojas Zorrilla, Vélez de Guevara, and many others. See, for example, Castro (1919, 184–5), Buceta (1920, 278–81), d'Ors Lois (2012, 84–7), and Spitzer (1922, 316–17).

40 "Part of his point in constructing the episode as he did may have been to indict the dancing master Rutilio who had seduced his young female pupil on the grounds of moral depravity, using as a litmus test his inability to see the witch in human form" (Kallendorf 2019, 4–5).

41 "[Y] que uno de ellos (como es la verdad) me dijo en voz clara y distinta y en mi propia lengua: 'Español, hazte a lo largo y busca en otra parte tu ventura, si no quieres en ésta morir hecho pedazos por nuestras uñas y dientes.'" (And that one of them spake unto me with an human and intelligible voice: yea more, in mine own language. "Spaniard, forsake this shore, and seek thy fortune elsewhere, if thou wilt not be rent and torn in pieces with our teeth"; Cervantes 2015b, 170.)

42 In this particular passage the earlier translation by Summers is very much like the newer one by Mackay: "The devil can deceive the human fancy so that a man really seems to be an animal [...] The apparent shape of a beast only exists in the inner perception, which, through the force of imagination, sees it in some way as an exterior object" (Kramer and Sprenger 1928, 62, 63).

43 "Three basic possibilities present themselves concerning transvection: (1) The flight actually took place; (2) Rutilio believed in the flight, although it was a demonic illusion; and (3) "an unreliable narrator (in Riley's terminology), Rutilio lied about transvection" (De Armas 1981, 303). Lozano Renieblas adds a fourth: "Cervantes quiere transitar por la rara

senda de la innovación simbólica hasta ganarse la aquiescencia del lector que cede ante la admiración que produce la magia del relato construido sobre el andamiaje de la novedad" (Cervantes wishes to take the unusual road of symbolic innovation until he can gain the reader's acquiescence, which yields when confronted by the admiration that stems from the magic of a story constructed on the scaffold of newness; 2016, 357).

44 Elsewhere I have suggested that this is the most plausible interpretation: "Rutilio's tale is as much a lie as the Northern environment; and the marvelous occurrences are a rejection of verisimilitude in favor of a different kind of truth: the presentation of a Christian conception of the perils of earthly exile and alienation. The lies of a poet have been metamorphosed into universal truths" (De Armas 1981, 307). Reynaldo C. Riva furthers this argument and asks why Cervantes would have Rutilio lie (2003, 350).

45 The (fictional) annals of brothers Nicolò and Antonio Zeno construct this fictional island from Iceland and the Faroe Islands. In Cervantes' novel Frislanda is closer to the pole than Tile (Thule), correcting Virgil and making Auristela/Sigismunda "Persiles' North Star" (Armstrong-Roche 2009, 69).

46 For Armstrong-Roche, Cervantes' Tile as Thule "registers a movement from margin or periphery to center, reversing the historic direction of empire" (2009, 68). But Persiles should not be related to the Augustus Caesar of Virgil's *Georgics*: "Thule's Caesar in *Persiles* is the northern Gothic Crown Prince Maximino" (70). His rulership will be taken up by Persiles/ Periandro and Auristela who "show themselves to be in possession of the better part of Christianity, giving Romans a lesson in the religion for which they are institutional custodians" (70). Alarcos Martínez, however, sees in Persiles Virgil's Augustus Caesar (2014, 275).

47 Early modern writers of Iberia often depicted the ship as dangerous and accused Jason, considered the first builder of boats, as inciting violence and warfare. See, for example, the invective against ships in *El burlador de Sevilla* (*The Trickster of Seville*) discussed in detail by B.B. Aschom (1943, 378–84)

8 Structures of Flight

1 "There is also the ekphrasis of an object that is being created, such as Vulcan['s] forging of Achilles' shield – a forging ekphrasis" (De Armas 2006, 10).

2 Vincent Parello (2015) mentions it briefly in his study of the praise of the city in *El burlador de Sevilla*. As stated, it serves to guard the estuary of the river Tagus.

3 An allusive ekphrasis is an almost paradoxical nomenclature because
the work of art or architecture is not described, nor is a narrative created
from its images. Instead, the poet playwright or novelist simply refers to a
painter, a work of art, the name of a statue or an architecture, or even to a
feature that may apply. This becomes an ekphrasis only in the mind of the
characters and / or readers or spectators who can view the work in their
memory and imagination (De Armas 2016, 10).

4 The pilgrims' effect on the inhabitants of the city was one of "espanto
y maravilla" (astonishment and marvel; Cervantes 2015b, 435). The
translation does not do full justice to the term *espanto*, which can relate also
to fright and anxiety.

5 "Cerca de Valencia llegaron, en la cual no quisieron entrar por escusar
las ocasiones del detenerse; pero no faltó quien les dijo la grandeza de
su sitio, la excelencia de sus moradores, la amenidad de sus contornos,
y, finalmente, todo aquello que la hace hermosa y rica sobre todas las
ciudades, no sólo de España, sino de toda Europa." (They came hard by
Valencia, where they would not enter, to avoid occasions of staying there;
but they wanted not some that knew how to inform them of the large
situation thereof, the excellency of the inhabitants, the pleasant places
round about it, and finally all that which made the same fair and rich *not
only* above all the cities in Spain, *but all of Europe*; Cervantes 2015b, 555.)
The praise of cities seems often tinged with some irony in Cervantes. We
need only recall the contrast between the praise of Barcelona's inhabitants
in part 2 of *Don Quixote* and the actual treatment that the knight received.
Here, the praise of Valencia does not come from the narrator or the
pilgrims, but from some unknown characters.

6 The number of gates in a city also recalls chapter 15 of part1 of *Don
Quixote*. Here the knight has to ride on Sancho's donkey, and, in order
for it not to appear as a comical or degrading transport, he recalls how
Bacchus' tutor, Silenus, rode a donkey into Thebes with its one hundred
gates. There is a fusion or confusion here between the Greek and the
Egyptian Thebes. The latter only had five gates.

7 For a discussion of this and other scenes in the canvas see Ignacio Arellano
Torres (2018, 231–42).

8 Childers contrasts her desecration at the hand of the Moors, then the
father and the brother of Feliciana assume this role in the new version
(2006, 88). For a comparison with the Guadalupe legend see Childers
(2006, 90–105).

9 Muñoz Sánchez has a different point of view: "No hay milagro mariano –
nada semejante se declara en el texto –, sino un pleito civil en la plaza
delante de la justicia y del pueblo de Guadalupe, extramuros del
monasterio" (There is no Marian miracle – the text declares no such thing –

but a civil suit in the plaza, in front of the justices of the peace and of the people of Guadalupe, outside the walls of the monastery; 2015a, 179).

10 The translation leaves out Feliciana's verses.

11 See Juan José Pastor Comín who argues that this disruption in the patriarchal order is the reason why Cervantes places Feliciana's story at the very centre of the *Persiles* (2006, 497).

12 Muñoz Sánchez explains that this event together with the full tale derives from a series of models: "El de Claricia y Domicio presenta un caso de amor, envenenamiento y locura relacionado al parigual con la ficción caballeresca y la celestinesca, pero que alude al mito de Hércules y Deyanira, elaborado por Sófocles […] y por Ovidio" (The tale of Claricia and Domicio presents a love affair, a case of poisoning and the madness related equally to chivalric fiction and to celestinesque works, but alluding to the myth of Hercules and Deianira crafted by Sophocles […] and by Ovid; 2015b, 265).

13 The Chicago call number is f TJ144.V47 1595 c.1. The description states: "The University of Chicago Library's copy has engraved t.p. only. Wanting pl. 8–24, 45. Bookplate of Harrison Gray Otis 3d, Boston, Mass. Stamp of The Newberry Library on t.p.; deaccessioning stamp of same on verso. Manuscript on t.p. Discovery of this item made possible by a gift from Julie and Roger Baskes." The University of Chicago Library also has a 1965 facsimile of the 1615 edition, although it seemed to be missing when I last checked. For modern editions of the work see Boric (2016, 48n3).

14 It is quite possible that Cervantes was acquainted with *Veintiún libros de los ingenios y máquinas de Juanelo Turriano* (Twenty-one books of the devices and machines of Juanelo Turriano), a work attributed to him, although not published at the time (De Armas 2006, 146).

15 "La que con más gusto escuchaba a Periandro era la bella Sinforosa, estando pendiente de sus palabras como cadenas que salían de la boca de Hércules: tal era la gracia y donaire con que Periandro contaba sus sucesos" (She that harkened to Periander with most pleasure was the fair Synforosa, who hung on his words as those that were fastened to the chains of gold issuing from the tongue of Hercules, with such a grace did Periander recount his adventures; Cervantes 2015b, 356).

9 Roman Architectures

1 The translation I am using does not include the sonnet.

2 We may conceive of the many springs and rivulets that the pilgrims cross as a sign that they are in the gardens of Madama. After all, its carefully terraced gardens, waterfalls, fishponds, and fountains that were to be intricately connected were made possible by the constant water flowing

from several springs in the mountains and thanks to the care of the designers (Bedini 1997, 170).

3 "The site was thus well suited to the pursuit of Leo X's hedonistic pleasures and to the fulfillment of Raphael's dreams. In April that year he had been to visit Hadrian's Villa [...] Looking at classical architecture and the principles of Vitruvius, and paraphrasing Pliny the Younger's letters on villas [...] Raphael was to create an entirely original compendium, with antique and Renaisssance references, in a new villa" (Napoleone 2008, 25–6).

4 When Margaret of Austria married her second husband, Ottavio Farnese, the future Duke of Parma, he came to own it. She seems to have forgotten about the villa when she became governor of the Low Countries and later settled in her domain of Abruzzo, living in Cittaducale and Aquila at the time Cervantes was in Italy (Niwa 2005, 30).

5 The name Hanno is the English for *Annone*. The Italians called him thus because *aana* was "the word for elephant in his native Malayalam language, spoken in the Kerla state" (Bedini 1997, 80).

6 In medieval times the elephant was associated with Adam and Eve, "who never desired each other and possessed no knowledge of coitus before the snake led them into temptation" (Fontes da Costa 2009, 76). Periandro and Auristela, in their brotherly love, can be seen as human embodiments of the mythical elephant.

7 "Pero el estilo cervantino, está ligado a la oralidad y tiende precisamente a atenuar el ropaje retórico" (But Cervantes' style is tied to orality and tends to attenuate its rhetorical adornments; Lozano Renieblas 1998b, 507).

8 Equally damning are the decorations of the villa by Giovanni da Udine. Turning to the grottos or caverns that opened underground to display ancient palaces such as Nero's Domus Aurea, he morphed flora and fauna into captivating forms.

9 Although Michelangelo received the commission, he turned it over to Nanni di Baccio.

10 The figures of Saint Peter and Saint Paul were not added until 1636. Built for the Basilica of Saint Paul, they had been rejected and ended up here.

11 For a vision of life in the Roman ghetto see Kenneth Stow (2001).

12 There may also be another point of contact between Manasseh/Manasses and Periandro, one that links the Jewish house with Hipólita's palace. At the courtesan's abode, "[l]ike his biblical ancestor, Joseph, Periandro flees the ardent advances of the temptress leaving behind his cloak" (Forcione 1972, 103). In the Bible, Manasseh/Manasses was Joseph's first-born son.

13 Juan Ramón Muñoz Sánchez discusses the truly extraordinary nature of this narrative that is told in so many bits throughout the novel: "se disemina por un amplio número de capítulos de los libros tercero y cuarto,

a saber: por los capítulos vi, vii, xvi, xviii y xix del libro tercero y el i, el v, el viii y el xiv del libro cuarto" (it is disseminated through a large number of chapters in the third and fourth books, which are: chapters 6, 7, 16, 18 and 19 of the third book and chapters 1, 5, 8 and 14 of the fourth; 2007, 128). In addition, the tale is told through three different narrators and takes place in three geographical spaces: Spain, France, and Italy (132). The story actually extends its geography to Portugal and the Indies (in the tale of Ortel Banedre).

14 Every so often, some repairs were accomplished: "S. Celso appears to have been the only building on the new piazza directly restored by Nicholas, perhaps by virtue of its status as a cappella papalis. Repairs of 1450 are documented, however, on the nearby Tor di Nona, the papal prison and base of the *soldano* (law enforcement officer). Though the repairs predate the clearing of the piazza, it is probable that the tower was later visible from the latter, if it did not indeed adjoin it" (Burroughs 1982, 103).

15 "In 1667 she assisted with the transformation of the Teatro Tor di Nona, later the Teatro Apollo, from a jail to a theater. The Queen was the primary patron of the theater and used it as a social space, hosting foreign visitors, cardinals, and members of Roman society in her royal box" (Kutasz Christensen 2018, 35).

16 On the *stella maris* as the Neoplatonic Venus and the Virgin Mary, see Warner (2013, 270).

17 In a doubly focused image, Auristela may be regarded as the Pole Star, but also as one of the two guardian stars in the Ursa Minor constellation. They revolve around the North Star and aid mariners in their nightly navigations. These guardian stars, as stated in a previous chapter, could be linked to Periandro and Auristela.

18 In the third part of the novel we read that Auristela insists on continuing the pilgrimage on foot rather than in carriages, for that had been her promise. Thus she will not need her jewels: "de no disponer de la cruz de diamantes que Auristela traía, guardándola, con las inestimables perlas, para mejor ocasión" (Cervantes 2015b, 440).

19 Forcione, turning to an early critic, Anton Rothbauer (1963, 58–83), suggests that Cervantes wanted to link the pilgrims in his novel to "the travels of St. Paul in the New Testament [...] There is a strong ecumenical message in the *Persiles*. The northern Europeans must be reconciled with the Catholic Church through instruction and not through war" (Forcione 1972, 104). Armstrong-Roche explains: "Paul was not only associated with converts on account of his dramatic vision and fall on the Road to Damascus – partly explaining the devotion of Jewish *conversos* [...] He was also linked with an emphasis on the spiritual, on inner religion or grace

over law, on humility, self-examination, and priority of compassionate over ritually sanctioned behavior" (2009, 122).

20 Although in 1554 Andrea Palladio published a volume on the *Antiquities of Rome* together with a second one describing the churches to be visited, Cervantes is clear that his pilgrims followed the route of the seven churches. Palladio added a large number to the initial seven, creating an itinerary with four different circuits (1991, xv).

21 The schedule ironically included rest and a basic meal at the gardens and vineyards of the Mattei family, where would later be erected a luxurious Renaissance villa. The Villa Celimontana, then called Villa Mattei for its owner, was built by Giacomo del Duca, a pupil of Michelangelo, in 1580. The grounds and gardens were acquired by the Mattei in 1552. Cervantes may have seen the gardens but not the villa because he left Italy in 1575.

22 Periandro visits the seven churches once the case of Auristela's portrait has been resolved (Cervantes 2015b, 663). At the end of the novel, after his brother's death, "Persiles […] volvió a visitar los templos de Roma" (Persiles […] visited again the temples in Rome; 713).

23 Armstrong-Roche sees this moment in religious terms: "A Pauline resurrection in the spirit […] Persiles' second-born triumph over first-born's rights to Sigismunda is, to use the terms Persiles relies on to explain their journey to Rome, a kind of triumph of 'elección' (choice) over 'destino' (destiny)" (2009, 298).

24 According to Rachel Schmidt, Cervantes portrays himself as the "hombre curioso" (curious man) who borrows proverbs from others and was born under Mars, Mercury, and Apollo (2014, 257). Mercury provides him with wit and invention among other qualities that are useful for writing (259).

25 Forcione argues that Maximino is a negative and demonic figure: "Moreover, the oppressive ruler, Prince Magsimino, […] in the cycle of the total action has a role analogous to that of the various demonic agents in the individual adventures" (1972, 105). In a footnote he adds: "Magsimino is constantly occupied in waging war. His ailment is symbolic of his sinister role" (105n27). I don't see his role as sinister but as representative of the old epic. Maximino may well be a new Achilles. To this interpretation I add a second: Maximino represents Cervantes who did indeed devote himself to war for a number of years and then wrote about a would-be knight. It is a Cervantes, hero of Lepanto, who, after enabling the action, now appears for purposes of reconciliation and redemption.

26 Frazer explains: "The teachings of St Paul on Christ's Incarnation and Resurrection determine the door's iconography […] The door is divided into four groups of four panels each illustrating in silver and enamel inlay a cycle of the twelve feasts from the Annunciation to the Descent of the Holy Ghost; twelve prophets holding scrolls inscribed with their

prophecies; twelve apostles, the panel with St. Paul, including Christ and Pantaleone; twelve scenes of the death and martyrdom of the apostles" (1973, 155).

Epilogue

1 https://www.maharishivastu.org/principles-of-maharishi-vastu-architecture.

2 In Sthapatya Veda we read: "Modern architecture and planning does not have this knowledge of orientation. In an average city buildings are facing random directions [...] From eight possible directions, only two directions – East and North – produce auspicious influences" (Maharishi Mahesh Yogi 1998, 12, 17). Vitruvius warns that in order for one to plan and build a city, streets and alleys need to be "properly laid out if foresight is employed to exclude the winds from the alleys" (1960, 24). Vitruvius then discusses the winds that blow from the four cardinal points and their influence, further refining this to include eight winds (26–8).

3 Da Vinci did not follow the Vitruvian model exactly, following instead his own measurements of human limbs. Furthermore, modern critics question both the name and the perfection of the drawing. Emanuele Lugli states that Leonardo's drawing is a "riflessione" (reflection) of multiple traditions on the nature of perfection (2019, 87).

4 This image also appears in Petronius' *Satyricon*: "Following a description of the zodiac, Trimalchio declares 'so the world turns like a mill (stone), and always brings some evil to pass, causing the birth of men or their death" (Watts 2014, 62).

5 https://www.curbed.com/maps/frank-lloyd-wright-best-buildings-map. The Meeting House's roof was designed in 1994 by Prairie Architects (no longer existing but formerly located in Fairfield, Iowa). Jonathan Lipman, who was part of the team, wrote a historic structures report on the roof of the building. He is specialized in Maharishi Sthapatya Veda and has written on Frank Lloyd Wright (1986). It would be interesting to follow up the connection between modern and ancient architectures in his work.

6 "It is impossible to overemphasize the paradox represented by every hierophany, even the most elementary. By manifesting the sacred, any object becomes something else, yet it continues to remain itself, for it continues to participate in its surrounding cosmic milieu. A sacred stone remains a stone" (Eliade 1959, 12).

7 Feliciana de la Voz can be described as being in a state of transcendental consciousness, "a state in which the inner awareness retires from all objects of perception and from all mental fluctuations or activity to a state of pure, inner wakeful silence" (Dillbeck and Alexander 1989, 310).

8 Indeed, this also echoes the ancient Sthapatya Veda. In Maharishi Vastu architecture the elevation of a building is divided into horizontal layers that correspond to the parts of the human body from bottom to top.

9 Many critics of Henry James' story discard the Count and praise the narrator. Jane Thomas asserts: "The Count's 'corporeality' is seen as a manifestation of his pagan heritage, which is objectified through the use of racial stereotypes and sculptural metaphors [...] His appearance is likened to 'the familiar bust of the Emperor Caracalla,' who epitomized for many the depravity, cruelty and barbarism of pre-Christian Rome" (2010, 256). Although very different from the emaciated knight, the Count in a quixotic enterprise comes to desire an ancient statue.

Works Cited

Acero Yus, Francisco. 2006. "Los gigantes en el *Quijote* de Cervantes: Revisión de un motivo de la literatura caballeresca." *Espéculo: Revista de Estudios Literarios* 32:n.p.

Aeschylus. 1988. *Suppliant Maidens, Persians, Prometheus, Seven against Thebes.* Edited by H. Weier Smyth. Cambridge, MA: Harvard University Press.

Aguilar Perdomo, María del Rosario. 2007. "La arquitectura maravillosa en los libros de caballerías españoles: A propósito de castillos, torres y jardines.' *Revista de Lingüística y Literatura* 51:127–48.

Aladro-Font, Jorge, and Ricardo Ramos Tremolada. 1996. "Ausencia y presencia de Garcilaso en el *Quijote*." *Cervantes: Bulletin of the Cervantes Society of America* 16 (2): 89–106.

Alarcos Martínez, Miguel. 2014. "Un caso de influencia virgiliana en el *Persiles*, la invención de Tile, lugar de origen del héroe." *Revista de Filología Española* 94:265–78.

Alcalá-Galán, Mercedes. 2009. *Escrituras desatadas: Poética de la representación en Cervantes.* Alcalá de Henares, Spain: Centro de Estudios Cervantinos.

– 2013. "Las piernas de la duquesa: Praxis médica y claves hermenéuticas en el *Quijote* de 1615." *Cervantes: Bulletin of the Cervantes Society of America* 33 (2): 11–44.

– 2016a. "Cartografías imaginarias en el *Quijote*, II." In *El "Quijote" de 1615: Dobleces, inversiones, paradojas, desbordamientos e imposibles*, edited by Gustavo Illades, Francisco Ramírez, and Antonio Cortijo, 11–31. Santa Barbara, CA: Publications of eHumanista.

– 2016b. "Hacia una teoría de la representación artística en el *Persiles*: 'Pinturas valientes' en el museo de Hipólita/Imperia." *eHumanista/Cervantes* 5:1–25.

Allen, John J. 1969. *Don Quixote: Hero or Fool? A Study of Narrative Technique.* Gainesville: University of Florida Press.

Alonso, Dámaso. 1971. *Poesía española: Ensayo de métodos y límites estilísticos.* Madrid: Gredos.

Alonso Romero, María Paz. 1982. *El proceso penal en Castilla (siglos xiii–xviii).* Salamanca: Ediciones de la Universidad de Salamanca.

Alvar Ezquerra, Alfredo, and Fabien Montcher. 2014. "Cervantes and the Turn of History (c1570–1615)." *Cervantes: Bulletin of the Cervantes Society of America* 34 (2): 15–36.

Amudsen, Michael. 2018. "Q&A with Juhani Pallasmaa on Architecture, Aesthetics of Atmospheres and the Passage of Time." *Ambiances.* Journals. openedition.org/ambiances/.

Andrés, Christian. 2004. "El sistema de los objetos y su función novelística en *Los trabajos de Persiles y Sigismunda*." In *Actas del V Congreso Internacional de Cervantistas (Lisboa 2003)*, edited by Elicia Villar Lecumberri, 179–206. Asociación de Cervantistas:

Arellano, Ignacio. 2004. "Elementos emblemáticos en *La Galatea* y el *Persiles*." *Bulletin of Spanish Studies* 81 (4–5): 571–83.

Arellano Torres, Ignacio. 2018. "Estrategias visuales en *Los trabajos de Persiles y Sigismunda*." *Hispanófila* 183:231–42.

Aresti, Nerea. 2007. "The Gendered Identities of the 'Lieutenant Nun': Rethinking the Story of a Female Warrior in Early Modern Spain." *Gender & History* 19:401–18.

Armstrong-Roche, Michael. 2004. "Europa como bárbaro Nuevo Mundo en la novela épica de Cervantes." In *Peregrinamente peregrinos: Actas del V Congreso Internacional de Cervantistas (Lisboa 2003)*, edited by Elicia Villar Lecumberri, 1123–38. Asociación de Cervantistas.

– 2009. *Cervantes' Epic Novel: Empire, Religion and the Dream Life of Heroes in "Persiles."* Toronto: University of Toronto Press.

– 2019. "Las paradojas de *Persiles y Sigismunda* (con *Don Quijote* y *Viaje del Parnaso*)." In *Cervantes en el Septentrión*, edited by Randi Lisa Davenport and Isabel Lozano Renieblas, 17–50. Colección Batihoja 57. New York: IDEA.

Aschom, B.B. 1943. "The First Builder of Boats in *El burlador de Sevilla*." *Hispanic Review* 11:378–84.

– 1951. "A Note on Garcilaso and Cervantes." *Hispanic Review* 19 (1): 61–3.

Aste, Kristina. 2008. "Music as Mirror: Dante's Treatment of Music in the *Divine Comedy*." *Elements* 4 (2): 67–73.

Austin, Norman. 1994. *Helen of Troy and Her Shameless Phantom.* Ithaca, NY: Cornell University Press.

Avalle-Arce, Juan Bautista. 1974. *La novela pastoril española.* Madrid: Ediciones Istmo.

Avery, William T. 1961–2. "Elementos dantescos del Quijote." *Anales cervantinos* 9:1–28.

Ávila, Ana. 1993. *Imágenes y símbolos en la arquitectura pintada española (1470–1560)*. Madrid: Anthropos.

Avilés, Luis. 2016. "Piratas justicieros: Una paradoja cervantina en el *Persiles y Sigismunda*." *eHumanista/Cervantes* 5:51–68.

– 2019. "Lidiar con la complejidad del otro: Confiar y desconfiar en el *Persiles y Sigismunda*." In *Cervantes en el Septentrión*, edited by Randi Lisa Davenport and Isabel Lozano Renieblas, 51–65. Colección Batihoja 57. New York: IDEA.

Ayala, Francisco. 1965. "Los dos amigos." *Revista de Occidente* 3:287–307.

Bachelard, Gaston. 1994. *The Poetics of Space*. Translated by Maria Jolas, with an introduction by John R. Stilgoe. Boston: Beacon Press.

Bakhtin, Mikhail. 1984. *Rabelais and His World*. Translated by Hélène Iswolsky. Bloomington: Indiana University Press.

Barnés Vázquez, Antonio. 2018. "Función de Ovidio en la construcción del *Quijote*." Anejo, *Ovidio dos mil años después: Estudios clásicos*, 4:177–90.

Barolsky, Paul. 1993. "Cellini, Vasari and the Marvels of Malady." *The Sixteenth Century Journal* 44 (1): 41–5.

Bass, Laura R. 2008. *The Drama of the Portrait: Theater and Visual Culture in Early Modern Spain*. University Park: Pennsylvania State University.

Bassegoda i Hugas, Buenaventura. 1985. "Notas sobre las fuentes de las *Medidas del Romano* de Diego de Sagredo." *Boletín del Museo e Instituto Camón Aznar* 22:117–25.

Bauman, Lissa Passaglia. 2007. "Piety and Public Consumption: Domenico, Girolamo and Julius II della Rovere at Santa Maria del Popolo." In *Patronage and Dynasty: The Rise of the Della Rovere in Renaissance Italy*, edited by Ian Verstegen, 19–62. Kirksville, MO: Truman State University Press.

Bearden, Elizabeth. 2006. "Painting Counterfeit Canvases: American Memory *Lienzos* and European Imaginings of the Barbarian in Cervantes' *Los trabajos de Persiles y Sigismunda*." *PMLA* 121 (3): 735–52.

Becherer, Joseph Antenucci. 1997. *Pietro Peruggino, Master of the Italian Renaissance*. Grand Rapids, MI: Grand Rapids Art Museum.

Bedini, Silvio A. 1997. *The Pope's Elephant*. Manchester, UK: Carcanet Press.

Benjamin of Tudela. 1907. *The Itinerary of Benjamin of Tudela*. Edited by Marcus Nathan Adler. London and Oxford: Henry Frowde and Oxford University Press.

Blanco, Mercedes. 1995. "Literatura e ironía en *Los trabajos de Persiles y Sigismunda*." In *Actas del II Congreso Internacional de la Asociación de Cervantistas*, edited by Giuseppe Grilli, 625–35. Naples, Italy: Societá Editrice Gallo.

Blecua, José Manuel. 1948. "Garcilaso y Cervantes." In *Homenaje a Cervantes*, 141–50. Madrid: Insula.

Boase, Roger. 2017. *Secrets of Pinar's Game: Court Ladies & Courtly Verse in Fifteenth-Century Spain*. 2 vols. Leiden: Brill.

Boric, Marijana. 2016. "Faust Vrančić: 400 Years after the Publication of His Work *Machinae novae*." *Croatian Studies Review* 12:45–70.

Borst, Arno. 1993. *The Ordering of Time from the Ancient Computus to the Modern Computer*. Translated by Andrew Winnard. Chicago: University of Chicago Press.

Botello, Jesús. 2016. *Cervantes, Felipe II y la España del Siglo de Oro*. Biblioteca Áurea Hispánica 111. Madrid: Iberoamericana.

Bramante, Donato. 2004. *Antiquarie prospettiche romane*. Edited by G. Agosti and D. Isella. Busto Arsizio, Italy.

Brito Díaz, Carlos. 1999. "Cervantes al pie de la letra: *Don Quijote* a lomos del 'Libro del Mundo.'" *Cervantes: Bulletin of the Cervantes Society of America* 19:37–54.

Brothers, Cammy. 2001. "Architecture, History, Archaeology: Drawing Ancient Rome in the Letter to Leo X and in Sixteenth-Century Practice." In *Coming About … A Festschrift for John Shearman*, edited by Lars R. Jones and Louisa C. Matthews, 135–40. Cambridge, MA: Harvard University Art Museum.

Brown, Jonathan, and John H. Elliott. 1980. *A Palace for a King: The Buen Retiro and the Court of Philip IV*. New Haven, CT: Yale University Press.

Brown, Jonathan, and Richard L. Kagan. 1982. "View of Toledo." In *Figures of Thought: El Greco as Interpreter of History, Tradition, and Ideas*, edited by Jonathan Brown, 19–30. Washington, DC: National Gallery of Art.

Brown, Kenneth. 1980. *Anastasio Pantaleón de Ribera (1600–1629): Ingenioso miembro de la republica literaria española*. Potomac, MD: Studia Humanitatis.

Brownlee, Kevin. 1986. "Ovid's Semele and Dante's Metamorphosis: Paradiso XXI–XXIII." Italian issue, *MLN* 101 (1): 147–56.

– 2005. "Zoraida's White Hand and Cervantes' Rewriting of History." *Bulletin of Hispanic Studies* 82 (5): 569–85.

Buceta, Erasmo. 1920. "Más sobre Noruega símbolo de la oscuridad." *Revista de Filología Española* 7:278–81.

Buck, Lawrence. 2014. *The Roman Monster: An Icon of the Papal Antichrist in Reformation Polemics*. Kirksville, MO: Truman State University Press.

Burningham, Bruce R. 2008. *Tilting Cervantes: Baroque Reflections on Postmodern Culture*. Nashville, TN: Vanderbilt University Press.

Burroughs, Charles. 1982. "Below the Angel: An Urbanistic Project in the Rome of Pope Nicholas V." *Journal of the Warburg and Courtauld Institutes* 45:94–124.

Burton, Robert. 1938. *The Anatomy of Melancholy*. Edited by Floyd Dell and Paul Jordan-Smith. New York: Tudor.

Byrne, Susan. 2007. *El Corpus Hermeticum y tres poetas españoles: Francisco de Aldana, San Juan de la Cruz y Fray Luis de León*. Newark, DE: Juan de la Cuesta.

Cacho Casal, Rodrigo. 2006. "Cervantes y la sátira: Clodio el maldiciente en el *Persiles*." *MLN* 121 (2): 299–321.

Camamis, George. 1988. "The Concept of Venus-*Humanitas* in Cervantes and Botticelli." *Cervantes* 8:183–223.

Cammarata, Joan, and Ana María Laguna. 2020. "Egocentricity versus Persuasion: *Eros, Logos*, and *Pathos* in Cervantes's Marcela and Grisóstomo Episode." In *Goodbye Eros: Recasting Forms and Norms of Love in the Age of Cervantes*, edited by Ana María Laguna and John Beusterien, 33–52. Toronto: University of Toronto Press.

Campo Baeza, Alberto. 2019. "On the Pantheon in Rome." In *Sharpening the Scalpel*, 115–24. Madrid: Arcadia Mediática, Escuela Técnica Superior de Arquitectura de Madrid.

Canavaggio, Jean. 1990. *Cervantes*, Translated by J.R. Jones. New York and London: W.W. Norton.

– 2007. "Cervantes y Barcelona." In *Cervantes, el 'Quijote' y Barcelona*, edited by Carmen Riera and Guillermo Serés, 49–58. Barcelona: Fundació Caixa Catalunya.

Candelaria, L. 2005. "Hercules and Albrecht Dürer's *Das Meerwunder* in a Chantbook from Renaissance Spain." *Renaissance Quarterly* 58 (1): 1–44.

Caramuel y Lobkowitz, Juan. 1984. *Arquitectura civil recta y oblicua*. Facsimile from the 1678 edition. Prefaced and edited by Antonio Bonet Correa. Madrid: Turner.

Cascardi, Anthony J. 1986. *The Bounds of Reason: Cervantes, Dostoyevsky and Flaubert*. New York: Columbia University Press.

Castro, Américo. 1919. "Noruega, símbolo de la oscuridad." *Revista de Filología Española* 6:184–5.

– 1925. *El pensamiento de Cervantes*. Madrid: Hernando, 1925.

– 1957. *Hacia Cervantes*. Madrid: Taurus.

Cave, Terence. 1976. "*Enargeia*: Erasmus and the Rhetoric of Presence in the Sixteenth Century." *L'Esprit Créateur* 16 (4): 5–19.

Cellauro, Louis. 2004. "Daniele Barbaro and Vitruvius: The Architectural Theory of a Renaissance Humanist and Patron." *Papers of the British School at Rome* 72:293–329.

Cellini, Benvenuto. 1956. *Autobiography*. Translated by George Bull. London: Penguin.

Cervantes, Miguel de. 1833. *El ingenioso hidalgo don Quijote de la Mancha*. Edited by Diego Clemencín. 3 vols. Madrid: D.E. Aguado, impresor de la Cámara de S. M. y de su Real Casa.

– 1892, *Galatea. A Pastoral Romance*. Translated by Gordon Willoughby and James Gyll. London: Bell & Daldy.

– 1973. *Viaje del Parnaso*. Edited by Vicente Gaos. Madrid: Castalia.

– 1978. *El ingenioso hidalgo don Quijote de la Mancha*. Edited by Juan Andrés Murillo. 2 vols. Madrid: Castalia.

– 1995. *La Galatea*. Edited by Francisco López Estrada and María Teresa López García-Berdoy. Madrid: Cátedra.

– 2007. *Don Quijote de la Mancha*. Edited by Francisco Rico. Madrid: Punto de Lectura.

– 2008. *Don Quixote*. Edited by E.C. Riley. Translated by Charles Jarvis. Oxford: Oxford University Press.

– 2014. *La Galatea*. Edited by Juan Montero, in collaboration with Francisco J. Escobar and Flavia Gherardi. Madrid: Real Academia Española.

– 2015a. *Novelas ejemplares*. Edited by José Montera Reguera. Barcelona: Penguin.

– 2015b. *Los trabajos de Persiles y Sigismunda*. Edited by Carlos Romero Muñoz. 6th edition. Madrid: Cátedra,

– 2017. *Los trabajos de Persiles y Sigismunda*. Edited by Laura Fernández, Ignacio García Aguilar, and Carlos Romera Muñoz. Madrid: Real Academia Española.

– n.d. *The Travels of Persiles and Sigismunda: A Northern Story*. Edited and translated by T.L. Darby and B.W. Ife.   http://www.ems.kcl.ac.uk.

Céspedes y Meneses, Gonzalo. 1970. *Historias peregrinas y ejemplares*. Edited by Yves-René Fonquerne. Madrid: Castalia.

Chamberlin, Vernon, and Jack Weiner. 1969. "Color Symbolism: A Key to a Possible New Interpretation of Cervantes' Caballero del Verde Gabán." *Romance Notes* 10:342–7.

Chastel, André. 1983. *The Sack of Rome, 1527*. Translated by Beth Archer. Princeton, NJ: Princeton University Press.

Cheng, Sandra. 2012. "The Cult of the Monstrous: Caricature, Physiognomy, and Monsters in Early Modern Italy." *Preternature: Critical and Historical Studies on the Preternatural* 1 (2): 197–231.

Childers, William. 1999. Review of Carlos Romero Muñoz, *Los trabajos de Persiles y Sigismunda*. *Cervantes: Bulletin of the Cervantes Society of America* 19:197–9.

– 2006. *Transnational Cervantes*. Toronto: University of Toronto Press.

Civil, Pierre. 1990. "Erotismo y pintura mitológica en la España del Siglo de Oro." *Edad de Oro* 9:39–49.

Close, Anthony. 2007. "La comicidad del episodio barcelones del 'Quijote.'" In *Cervantes, el "Quijote" y Barcelona*, edited by Carmen Riera and Guillermo Seres, 59–73. Barcelona: Fundacio Caixa Catalunya.

Clouse, Michel L. 2011. *Medicine, Government and Public Health in Philip II's Spain: Shared Interests, Competing Authorities*. Farnham, UK: Ashgate.

Clydesdale, Ruth. 2011. "'Jupiter Tames Saturn': Astrology in Ficino's *Epistolae*." In *Laus Platonici Philosophi: Marsilio Ficino and His Influence*, edited by Stephen Clucas, Peter J. Forshaw, and Valery Rees, 117–32. Leiden: Brill.

Colahan, Clark. 1994. "Towards an Onomastic of Persiles/Periandro and Sigismunda/Auristela." *Cervantes: Bulletin of the Cervantes Society of America* 14 (1): 19–40.

Coller, Alexandra. 2006. "The Sienese Accademia degli Intronati and Its Female Interlocutors.' *The Italianist* 26:223–46.

Collins, Marsha S. 2016. *Imagining Arcadia in Renaissance Romance*. London: Routledge.

Coolidge, J.S. 1965. "Great Things and Small: The Virgilian Progression." *Comparative Literature* 17:1–23.

Copete, Marie-Lucie, and E.J. Verger. 1990. "Criminalidad y espacio carcelario en una cárcel del Antiguo Régimen: La cárcel de Sevilla a finales del siglo XVI." *Historia Social* 6:105–25.

Copete, Marie-Lucie, and Bernard Vincent. 2007. "Missions en Bétique: Pour une typologie des missions intérieures." In *Missions religieuses modernes: 'Notre lieu est le monde,'* edited by Pierre-Antoine Fabre and Bernard Vincent, 261–86. Rome: École Française de Rome.

Covarrubias, Sebastián de. 1611. *Tesoro de la lengua castellana o española*. Madrid: Luis Sánchez.

– 1943. *Tesoro de la lengua castellana o española*. Edited by Martín de Riquer. Barcelona: Horta.

Cowie, Jonathan. 2007. *Climate Change: Biological and Human Aspects*. Cambridge: Cambridge University Press.

Cresswell, Tim. 2015. *Place: An Introduction*. 2nd edition. Oxford: John Wiley & Sons.

Cruz, Anne J. 2005. "Dorotea's Revenge." *Bulletin of Hispanic Studies* 82:615–32.

Cruz Casado, Antonio. 1992. "Auristela hechizada: Un caso de maleficia en el *Persiles*." *Cervantes: Bulletin of the Cervantes Society of America* 12 (2): 91–104.

Cull, John T. 1992. "Emblem Motifs in *Persiles y Sigismunda*." *Romance Notes* 32:200–8.

Dacos, Nicole. 1969. *La découverte de la Domus Aurea et la formation des grotesques a la Renaissance*. London: Warburg Institute.

Dante Alighieri. 1975. *Paradiso*. Translated by Charles Singleton. Princeton, NJ: Princeton University Press.

– 1980. *Inferno*. Translated by Allen Mandelbaum. New York: Bantam.

– 1982. *Purgatorio*. Translated by Allen Mandelbaum. New York: Bantam.

Davenport, Randi L., and Carlos Cabanillas Cárdenas. 2017. "Noruega en la literatura española del Siglo de Oro." *Ínsula* 71 (837): 15–18.

Davidson, Robert. 2018. *The Hotel: Occupied Space*. Toronto: University of Toronto Press.

De Armas, Frederick A. 1981. "Metamorphosis as Revolt: Cervantes' *Persiles y Sigismunda* and Carpentier's *El reino de este mundo*." *Hispanic Review* 49 (3): 297–312.

– 1993. "A Banquet of the Senses: The Mythological Structure of *Persiles y Sigismunda, III*." *Bulletin of Hispanic Studies* 70:403–14.

– 1998. *Cervantes, Raphael and the Classics*. Cambridge: Cambridge University Press.

– 1999. "Galileo, Kepler and Pantaleón de Ribera's *Vexamen de la luna*." *Calíope* 5 (1): 59–72.

– 2000. "Ekphrasis and Eros in Cervantes' *La Galatea*: The Case of the Blushing Nymphs." In *Cervantes for the 21st Century: Studies in Honor of Edward Dudley*, edited by Francisco LaRubia-Pardo, 33–48. Newark, DE: Juan de la Cuesta.

– 2002a. "Cervantes and the Italian Renaissance." In *The Cambridge Companion to Cervantes*, edited by Anthony Cascardi, 32–57. Cambridge: Cambridge University Press.

– 2002b. "Cervantes and the Virgilian Wheel: The Portrayal of a Literary Career." In *European Literary Careers: The Author from Antiquity to the Renaissance*, edited by Patrick Cheney and Frederick A. De Armas, 268–86. Toronto: University of Toronto Press.

– 2005. "Cervantes and Della Porta: The Art of Memory in *La Numancia, El retablo de las maravillas, El licenciado Vidriera* and *Don Quijote*." *Bulletin of Hispanic Studies* 82 (5): 633–48.

– 2006. *Quixotic Frescoes: Cervantes and Italian Renaissance Art*. Toronto: University of Toronto Press.

– 2008. "To See What Men Cannot: Teichoskopia in *Don Quijote, I*." *Cervantes: Bulletin of the Cervantes Society of America* 28 (1): 83–102.

– 2009. "Don Quijote's Barcelona: Echoes of Hercules' *Non Plus Ultra*." *Cervantes* 29 (2): 107–29.

– 2011. *Don Quixote among the Saracens: A Clash of Civilizations and Literary Genres*. Toronto: University of Toronto Press.

– 2014. "Don Quixote as Ovidian Text." In *A Handbook to the Reception of Ovid*, edited by John F. Miller and Carole Newlands, 277–90. New York: Wiley-Blackwell.

– 2019. "Fainting Men and Forward Women: Gender Instability and Sexual Equivocations in *La Galatea*." In *De Sexo y género en Cervantes / Sex and Gender in Cervantes*, edited by Esther Fernandez and Mercedes Alcalá Galán, 17–30. Kassel, Germany: Reichenberger.

De Armas Wilson, Diana. 1987. "'Passing the Love of Women': The Intertextuality of *El curioso impertinente*." *Cervantes: Bulletin of the Cervantes Society of America* 7 (2): 9–28.

– 1991. *Allegories of Love: Cervantes's Persiles y Sigismunda*. Princeton, NJ: Princeton University Press.

– 2003. *Cervantes, the Novel, and the New World*. Oxford: Oxford University Press.

De Lollis, Cesare. 1924. *Cervantes reazionario*. Rome: Fratelli Treves.

Díaz de Revega, Francisco Javier. 2014. "Ángel Valbuena Briones, tras la estela de Calderón de la Barca." *Revista de Estudios Filológicos*, 27. https://www.um.es.

Díez, J. Ignacio, 2019. "El gato de los Siglos de Oro y sus variables impregnaciones eróticas: Los aruños de don Quijote." In *Sex and Gender in Cervantes / Sexo y género en Crvantes: Essays in Honor of Adrienne Laskier Martín*, 91–112. Kassel, Germany: Reichenberger.

Di Giorgio Martini, Francesco. 1967. *Trattati di architettura ingegneria e arte militare*. Milan: Il Polifilo.

Dillbeck, Michael C., and Charles N. Alexander. 1989. "Higher States of Consciousness: Maharishi Mahesh Yogi's Vedic Psychology of Human Development." *Journal of Mind and Behavior* 10 (4): 307–34.

Domínguez, Julia. 2009. "'Coluros, líneas, paralelos y zodíacos': Cervantes y el viaje por la cosmografía en el *Quijote*." *Cervantes: Bulletin of the Cervantes Society of America* 29 (2): 139–57.

– 2016. "The 'Janus Hypothesis' in *Don Quixote*: Memory and Imagination in Cervantes." In *Cognitive Approaches to Early Modern Spanish Literature*, edited by Isabel Jaen and Julien Jacques Simon, 74–90. Oxford: Oxford University Press.

Donaldson, Ian. 1982. *The Rapes of Lucretia*. Oxford: Clarendon Press.

D'Onofrio, Julia. 2006. "Don Quijote acuático: Sentido simbólico y representación cervantina en la aventura del barco encantado." In *El Quijote en Buenos Aires*, edited by Alicia Parodi, Julia D'Onofrio, and Juan Diego Vila, 355 63. Buenos Aires: Universidad de Buenos Aires.

D'Ors Lois, Miguel. 2012. *De Grecia a Grecia (Escritos sobre literatura)*. Seville, Spain: Renacimiento.

Duce García, Jesús. 2002. *Olivante de Laura de Antonio de Torquemada: Guía de lectura*. Alcalá de Henares, Spain: Centro de Estudios Cervantinos.

– 2008. "Magia y maravillas en los libros de caballerías hispánicos." In *Amadís de Gaula: Quinientos años después; Estudios en homenaje a Juan Manuel Cacho Blecua*, edited by José Manuel Lucía Megías and María Carmen Marín Pina, 191–200. Alcalá de Henares, Spain: Centro de Estudios Cervantinos.

Dudley, Edward. 1995. "Goddess on the Edge: The Galatea Agenda in Raphael, Garcilaso and Cervantes." *Caliope* 1 (1995): 27–45.

– 1997. *The Endless Text: Don Quixote and the Hermeneutics of Romance*. Albany: State University of New York Press.

Dudley, Scott. 1999. "Conferring with the Dead: Necrophilia and Nostalgia in the Seventeenth Century,' *ELH* 66 (2): 277–94.

Dupont, Florence. 1993. *Daily Life in Ancient Rome*. Translated by Christopher Woodall. Oxford: Blackwell.

Egido, Aurora. 1994. *Cervantes y las puertas del sueño*. Barcelona: Promociones y Publicaciones Universitarias.

– 1998. "Poesía y peregrinación en el *Persiles*: El templo de la Virgen de Guadalupe." In *Actas del Tercer Congreso Internacional de la Asociación de Cervantistas*, edited by Antonio Bernat Vistarini, 13–41. Palma de Mallorca: Universitat de les Illes Balears.

– 2007. "Alba y albergue de don Quijote en Barcelona." In *Cervantes, el "Quijote" y Barcelona*, edited by Carmen Riera and Guillermo Serés, 91–132. Barcelona: Fundació Caixa Catalunya.

Eliade, Mircea. 1959. *The Sacred and the Profane*. New York: Harcourt.

– 1963. *Myth and Reality*. Translated by Willard R. Trask. New York: Harper & Row.

Ettinghousen, Henry. 2007. "Barcelona, un centro mediático a principios del XVII." In *Cervantes, el "Quijote" y Barcelona*, edited by Carmen Riera and Guillermo Serés, 149–167. Barcelona: Fundació Caixa Catalunya.

Everitt, Anthony. 2006. *The Life of Rome's First Emperor Augustus*. New York: Random House.

Fajardo, Salvador J. 1984. "Unveiling Dorotea or the Reader as Voyeur." *Cervantes: Bulletin of the Cervantes Society of America* 4 (2): 89–108.

– 1986. "The Enchanted Return: On the Conclusion of *Don Quijote* I." *Journal of Modern and Renaissance Studies* 16:233–51.

– 2002. "Don Quijote Wins by a Nose." *Hispanic Review* 70:191–205.

Falcón Márquez, Teodoro. 1996. "La Cárcel Real de Sevilla." *Laboratorio de Arte: Revista del Departamento de Historia del Arte* 9:157–70.

Fernández Morera, Darío. 1987. "Phenomenology of an Encounter: Don Quijote Meets the Knight of the Green Cloak." *Revista Canadiense de Estudios Hispánicos* 12 (1): 125–33.

Fernández Mosquera, Santiago. 2006. *La tormenta en el Siglo de Oro: Variaciones funcionales de un tópico*. Madrid/Frankfurt: Iberoamericana/Vervuert.

Ficino, Marsilio. 1975. *The Letters of Marsilio Ficino*. Preface by Oskar Kristeller. Vol. 2. London: Shepeard-Walwyn.

– 1989. *Three Books on Life*. Translated and edited by Carol V. Kaske and John R. Clark. Binghamton, NY: Medieval and Renaissance Texts and Studies.

Flórez, Enrique. 1775. *Contiene el estado antiguo de la Santa Iglesia de Barcelona … Obra póstuma que publica el P. Fr. Manuel Risco*. Vol. 29 of *España Sagrada: Theatro geográphico-histórico de la Iglesia de España: Origen, divisiones, y términos de todas sus provincias; Antigüedad, traslaciones, y estado antiguo y*

presente de sus sillas, en todos los dominios de España, y Portugal. Madrid: Don
Antonio de Sancha.

Fontes Da Costa, Palmira. 2009. "Secrecy, Ostentation and Illustration of
Exotic Animals in Sixteenth-Century Portugal." *Annals of Science* 66 (1):
59–82.

Forcione, Alban K. 1970. *Cervantes, Aristotle and the Persiles.* Princeton, NJ:
Princeton University Press.

– 1972. *Cervantes' Christian Romance: A Study of the "Persiles y Sigismunda."*
Princeton, NJ: Princeton University Press.

Fox, Dian. 2019. *Hercules and the King of Portugal: Icons of Masculinity and Nation
in Calderón's Spain.* Lincoln and London: University of Nebraska Press.

Frazer, Margaret English. 1973. "Church Doors and the Gates of Paradise:
Byzantine Bronze Doors in Italy." *Dumbarton Oaks Papers* 27 (1973):
145–62.

Friederich, Werner Paul. 1950. *Dante's Fame Abroad, 1350–1850: The Influence
of Dante Alighieri on the Poets and Scholars of Spain, France, England, Germany,
Switzerland, and the United States; A Survey of the Present State of Scholarship.*
Chapel Hill: University of North Carolina Studies in Comparative
Literature.

Fuchs, Barbara. 2003. "Empire Unmanned: Gender Trouble and Genoese Gold
in *Las dos doncellas.*" In *Passing for Spain: Cervantes and the Fictions of Identity,*
47–62. Champaign-Urbana: University of Illinois Press.

Fustel de Coulanges, Numa Denis. 1980. *The Ancient City: A Study on the
Religion, Laws, and Institutions of Greece and Rome.* Baltimore, MD: Johns
Hopkins University Press.

Gallego Zarzosa, Alicia. 2019. "El despertar sexual de don Quijote:
Construcción literaria y parodia erótica en el romance de Altisidora."
Calíope 24 (2): 128–47.

Garcés, María Antonia. 2002. *Cervantes in Algiers: A Captive's Tale.* Nashville,
TN: Vanderbilt University Press.

– 2009. "'Grande amigo mío': Cervantes y los renegados." In *USA Cervantes:
39 Cervantistas en Estados Unidos,* edited by Georgina Dopico Black and
Francisco Layna Ranz, 545–82. Madrid: CSIC and Polifemo.

García-Diego, José Antonio. 1974. "La cueva de Hércules." *Revista de Obras
Públicas* 121 (3114): 683–700.

García Santo-Tomás, Enrique. 2000. "Artes de la ciudad, ciudad de las artes:
La invención de Madrid en *El diablo cojuelo.*" *Revista Canadiense de Estudios
Hispánicos* 25 (1): 117–35.

– 2017. *The Refracted Muse: Literature and Optics in Early Modern Spain.*
Translated by Vicent Barletta. Chicago and London: University of Chicago
Press.

Gerli, Michael E. 1995. "The Dialectics of Writing: *El licenciado vidriera* and the Picaresque." In *Refiguring Authority: Reading, Writing and Rewriting in Cervantes*, 10–24. Lexington: University of Kentucky Press.

– 2012. "From Babel to Paradise: Typologies of Speech, Language, and the Quest for the Word in the *Persiles*." *eHumanista/Cervantes* 1:346–65.

Giles, Ryan D. 2015. "The Chancellor's Chains: Ex-Votos and Marian Devotion in the *Rimado de Palacio*." *Medievalia* 18 (2): 27–42.

Gil-Oslé, Juan Pablo. 2009. "Early Modern illusions of Perfect Male Friendship: The Case of Cervantes's *El curioso impertinente*." *Cervantes: Bulletin of the Cervantes Society of America* 29 (1): 85–115.

– 2013. *Amistades imperfectas: Del Humanismo a la Ilustración con Cervantes*. Biblioteca Áurea Hispánica 83. Navarra/Madrid/Frankfurt: Universidad de Navarra / Iberoamericana/Vervuert.

– n.d. "Renaissance Exchanges & Baroque Crisis: An Environmental Reading of Early Modern Iberian Globalism." Manuscript.

Gingras, Gerald L. 1985. "Diego de Miranda, 'bufón' or Spanish Gentleman? The Social Background of His Attire." *Cervantes: Bulletin of the Cervantes Society of America* 5 (2): 129–40.

Giontella, Massimo, and Riccardo Fubini. 2006. 'L'uomo con il compasso e la sfera: Note sulla recente edizione delle *Antiquarie prospetiche romane* attribuite a Bramante.' *Archivio Storico Italiano* 164 (2): 325–34.

Golden, Lauren. 2007. "A *fantasia* of Pagan myth in the Villa Farnesina: Agostino Chigi's homage to his lover, Imperia." In *Pagans and Christians – from Antiquity to the Middle Ages: Papers in Honour of Martin Henig, Presented on the Occasion of His 65th Birthday*, edited by Lauren Gilmour, 319–26. Oxford: British Archaeological Reports, International Series 1610.

Gómez, Benito. 2016. "La función de la casa y el contradictorio concepto de cordura en *Don Quijote*." *Cervantes: Bulletin of the Cervantes Society of America* 36 (1): 105–22.

González Echevarría, Roberto. 2005. *Love and the Law in Cervantes*. New Haven, CT: Yale University Press.

– 2019. *El estrellado establo: Infinito e improvisación en el Siglo de Oro*. Madrid: Cátedra.

González Galván, Manuel. 2006. *Trazo, proporción y símbolo en el arte virreinal: Antología personal*. Mexico City: Universidad Nacional Autónoma de México.

González Ruiz, Julio. 2009. *Amistades peligrosas: El discurso homoerótico en el teatro de Lope de Vega*. New York: Peter Lang.

González Urdáñez, Carmen. 2010. "Vitruvio según Cervantes: Arquitectos y oficiales en la construcción en el siglo del Renacimiento." In *Arquitectura en construcción en Europa en las épocas medieval y moderna*, edited by A. Serra

Desfilis, 255–85. Valencia, Spain: Universitat de Valencia, Ministerio de Ciencia e Innovación.

Goodrich, Peter H. 2003. Introduction to *Merlin: A Casebook*, edited by Peter H. Goodrich and Raymond H. Thompson, 1–89. New York: Routledge.

Gordon, Michael. 2011. "Presencia, papel y propósito: Los personajes judíos de Cervantes en el *Persiles*." *Iberoamerica Global* (The Hebrew University of Jerusalem) 4 (1): 68–75.

Green, Otis H. 1933. "The Literary Court of the Conde de Lemos at Naples, 1610– 1616." *Hispanic Review* 1 (4): 290–308.

Greer, Margaret R. 2002. "Calderón de la Barca, Playwright at Court." In *Cambridge Companion to Velázquez*, edited by Suzanne Stratton-Pruitt, 149–69. Cambridge: Cambridge University Press.

Groult, Pierre. 1954. "Don Quijote místico." In *Estudios dedicados a Ramón Menéndez Pidal*, vol. 5, 231–51. Madrid: CSIC.

Guntert, Georges. 2015. "*El curioso impertinente*: Nuevas perspectivas críticas." *Anales Cervantinos* 47:182–208.

Gutiérrez de los Ríos, Gaspar. 2000. *Noticia general para la estimación de las artes*. Edited by Alegría Alonso González. Salamanca: CILUS.

Hall, Marcia. 1999. *After Raphael: Painting in Central Italy in the Sixteenth Century*. Cambridge: Cambridge University Press.

Hall, H. Gaston. 1974. "Castiglioni's 'Superbi Colli' in Relation to Raphael, Petrarch, Du Bellay, Spenser, Lope de Vega and Scarron." *Kentucky Romance Quarterly* 21 (2): 159–81.

Hallowell, Robert E. 1962. "Ronsard and the Gallic Hercules Myth." *Studies in the Renaissance* 9:242–55.

Harmon, Katherine. 2010. "How Important Is Physical Contact with Your Infant?" *Scientific American*, 6 May 2010. https://www.scientificamerican. com.

Harrison, Stephen. 1993. *La composición de "Los trabajos de Persiles y Sigismunda."* Madrid: Pliegos.

Hart, Vaughan, and Peter Hicks. 1998. *Paper Palaces: The Rise of the Renaissance Architectural Treatise*. New Haven, CT: Yale University Press.

Hathaway, Robert L. 1995. "Leandra and That Nagging Question." *Cervantes: Cervantes Society of America* 15 (2): 58–74.

Heckscher, William S. 1987. "The Anadyomene in the Medieval Tradition." In *Art and Literature: Studies in Relationship*, 127–64. Durham, NC: Duke University Press.

Hekster, Olivier J. 2005. "Propagating Power: Hercules as an Example for Second-Century Emperors." In *Herakles and Hercules*, edited by H. Bowden and L. Rawlings, 203–17. Swansea, UK: Blackwell / Classical Press of Wales.

Heredia Moreno, María del Carmen, and Amelia López-Yarto Elizalde. 2001. *La edad de oro de la platería complutense*. Madrid: CSIC.

Herodotus. 1990. *Histories*. Edited and translated by A.D Godley. Vol. 1. Cambridge, MA: Harvard University Press.

Herrero, Javier. 1985. *Who Was Dulcinea?* New Orleans, LA: Graduate School of Tulane University.

Hersey, George L. 1993. *High Renaissance Art in St. Peter's and the Vatican*. Chicago: University of Chicago Press.

Hessel, Stephen. 2020. "Northworld: Peregrinages, Prisons, and the In(escapable) Loops of the Open Road." In "Confined Women: The Walls of Female Space in Early Modern Spain." Special issue, *Hispanic Issues Online* 25:226–49.

Hibbard, Howard. 1974. *Michelangelo*. 2nd. ed. Cambridge, MA: Harper & Row.

Hodder, Ian. 1990. *The Domestication of Europe: Structure and Contingency in Neolithic Societies*. Oxford: Basil Blackwell.

Homer. 1988. *The Iliad*. Translated by A.T. Murray. 2 vols. Cambridge, MA: Harvard University Press.

Honess, Claire. 1994. "Expressing the Inexpressible: The Theme of Communication in the Heaven of Mars." *Lectura Dantis* 14/15:42–60.

Horace. 1968. *Odes and Epodes*. Translated by C.E. Bennett. Cambridge, MA: Harvard University Press.

Hourihane, Colum. 2012. "Door/Bronze." In *The Grove Encyclopedia of Medieval Art and Architecture*, 2:315–18. Oxford: Oxford University Press.

Howard, Jean E. 1986. "The New Historicism in Renaissance Studies." *English Literary Renaissance* 16 (1): 13–43.

Hutchinson, Steven. 1992. *Cervantine Journeys*. Madison: University of Wisconsin Press.

Immerwahr, Raymond S. 1958. "Structural Symmetry in the Episodic Narratives of *Don Quijote*, Part One." *Comparative Literature* 10:121–35.

Institoris, Henricus, and Jacobus Sprenger. 2006. *Malleus maleficarum*. Edited and translated by Christopher S. Mackay. 2 vols. Cambridge: Cambridge University Press.

Irigoyen-García, Javier. 2014. *The Spanish Arcadia: Sheep Herding, Pastoral Discourse, and Ethnicity in Early Modern Spain*. Toronto: University of Toronto Press.

– 2017. *Moors Dressed as Moors: Clothing, Social Distinction and Ethnicity in Early Modern Iberia*. Toronto: University of Toronto Press.

Issacharoff, Dora. 1981. "Imágenes manieristas en *La Galatea* de Cervantes." In *Cervantes: Su obra y su mundo*, edited by Manuel Criado de Val, 327–36. Madrid: Edi-6.

James, Henry. 1875. "The Last of the Valerii." In *A Passionate Pilgrim and Other Tales*, 125–78. Boston: James R. Osgwood.

– 1998. *The Turn of the Screw and Other Stories*. Oxford World's Classics. Oxford: Oxford University Press.

Jeanneret, Michel. 1991. *A Feast of Words: Banquets and Table Talk in the Renaissance*. Translated by Jeremy Whiteley and Emma Hughes. Cambridge: University of Chicago Press.

Jiménez Savariego, Juan. 1602. *Tratado de peste, donde se contienen las causas, preservación y cura, con algunas cuestiones al propósito*. Antequera, Spain: Claudio Bolan.

Johnson, Paul Michael. 2016. "The Trials of Language: Apophasis, Ineffability and the Mystical Rhetoric of Love in the *Persiles*." *eHumanista/Cervantes* 5:297–316.

Joly, Monique. 1991. "Las burlas de Don Antonio en torno a la estancia de Don Quijote en Barcelona." In *Actas del Segundo Coloquio Internacional de la Asociación de Cervantistas (Alcalá de Henares, 6–9 noviembre 1989)*, 71–81. Barcelona: Anthropos.

– 1996. "Sémiologie du vetement et interprétation du texte." In *Etudes sur le Quichotte*, 49–65. Paris: Publications de la Sorbonne.

Jones, Roger, and Nicholas Penny. 1983. *Raphael*. New Haven, CT: Yale University Press.

Kallendorf, Hilaire. 2003. *Exorcism and Its Texts: Subjectivity in Early Modern England and Spain*. Toronto: University of Toronto Press.

– 2005. "La Inquisición ¿por qué deshace la cabeza encantada?" In *Actas del XI Coloquio Internacional de la Asociación de Cervantistas (Seúl, 17–20 de noviembre, 2004)*, edited by Chul Park, 173–86. Seoul: University of Hankuk.

– 2019. "Lycanthropy and Free Will: The Female Werewolf in Cervantes' *Persiles*." *eHumanista: Journal of Medieval and Early Modern Iberian Studies* 42:1–19.

Kay, Richard. 2002. "Vitruvius and Dante's Giants." *Dante Studies* 120:17–34.

Kennedy, William J. 2002. "Versions of a Career: Petrarch and His Renaissance Commentators." In *European Literary Careers: The Author from Antiquity to the Renaissance*, edited by Patrick Cheney and Frederick De Armas, 146–64. Toronto: University of Toronto Press.

Kepler, Joannes. 1967. *Kepler's Somnium: The Dream or Posthumous Work on Lunar Astronomy*. Edited and translated by Edward Rosen. Madison: University of Wisconsin Press.

Kim, Kwang-ho. 2002. "A Study on the Concept of Prospect in Frank Lloyd Wright's Works." *Journal of Asian Architecture and Building Engineering* 1 (1): 297–301.

Klibansky, Raymond, Erwin Panofsky, and Fritz Saxl. 1964. *Saturn and Melancholy: Studies in the History of Natural Philosophy, Religion and Art*. London: Thomas Nelson.

Klooster, Jacqueline, and Jo Heirman. 2013. Introduction to *The Ideologies of Lived Space in Literary Texts Ancient and Modern*, 3–11. Ghent, Belgium: Academia Press.

Kramer, Henry, and James Sprenger. 1928. *Malleus maleficarum*. Translated by Montague Summers. New York: Benjamin Blom.

Krieger, Murray. 1992. *Ekphrasis. The Illusion of the Natural Sign*. Baltimore, MD: Johns Hopkins University Press.

Kriegeskorte, Werner. 1993. *Giuseppe Arcimboldo, 1527–1593*. Cologne: Benedikt Taschen.

Kruft, Hanno-Walter. 1994. *History of Architectural Theory from Vitruvius to the Present*. Translated by Ronald Taylor, Elsie Callander, and Anthony Wood. New York: Princeton Architectural Press.

Kuhn, Annette. 1985. *The Power of the Image: Essays on Representation and Sexuality*. London and New York: Routledge.

Kutasz Christensen, Theresa A. 2018. "Queen Christina of Sweden's Development of a Classical Persona through Allegory and Antiquarian Collecting." PhD diss., Pennsylvania State University.

Lacarta, Manuel. 2005. *Cervantes: Biografía razonada*. Madrid: Silex.

Lacy, Norris J. 1987. "French Arthurian Literature." In *The Arthurian Encyclopedia*, edited by Norris J. Lacy, 187–93. New York: Bedrick Books.

Laspuertas Sarvisé, Carmen. 2000. *Amadís de Grecia de Feliciano de Silva: Guía de lectura*. Alcalá de Henares, Spain: Centro de Estudios Cervantinos.

Lasso de la Vega, Ángel. 1871. *Historia y juicio crítico de la escuela poetica sevillana en los siglos XVI y XVII*. Madrid: Imprenta de la Viuda e Hijos de Galiano.

Lathrop, Tom. 2006. "Edith Grossman's Translation of *Don Quixote*." *Cervantes: Bulletin of the Cervantes Society of America* 26:237–56.

Lee, Christina H. 2005. "El encantamiento de don Quijote en Barcelona." In *Actas del XI Coloquio Internacional de la Asociación de Cervantistas (Seúl, 17–20 de noviembre, 2004)*, edited by Chul Park, 207–14. Seoul: University of Hankuk.

Lefebvre, Henri. 1991. *The Production of Space*. Translated by Donald Nicholson-Smith. Oxford: Blackwell.

León, Pedro de. 1981. *Compendio de algunas experiencias en los ministerios de que usa la Compañía de Jesús, con que prácticamente se muestra con algunos acontecimientos y documentos el buen acierto en ellos, por orden de los superiores*. In *Grandeza y miseria en Andalucía: Testimonio de una encrucijada histórica (1578–1616)*, edited by Pedro Herrera Puga. Granada, Spain: Facultad de Teología.

Lester, Toby. 2012. "The Other Vitruvian Man: Was Leonardo da Vinci's Famous Anatomical Chart Actually a Collaborative Effort?' *Smithsonian Magazine*, February 2012. https://www.smithsonianmag.com.

Levisi, Margarita. 1968. "Las figuras compuestas en Archimboldo y Quevedo." *Comparative Literature* 20:217–35.

– 1972. "La pintura en la narrativa de Cervantes." *Boletín de la Biblioteca Menéndez Pelayo* 48:293–325.

Lima, Robert. 2003. *The Dramatic World of Valle-Inclán*. Woodbridge, UK: Tamesis.

– 2005. *Stages of Evil: Occultism in Western Theater and Drama*. Lexington: University Press of Kentucky.

Lindemann, Mary. 1999. *Medicine and Society in Early Modern Europe*. Cambridge: Cambridge University Press.

Lipking, L. 1981. *The Life of the Poet: Beginning and Ending Poetic Careers*. Chicago: University of Chicago Press.

Lipman, Jonathan. 1986. *Frank Lloyd Wright and the Johnson Wax Buildings*. New York: Rizzoli.

Listri, Massimo. 2008. "Villa Madama." In *Villa Madama: Raphael's Dream*, edited by Caterina Napoleone and Massimo Listri, 69–124. Turin and New York: Umberto Allemandi.

Livy. 1919. *History of Rome, Books 1–2*. Translated by B.O. Foster. Vol. 1. Cambridge, MA: Harvard University Press.

Lope de Vega Carpio, Félix. 2001. *El nuevo mundo descubierto por Cristóbal Colón*. Translated by Robert M. Shannon. New York: Peter Lang.

López Alemany, Ignacio. 2005. "A Portrait of a Lady: Representations of Sigismunda-Auristela in Cervantes's Persiles." In *Ekphrasis in the Age of Cervantes*, edited by Frederick A. de Armas, 202–16. Lewisburg, PA: Bucknell University Press.

– 2008. "*Ut pictura non poesis: Los trabajos de Persiles y Sigismunda* and the Construction of Memory." *Cervantes: Bulletin of the Cervantes Society of America* 28 (1): 103–18.

López Estrada, Francisco. 1952. "La influencia italiana en *La Galatea* de Cervantes." *Comparative Literature* 4.2: 161–9.

– 1999. "La 'Embajada a Tamorlán' castellana como libro de relación entre occidente y oriente en la Edad Media." In *Mélanges: María Soledad Carrasco Urgoiti*, vol. 1, 73–80. Zaghouan, Tunisia: Fondation Temimi pour la recherche scientifique et l'information.

– 2006. "La época de los viajeros y el redescubrimiento: Los viajeros medievales y el reencuentro con Oriente: González de Clavijo." In *La aventura española en Oriente (1166–2006)*, edited by Joaquín María Córdoba and María del Carmen Pérez-Díe, 65–70. Madrid: Ministerio de Cultura.

Lorenzo Domínguez, Javier. 2017. "Una adelfa en tierras extrañas: Emblemática y misoginia en la *Comedia famosa de los guanches de Tenerife y conquista de Canaria.*" *Anuario Lope de Vega* 23:484–98.

Losada Varela, Celestina. 2007. *La arquitectura en el otoño del Renacimiento: Juan de Naveda 1590–1638.* Santander, Spain: Universidad de Cantabria.

Lozano Renieblas, Isabel. 1998a. *Cervantes y el mundo del "Persiles."* Alcalá de Henares, Spain: Centro de Estudios Cervantinos.

– 1998b. "La función de la écfrasis en el *Persiles.*" In *Actas del Tercer Congreso Internacional de la Asociación de Cervantistas,* edited by Antonio Pablo Bernat Vistarini, 507–15. Palma de Mallorca: Universitat de les Illes Balears.

– 2008. "El *Persiles* hermético." *Cervantes: Bulletin of the Cervantes Society of America* 26 (1): 277–84.

– 2016. "Más para ser admirado que creído: Admiración y novedad en los episodios de licántropos en el *Persiles.*" *eHumanista/Cervantes* 5:349–59.

Lucía Megías, José Manuel. 2019. *La plenitud de Miguel de Cervantes: Una vida en papel (1604–1616).* Madrid: Edaf.

Lugli, Emanuele. 2019. "In cerca della perfezione: Nuovi elementi per l'Uomo Vitruviano din Leonardo da Vinci." In *Leonardo e Vitruvio: Oltre il cerchio e il quadrato,* edited by Francesca Borgo, 69–91. Venice: Marsilio.

Macaya, Emilia. 1992. *Cuando estalla el silencio: Para una lectura femenina de textos hispánicos.* San José: Editorial de la Universidad de Costa Rica.

Maharishi Mahesh Yogi. 1998. *Building for the Health and Happiness of Everyone: Creating Ideal Housing in Harmony with Natural Law.* Vlodrop, Netherlands: Maharishi Vedic University, 1998.

Maiorino, Giancarlo. 1991. *The Portrait of Eccentricity: Arcimboldo and the Mannerist Grotesque.* University Park and London: Pennsylvania State University Press.

Marasso, Antonio. 1954. *Cervantes: La invención del Quijote.* Buenos Aires: Hachette.

Marchante-Aragón, Lucas A. 2016. "*Don Quixote*'s Ana Félix: The Virile *Morisca* Maiden and the Crisis of Imperial Masculinity." *Hispanófila* 176:3–18.

Marder, Tod A. 1989. "Bernini and Alexander VII: Criticism and Praise of the Pantheon in the Seventeenth Century." *Art Bulletin* 71 (4): 628–45.

Marías, Fernando. 1986. *La arquitectura del Renacimiento en Toledo (1541–1631).* Vol. 4. Madrid: CSIC.

Márquez-Villanueva, Francisco. 1975. *Personajes y temas del "Quijote."* Madrid: Taurus.

Martínez Montiel, Luis, and Alfredo J. Morales. 1999. *The Cathedral of Seville.* London: Scala.

Martínez Sobrino, Alejandro. 2013. "La empresa 60 de las *Empresas Morales* de Juan de Borja: Posible origen textual de la imagen del caracol." *IMAGO Revista de Emblemática y Cultura Visual* 5:91–9.

Martín Fernández, María Amor. 1988. *El mundo mitológico y simbólico de Juan de Padilla "El Cartunaj."* Córdoba, Spain: Publicaciones del Monte de Piedad y Caja de Ahorros de Córdoba.

Martín Moran, José Manuel. 1991. "Tópicos especiales en los libros de caballerías." *Filología Románica* 10:279–92.

– 2008. *Cervantes y el Quijote: Hacia la novela moderna.* Alcalá de Henares, Spain: Centro de Estudios Cervantinos.

Martin Vide, Javier, and Jorge Olcina Campos. 2001. *Climas y tiempos de España.* Madrid: Alianza Editorial.

Mays Merrill, Elizabeth. 2013. "The *Trattato* as Textbook: Francesco di Giorgio's Vision for the Renaissance Architect." *Architectural Histories* 1 (1), Art. 20. https://journal.eahn.org.

McCallister, Timothy. 2011. "Intercalated Grace at Juan Palomeque's Inn." *Cervantes: Bulletin of the Cervantes Society of America* 31 (1): 109–33.

McClure, Christopher Scott. 2016. "Sculpting Modernity: Machiavelli and Michelangelo's *David.*" *Interpretation: A Journal of Political Philosophy* 43 (1): 111–24.

McGaha, Michael. 1980. "Cervantes and Virgil." In *Cervantes and the Renaissance,* edited by Michael McGaha, 34–50. Easton, PA: Juan de la Cuesta.

McKay, Ruth. 2019. *Life in Times of Pestilence: The Great Castilian Plague of 1598–1601.* Cambridge: Cambridge University Press.

Menéndez Pelayo, Marcelino. 1944. *Antología de poetas líricos castellanos.* Vol. 3. Madrid-Santander: Viuda de Hernando.

Meserve, Margaret. 2018. "A Roman Monster in the Humanist Imagination." In *Et Amicorum: Essays on Renaissance Humanism and Philosophy,* edited by Anthony Ossa-Richardson and Margarest Meserve, 118–33. Leiden : Brill.

Mexía, Pedro, 1989. *Silva de varia lección.* Edited by Antonio Castro. Madrid: Castalia.

Miller, Francis Trevelyan. 1930. *The World in the Air: The Story of Flying in Pictures.* New York: G.P. Putnam's Sons.

Mitrovic, Branko. 2019. Daniele Barbaro's Architectural Theory." In *Daniele Barbaro's Vitruvius of 1567,* edited by Kim Williams, ix–xxxviii. Cham, Switzerland: Birkhauser.

Molina, Francisco. 1981. *El Giraldillo.* Seville, Spain: Monte de Piedad y Caja de Ahorros de Sevilla.

Moner, Michel. 1989. *Cervantes conteur: Escrits et paroles.* Madrid: Casa de Velázquez.

Montero Delgado, Juan. 2000. "La tinaja de Pandora: El Giraldillo y sus artífices en la Sátira de Francisco Pacheco." *Calamus Renascens* 1:229–46.

Montero Reguera, José. 1996. "Miguel de Cervantes: El Ovidio español." In *Studia Aurea: Actas del III Congreso de la AISO,* edited by I. Arellano,

M.C. Pinillos, F. Serralta, and M. Vitse, 3:327–34. Toulouse-Pamplona: LEMSO-GRISO.

Morales, Alfredo J. 1996. *Hernán Ruiz "el joven."* Madrid: Akal.

Morales, Ángela. 2014. "Nuevas consideraciones sobre el personaje de don Diego Miranda: La identidad religiosa de Caballero del Verde Gabán." In *Comentarios a Cervantes: Actas selectas del VIII Congreso Internacional de la Asociación de Cervantistas (Oviedo, 11–15 de junio de 2012)*, edited by Emilio Martínez Mata and María Fernández Ferreiro, 494–503. Oviedo, Spain: Fundación María Cristina Masaveu Peterson.

Mulvey, Laura. 1997. "Visual Pleasure and Narrative Cinema." In *Feminisms: An Anthology of Literary Theory and Criticism*, edited by Robyn R. Warhol and Diane Price Herndil, 438–48. New Brunswick, NJ: Rutgers University Press.

Muñoz Sánchez, Juan Ramón. 2003. "Hacia una nueva visión de la estructura de *La Galatea*." *Epos* 19:91–101.

– 2007. "Ortel Banedre, Luisa y Bartolomé: Análisis estructural y temático de un episodio del *Persiles*." *Criticón* 99:125–58.

– 2008. "'Los vírgenes esposos' del *Persiles*: El episodio de Renato y Eusebia." *Anales Cervantinos* 40: 205–28.

– 2015a. "El episodio de Feliciana de la Voz (*Persiles*, III, 2–5) en el conjunto de la obra de Cervantes." *Artifara* 15:157–83.

– 2015b. "Reflexiones sobre *Los trabajos de Persiles y Sigismunda, historia setentrional*." *Anales cervantinos* 47:249–88.

Murante, Joseph. 2020. "Let Him Cast the First Stone." In "'Cancel Culture': Views from the Campus; Students Debate the Merit of the Latest Export from the Universities." *Wall Street Journal*, 15 July 2020. https://www.wsj.com.

Nabokov, Vladimir. 1983. *Lectures on Don Quixote*. Edited by Fredson Bowers, with foreword by Guy Davenport. San Diego, New York, and London: Harcourt, Brace & Jovanovich.

Nadeau, Carolyn A. 2016. *Food Matters: Alonso Quijano's Diet and the Discourse of Food in Early Modern Spain*. Toronto: University of Toronto Press.

Napoleone, Caterina. 2008. "Raphael's Dream." In *Villa Madama: Raphael's Dream*, edited by Caterina Napoleone and Massimo Listri, 19–68. Turin and New York: Umberto Allemandi.

Navarro, Rosa. 2002. "Dos burladores: Don Juan Tenorio en la estela de Eneas." *Scriptura* 17:263–77.

Navascués Palacios, Pedro. 1971. "El manuscrito de arquitectura de Hernán Ruiz el Joven." *Archivo Español de Arte (CSIC)* 44 (175): 295–331.

Nelson, Benjamin J. 2017. "Pilgrimaging to the Temple of Diana: Jorge de Montemayor, Merida, and the Septizodium." In *"Los cielos se agotaron de prodigios": Essays in Honor of Frederick A. de Armas*, edited by Christopher B.

Weimer, Kerry K. Wilks, Benjamin J. Nelson, and Julio Vélez Sainz, 245–56. Newark, DE: Juan de la Cuesta.

Nelson, Bradley J. 2005. *"Los trabajos de Persiles y Sigismunda*: Una crítica cervantina de la alegoresis emblemática." *Cervantes: Bulletin of the Cervantes Society of America* 24 (2): 43–69.

Neri, Stefano. 2007. *Antología de las arquitecturas maravillosas en los libros de caballerías*. Alcalá de Henares, Spain: Centro de Estudios Cervantinos.

Nesselrath, Christiane Denker. 1993. "Raphael's Loggia." In *Raphael in the Apartments of Julius II and Leo X*, edited by Robert Caravaggi, 39–79. Milan: Electa.

Nevoux, Pierre. 2011. "El *Persiles* como novela épica." *Criticón* 111–12:237–59.

Newlands, Carole E. 1995. *Playing with Time: Ovid and the Fasti*. Ithaca, NY, and London: Cornell University Press.

Niwa, Seishiro. 2005. "'Madama' Margaret of Parma's Patronage of Music." *Early Music* 33 (1): 25–38.

Noel, Gerard. 2006. *The Renaissance Popes: Statesmen, Warriors and the Great Borgia Myth*. New York: Carroll & Graff.

Nonnus. 1940. *Dionysiaca: Books I–XV*. Translated by W.H.D. Rouse. Cambridge, MA: Harvard University Press.

Nuñez Rivera, Valentín. 2015. *Cervantes y los géneros de la ficción*. Prosa Barroca. Madrid: SIAL.

Ordoñez, Elizabeth. 1985. "Woman and Her Text in the Works of María de Zayas and Ana Caro." *Revista de Estudios Hispánicos* 19:3–15.

Ovid. 1986. *Metamorphoses*. Translated by A.D. Melville. Oxford and New York: Oxford University Press.

– 1989. *Fasti*. Translated by Sir James George Frazer; rev. G.P. Goold. Cambridge: Harvard University Press.

Padilla, Juan de (El Cartuxano). 1891. *Los doze triumphos de los doze apóstoles fecho por el Cartujano*. Edited by Miguel del Riego. London: D. Carlos Wood.

Palladio, Andrea. 1991. *The Churches of Rome*. Edited and translated by Eunice D. Howe. Binghamton, NY: Medieval and Renaissance Texts and Studies.

Parello, Vincent. 2015. "La *relación sucinta* de la ciudad de Lisboa en *El burlador de Sevilla*: Un viaje a través del género corográfico." *Criticón* 124:165–83.

Parker, Geoffrey. 2013. *Global Crisis: War, Climate Change and Catastrophe in the Seventeenth Century*. New Haven, CT: Yale University Press.

Parra Luna, Francisco, M. Fernández Nieto, S. Petschen Verdaguer, J.A. Garmendia, J.P. Garrido, J. Montero de Juan, G. Bravo, M.J. Ríos Insua, and J. Maestre Alfonso. 2005. *El lugar de La Mancha es: El Quijote como un sistema de distancias, tiempo*. Madrid: Editorial Complutense.

Pascual Barea, Joaquín. 1998. "Un poema inédito de Arias Montano a Don Hernando de su etapa complutense influida por Marcial." *Revista Augustiniana* 39 (120): 1017–27.

Pastor Comín, Juan José. 2006. "Música callada: La resonancia del hecho musical en la obra cervantina." In *Edad de Oro Cantabrigense: Actas del VII Congreso de la Asociación Internacional Siglo de Oro*, edited by Anthony Close, 495–501. Madrid: AISO.

Paulson, Ronald. 1984. "Hogarth's *Country Inn Yard* at Election Time: A Problem in Interpretation." In *English Satire and the Satiric Tradition*, edited by C.J. Rawson, 196–208. Oxford: Blackwell.

Pedrocco, Filippo. 2001. *Titian*. New York: Rizzoli.

Percas de Ponseti, Helena. 1968. "La cueva de Montesinos." *Revista Hispánica Moderna* 34:376–99.

– 1975. *Cervantes y su concepto del arte: Estudio crítico de algunos aspectos y episodios del Quijote*. 2 vols. Madrid: Gredos.

Pérez de León, Vicente. 2010. *Cervantes y el cuarto misterio*. Alcalá de Henares, Spain: Centro de Estudios Cervantinos.

Pérez de Moya, Juan. 1995. *Philosofía Secreta*. Edited by Carlos Clavería. Madrid: Cátedra.

– 2002. *Comparaciones o símiles para los vicios y virtudes: Philosophía secreta*. Edited by Consolación Baranda. Madrid: Biblioteca Castro.

Pérez Martínez, Ángel. 2012. *El Quijote y su idea de virtud*. Madrid: CSIC.

Pericoli, Matteo. 2013. "Writers as Architects." *New York Times*, 3 August 2013. https://opinionator.blogs.nytimes.com.

Perry, Mary Elizabeth. 1980. *Crime and Society in Early Modern Seville*. Hanover, NH: University Press of New England.

Pico della Mirandola, Giovanni.1956. *Oration on the Dignity of Man*. Chicago: Henry Regnery Co.

Pietrangeli, Carlo. 1976. *Sant'Angelo: Guide rionali di Roma*. Rome: Fratelli Palombi.

Pike, Ruth. 1975. "Crime and Criminals in Sixteenth-Century Seville." *Sixteenth Century Journal* 6 (1): 3–18.

– '1981. Review of Mary Elizabeth Perry's *Crime and Society in Early Modern Seville. American Historical Review* 86 (2): 406–7.

Plato. 1979. *The Republic*. Translated and edited by Francis McDonald Cornford. Oxford: Oxford University Press.

Platt, Peter G. 1992. "'Not Before Either Known or Dreamt of': Francesco Patrizi and the Power of Wonder in Renaissance Poetics." *Review of English Studies* 43 (171): 387–94.

Pliny. 1952. *Natural History: Books XXXIII–XXXV*. Translated by H. Rackham. Cambridge, MA: Harvard University Press.

Poggioli, Renato. 1959. "The Pastoral of the Self." *Daedalus* 88 (4): 686–99.

– 2008. "Envidia y conciencia creativa en el Siglo de Oro." Special issue, *Anales de Historia del Arte*, 135–49.

Powers, Katrina. 2016. "Marion, Venus and Susanna in the Mirror: The Paintings in the Parlor of the Bates Motel." *Americana: The Journal of*

American Popular Culture 15 (2). https://www.americanpopularculture.com/journal/

Prem, Hanns. 1991. "Disease Outbreaks in Central Mexico during the Sixteenth Century." In *"Secret Judgments of God": Old World Disease in Colonial Spanish America*, edited by David Noble Cook and W. George Lovell, 20–48. Norman: University of Oklahoma Press.

Presberg, Charles. 2001. *Adventures in Paradox: Don Quixote and the Western Tradition*. University Park: Pennsylvania State University Press.

Prescott, Anne Lake. 2002. "Divine Poetry as a Career Move: The Complexities and Consolations of Following David." In *Europan Literary Careers: The Author from Antiquity to the Renaissance*, edited by Patrick Cheney and Frederick A. de Armas, 206–31. Toronto: University of Toronto Press.

Puig, Idoya. 2011. "Relationships in *Los trabajos de Persiles y Sigismunda*: Parental Authority and Freedom of Choice." *Anuario de Estudios Cervantinos* 7:211–22.

Pujades, Geronimo. 1829. *Crónica universal del principado de Cataluña: Escrita a principios del siglo XVII*. Vol. 1. Barcelona: Jose Torner.

Puttfarken, Thomas. 2005. *Titian and Tragic Painting*. New Haven, CT: Yale University Press.

Quevedo, Francisco de. 1997. *Casa de locos de amor*. In *Prosa completa: Obras satíricas y festivas*, edited by José Bergua, 155–67. Madrid: Ediciones Ibéricas.

Quinlan-McGrath, Mary. 1997. "Caprarola's Sala della Cosmografía." *Renaissance Quarterly* 50 (4): 1045–100.

Quint, David. 2003. *Cervantes's Novel of Modern Times: A New Reading of Don Quijote*. Princeton, NJ, and Oxford: Princeton University Press.

Randell, Thomas James. 2001. *Spanish Rome: 1500–1700*. New Haven, CT, and London: Yale University Press.

Raynié, Florence. 2004. "Silencio pro Deo y elocuencia *pro domo*: San Bruno instrumentalizado por Lope de Vega." *Criticón* 92:65–84.

Redondo, Augustin. 1998a. "Fiestas burlescas en el palacio ducal: El episodio de Altisidora." In *Actas del tercer congreso internacional de la Asociación de Cervantistas*, edited by Antonio Bernat Vistarini, 49–62. Palma de Mallorca: Universitat de les Illes Balears.

– 1998b. *Otra manera de leer el Quijote*. Madrid: Castalia.

Reed, Cory A. 2004. "Ludic Revelations in the Enchanted Head Episode in *Don Quijote*." *Cervantes: Bulletin of the Cervantes Society of America* 24.1: 189–216.

– 2016. "*Máquinas de peregrinaciones*: Cosmography, Empire and the *Persiles*." *eHumanista/Cervantes* 5:444–59.

Regula, DeTraci. 2001. *The Mysteries of Isis: Her Worship and Magic*. St. Paul, MN: Llewellyn Publications.

Reyes, Matías de los. 1640. *Para algunos*. Madrid: Viuda de Juan Sánchez.

Richter, David F. 2010. "Don Quixote's Demise: Games, Cruelty, and the Closure of Representation on the Ducal Stage." *Confluencia* 25 (2): 43–55.

Río, Martín del. 1991. *La magia demoníaca*. Translated and edited by Jesús Moya, with preliminaries by Julio Caro Baroja. Madrid: Hiperión.

Riva, Reynaldo C. 2003. "Apuntes para una solución: La narración de Rutilio." *Cervantes: Bulletin of the Cervantes Society of America* 23 (2): 343–55.

– 1983. "Cervantes y Garcilaso." In *Homenaje a José Manuel Blecua*, 565–70. Madrid: Gredos.

Robbins, Jeremy. 2004. "The False Captives and the Representation of History and Fiction in *Los trabajos de Persiles y Sigismunda*." *Bulletin of Spanish Studies* 81 (4–5): 627–39.

Roberts, Jennifer T. 2011. *Herodotus: A Very Short Introduction*. Oxford: Oxford University Press.

Rodríguez, Alfredo, S. Tisinger, and G. Utley. 1995. "La creatividad de Cervantes en 'El cuento de Leandra.'" *Cervantes: Bulletin of the Cervantes Society of America* 15 (2): 84–9.

Rodríguez de Monforte, Pedro. 1687. *Sueños misteriosos de la escritura en discursos sagrados, políticos y morales*. Madrid: Antonio Román.

Rodríguez de Montalvo, Garcí. 1987. *Amadís de Gaula*. Edited by Juan Manuel Cacho Blecua. 2 vols. Madrid: Cátedra.

Rodríguez Marín, F. 1907. "Una sátira sevillana del licenciado Francisco Pacheco." *Revista de Archivos, Bibliotecas y Museos* 17:1–25, 433–54.

Rodríguez Ramos, L. 1990. "Los galeotes de los Austrias: La penalidad al servicio de la Armada." *Historia Social* 6:127–40.

Rodríguez Valles, Nieves. 2007. "'Debajo de mi manto al rey mato': La protección que ofrecen a Cervantes los refranes en el *Quijote* I." In *Las dos orillas: Actas del XV Congreso de la Asociación Internacional de Hispanistas (México del 19 al 24 de julio de 2004)*, coordinated by Beatriz Mariscal and María Teresa Miaja de la Peña, 2: 501–8. Mexico: Fondo de Cultura Económica.

Roettgen, Steffi. 1997. *Italian Frescoes: The Flowering of the Renaissance, 1470 – 1510*. New York, London, and Paris: Abbeville Press.

Rogers, Edit. 1974. "The Hunt in the *Romancero* and other Traditional Ballads." *Hispanic Review* 42 (2): 133–71.

Romero Díaz, Nieves. 2002. *Nueva nobleza, nueva novela: reescribiendo la cultura urbana del barroco*. Newark, DE: Juan de la Cuesta.

Rosario, Medardo. 2015. "El abrazo de Persiles y Sisgismunda como metáfora de la armonización última del alma." *Anuario de Estudios Cervantinos* 11:343–56.

Rosenthal, Earl. 1971. "*Plus ultra, Non Plus Ultra,* and the Columnar Device of Emperor Charles V." *Journal of the Warburg and Courtland Institutes* 34:204–28.

Rothbauer, Anton M. 1963. *Die Muhen und Leiden des Persiles und der Sigismunda.* Stuttgart, Germany: Goverts.

Rowland, Ingrid D. 1998. *The Culture of the High Renaissance: Ancients and Moderns in Sixteenth-Century Rome.* Cambridge: Cambridge University Press.

Rueda, Lope de. 1992. *Pasos.* Edited by José Luis Canet Vallés. Madrid: Castalia.

Ruiz Pérez, Pedro. 2010. "El *Canto de Calíope*: Entre la Arcadia, el Parnaso y la república literaria." In *Cervantes en el espejo del tiempo,* edited by M. Carmen Marín Pina, 393–429. Zaragoza, Spain: Universidad de Zaragoza.

Rupp, Stephen. 2014. *Heroic Forms: Cervantes and the Literature of War.* Toronto: University of Toronto Press.

Saavedra Fajardo, Diego. 1986. *España y Europa en el siglo XVII: Correspondencia de Saavedra Fajardo, 1631–33.* Edited by Quintín Aldea Vaquero. Madrid: CSIC.

Sáez, Adrián J. 2019a. "Epitafios de novela: La poesía funeral de Cervantes en *La Galatea,* los *Quijotes* y el *Persiles.*" In *Cervantes y la posteridad: 400 años de legado cervantino,* edited by A. Moro Martín, 178–90. Madrid/Frankfurt: Iberoamericana/ Vervuert.

– 2019b. *Godos de papel: Identidad nacional y reescritura en el Siglo de Oro.* Madrid: Cátedra.

Sagredo, Diego de. 1526. *Medidas del romano.* Toledo, Spain: Remón de Petras.

Sales Dasí, Emilio J. 2009–10. "Pinturas, tapices y libros de caballerías." *Destiempos* 4 (23): 41–68.

Sallers, Robert. 2002. *Malaria and Rome: A History of Malaria in Ancient Italy.* Oxford: Oxford University Press.

Sánchez, Alberto. 1998. "Historia y poesía: El mito de Píramo y Tisbe en el *Quijote.*" *Anales Cervantinos* 34:9–22.

Sánchez Jiménez, Antonio. 2006. *Lope pintado por sí mismo: Mito e imagen del autor en la poesía de Lope de Vega Carpio.* London: Tamesis.

Sánchez Jiménez, Antonio, and Julián Olivares. 2011. "Lope de Vega y El Greco: *Ut pictura poesis* en el Toledo del siglo XVI." *Bulletin of Hispanic Studies* 88 (1): 21–41.

Sánchez Robayna, Andrés. 2000. "La epístola moral en el Siglo de Oro." In *La epístola: V encuentro sobre la poesía del Siglo de Oro,* edited by Begoña López Bueno, 129–50. Seville, Spain: Universidad de Sevilla.

Santiago Álvarez, Cándido. 2011. "Refranes sobre animales invertebrados no artrópodos." *Revista de Folklore* 355:32–45.

– 2017. "Los animales invertebrados mencionados en los escritos de Cervantes: (I), El *Quijote*." *Revista de Folklore* 429:57–83.

Santore, Cathy. 1991. "Danaë: The Renaissance Courtesan's Alter Ego." *Zeitschrift für Kunstgeschichte*, 54 (3): 412–27.

Sarduy, Severo. 1973. "Suelo del barroco." *Diálogos: Artes, Letras, Ciencias humanas*, 9 (4) (52): 23–7.

Schaffer, Anna Katharina. 2016. *Exhaustion: A History*. New York: Columbia University Press.

Schmidt, Rachel. 2014. "Nacido bajo Marte, Mercurio y Apolo: ¿Un posible autorretrato de Cervantes hacia el final del *Persiles*?" *Anuario de Estudios Cervantinos* 10:257–70.

– 2016. "The Stained and the Unstained: Feliciana de la Voz's Hymn to Mary in the Context of the Immaculist Movement." *eHumanista/Cervantes* 5:478–95.

Scobie, A. 1976. "*El curioso impertinente* and Apuleius." *Romanische Forschungen* 88:75–6.

Scotti, R.A. 2006. *Basilica: The Splendor and the Scandal; Building St. Peter's*. New York: Penguin.

Seneca. 2014. *Epistles 66–92*. Translated by Richard M. Gummere. Cambridge, MA: Harvard University Press, 2014.

Severa Baños, José. 1990. "El paisaje soñado en el *Persiles y Sigismunda*." In *Actas del I Coloquio Internacional de la Asociación de Cervantistas (Alcalá de Henares, 29–30 noviembre y 1–2 diciembre, 1988)*, 295–305. Barcelona: Anthropos.

Severin, Dorothy. 1997. "Diego de San Pedro's *Arnalte y Luscenda*: Subtext for the Cardenio Episode of *Don Quijote*." In *Studies on the Spanish Sentimental Romance (1440–1550): Redefining the Genre*, edited by Joseph J. Gwara and Michael E. Gerli, 145–51. London: Tamesis.

Seznec, Jean. 1972. *The Survival of the Pagan Gods*. Translated by Barbara F. Sessions. Princeton, NJ: Princeton University Press.

Sgarbi, Claudio. 1993. "A Newly Discovered Corpus of Vitruvian Images." *RES: Anthropology and Aesthetics* 23:31–51.

Shakespeare, William. 2016. *The Tempest*. In *The Norton Shakespeare: Romances and Poems*, edited by Stephen Greenblatt, Walter Cohen, Suzanne Gossett, Jean E. Howard, Katharine Eisaman Maus, and Gordon McMullan, 4 vols., 387–448. New York and London: W.W. Norton.

Shepherd J.C., and G.A. Jellicoe. 1993. *Italian Gardens of the Renaissance*. New York: Princeton Architectural Press.

Singer, Charles L. 1985. *The Renaissance in Rome*. Bloomington: Indiana University Press.

Slater, John. 2014. "The Theological Drama of Chymical Medicine in Early Modern Spain." In *Medical Cultures of the Early Modern Spanish Empire*, edited by John Slater, María Luz López-Terrada, and José Pardo Tomás, 213–30. Farnham, UK: Ashgate.

Sletsjöe, Leif. 1959–60. "Cervantes: Torquemada y Olao Magno." *Anales Cervantinos* 8:139–50.

Sliwa, Krysztof. 2005. *Vida de Miguel de Cervantes Saavedra*. Kassel, Germany: Reichenberger.

Solís de los Santos, José. 2016. "Cervantes y el entorno humanístico de los Ramírez de Prado." *Edad de Oro* 35:97–120.

Soto, Hernando de. 1983. *Emblemas moralizadas*. Edited by Carmen Bravo Villasante. Madrid: Fundación Universitaria Española.

Spitzer, Leo. 1922. "La Norvege comme symbole de l'obscurité." *Revista de Filología Española* 9:316–17.

Spurr, David. 2012. *Architecture and Modern Literature*. Ann Arbor: University of Michigan Press.

Squire, Michael. 2012. "'Fantasies So Varied and Bizarre': The Domus Aurea, the Renaissance, and the 'Grotesque.'" In *The Blackwell Companion to the Age of Nero*, edited by M. Dinter and E. Buckley, 444–64. Malden, MA: Wiley-Blackwell.

Stagg, Geoffrey. 1959. "Plagiarism in *La Galatea*." *Filologia Romanza* 6:255–76.

Stinger, Charles L. 1985. *The Renaissance in Rome*. Bloomington: Indiana University Press.

Stoichita, Victor I. 2000. *La invención del cuadro: Arte, artífices y artificios en los orígenes de la pintura europea*. Barcelona: Ediciones del Serbal.

Stone, Robert. 2017. "Reflections on Knights and Mirrors: *El Caballero del Verde Gabán*." In *52nd International Conference on Medieval Studies (Western Michigan University, May 11–14, 2017)*. https://www.academia.edu.

Stow, Kenneth. 2001. *Theater of Acculturation: The Roman Ghetto in the Sixteenth Century*. Seattle: University of Washington Press.

Sullivan, Henry W. 1996. *Grotesque Purgatory: A Study of Cervantes's Don Quixote, Part II*. University Park: Pennsylvania State University Press.

– 1998. "Cervantes and the Genealogy of Merlin: 'That French Wizard.'" *Romance Notes* 38 (2): 223–32.

Summers, David. 1977. "Contrapposto: Style and Meaning in Renaissance Art." *Art Bulletin* 59 (3): 336–61.

Sylvaine, Hansel. 1999. *Benito Arias Montano: Humanismo y arte en España*. Translated by Daniel Romero Álvarez and Jesús Espino Nuñez. Huelva, Spain: Universidad de Huelva.

Talvacchia, Bette. 1999. *Taking Positions: On the Erotic in Renaissance Culture*. Princeton, NJ: Princeton University Press.

Tate, Brian. 2002. "*Laus Urbium*: Praise of Two Andalusian Cities in the Mid-Fifteenth Century." In *Medieval Spain: Conflict and Coexistence; Studies in Honour of Angus MacKay*, edited by Angus MacKay, Roger Collins, and Anthony Goodman, 148–59. New York: Macmillan.

Thomas, Jane. 2010. "Icons of Desire: The Classical Statue in Late Victorian Literature." *The Yearbook of English Studies* 40 (1–2): 246–72.

Tomás García, Jorge. 2019. "Classical Tradition and the Painting of Giovanni da Udine." *RES Antiquitatis* 1:14–28.

Triplett, Kyle. 2012. "Rare Books: *Machinae Novae* 1595." *New York Public Library* (blog). May 18, 2012.   https://www.nypl.org/blog/2012/05/18/rare-books-machinae-novae.

Tuan, Yi-Fu. 1977. *Space and Place: The Perspective of Experience*. Minneapolis: University of Minnesota Press.

– 1979. *Landscapes of Fear*. New York: Pantheon Books.

– 1990. *Topophilia: A Study of Environmental Perception, Attitudes and Values*. Morningside Edition. New York: Columbia University Press.

– 2014. "Space, Place and Nature: The Farewell Lecture." 4 April 2014.   http://www.yifutuan.org/dear_colleague.htm.

Turney, Alexandra. 2016. "Torture by the Tiber: Tor di Nona Prison in Rome." *Through Eternity Tours* (blog), 22 December 2016.   https://www.througheternity.com/en/blog/history/torture-by-the-tiber.html#.

Turriano, Juanelo. 1983. *Los veintiún libros de los ingenios y las máquinas*. Edited by José A. Garcia Diego. 2 vols. Colegio de Ingenieros de Caminos, Canales y Puertos. Madrid: Ediciones Turner.

Urbina, Eduardo, and Fernando González Moreno. *Cervantes Project*.   http://cervantes.dh.tamu.edu.

Valbuena Briones, Ángel. 1958. *Ensayo sobre la obra de Calderón*. Madrid: Ateneo.

– 1965. *Perspectiva crítica de los dramas de Calderón*. Madrid: RIALP.

Valsecchi, Maria Cristina. 2007. "Mass Plague Graves found on Venice 'Quarentine' Island." *National Geographic*, 29 August 2007.   https://www.nationalgeographic.com.

Van Baak, Joost. 2009. *The House in Russian Literature: A Mythopoetic Exploration*. Amsterdam and New York: Rodopi.

Van den Doel, Marieke. 2010. "Ficino, Diacceto and Michelangelo's Presentation Drawings." In *The Making of the Humanities*, vol. 1, *Early Modern Europe*, edited by Rens Bond, Jaat Maap, and Thijs Weststeijn, 107–32. Amsterdam: Amsterdam University Press.

Varo Zafra, Juan. 2009. *Ironía trágica de la Guerra de Granada de Don Diego Hurtado de Mendoza*. Discurso 47. Granada, Spain: Academia de Buenas Letras de Granada.

– 2012. *Diego Hurtado de Mendoza y la Guerra de Granada en su contexto histórico*. Valladolid, Spain: Universidad de Valladolid.

Vasari, Giorgio. 1996. *Lives of the Painters, Sculptors and Architects*. Translated by Gaston du C. de Vère. 2 vols. New York: Knopf.

Velázquez de Castro, María. "Pedro de León." *Real Academia de la Historia*. http://dbe.rah.es/biografias/20525/pedro-de-leon.

Vicente García, José Luis. 1992. "La astrología en *Los doce triunfos de los doce apóstoles* del Cartujano." *Revista de Literatura* 54 (107): 47–73.

Viola Zanini, Gioseffe. 1629. *Della architectura, libre due*. Padua, Italy: Francesco Bolzetta.

Virgil. *Eclogue X*. The Internet Classics Archive. http://classics.mit.edu/ Virgil/eclogue.10.x.html.

Vitruvius. 1960. *The Ten Books on Architecture*. Translated by Morris Hicky Morgan. New York: Dover.

Von Barghahn, Barbara. 1985. *Age of Gold, Age of Iron: Renaissance Spain and Symbols of Monarchy*. 2 vols. Lanham, MD: University Press of America.

Vosters, Simon A. 1990. *Rubens y Espana Estudio artístico-literario sobre la estética del Barroco*. Madrid: Cátedra.

Wagschal, Steven. 2005. "From Parmigianino to Pereda: Góngora on Beautiful Women and *Vanitas*." In *Ekphrasis in the Age of Cervantes*, edited by Frederick A. de Armas, 102–23. Lewisburg, PA: Bucknell University Press.

– 2018. *Minding Animals in the Old and New Worlds: A Cognitive Historical Analysis*. Toronto: University of Toronto Press.

Ward, Benedicta. 2010. "Relics and the Medieval Mind." *International Journal for the Study of the Christian Church* 10 (4): 274–86.

Wardropper, Bruce W. 1984. "The Butt of Satire in *El retablo de las maravillas*." *Cervantes: Bulletin of the Cervantes Society of America* 4:25–33.

Warner, Marina. 2013. *Alone of All Her Sex: The Myth and the Cult of the Virgin Mary*. Oxford: Oxford University Press.

Waxman, Samuel M. 1916. "Schools of Magic in Toledo and Salamanca." In "Chapters on Magic in Spanish Literature," *Revue Hispanique* 38:1–42.

Watt, Ian. 1996. *Myths of Modern Individualism: Faust, Don Quixote, Don Juan, Robinson Crusoe*. Cambridge: Cambridge University Press.

Watts, Susan. 2014. "The Symbolism of Querns and Millstones." *AmS-Skrifter* 24:51–4.

Weiger, John G. 1979. *The Individuated Self: Cervantes and the Emergence of the Individual*. Athens, OH: Ohio University Press.

– 1985. *The Substance of Cervantes*. Cambridge: Cambridge University Press.

Weinrich, Harald. 2005. *The Linguistics of Lying and Other Essays*. Seattle: University of Washington Press.

Whitenack, Judith. 1990. "Ana Caro's *Partinuplés* and the Chivalric Tradition." In *Engendering the Early Modern Stage: Women Playwrights in the Spanish Empire*, edited by Valerie Hegstrom and Amy R. Williamsen, 51–74. New Orleans, LA: University Press of the South.

Whitney, Geffrey. 1866. *Whitney's Choice of Emblemes: A Facsimile Reprint*. Edited by Henry Green. London: Lovell Reeve & Co.

Wilson Bowers, Kristy. 2013. *Plague and Public Health in Early Modern Seville*. Rochester, NY: University of Rochester Press.

Wilson Jones, Mark. 2000. *Principles of Roman Architecture*. New Haven, CT: Yale University Press.

Witt, R.E. 1971. *Isis and the Ancient World*. Baltimore, MD, and London: Johns Hopkins University Press.

Worden, William. 2010. "Cervantes Transforms Ovid: The Dubious Metamorphoses in Don Quixote." In *Ovid in the Age of Cervantes*, edited by Frederick A. de Armas, 116–35. Toronto: University of Toronto Press.

Zalamea, Patricia. 2018. "Pinturas de malísima mano: Usos y paradojas de la narrativa visual en Cervantes." *Hipogrifo* 6 (2): 345–63.

Zumthor, Paul. 1993. *La mesure du monde: Représentations de l'espace au Moyen Age*. Paris: Seuil.

Index

Toronto Iberic

Milton Keynes UK
Ingram Content Group UK Ltd.
UKHW022301040324
438897UK00017B/111/J